TO THE HEBREWS

THE ANCHOR BIBLE is a fresh approach to the world's greatest classic. Its object is to make the Bible accessible to the modern reader; its method is to arrive at the meaning of biblical literature through exact translation and extended exposition, and to reconstruct the ancient setting of the biblical story, as well as the circumstances of its transcription and the characteristics of its transcribers.

THE ANCHOR BIBLE is a project of international and interfaith scope: Protestant, Catholic, and Jewish scholars from many countries contribute individual volumes. The project is not sponsored by any ecclesiastical organization and is not intended to reflect any particular theological doctrine. Prepared under our joint supervision, THE ANCHOR BIBLE is an effort to make available all the significant historical and linguistic knowledge which bears on the interpretation of the biblical record.

THE ANCHOR BIBLE is aimed at the general reader with no special formal training in biblical studies; yet, it is written with the most exacting standards of scholarship, reflecting the highest technical accomplishment.

This project marks the beginning of a new era of co-operation among scholars in biblical research, thus forming a common body of knowledge to be shared by all.

William Foxwell Albright
David Noel Freedman
GENERAL EDITORS

Following the death of senior editor W. F. Albright, The Anchor Bible Editorial Board was established to advise and assist David Noel Freedman in his continuing capacity as general editor. The three members of the Editorial Board are among the contributors to The Anchor Bible. They have been associated with the series for a number of years and are familiar with its methods and objectives. Each is a distinguished authority in his area of specialization, and in concert with the others, will provide counsel and judgment as the series continues.

THE ANCHOR BIBLE

TO THE HEBREWS

Translation, Comment
and Conclusions
by
George Wesley Buchanan

1972
DOUBLEDAY & COMPANY, INC.
GARDEN CITY, NEW YORK

ISBN: 0-385-02995-0
Library of Congress Catalog Card Number 72–76127

Printed in the United States of America
First Edition

To My Wife
Harlene

PREFACE

This commentary is the result of a practical examination of a document composed by an early Jewish Christian scholar. The research has involved a study of the Old Testament, which was familiar to the author of this homily, the writings of Philo, Josephus, the Dead Sea scrolls, rabbinic literature, and Samaritan documents that were composed before, during, or after the composition of New Testament literature. The history, practices, literary forms, and beliefs reflected in this and other Jewish, Samaritan, and Christian literature provide a necessary background for understanding "To the Hebrews." The first draft of this commentary was written without consulting the available secondary sources in an effort to avoid the conscious or unconscious imitation of earlier commentators. After tentative conclusions had been reached on the basis of primary sources, many secondary sources were consulted, and the second draft was modified accordingly, utilizing many insights from earlier scholars acknowledged in footnotes throughout the commentary. Reference has been made only to those sources that seemed directly relevant to the discussion here. This policy caused the omission of many excellent works on Hebrews and does not necessarily reflect any adverse appraisal of these scholarly contributions. The outline of this commentary has been modified in several places to concur with the insights on structure published by Albert Vanhoye. Westcott's masterful study of the church fathers and the Old Testament in relationship to Hebrews is still useful. Vaughan and Stuart are both helpful for their analyses of Greek words used in Hebrews. The well-balanced works of Moffatt and Michel were consulted verse by verse and utilized more often than footnotes can show. Spicq's extensive study is useful from many points of view, and his interpretation of Philo has been accurately corrected at some points by Williamson. These works and others that were consulted frequently are listed in the abbreviated reference section together with all of the necessary bibliographical data about them, so they are referred to only by name, volume, and page number throughout the commentary. I am grateful to all of these and other colleagues in New Testament research who have made it impossible for anyone to write a completely original commentary on this important document.

In addition to other authors I am grateful to Hebrew Union College-Jewish Institute of Religion from which I received the training in Jewish literature necessary for understanding New Testament documents. Time spent in discussion with the late Professor W. F. Albright in his home was both enlightening and enjoyable. Dr. David Noel Freedman, general editor of the Anchor Bible series, has been unusually generous and judicious in his assistance throughout this project. He has not only helped me to improve the style and scholarship of this volume, but he has made suggestions that should continue to be helpful to me in research and writing. My esteemed colleague, Dr. James T. Clemons, has read the entire manuscript and made helpful suggestions for improving its style and presentation. Miss Margaret Balcom and Mrs. Louise Risk have jointly checked all biblical references for accuracy. To all of these I am grateful. My wife, Harlene, has spent countless hours reading proofs, and she has provided the kind of moral support that makes research a joy. To her and for her I am very thankful, and it is to Harlene that I dedicate this commentary.

The introduction is very brief, including only a few definitions that are necessary for understanding the commentary. The book was written to help the reader understand this document from chapter to chapter without forcing conclusions upon him before he has read the evidence. Because the author of Hebrews made his case stronger as he wrote, frequently repeating, reinforcing, and summarizing his earlier expressions, this commentary follows in much the same way. Interpretations of earlier chapters may not satisfy the reader because the evidence at that point is often insufficient to be convincing. If he will be patient and read further, he may find that the case becomes stronger as the commentary progresses, but the conclusions that are normally considered "introductory" will be placed at the end with the assumption that the reader will not read these until he has read the text and commentary intended to justify the conclusions about the author and the original readers.

CONTENTS

ABBREVIATIONS AND REFERENCES

Briggs	C. A. and E. G. Briggs, *A Critical and Exegetical Commentary on the Book of Psalms,* 2 vols., New York, 1917
Bruce	F. F. Bruce, *The Epistle to the Hebrews,* Grand Rapids, 1964
Bultmann	Rudolf Bultmann, *Theology of the New Testament,* I, tr. K. Grobel, New York, 1951
CC	*The Consequences of the Covenant* by George Wesley Buchanan, Leiden, 1970
Dahood	Mitchell Dahood, *Psalms I, 1–50; II, 51–100; III, 101–150,* AB, vols. 16, 17, and 17A, Garden City, N.Y., 1966, 1968, 1970
Davidson	A. B. Davidson, *The Epistle to the Hebrews,* Edinburgh, n.d.
Delitszch	Friedrich Delitszch, *Commentary on the Epistle to the Hebrews 1876,* tr. T. L. Kingsbury, 2 vols., Grand Rapids, 1952
Eliade	M. Eliade, *Cosmos and History,* tr. W. R. Trask, New York, 1959
Grässer	E. Grässer, *Der Glaube im Hebräerbrief,* Marburg, 1965
Hanson	A. T. Hanson, "Christ in the OT According to Hebrews," *Studia Evangelica* II (1964), 393–407
Jeremias	J. Jeremias, *New Testament Theology,* I, tr. J. Bowden, London, 1971
Keil	K. F. Keil, *Commentar über den Brief an die Hebräer,* Leipzig, 1885
Kuss	O. Kuss, *Der Brief an die Hebräer,* Regensburg, 1966
Lenski	R. C. H. Lenski, *The Interpretation of the Epistle to the Hebrews and of the Epistle of James,* Columbus, 1938
Manson	T. W. Manson, *The Epistle to the Hebrews,* London, 1951
Marshall	I. H. Marshall, "The Synoptic Son of Man Sayings in Recent Discussion," NTS 12 (1965–66), 327–51
Michel	Otto Michel, *Der Brief an die Hebräer,* Göttingen, 1957
Moffatt	James Moffatt, *A Critical and Exegetical Commentary on the Epistle to the Hebrews,* Edinburgh, 1924
Montefiore	Hugh Montefiore, *A Commentary on the Epistle to the Hebrews,* New York, 1964
Mowinckel	Sigmund Mowinckel, *The Psalms in Israel's Worship,* tr. D. R. Ap-Thomas, 2 vols., New York, 1962

Schröger	F. Schröger, *Der Verfasser des Hebräerbriefs als Schriftausleger,* Regensburg, 1968
Sowers	S. G. Sowers, *The Hermeneutics of Philo and Hebrews,* Zürich, 1965
Spicq	C. Spicq, *L'Épître aux Hébreux,* 2 vols., Paris, 1953
Stuart	M. Stuart, *Commentary on the Epistle to the Hebrews,* 2 vols., Andover, 1828
Turner	S. H. Turner, *The Epistle to the Hebrews in Greek and English,* New York, 1852
Vanhoye	A. Vanhoye, *La Structure Littéraire de l'Épître aux Hébreux,* Paris, 1962
Vaughan	C. J. Vaughan, *The Epistle to the Hebrews,* London, 1890
Westcott	B. F. Westcott, *The Epistle to the Hebrews,* London, 1892
Williamson	R. Williamson, *Philo and the Epistle to the Hebrews,* Leiden, 1970
Windisch	Hans Windisch, *Der Hebräerbrief,* Tübingen, 1931

Abbreviations for Tractates, Journals, etc.

AB	The Anchor Bible
Aboth	The Fathers—mishnaic tractate
Abr.	Philo, *De Abrahamo*
Ant.	Josephus, *Antiquities of the Jews*
Apol.	Justin Martyr, *First Apology*
Apos. Cons.	*Apostolic Constitutions*
ARN	*The Fathers according to Rabbi Nathan*
AZ	*Abodah Zarah* (Idolatry)—mishnaic and talmudic tractate
BA	*Biblical Archaeologist*
BASOR	*Bulletin of the American Schools of Oriental Research*
BB	*Baba Bathra* (The Last Gate)—mishnaic and talmudic tractate
Ber.	*Berakoth* (Blessings)—mishnaic tractate
BJRL	*Bulletin of the John Rylands Library*
CBQ	*Catholic Biblical Quarterly*
CDC	Damascus Document (Zadokite Document)
CJT	*Canadian Journal of Theology*
CL	Philo, *De Confusione Linguarum*
Decal.	Philo, *De Decalogo*
Dial.	Justin, *Dialogue with Trypho*
Ebr.	Philo, *De Ebrietate*
Exod R.	*Exodus Rabbah*
Fuga	Philo, *De Fuga et Inventione*
Gen R.	*Genesis Rabbah*
Hag.	*Hagigah* (The Festal Offering)—mishnaic and talmudic tractate

HE	Eusebius, *The Ecclesiastical History*
Heres	Philo, *Quis Rerum Divinarum Heres*
Hom.	*Clementine Homilies*
HTR	*Harvard Theological Review*
HUCA	*Hebrew Union College Annual*
Hyp.	Philo, *Hypothetica*
IDB	The Interpreters' Dictionary of the Bible, 4 vols.
IEJ	*Israel Exploration Journal*
Ios.	Philo, *De Iosepho*
JTaan.	Jerusalem Talmud *Taanith*
JAAR	*Journal of the American Academy of Religion*
JBL	*Journal of Biblical Literature*
Jub	Jubilees
Keth.	*Kethuboth* (Marriage Deeds)—mishnaic and talmudic tractate
Kid.	*Kiddushim* (Betrothals)—mishnaic and talmudic tractate
LA	Philo, *Legum Allegoriae*
LumVie	*Lumière et Vie*
LXX	The Septuagint
Mand.	Shepherd of Hermas, *Mandates*
Meg.	*Megillah* (The Scroll of Esther)—mishnaic and talmudic tractate
Men.	*Menahot* (Meal Offerings)—mishnaic and talmudic tractate
Mid.	*Middot* (Measurements)—mishnaic and talmudic tractate
Mos.	Philo, *De Vita Mosis*
MT	Massoretic Text
Ned.	*Nedarim* (Vows)—mishnaic and talmudic tractate
NEV	New English Version
NTS	*New Testament Studies*
Num R.	*Numbers Rabbah*
Op.	Philo, *De Opificio Mundi*
PG	Migne, *Patrologia Graeca*
Philos.	Hippolytus, *Philosophumena*
PR	*Pesikta Rabbati*
PRE	*Pesikta de Rabbi Eleazar*
PRK	*Pesikta de Rav Kahana*
Prob.	Philo, *Quod Omnis Probus Liber Sit*
1Q, 4Q, et al.	Caves 1, 4, et al. of Qumran
1QM	Cave 1, The War Scroll of Qumran
1QpHab	Cave 1, Qumran Pesher on Habakkuk
1QS	Cave 1, *The Rule of the Community* or *Manual of Discipline*
1QSa	Cave 1, Samuel
QDPIS	Philo, *Quod Deterius Potiori Insidiari Solet*
RB	*Revue Biblique*
Recog.	*Clementine Recognitions*

RH	*Rosh ha-Shanah* (Feast of the New Year)—mishnaic and talmudic tractate
RQum	*Revue de Qumrân*
RSV	Revised Standard Version
San.	*Sanhedrin*—mishnaic and talmudic tractate
Shab.	*Shabbat*—mishnaic and talmudic tractate
Sheb.	*Shebuoth* (Oaths)—mishnaic and talmudic tractate
Shek.	*Shekalim* (Shekal dues)—mishnaic and talmudic tractate
Sim.	Shepherd of Hermas, *Similitudes*
Sir	*The Wisdom of Sirach*
SJT	*Scottish Journal of Theology*
SO	*Sibylline Oracles*
Som.	Philo, *De Somniis*
Spec.	*De Specialibus Legibus*
StEv	*Studia Evangelica*
Strom.	Clement of Alexandria, *Stromateis*
Suk.	*Sukkah* (The Feast of Tabernacles)—mishnaic and talmudic tractate
T. Levi	Testament of Levi in *The Twelve Patriarchs*
TBK	Tosephta, *Baba Kamma* (The First Gate)
TYoma	Tosephta, *Yoma* (The Day of Atonement)
TWZNT	*Theologisches Wörterbuch zum Neuen Testament*
Virt.	Philo, *De Virtutibus*
Vis.	Shepherd of Hermas, *Visions*
VT	*Vetus Testamentum*
Wars	Josephus, *The Wars of the Jews*
Wis	Wisdom of Solomon
Zeb.	*Zebahim* (Animal offerings)—mishnaic and talmudic tractate
ZNTW	*Zeitschrift für die Neutestamentliche Wissenschaft*

INTRODUCTION

The document entitled "To the Hebrews" is a homiletical midrash based on Ps 110. Some of the concepts and literary forms considered in the commentary are defined below:

1. *Midrash.* The midrashic method of biblical exegesis, employed by the author of Hebrews, was basic to the Samaritan, Jewish, and Christian understanding of the role of scripture in religious life. The scripture was always closely related to the worshiping community. Once a certain body of literature was considered to be sacred, later covenanters accepted it and prepared their teachings for their contemporaries on the basis of this sacred text. For example, the Book of Deuteronomy is basically structured around the ten commandments in chapter five. Chapter six begins with an exhortation on keeping these commandments as the central guiding force of Israel's ethics. Parents were admonished to teach these laws to their children and talk of them when they were at home, when they were walking by the way, and when they were lying down or rising up. The commandments should be prepared in written form and put in places where they could be seen frequently (Deut 6:4–9). At some later time, the rest of Deuteronomy also became sacred scripture, and an unknown author of Prov 2–7 prepared a midrashic exegesis based on the exhortatory portion of Deuteronomy (6:4–9 || 11:18–22), illustrating the ethical implications involved in lying down, rising up, and walking by the way. The homily in Proverbs, then, is a midrash upon a midrash. Psalm 8 was expounded positively by another psalmist (144:3–4), satirized by Job (7:17–18; 14:1, 4; 15:14; 25:4–6), and used as the basis of a later hymn (1QS 11:15–22). All of these later authors quoted words from Ps 8 and midrashically paraphrased its message for their own needs. In a similar way the beautiful priestly benediction (Num 6:24–26) was paraphrased over and over again in later literature (Pss 4:1, 6; 13:1, 3; 29:11; 31:16, 21–23; 41:2, 4, 10–13; 67:1, 6–7; 80:3, 7, 19; 118:26–27; 119:29, 132, 135; Dan 9:17; Enoch 61:7–12; 1QSa 2:1–9; II Macc 1:2–5; 1QH 9:33–34; PRK 13:13).[1]

[1] For a more extensive treatment of this subject see "Midrashim Pre-tannaïtes," RB 72 (1965), 229–39.

The word "midrash" comes from the Hebrew root *drš,* which means to "examine," "question," or "search." A person preparing a midrash was one who searched the scripture to find its true meaning, which he then expounded, so the word came to mean to "expound" or "interpret." Another closely related word is *pšr,* which means to "interpret." Some of the documents found among the Dead Sea scrolls contain running commentaries on some biblical texts. These texts have brief explanations which begin "Its interpretation (*pšrw*) is . . ." Because of this characteristic, these are called *pᵉšārīm.* Authors of Dead Sea scrolls *pᵉšārīm* made almost no attempt to clarify the text itself but only to reinterpret it to suit the situation facing the midrashic author's generation. Other midrashim also did this sometimes, but not always. The *pšr* is a distinctive type of commentary or "midrash."[2] Two major types of midrash are running commentaries and expositions on special texts. Under these two major headings are many other variations.

Running commentaries—Among the running commentaries composed in New Testament times were some of the writings of Philo ("Questions and Answers in Genesis" and "Questions and Answers in Exodus") and the Tannaitic midrashim: Mekilta (on parts of Exodus), Sifra (on Leviticus), and Sifré (on parts of Numbers and Deuteronomy). These all disclose the work of rabbis who were well versed in the Old Testament. They were basically organized in consecutive order, with the commentary on one verse following that of the verse just preceding in the scripture. Sometimes the comment is brief and sometimes it is elaborate, but the appraisal of any one verse can seldom be completely appreciated by checking that verse alone. These commentators composed their literary works the way a musical composer might, with many themes woven throughout. As one melody fades into the background, another theme is raised into prominence so as to blend, vary, and move from one score to another. Thus the commentators, while expounding on one verse, sometimes examined one word after another. While studying a certain term or phrase in passage B, for instance, the author may have been reminded of another use of the same expression in passage A on which he had already commented, or in passage C, several verses or chapters further on in the text. In either case, he might choose to explain some detail of another verse (A or C) while interpreting B, even though the commentary might have dealt with it rather briefly or omitted it entirely in direct relationship to the passage A or C. He also frequently supported a point by scripture passages from other

[2] See A. G. Wright, "The Literary Genre Midrash," CBQ 28 (1966), 116–17, 418–22.

books, which he quoted and on which he sometimes commented briefly in the process. Repetition, collections of similar illustrations, and summary statements were standard literary devices for the composition of midrashim.[3]

Homiletic midrashim. Homiletic midrashim are sermons or essays which expound important subjects or texts in the Old Testament. Philo composed some of these ("On the Creation of the World," "Allegorical Interpretation," "On the Cherubim," "The Tower of Babel," "Moses," and "The Ten Commandments"). Others are included in such collections as Pesikta de Rav Kahana, Tanḥuma, and Pesikta Rabbati. These exegetes used the same basic methodology of interpretation as that employed by the authors of running commentaries. The main difference is that these are principally based on one text throughout each exposition, even though the authors quoted many other biblical passages as well as illustrations. They even commented briefly on these other texts when they chose, but all other comments and texts were subordinated to the main text. To this classification belongs Prov 2–7, which is a midrashic exposition of Deut 11:18–22//6:4–9, and "To the Hebrews," which is based on Ps 110. Those scholars who prepared midrashim were not just objective, dispassionate interpreters whose only purpose was to present the text fairly. They were primarily dogmatic theologians who used the scripture to prove points they wanted to defend. Midrashic composers were resourceful apologists with amazing skill in manipulating words, phrases, and passages to suit their own needs in ways that were far removed from the original meaning of the text. The reason such a method was necessary was that the official interpreter had to relate an ancient text that was considered sacred to the needs of a worshiping community in a different period of time and under situations that differed from those that prompted the writing of the scripture on which they depended. Authors of midrashim were not free to ignore the text and present their ideas on the basis of contemporary need and normal logic. The scripture gave them their authority to speak. Their use of scripture represents their skill in presenting their own views on the basis of the sacred text. Rabbis had numerous, well-established rules for doing this,

[3] Renée Bloch, "Midrash," in *Dictionnaire de la Bible, Supplement V,* ed. Henri Cazelles (Paris, 1957), cols. 1265–67, pointed out the following characteristics of rabbinic midrash: (1) it has its point of departure in the scripture; (2) it is of a homiletical character; (3) it is an attentive study of the text; (4) it is adapted to the present; and (5) it includes *aggadah* and *halakah.* Wright, CBQ 28 (1966), 133–38, has defined the characteristics of midrash too sharply to be applied generally. He is correct in saying that a midrash is a literature about a literature, but the precise form this literature takes varies widely.

and some of them were employed by the author of Hebrews. The midrash on Ps 110 is limited to the first twelve chapters of Hebrews. It is well organized; it includes many passages of scripture and some poetry which was treated midrashically as if it were scripture; and it is logically sound, once the author's presuppositions are understood and accepted. This logic will be explained in the commentary, passage by passage, but the following terms will be defined at the outset to prepare the reader to understand the midrashic literature that follows.

2. *Prophecy and the Messiah.* R. Yoḥanan said, "Every prophet prophesied only for the days of the Messiah" (Ber. 34b). The author of the Habakkuk Commentary said the prophecy of Habakkuk was for the end of days (2:5–6). God had told Habakkuk to write down the things that would happen to the last generation (7:1–2). This opinion was widely accepted, and rabbis frequently took statements made about Old Testament personages, changed them into future expectations, and applied them to the Messiah. The author of Hebrews did the same. In the first two chapters alone, the author of Hebrews understood Jesus, the Messiah, to be the subject of statements originally made about some unknown Jewish or Israelite king being enthroned, the children of Israel, Solomon, a warrior king, God, and man.

3. *Introductions to scripture.* The author of Hebrews never referred to the Old Testament as something written. Even when he referred to a quotation "in David" (i.e., in the Psalter), he said, "Just as it is prophesied," rather than saying, "David wrote" or "David said." He understood that all scripture, even that which he believed had been written by David or Moses, was the word of God, spoken by either God or the Holy Spirit (3:7). By using the passive voice, he avoided the use of the divine name. The usual introduction is "just as the Holy Spirit says" (3:7); "just as he said" (4:3); "just as it also says" (5:6); "it says" (1:7, 8); "he says" (10:5); "he said" (1:5; 4:3, 4; 8:14); or "saying" (2:12). In these cases the subject was understood to have been God or the Holy Spirit, although the author never used the expression "God said." Like other Jews and Christians who avoided the use of the divine name, he used such terms as "the one who says to him," (7:21), "the one who said" (5:5; 10:30), or he used passive verbs (3:15; 7:13; 11:18). Sometimes introductions conclude with the repetitious word "saying" (2:6, 12; 6:13; 12:26). These reflect introductions similar to those found numerous times in rabbinic literature. "As it is said" or "just as it is said" (*šene'ᵉmar*) occurs frequently. The

repetitious "saying" is like the Mishnaic *lē'mōr,* as in Yoma 6:2, "As it is written in the law of your servant Moses, saying (*lē'mōr*)."

4. *Florilegia.* One of the practices of Jews and Christians of New Testament times was to gather proof texts on various subjects. These are called *florilegia.* One of the Dead Sea scrolls is called 4Q Florilegium because it contains the following Old Testament passages regarding the Messiah: II Sam 7:11–14; Exod 15:17–18; Amos 9:11; Ps 1:1; Isa 8:11; Ezek 37:23(?); Ps 2:1; Dan 11:32; 12:10. In the midrash on Ps 2:9 there is a similar florilegium. Rom 9:15–22 contains a collection of passages on God's unalterable will, and 9:25–29 and 10:18–21 are parts of a florilegium on God's rejection of Israel. Rom 3:10–18 is a florilegium on the universality of sin. Heb 1:5–13 contains passages from a florilegium on sonship, to which have been added some passages on angels. These are joined by typical midrashic introductions: "has he ever said? . . . and again . . . he said . . . it says . . . to the Son . . . and . . . and . . . has he ever said?" In other places the author of Hebrews listed two or more Old Testament passages together, but they do not seem to represent florilegia of passages on one important topic (see 2:12–13; 5:5–6).

5. *Parables.* A parable is one kind of analogy. When trying to explain something difficult, usually religious or ethical, Jews and Christians found practical situations that could easily be understood, and they compared the unknown with these for clarification. Rabbis frequently introduced such parables by the formula, "To what can the matter be compared" (*lmh hdbr dwmh*)? (Mekilta *Pisha* 16:68 *et passim*). This is similar to the formula used by Jesus, "To what shall I compare this generation" (*tini de homoiōsō tēn genean tautēn*)? (Matt 11:16). The author of Hebrews used few analogies; only one of these was a parable, and it lacks the normal introduction. The analogy compares believers to land that receives rain from heaven. If the land produces only thorns and thistles as a result, it is burned off. In the same way, covenanters who accept the advantages of the covenant and then become apostate can expect severe treatment from God (6:7–8). The most frequently used analogy in Hebrews is the *a fortiori* argument.

6. *A fortiori.* An *a fortiori* argument is a type of analogic reasoning to make a case "for the stronger" reason. It is sometimes called *a minore ad maius,* "from the lesser to the greater." In Hebrew it is called *qal wᵉḥōmer,* "light and heavy." This is an argument which describes a situation related to something small, light, or unimportant (A), and

then reasons that the same would be all the more applicable to something great, heavy, or important (B). One Old Testament example was the response of Jacob's sons when Joseph's servants accused them of stealing a silver cup belonging to Joseph:

A. "Behold the money which we found in the mouth of our sacks, we brought back to you from the land of Canaan,
B. how then should we steal silver or gold from your master's house?" (Gen 44:8).

Since they were honest in a situation where it was not expected, they should be understood to be all the more honest when dealing in a situation where honesty was required.

In commenting on the manna provided for the rebellious exodus generation, rabbis said:

A. "If God thus provided for those who irritated him,
B. how much more (*'l 'ḥt kmh wkmh*) will he pay a good reward in the future to the righteous?" (Mekilta *Vayassa'* 4:43–45).

In a very similar way, Jesus assured his disciples of God's providence:

A. "Consider the lilies of the field, how they grow. They neither toil nor spin, but I tell you not even Solomon in all his glory was clothed like one of these. If the grass of the field which is today and tomorrow is cast into the oven, God thus clothes,
B. will he not much more (*pollǭ mallon*) clothe you, [O people of] little faith" (Matt 6:28–30; see also 7:9–11; 12:11–12; for examples in Romans, see 5:8–9, 10, 17, 18, 21; 11:12, 15, 24).

There are several *a fortiori* arguments in Hebrews (2:2–4; 9:13–14; 10:28–29; 12:9; 12:25). The first example is as follows:

A. "For if the word which was spoken through angels became steadfast, and every transgression and disobedience received just recompense;
B. how shall we escape, having neglected so great a salvation [as this], which had its beginning when it was spoken through the Lord, was confirmed to us by those who heard, while God supported the testimony with signs, wonders, and various kinds of miracles, and by the distribution of the Holy Spirit according to his will?"

7. *Typology*. A typology is a belief that objects, events, persons, and institutions exist and occur in relationship to other corresponding objects, events, persons, and institutions. For earthly things, when considered antitypes, there are prior and corresponding heavenly prototypes or archetypes which were the patterns by which the earthly

things were created. For instance, according to Hebrews, there was a heavenly temple not made with hands which was a prototype for the temple made with hands at Jerusalem, which was its inferior antitype. When the typology dealt with earthly things, the pattern was usually referred to as a "type," rather than a "prototype," and its corresponding antitype was also earthly and historical. Typological exegesis was not allegorical. The antitype was not designed to give a hidden meaning to the type or to change the meaning originally intended by it. Rather it anticipated a later event, person, object, or institution which corresponded in some imitative fashion to its earlier type. For instance, the exodus from Egypt was a type of deliverance of which the deliverance from Babylon and the future anticipated deliverances were understood as antitypes. Frequently the type was expected to be followed by a superior antitype. Moses was an inferior type to be succeeded by his antitype, the Son (see *Mos.* I. 27–158); the levitical priesthood was a type to be succeeded by a superior high priest of the order of Melchizedek; the old covenant and Mount Sinai were types for the superior covenant and revelation at Mount Zion. Platonic philosophy includes a typology in which all earthly things are but shadows of the heavenly pattern or original. The typology in Hebrews, however, is different. There are heavenly prototypes, to be sure, but they are understood in terms of historical sequence and faith that is foreign to Platonism. Most types were historical and earthly, and they anticipated antitypes that were also historical and earthly.

8. *Treasury of merits.* An important concept in Jewish and Christian theology is the belief that sins and virtues accumulate and are "stored" the way money might be stored in a treasury. The Lord was believed to keep records of every sin and virtue and require that the books be balanced from time to time. Not only were the individual Israelite's sins recorded, but all Israel's good and bad deeds were under one classification so that excess virtues from one Israelite might be used to balance some other Israelite's excess sins. On this basis were developed doctrines of atonement, redemption, and eschatological expectations. The author of Hebrews accepted the treasury of merits as part of his theology.

9. *Inclusion.* An inclusion (Latin *inclusio*) is a literary form that brings the reader to the beginning of a passage when he reaches its conclusion. This formula is a signal to the reader that the unit is complete. Sometimes an inclusion "frames" a very small unit, as in Matt 6:19–20:

"Do not lay up for yourselves treasures . . .
but lay up for yourselves treasures . . ."

A larger unit is Matt 7:16–20, which begins and ends as follows:

"from their fruits you shall know them."

In between is a short discussion on the relationship of plants to fruits they produce. Whatever the content of the section between the beginning and concluding statements, it takes the center position like meat or cheese in a sandwich. The beginning and concluding parts of the inclusion are like the bread on the outside of a sandwich.

Hebrews contains many short and long sections marked off by inclusions. The author did not always place the key words at the very beginning and the very end of a unit, because he frequently followed the final part of the inclusion with a connecting sentence, relating one unit to the next. The connecting sentences frequently also affected the opening sentence of a unit in the same way. For instance, Heb 1:4 is a connecting clause relating the introduction (1:1–3) to the following unit, and it includes a catchword, "angels," to prepare the reader for the following unit which is sandwiched in between the two parts of the inclusion, "to which of the angels has he ever said" (1:5, 13). The unit, however, also includes 1:14, which completes the sense of the unit. In the same way, the phrase "not to angels" in 2:5 and 2:16 forms an inclusion, but the unit is not complete without 2:17–18, which has a summarizing and introductory purpose of its own. The author of Hebrews used inclusions like this, but he also used catch words and transition sentences along with them to relate units together to blend one unit into the next. These will be noted throughout the commentary.[4]

10. *Chiasm.* Chiasm (Latin *chiasmus*) is derived from the Greek *chiazein,* to mark with a *chi,* which looks like the Latin X. The literary form, chiasm, is one which includes at least two units, whether they are words, lines, ideas, or paragraphs, and each of these units must have at least two parts, so that there are four parts to form the four points of a *chi.* Like the inclusion, these form a sandwich-like expression, but in a much more precise way than the inclusion requires. The *chi* is formed by arranging the words of the first unit in one sequence and those of the second in reverse order, to form an arrangement such as this:

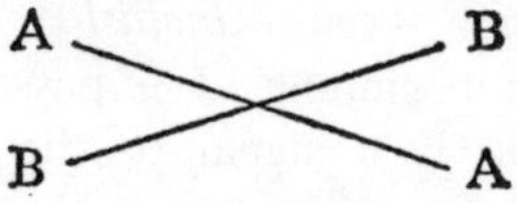

[4] See B. C. Butler, *The Originality of St. Matthew* (Cambridge, 1951), p. 150, and F. C. Fenton, "Inclusio and Chiasmus in Matthew," StEv I (1959), 174–79.

An example of this is Matt 19:30:

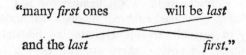

"many *first* ones — will be *last*

and the *last* — *first*."

The chiasm in Matt 19:30 is repeated in 20:16, thus forming an inclusion with a chiasm at both ends (see also Matt 10:28; 12:49–50).

In addition to words, phrases are sometimes put together chiastically, such as Matt 7:6:

A. "Do not give dogs what is holy,
B. and do not throw your pearls before swine:
B. lest they [the swine] trample them underfoot,
A. and [the dogs] turn to attack you."

A euphonic chiasm in Hebrews is 4:16b[5]:

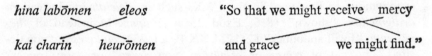

hina labōmen — *eleos* — "So that we might receive — mercy

kai charin — *heurōmen* — and grace — we might find."

"Mercy" and "grace" are synonymous and form a hendiadys here. Concepts and literary forms that have been discussed in this introduction will be illustrated as occasions arise in the commentary.

11. *The author's use of the Old Testament.* This homiletic midrash has been generously interspersed with Old Testament allusions and direct quotations. Although the text on which the entire homily was based is Ps 110, the citation from Jer 31:31–34 is the longest quotation in the entire New Testament (8:8–12). According to Westcott, in addition to many allusions, there are twelve direct quotations from the Pentateuch, eleven from the Psalms, four from the prophets, and two from the writings and historical books.[6]

For many years scholars have thought the author had access to the LXX alone. Recent studies, however, indicate a far more complex situation. Howard concluded that of forty-one possible sources for thirty-five quotations, twenty-four are unlike either the MT or the LXX,

[5] Fenton, StEv I (1959), 174–79, and J. M. Moulton, *A Grammar of New Testament Greek* (Edinburgh, 1963), III, 345–47. Some scholars say the chiasm is first of all a Semitic form, evident in MT Pss 3:8–9; 7:17; 58:7. It is very common in the MT and in Ugaritic literature (see D. N. Freedman, "The Structure of Psalm 137," in *Near Eastern Studies,* ed. H. Goedicke [Baltimore, 1971], pp. 188, 203–4) and in Syriac literature (so J. T. Clemons in personal conversation).

[6] Westcott, p. 472.

eight are identical to both, six are identical to MT against LXX, and only two are identical to the LXX against the MT.[7] The discovery of the Dead Sea scrolls has enabled scholars to understand better the wide variety of textual versions available to biblical scholars in New Testament times. Of course, there are still only a few texts that can actually be compared, but there are enough to remind scholars that any study of the texts used by New Testament authors must consider the possibility that many texts that are no longer extant might have been used then. Among those now available for comparison, Hebrews sometimes agrees with one and sometimes another. In Heb 2:7, 10:5, and 12:6, for instance, the author's argument depends on the LXX. In 1:6 he may have translated the same version as 4Q Deuteronomy, or he may have had access to a LXX translation of that text. Sometimes the author seems to have used a LXX version different from any extant text, and, for his purposes, inferior both to the LXX and to the MT (2:16). In some cases the author used a Greek word that is synonymous to that used in the LXX, such as *deichthenta* instead of *dedigmenon,* "shown" (8:5; Exod 25:40); *apaggelō* instead of *diēgēsomai,* "I will announce" (2:12; LXX Ps 21:23); *eudokēsas,* "you desired," instead of *ḗtēsas* or *ezētēsas,* "you asked" or "you sought" (10:6; LXX Ps 39:7). These synonyms used by the author of Hebrews might suggest the use of a variant LXX text, but there are other variations that require a different explanation. In his use of Jer 31:31–34, the author used *diathēsomai* for "I will covenant" in 10:16, consistent with the LXX. In 8:8, however, he substituted *syntelesō* for *diathēsomai.* Other differences between these two references are: In 8:10, the author followed the LXX, "with the house of Israel" (*tō̧ oikō̧ Israēl*); in 10:16, he substituted "to them" (*pros autous*). In 8:10, he quoted the LXX,

> "[I will] put my laws in their minds
> and on their hearts I will write them."

In 10:16, he altered the quotation to read as follows:

> "[I will] put my laws on their hearts
> and on their minds I will write them."

The important difference between these two quotations in the Greek is the reversal of "minds" and "hearts," forming a chiasm of the statement.[8]

[7] G. Howard, "Hebrews and the Old Testament Quotations," *Novum Testamentum* 10 (1968), 211. Analysts vary somewhat in their judgment and count. See also Schröger, pp. 247–66.

[8] For a fuller discussion on these texts and others that may have been altered by the author of Hebrews himself, see K. J. Thomas, "The Old Testament Citations in Hebrews," NTS 11 (1964–65), 303–25.

It is very unlikely that the author of Hebrews used one LXX text for the composition of chapter eight and a different one for chapter ten. It seems rather that he used the same text in both cases and that he paraphrased it as he chose. Since the possibility is great that the author of Hebrews made changes like this in these instances, this provides another variable factor to consider. He may have made all of the changes listed above that might otherwise be attributed to variant texts, but that does not exclude the possibility that he used variant texts. It just raises more doubts and requires careful consideration of the possibilities in each case. These will be treated in the commentary.

Westcott is correct in observing that the author of Hebrews used passages from all parts of the Old Testament as proof texts, considering them all authoritative representations of the word of God, but he did not consider them all "law" as Westcott implies.[9] Paul and John both referred to passages from the prophets or Psalter as "law," but for the author of Hebrews the law was the Pentateuch. This was the code that governed the Levites (7:5) and must be changed (7:12). It was fleshly (7:16); it perfected nothing (7:19); and it was responsible for establishing as high priests men who are weak (7:28). Jesus was different from those priests who offered gifts according to the law (8:4). The first covenant was renewed according to the law of Moses (9:19) which required blood for cleansing almost everything (9:22). That law of Moses, however, had only a shadow of the coming good things (10:1). The sacrifices which the psalmist prohibited were offered according to the law (10:8). The law of Moses was rated in an inferior position in comparison with the new covenant of Christ (10:28–29). The rest that was promised in Ps 95 together with an oath was superior to the rest promised in the Pentateuch without an oath (3:7–4:10). The new covenant promised by the prophet Jeremiah took precedence over the old covenant established in the Pentateuch (8:8–13). The priesthood of Melchizedek established with an oath in Ps 110 replaced the levitical priesthood established in the Pentateuch (see ch. 7). Although the author used passages from the Pentateuch for proof texts and supportive texts, he considered the Pentateuch to be the law of Moses, associated with the old covenant, the old priesthood, and the temple made with hands. It was an inferior type to be succeeded by something superior, which nevertheless would be of the same general kind. He used Num 18 to explain Ps 110 and Exod 15–17||Num 14–20 to explain Ps 95, but his defense was built on the Psalter and not on the Pentateuch. Westcott thought it was remarkable that, "with two exceptions (II Sam 7:14; Isa 8:17f.), all the primary passages which

[9] Westcott, p. 473.

are quoted to illustrate the true nature of the Person and Work of Christ are taken from the Psalms."[10] This consistency *is* remarkable, but it fits in well with the author's general outlook. He considered the Psalms to have been written by David. David and the prophets were all composed after the Pentateuch and therefore reflected a later word of God. Whenever they contradicted the Pentateuch, this meant that the Pentateuch had been superseded. The author seemed to relate the prophets and the Psalter to the new covenant prophesied by Jeremiah and considered that all the prophets prophesied only for the days of the Messiah. Jesus was the Messiah, therefore these prophecies were to be applied directly to the time of the author of Hebrews and the new covenant established by Jesus. On the other hand, the Pentateuch was associated with the exodus generation which had been given a fair opportunity to receive the promised rest, but failed because of disobedience. That was the reason why a new opportunity was given later. The author tended to group his concepts into typologies, and this is one of the ramifications of this tendency. The Pentateuch was classed with the old covenant, the law of Moses, the disobedient generation, the inferior priesthood, and the temple made with hands. The Psalms and at least some of the prophets were associated with the new covenant, the new priesthood, the new law, the days of the Messiah, the temple not made with hands, and the perfect sacrifice. Even the author's use of scripture reflected these contrasts.

[10] Westcott, p. 473.

OUTLINE

I. GOD'S LATEST WORD
(1:1–4)

1 1 In many places and ways God spoke in antiquity to the fathers
through the prophets; 2 in the last of these days he has spoken to us
through a Son, whom he established heir of all, through whom he
also made the ages;

3 who, being a reflection of the glory and stamp of his nature,
bearing everything by the word of his power,
when he had made a purification for [his] sins,
sat down at the right hand of the Majesty in exaltation

4 being so much greater than the angels that he inherited a name
more excellent than theirs.

COMMENT

1:1. The opening verse of Hebrews prepares the reader for all the substance of the document from 1:1–12:29. The Greek words rendered "many places and ways" are adverbs for which there are no good English equivalents. The force intended is that God's speaking in the past has been diverse both in geographical location and in method of disclosure. He appeared in visions, dreams, symbols, Urim and Thummim, angels, natural events, ecstasy, the column of smoke or fire, and occasionally face to face. These revelations occurred to different people at different periods of history—in Ur of the Chaldees, Haran, Canaan, the Wilderness, Egypt, and Babylon. The "fathers" were probably not only Abraham, Isaac, and Jacob, who preceded the prophets, but rather all of the religious ancestors listed in 11:4–38, which list the author noted as being incomplete. The intended readers depended on all these "fathers" for their tradition. "Through the prophets" renders the Greek *en tois prophētais,* literally "in" the prophets, but this is a Hebrew idiom, *dābār* b^e translated as in "the Spirit of the Lord speaks through me" (II Sam 23:2 *et passim*). The b^e in Hebrew in this usage has the force of "through" or "by" rather than "in." Therefore the translation given is "through." This verse includes the beautifully alliterative Greek words, *polymerōs, polytropōs, palai, patrasin* and *prophētais.*

2. "In the last of these days" is a very literal translation of the Greek *ep' eschatou tōn hēmerōn toutōn.* A few texts read *eschatōn,* probably because of scribal memory of the idiom as it occurs in Gen

49:1; Deut 4:30; Jer 37[30]:24; Ezek 38:16; Dan 2:28; Hosea 3:5; Micah 4:1; and II Peter 3:3. The idiom "in the last of these days" reflects a Semitic attitude toward time. Semitic words for past are words meaning "before" or "in front of" (*qdm, lpnym*) as if the Semite were looking toward his ancestral origins when he talked of the past. The past had happened; it was known and could be faced. The future, on the other hand, could not be seen, so it was considered "behind" or "in back of" the person who stood in the present. Words for "tomorrow," "later," "future," and "last" were words like *māḥār, 'aḥar, 'aḥ^{a}rīt,* or *'aḥ^{a}rōn*—all of which refer to something behind. This does not mean the Semite viewed time as either a circular or a horizontal phenomenon, but that he was a realist. He understood his world as it appeared to him. He could not see the future. On the basis of this concept, the author of Hebrews spoke of the future hope as "things not seen" (11:1). Noah prepared for the future "not yet seen" (11:7). Christians could look to Jesus whose activity took place in the past (12:2). This does not mean the Semite was not interested in the future, but that his only basis for understanding what the future might be was the past, from which he deduced the future in terms of typologies or patterns of historical events. This is why his eschatological beliefs were inseparably tied to history. The Semite thought of the future as the "behind" aspect of time. One of the idioms that expresses this is *b^{e}'aḥ^{a}rīt hayyāmīm,* "in the afterness of days." "In the last of these days" refers to the last days of this undesirable age which would be followed by a better future.

The Son here is also heir, as might be expected. The word "heir" in other contexts is also associated with "lord." The word *klēronomos,* rendered "heir," is derived from the Greek word *klēros,* meaning "lot." In a situation in which lots were drawn to divide property or select a winner, the one who drew the lot was the heir. This word came to be used for dividing the property that a father left to his children when he died. Hebrew traditions were probably identical to the Assyrian customs in which lots were drawn to determine which son received which portion of property. When there was only one son, of course, there would also normally be only one *heir*. Where there were more sons than one, however, the eldest son would choose and take the first portion, after which he and the other sons would draw lots to determine which share of the property fell to which son. This gave the first-born the advantage of receiving both the choice share and a normal share of the property.[1] A king's dynastic succession, however, was normally given to only one son. The heir to the throne was usually the oldest son, but the king might choose a different son to succeed him, as David did (I Kings 1:1–40). Many times sons fought over this position. Heritage was closely related to sonship. Paul observed that an heir, while a minor, was no different in position from a slave, even though he was the lord of all (Gal 4:1). It was after he became an adult and received his heritage

[1] G. R. Driver and J. C. Miles, *The Assyrian Laws* (Oxford, 1935), pp. 295–97.

that his status changed radically. The authority of the son and heir in comparison to other messengers or servants was shown in the attitude of the farmers, who, after they had killed the son and heir, hoped to be able to take over the father's property for themselves (Matt 21:33–41). Had Abraham's servant not succeeded in finding a wife for Isaac, Abraham's seed would have discontinued, and Abraham's property would probably have fallen to the family of the servant (Gen 24). It was as a king coming into his inheritance that one like a son of man appeared before the Ancient of Days and "was given dominion and glory and a kingdom" (Dan 7:13–14). It was in similar terms of royalty that Jesus said, "All things have been delivered to me by my Father" (Matt 11:27; cf. Luke 10:22). The angel who spoke to Mary said of Jesus, "He will be great, and will be called the Son of the Most High; and the Lord God will give him the throne of his father David . . . and of his kingdom there shall be no end" (Luke 1:32–33). Jesus' status as Son and heir is evident in the New Testament (John 3:35; 5:22; 13:3; 17:2), and Christians, who are also sons, are by that token "joint heirs with Christ" (Rom 8:17). The younger brother, Jacob, partly out of courtesy and deference, referred to his older brother, Esau, as "lord" (*'adōn—kyrios*), and himself as "servant" (Gen 32:4, 18; 33:13–14). The relationship of David to the Lord was that of a first-born, a chosen one, to a father. The Father was the one who covenanted to give his first-born the throne (Ps 89). Paul said the heir was "lord of all" (Gal 4:1), and Acts 10:36 described Jesus, the Messiah, as Lord of all. Hebrews is consistent with this usage, describing Jesus, the Son, as heir of all.

RSV renders *aiōnas* "the world," even though it is plural. There is some basis for translating it "worlds," because some rabbis and early Christians believed that there were more worlds than one of which the Lord was in charge (Mid. Ps 18:15; cf. *Recog.* II. 68, 70). Furthermore, the "all" over which Jesus was made heir appears to be the same as *tous aiōnas,* which the RSV has rendered "the world." A stronger reason is the parallel between 1:2 and 11:3. In 11:3 the claim is made that *tous aiōnas* "have been put in order by [the] word of God." This clearly refers to the creation, coming first in order of events listed in Genesis, followed by the Cain and Abel story (11:4), Enoch (11:5–6), Noah (11:7), etc. RSV has the support of Moffatt[2] in its translation, but many scholars think the temporal force of *aiōnas* governs here,[3] for the following reasons: It is true that the Greek *aiōn* and the corresponding Hebrew *'ōlām* can be rendered "world," but the sense of "age" is more frequent in both. Thus "the age to come" (*hā'ōlām habbā'*) refers to the period when the Messiah will rule. Just as Jews believed that God created the world, so also they believed that he established the ages, the days of the week, the holiday seasons, sabbaths, and jubilees. Some thought

[2] Moffatt, p. 5.
[3] Keil, pp. 28–29; Lenski, pp. 29–36; Turner, p. 19; Vaughan, p. 5; Westcott, pp. 8–9.

that all periods were decreed, established once-for-all, finalized so that life consisted only in living out the foreordained periods which God established. According to IV Ezra 4:37:

"With a measure he has measured the times;
by number he numbered the times;
he will neither move nor stir
until the predicted measure is fulfilled."

According to Pss of Sol 18:12–14:

"He has established the lights in their courses
for determining the seasons from day to day,
and they do not deviate from the path which he
commanded for them.
In the fear of God their path [is taken] each day,
from the day in which God created them until the
age [to come] (*eōs aiōnas*),
and they have not deviated since the day he created them,
from generations of old they have not left their courses
if God did not command them through his servants."

It is probably with this concept of time and creation in mind that the author wrote both Heb 1:2 and 11:3. He was clearly referring to the creation of "all" over which the Son was established heir, but "all" included not only substance and material; the first of God's creation was light, which was separated from darkness to begin units of time. The author here chose to emphasize the temporal sequence, the periods or ages ranging from Adam until Christ. It was "through a Son" that he "made the ages," putting them "in order" (11:3).

3. "The glory" refers to the presence of the Lord, usually identified either with the ark of the covenant or with the column of fire or smoke over the altar. After the tragedy of Israel's defeat by the Philistines, one of Eli's daughters-in-law named her newly born son "The glory has departed," because "The glory has departed from Israel, for the ark of God has been captured" (I Sam 4:21–22). In Ezekiel's vision the comment was made of the area over the altar, "Such was the appearance of the likeness of the glory of the Lord" (Ezek 1:28). In a vision, Ezekiel saw the glory of God move from the temple eastward, presumably toward Babylon where the people were (Ezek 11:23). The glory of God that was seen in the smoke pouring out from the tent of meeting where the Lord dwelt as he tented in the midst of his people, where they beheld his glory (*doxa*), was compared to the glory of "[the] only one from [the] Father" (John 1:14).

Hebrews also considered Jesus a "reflection of the glory" which meant the same as being a "stamp of his nature." The Greek word for "stamp" comes from the verb *charassein,* "to mark, engrave, or stamp." The stamp, accordingly, refers to the characteristic and distinctive form (see II Macc 4:10). Isaac was claimed to have features (*zīw 'iqōnīw*) like those of Abraham (Gen R. 21:2; 53 §6). This does not mean either that Isaac was actually identical to Abraham or that Jesus was identical to God. Both were reflections and had characteristics of their fathers. Jesus was the son, heir, and apostle of God (3:1). As apostle or agent he was sent with the full authority of the one who sent him. A man's agent is like the man himself, not *physically,* but *legally.* He has the power of attorney for the one who sent him. That which the apostle/agent does is in behalf of and has the approval and support of the one who sent him. He has the authority of an ambassador who speaks in behalf of a king in negotiating for his country (Ber. 5:5).[4] Jesus said that the one who received his apostles whom he had sent received Jesus himself, and not only Jesus, but the one who had sent him (Matt 10:40–42; John 13:20). This is true because legally a man's apostle is like the man himself. The New Testament apostles were apostles of Jesus, and Jesus was an apostle of God. It is against this background that Jesus, in the same context, could say both, "He who has seen me has seen the Father" (John 14:9) and "The Father is greater than I" (John 14:28). *Legally* Jesus was identical with the Father, but *physically* the Father was greater. Just as Christians thought of Jesus as an apostle of God, so Jews thought of Moses as the "apostle between Israel and their heavenly Father" (Sifra *beḥuqqōtai,* perek 8:12; Lev 26:46). As the great apostle (*magnus nuntius*), Moses prayed "every hour, both day and night . . . to him who rules all the world" (Assumption of Moses 11:17). Samaritans also thought of Moses as their apostle of God: they called him a good apostle, a righteous apostle, an apostle of God, and the apostle of the True One whom God specially chose for apostleship. As apostle, he was also called "Son of the house of God," God's "man," "savior," "prophet," "faithful one," "crown of the righteous of the world," and "light of prophethood." As an apostle, Moses was entrusted with the mysteries and honored in the things revealed. To Moses was revealed that which preceded creation and also that which follows the day of vengeance. To him was opened the gateway to the unseen. He had drawn near to the holy deep darkness where the Divine One was and had seen the wonders of the unseen (Memar Marqah 2 §12; 3 §6; 4 §4; 5 §3; 6 §§3, 11). There are many biblical illustrations of apostolic authority: Jehu was ritually made king when Elisha sent one of the sons of the prophets to anoint him. It was not necessary for Elisha to anoint him himself for the anointing to be authoritative (II Kings 9:1–10). Paul sent a message to the Corinthians, giving them authority to deliver to Satan the man who had been living with his father's wife, because Paul was "with them in spirit," meaning that his legal authorization was there (I Cor 5:1–5).

"Bearing everything by the word of his power" does not picture the Son playing the part of Atlas carrying the world on his shoulder, nor in the sense that God is the "sustainer of the world" or "age" (*sōbēl 'ōlām*) (Exod R. 64c, §36:4). Rather, as ambassador or apostle, the Son has

[4] See K. H. Rengstorf, "Apostolos," TWZNT, I, 406–48; R. M. Boyer, "God's Agent in the Fourth Gospel" (unpublished Th.M. thesis for Wesley Theological Seminary, 1965), summarized by P. Borgen, "God's Agent in the Fourth Gospel," in *Religions in Antiquity,* ed. J. Neusner (Leiden, 1968), pp. 137–48.

authority over everything since he is given legal authority and is supported in everything he does "by the word of [God's] power." He speaks for the One who sent him.[5]

There are some textual variants related to the purification. Texts DP[46] add "through his" purification, and other texts have "through his own" purification. These are probably interpretative additions which understood Jesus' crucifixion as a sin offering intended to cleanse the community of its sin. The addition of "our" to sins by some of the same texts makes this probability still greater. This is a normal interpretation of the later church that believed Jesus to be completely sinless and was therefore defensive about anything that might imply sinfulness. The author of Hebrews, however, seemed more interested in portraying Jesus as a king than in defending his original freedom from defilement, so he felt no difficulty either in composing a small verse of poetry or in utilizing one that described the Son as a king who would be purified to be ritually undefiled before he ascended his throne where he could sit at God's "right hand." Once purified, he was without sin (4:15).

"The Majesty" is a substantive, meaning "the majesty of God." To avoid unnecessary possibilities for blasphemy, many Jews and Christians used such words as Heaven (Luke 15:18), Power (Matt 26:64), The Throne of Majesty (Heb 8:1), The Mighty One (II Bar 85:2, 3), The Place [where God dwells] (Gen R. 68c; Exod R. 64a *et passim*), The Holy One blessed be He (Gen R. 68c; Exod R. 64c *et passim*), and other adjectives and descriptive expressions instead of the divine name.

"In exaltation" is not connected with "Majesty" but with the verb "he sat down." Of course "the Majesty" was also in a position of exaltation, but the point of the statement is that the Son sat down in exaltation at the right hand of the Majesty. The reason it was not said in just that way was the author's attempt to keep his quotations of scripture intact. The enthronement Ps 110 was the primary text for the entire exposition, 1:1–12:29. Verse 3 set the stage for the rest of the document by this initial quotation. Both in Egypt and in Mesopotamia the king was a son of the deity.[6] The author of Hebrews used Ps 110 as his text because he wanted to affirm that Jesus, as the Son, was raised to the position of a king when "he sat down at the right hand of the Majesty."

4. "Inherited" is the perfect tense, active voice of *klēronomein,* which in normal Greek means "to obtain a lot or portion," "to be an heir." In Jewish and Christian thought forms, however, it has a wider meaning. The heirs "inherit" the land, the cities, eternal life, the Kingdom of God, the promises, and salvation. The verb *klēronomein* frequently renders the Hebrew *yrš,* a more active term, which means to take possession, dispossess, succeed. When the Hebrews "inherited" the promised land, they

[5] *Contra* NEV, "Sustains the Universe." For other interpretations, see Williamson, pp. 96–97.

[6] Mowinckel, II, 54.

understood that God had allotted it to them, but they also dispossessed the Canaanites and took possession of their "inheritance." When Antiochus Epiphanes sacked Jerusalem, a Jewish author said of the siege: "They took women and children captive and they inherited (*eklēronomēsan*) the cattle" (I Macc 1:32, see also LXX II Sam 7:1, quoted in 4Q Florilegium 1:7). Jesus, as "heir" (*klēronomos*) (1:2), was made possessor, administrator, or ruler over "all" (1:2). A zealous Jew of pre-Christian times urged the Lord to raise up for Israel a king, who would cleanse Jerusalem from Gentiles, which meant driving the sinners out of the inheritance (Pss of Sol 17:23–25). For him, as for others, the inheritance was the promised land which the Messiah was to reconquer and rule. Since his inheritance was associated with his sonship, which name he inherited, he was evidently made Son, heir, apostle, and high priest (1:2; 3:1; 5:10) all at once. In this context, the translation "acquired" or "obtained" would be proper for *keklēronomēken* (1:4).

Summary.—This introduction was well written. It introduces a variety of contrasts to be developed throughout 1:1 – 12:29; it briefly defines the nature of the main character of the exposition; and it supplies a neat transition clause to prepare the reader for the next immediate topic of discussion. The contrasts are between: (1) the ages of antiquity and the age of the author, (2) the fathers and the believers of the author's day, and (3) the prophets and the Son.

Early Jewish and Christian eschatology thought of time as a sequence of days, weeks, generations, or ages, following one another. When one day or age ended, the next began. There were six days of labor each week before there was one day of rest. There were six years of produce before the sabbath year when the land was to receive its year of rest. The author of Hebrews thought of deliverance from Roman rule as the age of "rest."[7] The days of the Messiah were to be those in which Israel gained her freedom, before the period of "rest," during which *she* would rule the world, rather than Rome. Since Jesus was the Messiah, the author believed himself to be living at the end of the sixth "age," just before the age of rest. "In the last of these days" (1:2), then, had the same meaning as "at the end of the ages" (9:26), after the Messiah had "appeared" (9:26) and during which the author of Hebrews lived.[8] Rabbis said all the prophets prophesied only of the days of the Messiah

[7] The political nature of "rest" will be discussed in greater detail in chs. 3 and 4. Spicq, I, 14, is not justified in making a contrast between the entrance into the promised land as the hope of the old covenant and the entrance into the sabbatical rest (4:9) as the hope of the new covenant. To be sure, the new covenant was to be better than the old, but that was principally because it would be effective, whereas the old one was not. Like II Isa (44:24–28; 49:6–26), the author of Hebrews had dreams of better things, but they were all centered around Jerusalem and Palestine.

[8] For a more detailed account of sabbatical eschatology, see CC, pp. 9–18.

(Shab. 63a). The author of Hebrews considered Jesus to be the Messiah and the days of the Messiah to be "the last of these days" (1:2).

A less happy contrast between the earlier days and the days of the author is evident in II Bar 85:1–3:

> "In earlier times and in generations of old our fathers had assistants—righteous men, prophets, and saints. Furthermore, we were in our own land, and they assisted us when we sinned, and they made intercession for us with him who made us because they were confident in their works; and the Mighty One heard them and acted favorably toward us. But now the righteous ones are gathered and the prophets have died, and consequently we have left our land, and Zion is removed from us. Now we have nothing at all but the Mighty One and his law."

Michel has correctly called attention to the poetic nature of 1:3 and related it to other poetry in Hebrews (4:12–13; 7:3).[9] Here the verse was suitably incorporated into the author's description of the Son and seems to have been composed originally as a praise to the Son. This poem was particularly useful to the author because it contained a quotation from Ps 110. Rabbis applied Ps 110:1 to Abraham, who was called "king" after he had been victorious over all the kings and was then invited to sit at the Lord's right hand (Ps 110). They also said it referred to the Messiah for whom a throne was prepared (Isa 16:5) and for whom the Lord would make war as he did when he made war for Israel against Pharaoh at the Reed Sea (Yalqut HaMakiri on Ps 110). The author of Hebrews was interested in the royal enthronement character of Ps 110 because he wanted to present Jesus as a king. Like other kings, he held the position of favor with God, "at the right hand" (1:3). Christians frequently confessed that Jesus held this place of honor and quoted Ps 110 to show it (Mark 12:36; Acts 2:32–36; Rom 8:34; Eph 1:20; Col 3:1; I Peter 3:22. See also Mark 14:62; 16:19; Acts 7:56; I Cor 15:25). Jesus, the Son, was a true replica of the Father, acted as his agent, and spoke with the authority of the Father. As king he had a special place of honor with the Father that was even greater than that of the angels. This last point was to receive further demonstration.

[9] Michel, pp. 114–16.

II. SUPERIORITY OVER ANGELS (1:5–2:18)

Son has higher status

1 5 For to which of the angels has he ever said,
"You are my son. Today I have begotten you"?
and again,
"I will be his Father, and he will be my Son"?

Angels worship the Son

6 And again, when he led his first-born into the world, he said,
"Now, let all the angels of God prostrate themselves before him."

Angels, temporal; Son, eternal

7 Now [with reference] to the angels, it says,
"You, Lord, in the beginning laid the earth's foundation, and
"He makes his angels winds,
his ministers, flames of fire";
8 but [with reference] to the Son, [it says],
"Your throne, O God, is forever and ever,
and the staff of justice is the staff of his kingdom.

Son is anointed

9 "You loved justice and you hated lawlessness;
because of this, God, your God, anointed you [with] oil of joy, [ranking you greater] than your colleagues."

God's eternity

10 And
"You, Lord, in the beginning laid the earth's foundation,
and the heavens are the works of your hands.
11 "They perish, but you endure;
and they all grow old like a garment,
12 and like a robe you will roll them up;
(like a garment,) and they will be changed;
but you are the same and your years will not run out."

Son is at God's right hand

13 Now, to which of the angels has he ever said,
"Sit at my right hand
until I make your enemies a footstool for your feet"?
14 They are all ministering spirits, sent for service of those who are
about to inherit salvation, are they not?

Son is higher than the angels

2 1 Therefore we must pay closer attention to the things that were
heard, lest we drift away. 2 For if the word which was spoken
through angels became steadfast, and every transgression and disobedience received just recompense, 3 how shall we escape, having
neglected so great a salvation [as this], which had its beginning
when it was spoken through the Lord, was confirmed to us by those
who heard, 4 while God supported the testimony with signs, wonders, and various kinds of miracles, and by the distribution of the
Holy Spirit according to his will? 5 For [it was] not to angels [that]
he subjected the world to come, about which we speak, 6 but somewhere someone has testified saying:
"What is man that you pay attention to him
or the son of man that you consider him?
7 For a short time, you have made him lower than the angels,
[and] crowned him with glory and honor.
8 You have put all things under his feet."
In "putting all things under," he left nothing that was not made
subordinate to him. Now we do not yet see "all things made subject" to him, 9 but [with reference to the passage] "For a short time
having been made lower than the angels," we see Jesus, because of
the suffering of death, "crowned with glory and honor," so that, by
the grace of God, he might taste death for everyone.

The Son and the believers

10 For it was fitting for him, for whom were all things and through
whom were all things, to make perfect the pioneer of their salvation
through sufferings, leading many sons to glory. 11 For both he who
sanctifies and those who are sanctified are all from one. Therefore
he is not ashamed to call them "brothers," 12 saying,

"I will announce your name to my brothers,
in the midst of the congregation I will praise you in song";
13 and again:
"I will be confident of him":
and again:
"Behold, I and the children whom God has given me."
14 Since, therefore, the children share blood and flesh, he also
himself shared the same equally, so that he might incapacitate the
one who controls death, namely, the devil, 15 and release all those
who, through fear of death, were subject to slavery through every
aspect of life. 16 For he certainly does not prefer [take] angels but
he prefers [takes] the seed of Abraham. 17 Therefore he was obligated to be made like the brothers in every way, so that he might
become a merciful and faithful high priest [regarding] divine services, so that the sins of the people might be expiated. 18 For because he himself suffered, having been tempted, he is able to help
those who are being tempted.

Comment

Son has higher status

1:5. Both quotations in 1:5 are related to kings who are called God's sons. They are included as part of a rhetorical question, expecting a negative answer. It has the same meaning as if it said, "He has never said to any of the angels . . ." The first quotation (Ps 2:7) is from an enthronement Psalm. It pictures the kings of surrounding nations plotting against the Lord and his anointed one, meaning his anointed king. While they are doing that, the Lord from heaven laughs and mocks them. In anger he informs them that he has set his king on Zion, his holy hill. It is of that anointed king that he said, "You are my son, today I have begotten you" (Ps 2:7). He promised his anointed one (*mešîḥō*) that he would make the nations his heritage. This anointed king would break those nations with a rod of iron, dash them into pieces like a potter's vessel. If the kings of the earth were wise, they would submit immediately and serve the Lord with trembling, which means they should surrender unconditionally at once to the ruler whom the Lord appointed king over Zion. It is such a powerful king as this who is called God's Son and his anointed one. It is as a mighty king that he was enthroned to sit at God's right hand. As such a king he was called "Son," which is a greater name than any of the angels had acquired. The rabbis listed together Ps 2:7–8, Ps 110:1, and Dan 7:13–14. The first two references are enthronement Psalms, and the third pictures one like a son of man receiving the dominion, glory, and a kingdom while other nations were made subject to him. Rabbi Yudan said these were all promises which the Lord would fulfill for the Messiah (Midr. Ps 2 §9). This means that the rabbis considered the Messiah to be a king, Son of God, and Son of man. In Matt 16:17, 20, 27, Jesus was identified with the Messiah, Son of the living God, and Son of man (see also Matt 26:63).[1]

The words rendered "his" and "my" are literally "to him" and "to me," as the RSV renders. The Greek is a literal rendering of the Hebrew *lō l*^{e}*'āb . . . lī l*^{e}*bēn*. The *l*^{e} in each case might be rendered "as" or "for." In this case, God would act as a father in relationship to a son. The relationship of Jesus to God was certainly not understood by the author of Hebrews to be a physical relationship, whatever translation be accepted. For other examples of this kind of Semitism see Matt 19:5; Mark 10:8; Luke 3:5; I Cor 6:16; II Cor 6:18; Eph 5:31; Heb 8:10; James 5:3.

The second quotation (II Sam 7:14) also refers to Solomon in anticipation of his position as king over the united monarchy of Israel. Through Nathan, God promised David that God would establish Solomon on the throne, and he, as king over Israel, would be God's son and God would be his father (see also I Chron 17:13). I Chron 28:5 referred to the kingdom over which Solomon would rule as the kingdom of the Lord. The king was evidently believed to be in close relationship to the Lord. He was called God's son; he ruled over the Lord's kingdom and sat on the Lord's throne (I Chron 29:23). This further illustrates the significance of the name which Jesus inherited when he was called "Son." As Son he was the Messiah who was anointed to be king over the kingdom of the Lord. This has important implications which will receive further attention as Jesus' role is interpreted according to the author of Hebrews.

Among the Dead Sea scrolls is a collection of messianic passages (4Q Florilegium) which are closely related in subject matter to the first five verses of Hebrews. It contains three references to the expression "in the end of days" (*b*^{e}*'aḥ*^{a}*rīt hayyāmīm*), similar to Heb 1:2. The Massoretic reading of II Sam 7:1 is, "And the Lord gave him rest (*hēnīaḥ lō*) from all his surrounding enemies." The LXX renders the verb "rest" by the Greek for "inherit." "And the Lord made him heir (*kataklēronomēsen*) from all his surrounding enemies." This adds significance to the words "heir" and "inherit" used by the author of Hebrews (1:2, 4). In 4Q Florilegium, the statement is given as a direct address to David from the Lord: "And where he said to David, 'And I will [give] you [rest] from all your enemies'" (1:7). In the same document is a quotation from II Sam 7:14, also quoted in Heb 1:5: "I will establish the throne of his kingdom forever. I will be his Father and he will be my Son." The commentator explained this to mean: "He is the shoot of David

[1] See S. Mowinckel, *He That Cometh*, tr. G. W. Anderson (New York, 1954), pp. 123, 157–59.

(*ṣemāḥ Dāwīd*) who stands with the interpreter of the Torah, who [. . .] in Zi[on in] the end of days . . . who will arise to save Israel" (4Q Florilegium 1:10–13).

It is clear that the Old Testament passage from II Samuel refers to David's first successor on the throne, Solomon. It is also clear that the author of 4Q Florilegium expected a messiah from the son of David to fulfill this promise, and some scholars just assume that the author of Hebrews also expected a Davidic messiah when he used the same Old Testament quotation.[2] There is no direct evidence, however, that the author of Hebrews interpreted Jesus as belonging to the family of David, and there is very little indirect evidence that might even point in that direction. The author of Hebrews never mentioned David in relationship to Jesus or the Messiah. He portrayed a messiah who was a priest-king, which David and his successors certainly were not; but some Hasmoneans were, and the priest-king described in Hebrews resembles that type of messianic expectation much more closely than any messiahs from the families of David or Aaron.

Angels worship the Son

6. The quotation from Deuteronomy is not exactly like any text extant today. There are enough variants, however, to allow the possibility that the author had access to still others. The following editions of Deut 32:43 are available today:

Qumran Cave 4(4Q)[3]	*Massoretic Text* (*MT*)
1. Praise his people, *O heavens.*	1. Praise his people, *O nations,*
2. (and prostrate yourselves before him, all gods;)	
3. for he avenges the blood of his *sons*	3. for he avenges the blood of his *servants*
4. and returns vengeance on his adversaries	4. and returns vengeance on his adversaries
5. (and pays back those who hate him,)	
6. and he atones for the land of his people.	6. and atones for the land of his people.

The Septuagint (*LXX*)

1. Rejoice, *O heavens,* together with him (*hama autǭ*)
2. and let all the *sons of God* prostrate themselves before him;

[2] F. F. Bruce, "'To the Hebrews' or 'To the Essenes?'" NTS 9 (1962–63), 221.

[3] See P. W. Skehan, "A Fragment of the 'Song of Moses' (Deut 32) from Qumran," BASOR 136 (1954), 12–15. For a different conjecture on the relationship of these texts, see F. M. Cross, Jr., *The Ancient Library of Qumran and Modern Biblical Studies* (Garden City, 1958), pp. 135–37.

3. rejoice, *O nations,* with his people,
4. and let all the *angels of God* strengthen him,
5. because the blood of his *sons* will be avenged
6. and he will avenge and pay back justice against his enemies.
7. The Lord will both pay back those who hate him
8. and cleanse the land of his people.

The question is, how did these texts become so variant? Some conjectures are more likely than others. Since this is a poem, it is more likely that lines 2 and 5 of the 4Q text belonged to the original poem, providing parallels for the lines preceding. The Proto-MT may have contained these lines which some scribe omitted because they were redundant. It would be only an arbitrary guess to select whether "heavens" was more or less original than "nations," or "sons" than "servants." It seems likely, however, that the editor of this LXX passage had access to both the 4Q text and the Proto-MT, and that he quoted lines 1 and 2 from the 4Q text and lines 3 and 4 of the Proto-MT. In the 4Q text, line 1, there are two objects: "heavens" (*šāmayim*) and "his people" (*'ammō*). If it were not for the parallel with Deut 32:1, one might render this passage either "Praise his people, O heavens" or "Praise Heaven (—God), O his people." The LXX understood God as the object of praise and rendered *'ammō* (his people) as if it were pointed *'immō* and awkwardly translated it "together with him" (line 1) and "with his people" (line 3). The version of the 4Q text used by the LXX apparently read "sons of God" (*b^e^nē 'ēlīm*) rather than "gods" (*'^e^lohīm*). LXX, line 6, is evidently an abbreviation of lines 4 and 5 of the 4Q text, and LXX, line 7, is a similar abbreviation of lines 4 and 5 of the unabbreviated MT. The LXX translator and editor apparently did not want to choose between the two variants, so instead he included both, first lines 1 and 2 of 4Q and then the same two lines of Proto-MT. His line 5 agrees with 4Q, line 3, which was so similar to MT, line 3, that he did not quote the variant. Then, in the same sequence, he abbreviated first 4Q, lines 4 and 5, into his line 6 and then Proto-MT, lines 4 and 5, into his line 7. Since there was no variant between 4Q and MT, line 6, he quoted the line only once into his line 8, as he had done with 4Q and MT, line 3.

The author of Hebrews may either have used only the LXX and put the verb of line 2 into line 4, or he may have had access to a variant that is no longer extant in which line 2 read "angels of God" instead of "gods" (4Q) or "sons of God" (the LXX version of 4Q). These terms are sufficiently close in meaning to have been interchangeable. Perhaps one was substituted for the other in the course of transmission. One of these substitutions may have been made by the author of Hebrews himself. Angels were also called sons of God (Gen 6:4; Pss 29:1; 89:7; Job 1:6; 2:1; 38:7).

In Hebrew texts of Deut 32:43, the object of adoration was probably intended to be "his people," with the "heavens," "nations," "gods," "sons of

God" or "angels of God" doing the worshiping. The LXX translator understood God to be the object of worship throughout. He was probably dissatisfied with the theology that suggested any object of worship other than God, so he undersood *'ammō* to be pointed *'immō.* The author of Hebrews seems to have used either the Hebrew text similar to 4Q or a different LXX translation of that text, because he was able to change the object to first-born. It is easily understandable for a scribe to have changed "his people" to "his first-born," because Israel, God's people, was called the first-born (Exod 4:22). The next transfer involved understanding the "first-born" to mean the Messiah rather than Israel. Since it was understood also that all the prophets prophesied only for the time of the Messiah, this was a normal interpretation. Commenting on "Israel, my first-born son" (*bᵉkōrī*) (Exod 4:22), rabbis said, "Thus I shall make the king Messiah [the] first-born, as it is said, 'Also I will give him [the title of] first-born' (Ps 89:27[28])" (Exod R. 37b, 13:1, 19:7). Zechariah promised that a man whose name was "shoot" (*ṣemaḥ*) would build the temple of the Lord, bear the royal honor, and rule upon his throne (Zech 6:12–13). Philo, commenting on the LXX rendering for "shoot," which is "rising" (*anatolē*) (Zech 6:12), said, "For this man is the oldest son, whom the Father of all raised up (*aneteile*), whom he elsewhere called first-born (*prōtogonon*)" *CL* XIV. 62–63). The various titles that could be applied to the Messiah who was expected to rule Israel from Jerusalem seem to have been widely known in Jewish and Christian circles. He was referred to as the Son, first-born, heir, shoot/rising, and by other titles that will appear further on in the document "To the Hebrews." Pseudo-Clement observed that certain countries had their own names for kings:—Arsaces for the Persians, Caesar for the Romans, and Pharaoh for the Egyptians—"So with the Jews a king is called Christ" (*Recog.* I. 45). Some of these messianic titles could be used in public without non-Jews realizing that they referred to an anticipated military leader, promised in the scriptures. It seems to have been an acceptable practice for Jews to attribute to the Messiah passages that originally had different subjects or objects in mind.

The Greek word rendered "world" is *oikoumenē,* which occurs only twice in Hebrews (1:6 and 2:5). In the LXX, *oikoumenē* is used to describe the world which God created (LXX Pss 23:1; 88:12; 89:2; 92:1; Jer 10:12; 28:15). III Isaiah promised the Jews in Babylon:

> "You will no longer be called 'abandoned,'
> and your land will not be called 'wilderness' (*erēmos*);
> for you shall be called 'my will,'
> and your land, 'world' (*oikoumenē*)" (LXX Isa 62:4).

In this context, the *oikoumenē* is the land of the promise (Heb 11:9) to which the Jews expected to return when released from "captivity" in Babylon. Its capital city was Jerusalem or Zion (Isa 62:1). This may also be the meaning intended in the enthronement Psalm in which the Lord would "set straight the *oikoumenē,* which will not be shaken" (Ps 96[95]:10). Vanhoye said, "*Kosmos* designates the visible, material world; *oikoumenē* evokes a spiritual reality—the world of relationships among persons."[4] Whenever the Lord ruled over Palestine, Israel had a king and was free from foreign rule.[5] Enthronement Psalms were sung when kings were installed,[6] and the Lord ruled when Israel's king ruled. When the administration or the world situation was "set straight," from Israel's point of view, the Lord ruled (Ps 96[95]:10) and judged the *oikoumenē* (Ps 96[95]: 13). In contrast to abandonment was the Lord's will, and in contrast to wilderness was *oikoumenē* (Isa 62:4). When the Lord's salvation shone forth (Isa 62:1), the wilderness became an *oikoumenē*. The "world" which early Jews called *oikoumenē* seemed to have existed whenever the *kosmos* was under God's rule or administration. At such a time, God's kingdom would have come, and he would establish a king on the throne of Zion. This is just another way of saying he would lead his first-born into the *oikoumenē*. Such an understanding of *oikoumenē* as this would be consistent with the scriptural passages cited earlier in relationship to the Son and also to the text cited in the next verse.

Angels, temporal; Son, eternal

7. Ps 104 portrays God in his greatness, forming all creation and using it according to his will. He stretched out the heavens, laid the beams of his chambers on the waters, and made the clouds his chariot (Ps 104:2–3). In this context, it seems most likely that the passage quoted should read:

"He makes winds his messengers
flames of fire, his ministers" (Ps 104:4).

Since there are two objects in each line,[7] however, it is not certain whether God makes winds his messengers or his messengers, winds; flames of fire, his ministers or his ministers, flames of fire. Although most scholars think God used winds and fire for his messengers and ministers,[8] there are some who prefer the opposite reading, as the author of Hebrews did. Stuart paraphrased, "Who maketh his angels that serve him the ministers of his will, as the winds and lightning are."[9] Turner argued, "It is undeniable that the . . . view given in the epistle is at least as much if not more in keeping with the general representation."[10] A modification of the position taken by the author of Hebrews is the targum on the passage, which reads, "Who makes his messengers swift as the wind, his ministers mighty as flaming fire." In an ancient prayer, the Lord is described as One before whom a trained group of angels (*exercitus angelorum*) stand trembling (*cum tremore*), and at whose word they are changed into wind and

[4] A. Vanhoye, "L'oikouemenē dans l'épître aux Hébreux," *Biblica* 45 (1964), 248–53. See also G. Johnston, "OIKOUMENH and ΚΟΣΜΟΣ in the NT," NTS 10 (1963–64), 353–54.
[5] CC, pp. 60–62.
[6] Mowinckel, I, 125.
[7] As in LXX Deut 32:43 quoted in 1:6.
[8] Most recently Dahood, III, 31, 35.
[9] Stuart, p. 55.
[10] Turner, p. 35. See also Briggs, II, 329, 332.

fire (*in ventum et agnem convertuntur*) (IV Ezra 8:21–22). R. Helbo claimed that the Holy One, blessed be He, creates a new company of angels every day, who sing for him and then depart (Gen R. 32:27; 78:1).

The Greek word for "angels" means "messengers." Any human being who ran an errand was considered an angel. Angels of the Lord, of course, could be heavenly beings, but they never were given administrative power. They were responsible for carrying out orders, not for giving them. The Greek word for "ministers" is *leitourgoi* from the words *leitos,* "of the people," and *ergon,* "work." Therefore a minister of this kind, in secular life, would be a person holding some public office, one who had responsibilities for service to the state. In biblical terms, however, the word is almost always employed in relationship to the service of the priests in the temple. It is from this priestly office that the word "liturgy" is derived. These liturgists were ministers who fulfilled assigned tasks at specified times on prescribed days. Like the angels, they were not those who made the major decisions.

The Greek for "[with reference] to the angels" is *pros . . . tous aggelous,* literally, "to . . . the angels," but this makes no sense. The message was not *to* the angels but *about* them. Therefore the *pros* might be understood as a Semiticism, representing the *lᵉ* used to mean "with regard to," "with reference to," or "in respect to." When Abimelech finally learned that Sarah was Abraham's wife and called Abraham to account, Abraham admitted, "I said to her [Sarah], 'This is a kindness you must do with me: at every place where we come, *say about me* (*'imᵉrī lī*), "He is my brother"'" (Gen 20:13). The LXX renders these pertinent words "tell me" (*eipon eme*), a literal rendering, which, like "to . . . the angels" in Heb 1:7, makes no sense. The translator missed the significant meaning of this Hebrew preposition. Of King Solomon it is reported, "Now King Solomon became greater than all the kings of the world *with respect to wealth and wisdom*" *lᵉʻōšer ūlᵉḥokmāh* (I Kings 10:23). The intention of this sentence was not that King Solomon became greater . . . "to" wealth and wisdom any more than Abraham ordered Sarah to "tell" him. The preposition here must be understood to mean "in respect to."[11] These examples show both the force of the Hebraism and the way in which this meaning could be obscured or overlooked. But it is not only in a Semitic type of Greek that *pros* can bear this force. In classical literature, as well, *pros* can mean "in relation to," "according to," "with reference to."[12] Hence there is no difficulty with the translation given here.[13]

The subject represented by the supplied pronoun "it" is "the scripture" which *says* the quotation given. The author used the quotation because it helped him to depreciate the angels, which he was comparing un-

[11] See further *Gesenius' Hebrew Grammar,* ed. and enlarged by E. Kautzsch, rev. and tr. A. E. Cowley (Oxford, 1910), pp. 381–82, 458.

[12] W. W. Goodwin, *Greek Grammar,* rev. C. B. Gulick (New York, 1930), p. 260.

[13] See also RSV, Moffatt, p. 11, Westcott, p. 24, Vaughan, p. 15.

favorably to the Son. Had he chosen not to accept different primary and secondary objects, as many scholars do today, the Old Testament passage would have defeated his purpose.

8. The introduction to the quotations in this verse is exactly as it is in vs. 7. The *pros . . . ton huion* means "[with reference] to the Son" and not just "to . . . the Son." This is important for understanding the author's use of the quotations involved. Some scholars have taken this as a direct address to the Son and therefore believed the author of Hebrews thought Jesus was God. An old example of this reasoning is Turner, who said, "The only correct translation then is, 'Thy throne, O God.' As this title is never applied to any Hebrew monarch, it must relate to some superhuman personage. . . . The Messiah is really God, but is spoken of at the same time in such a way as presumes a human nature also."[14] More recently Montefiore said, "He is superior to them, for he has been raised above them when he was anointed as God."[15] This is not a necessary conclusion. As the *pros* in vs. 7 means "in reference to," and it seems most likely that *pros* in vs. 8 should be rendered in the same way, so it is *in reference to* the Son that the author quoted a scripture dealing with the eternity of God's throne, *upon which the Son would sit.* When Solomon, who was God's Son (II Sam 7:14), ruled over the Lord's kingdom (I Chron 29:11), he sat on the Lord's throne (*'al kissē' Yhwh*) (I Chron 29:23; see also Enoch 51:3; 55:4; 61:8; 62:2–3, 5; 69:26–27, 29). That did not mean that Solomon was God. It means that Solomon ruled over God's kingdom when he ruled over Palestine, and he sat on God's throne when he ruled from Jerusalem. Therefore, it is just as proper to speak of the eternity of God's throne with reference to the Son Jesus who was to sit on it as it was to speak of God's throne when Solomon, the son, sat on it. The point of the author's argument is that, in contrast to the angels, who are as temporal as wind and fire, the Son was destined for a throne which was "forever and ever," as the scripture says. At the end of the verse "his" has the stronger textual support (P⁴⁶Bℵ), although almost all other texts have "your" (*sou*) in conformity to the LXX (and MT). The RSV renders Ps 45:6, "Your divine throne"—the most likely rendering when the next line continues "*Your* royal scepter . . ."[16] and the address is clearly to the king. The same would be true here in Heb 1:8 if the reading "your" were accepted at the end of the verse. It seems more likely that the author of Hebrews spoke only *in reference to* the Son when he addressed God, mentioning the eternity of the throne on which the Son would sit. He then changed the pronoun from second to third person in the next line to describe *his* (the Son's) kingdom. "The staff" was the symbol of royal power and authority. As king, he was the highest judge in the land, so this staff was also a symbol of his legislative authority. Psalm 45 was a poem addressed to a

[14] Turner, p. 37. [15] Montefiore, p. 47.

[16] Dahood, III, 269–73, vocalized the Hebrew *kissē'ᵃkā,* called it a denominative piel, and rendered it, "has enthroned you." This is reasonable for the Hebrew text, but is irrelevant to Hebrews because the author of Hebrews did not understand it that way.

king, not to God. The king, whom God had blessed, was urged to gird on his sword in glory and ride forth victoriously (Ps 45:3–4). His enemies were destined to fall before his sharp arrows (Ps 45:5). In the Psalm the king was also addressed with reference to his throne and his scepter, but the words could be understood as addressed to God. Since the author of Hebrews wanted to use this royal Psalm, he had to deal with this difficulty in some way, just as commentators do today. He seems to have handled the problem by speaking in reference to the Son, just as he had spoken in reference to the angels (1:7) just before. Then, in reference to the Son he spoke of God's throne and the Son's kingdom. Next, in the following verse, he continued to deal with the Son in direct address as indicated by the Psalm quotation. It seems more likely that the author of Hebrews sensed a difficulty here than that he intentionally confused the Son with God. For the author, the Son was the first-born, the apostle of God, the reflection of God's glory, and the stamp of his nature (1:3, 6), but he was not God *himself*.

Son is anointed

9. The Son, referred to in the third person in vs. 8, was addressed in the second person in vs. 9. The king who had authority over the kingdom and the administration of justice for the land was one who "loved justice" and "hated lawlessness." It was for this reason that he was singled out from among his peers and given the high rank of king. Although his ability became evident to his contemporaries, his anointing came from God. This anointing was the rite by which he was made king. This rite was so significant that kings were called anointed ones or messiahs (*Recog.* I. 45). It would be difficult to deduce which Israelite or Jewish king was first addressed in this Psalm as God's anointed one when he was enthroned, but by the time of the author of Hebrews, Ps 45 was sacred scripture which described the power and authority of a king who had been anointed, and anointed ones were called messiahs. Thus when the author of Hebrews took the central figure of Ps 45 to be the Messiah, he expressed a commonly held opinion. He identified the central figure with Jesus, who, as Son, was also a king, the anointed one and, according to the author, a mighty one who was victorious in battle, who would crush his enemies and ascend to God's throne in his exalted position at God's right hand, from which he would rule justly.

God's eternity

10. The connective "and" relates verses 10–12 to verses 7–9. "Now, (on the one hand,) [with reference] to the angels, it says" (1:7) "but [with reference] to the Son, [it says]," (1:8) "and" (1:10). The "Lord" in Ps 102 clearly referred to God. Here it might also mean God, with the implication that since the Son was "heir of all" (1:2) and since it was through the Son that the Lord "made the ages" (1:2), any reference to the endurance of God would also be a reference to the endurance of the Son. In other places the author of Hebrews quoted Old Testament passages that mention the

name of the Lord, and in every case the author held the same meaning (7:21; 8:8, 9, 10, 11; 10:16, 30; 12:5, 6). On the other hand, the author did use the name "Lord" when referring to Jesus (2:3; 7:14). Like other scholars of his time, the author was also capable of taking an Old Testament passage out of context and attributing it to the Messiah. For example in LXX Deut 32:43, in which the object of worship for the sons of God according to the Proto-Massoretic text was Israel, the author of Hebrews applied it to the first-born, namely Jesus (1:6). Since the term "first-born" could be applied either to Israel (Exod 4:22) or to the Messiah, the author made the shift. By the same logic, since "the Lord" was a title of respect used both for God and for kings, such as Jesus, he may also have made the shift here to apply to Jesus the durability of God in contrast to the temporal nature of the angels. If this were the case, then Jesus would also have been thought of as a sort of demiurge through whom God created the heaven and earth as well as the ages (1:2, 10). In either case it does not mean that Jesus was believed to be God or was addressed as God.

11. The contrast here is between the endurance of God, which is related to the endurance of the Son, and the ephemeral nature of the creation, including even the heavens to which the angels belong.

12. The Greek for "roll them up" is *helixeis autous*. A variant (in original hands of אD and in Latin MSS) is *allaxeis*, which means "you will change" and is paralleled by *allagēsontai* in the following line. The variant agrees with the Massoretic text (*taḥᵃlīphēm wᵉyaḥᵃlōphū*) (Ps 102:27) and the LXX (*allaxeis autous, kai allagēsontai*) (LXX Ps 101:27). The smoother reading has the poorer textual support and agrees with LXX and MT. It is more natural to think of "changing" in relationship to "robes" than "rolling them up." Therefore it seems unlikely that a later scribe would have changed the text to make it more awkward, and it is easily understood why he might improve it, especially when he could do so by making it conform to the Old Testament. Why, then, would the author of Hebrews have changed the Old Testament text? He may have been influenced by Isa 34:4 (LXX), which is also partially quoted in Rev 6:14:

> "Heaven will be rolled up (*heligēsetai*) as a scroll,
> and all the stars will fall as leaves from a vine,
> and as leaves fall from a fig tree."

Since the contrast was being made between God and his Son, on the one hand, and the heavens where the angels dwelt, on the other, the author may have preferred the idiom more customarily used in relationship to heaven than to a garment. The phrase "like a garment" is an addition to the Old Testament text, supported by P46BאAD 1739, and would make more sense if the imagery from Isa 34:4 had been carried out completely in the first line, so that "garment" would need to be mentioned in the second line to make sense with "will be changed." Then it would have read as follows:

> "And like a scroll you will roll them up;
> like a garment also (and) they will be changed."

The only problem with this suggestion is that there is absolutely no textual support for "scroll." The conjunction could be translated "also," after the addition was made. It is perhaps best to assume that the author changed the text only by changing "you will change" to "you will roll . . . up" and by adding "as a garment," which does not change the sense of the passage.

"You," as in vs. 10, probably means God, as in the Psalm, but by implication it means that the Son, "through whom he also made the ages" (1:2), would not run out of years either.

Son is at God's right hand

13. "To which of the angels has he ever said" is a repetition in slightly different words of 1:5, employed here to form an inclusion of the material in between. The quotations that follow are different. Verse 5 introduces Ps 2, followed by other Old Testament passages that were used to contrast the inferiority of the angels to the superiority of the Son. Verse 13 reintroduces Ps 110, which is the basic text of his message. This ties the two enthronement Psalms together and helps clarify the role of the Messiah, according to the author. He is to be a powerful ruler who overcomes all his enemies in battle and forces them to become a "footstool for his feet" while he is elevated to the throne at Jerusalem, which means he is sitting at the Lord's "right hand." It thus echoes the "punch line" of the introductory section, assuring the reader that this is the main point of the discussion.

The position "at the right hand" was the preferred position in any gathering where people were classed according to status. The one who sat at the host's right hand at a banquet, for instance, was the guest of honor. In the ancient Near East it was customary for people to recline when they ate. The person at the host's right hand reclined so that his head was before the host where he and the host could converse most easily. He was reclining at the bosom of his host. This was the kind of setting implied in the statement, "Many will come from the east and the west and recline with Abraham, Isaac, and Jacob in the kingdom of heaven" (Matt 8:11). The importance attached to the position at a banquet is shown in the parable where the one who took the lowest place was invited before all the guests to take a position nearer to the host (Luke 14:8–11). In the parable of Lazarus and the rich man, Lazarus was finally rewarded by being placed at Abraham's bosom (Luke 16:23; see also Kid. 72b) and the rich man was punished by being placed at a distance. The disciple whom Jesus loved was pictured at the banquet reclining at Jesus' bosom (John 13:23). In earthly protocol there was no person of higher status than the king. He would always be at the head of the gathering, with the princes and closest allies at his right and left, but he was also thought to be the one closest to God. Therefore he was called God's "son" or "chosen one" (see Enoch 55:4; 61:8; 62:2–3). Since this was true, it was normal to describe his status in terms of earthly protocol and say that he was stationed at the Lord's right hand when he ascended his throne. In contrast to this position were his "enemies" who were to become his "footstool" and the angels who were mere servants, commissioned during their ephemeral existence to carry out the assignments he gave.

14. The "ministering spirits" were those who ministered at the altar rather than those who waited tables or performed other types of menial labor. Nonetheless, the "service" (*diakonia*) they rendered was the kind usually related to table serving. The author's use of the two terms for ministering probably reflects his own good taste in literary style, preferring to use synonyms rather than being repetitious. The distinction between the serving that took place at the altar (*leitourgia*) and that which took place at the meal (*diakonia*) was not very sharp, because those who served at the altar slaughtered and sacrificed livestock. Sacrificing involved cooking the beasts that had been slaughtered, most of which were then eaten. The "ministering spirits" are here pictured as the ones who administered the sacrifice in preparing a feast for God's chosen people who would "inherit" the "salvation" prepared for the children of Abraham. The "ministering spirits" are identical to the angels whom the Lord makes spirits, winds, or flames of fire when he chooses (1:7). The status of the angels is shown to be lower than that of the Son by their position and function. The angels minister in whatever task they "are sent." The Son sits at the Lord's "right hand" (1:13), like a king who sends messengers and gives orders. The one who sits on the throne is far superior to all court servants (see Rev 5:6–7).

The passage that began with a rhetorical question also ended with a rhetorical question (1:5, 14). The next part of this division is an admonition reminding the readers of their responsibility to the facts presented.

Son is higher than the angels

2:1. "Therefore," literally, "on account of this" (*dia touto*), refers to the superiority of Jesus over the angels. "Drift away" (*pararyōmen*) literally means to "flow by." This word is used to describe a river that flows by a place, or flows aside from its normal channel in the sense of flooding or escaping its channel. Metaphorically, it means to drift, to wander from the true path, to transgress. Thus, the son in Prov 3:21 was warned, "Son, do not drift away (*pararryęs*)," which means "Observe my counsel and intention." "The things that were heard" refers to the instruction that the readers had been taught and for which they were responsible (see Eph 1:13; 4:21; Col 1:6, 23; II Tim 1:13; 2:2; I John 2:7, 24).

2. "The word which was spoken through angels" was the law given to Moses. There was a widely held tradition that God delivered this through the medium of angels (*Ant.* XV. 136; Gal 3:19; Acts 7:53; Targ. Deut 33:2). The author had been depreciating angels in comparison to the Son. At this point he made the contrast of his *a fortiori* argument greater by calling attention to the accepted belief that angels delivered the law at Sinai. The association of the law given at Sinai to angels, in this context, makes the law seem relatively less important. But even this word of secondary importance delivered by beings of no higher status than messen-

gers was enforced to the letter. The expression "transgression and disobedience" may be a *hendiadys*—two synonyms describing one activity. The Greek, translated "transgression" (*parabasis*), literally means "stepping alongside" and refers to walking out of bounds or overstepping the prescribed limitations. The Greek for "disobedience" (*parakoē*), literally, "hearing alongside [that which was directed]" or "hearing amiss," means not hearing accurately or hearing something contrary to that which was spoken. Those who heard paid attention and obeyed the commandments heard. Those who ignored the commandments disobeyed them, which means they acted in a contrary way or transgressed.

3. "Escape" refers to the "just recompense" of "every transgression and disobedience" (2:2). The rhetorical question expects a negative answer and means, "We cannot escape . . ." "Salvation" in the Old Testament usually refers either to deliverance of a nation from the power of the enemy at war, or to receiving a pardon or verdict of "not guilty" in a court case. For the author of Hebrews it refers to the deliverance that the Son provides when God makes his "enemies a footstool for [his] feet" (1:13), and the Son utilizes "the staff of justice" (1:8) to rule over his people. As the document repeatedly reminds the readers, the opportunity for "so great a salvation" was available to them and should not be neglected. The revelation related to the salvation was contrasted to that related to the "word spoken through angels." One revelation came through the Mosaic law and the other through Jesus. It was to the latter that the author turned his attention. Its significance was made evident in various ways: first, it was initially "spoken through the Lord," which probably refers to the sayings of Jesus,[17] rather than a word from God himself. This came to the author and his contemporaries from "those who heard." This probably means they received it from the ear and eye witnesses—those who saw and heard the very words of Jesus. These would have been the apostles and their contemporaries who further supported the importance of the things Jesus said. The author of Hebrews was evidently not one of those witnesses himself, but rather was dependent upon "the things that were heard" (2:1) from reports he had received directly from the apostles themselves or else from the reports that they left.

The good news that was proclaimed by Jesus was accompanied by numerous "signs, wonders, and various kinds of miracles," which was God's way of corroborating the testimony of Jesus and his apostles. An additional testimony was provided by "the distribution of the Holy Spirit" (see Rom 12:3; I Cor 7:17; II Cor 10:13; Heb 7:2; Eph 4:7 for use of the term "distribute") which accompanied the preaching and miracles. This is especially reported in the account of the first Pentecost (Acts 2:1–41). Whereas the revelation given through Moses was spoken only by angels,

[17] K. Berger, "Zum Traditionsgeschichtlichen Hintergrund Christologischer Hoheitstitel," NTS 17 (1970–71), 413–22, compared Moses and Enoch to Jesus and some angels to show that the term "Lord" means apostle or messenger. This is consistent with the apostolic Christology of Hebrews.

the revelation associated with Jesus had four strong supports: (1) the authority of Jesus, (2) the approval and support of the apostles, (3) God's approval shown in various kinds of miraculous events, and (4) the provision of the Holy Spirit wherever God chose to reveal his presence. This fourfold description of divine evidence is more than was usually claimed. Usually only signs and wonders are given (Matt 24:24; Mark 13:22; John 4:48; Acts 2:19, 43; 4:30; 5:12; 6:8; 7:36; 14:3; 15:12). Sometimes signs and miracles (Acts 8:13), miracles, signs, and wonders (Rom 15:19), or signs, wonders, and miracles are listed (Acts 2:22; II Cor 12:12; II Thess 2:9). Acts 2:1–41 is the only other place in the New Testament where a fourfold description of divine evidence is reported. There signs, wonders, and miracles are listed (2:22), and the distribution of the Holy Spirit is described (2:1–21, 33). In the author's judgment, this was enough evidence to show that the revelation made known through Jesus the Son was far superior to that made known in the Mosaic law.

5. The expression translated "world to come" is the Greek *oikoumenē hē mellousa* (Syriac *'ālmā da'ᵃtīd*), which is the equivalent of the Hebrew *'ōlām habbā'*, "the age to come." "The world to come," or the age to come, did not refer to heaven, as some have thought.[18] Westcott recognized years ago: "The phrase is not to be understood simply of 'the future life' or, more generally, of 'heaven.' It describes, in relation to that which we may call its constitution, the state of things which, in relation to its development in time, is called 'the age to come' (*ho mellōn aiōn*), and, in relation to its supreme Ruler and characteristics, 'the Kingdom of God,' or 'the Kingdom of heaven,' even the order which corresponds with the completed work of Christ."[19] To be still more specific "the world to come" was the messianic age, the time when the Romans would be subdued, and the Messiah would rule as king from his throne at Jerusalem (see COMMENT on 1:6–8). An "age" was a chronological period, an era characterized in some distinctive way, such as an evil age, a good age, an age of prosperity, or an age of oppression. It could describe the period of a certain rule, dynasty, or political control.[20] R. Joshua interpreted "generation generation" (*dōr dōr,* as Mekilta quoted it from Ps 72:5; MT has *dōr dōrīm*) to mean "[a succession] from life in this age" to "life in the age to come" (Mekilta *Amalek* 2:186–88). Ages were considered to be in temporal sequence. Whenever one age ended, the age to come began. Thus the age of Esau-Edom-Rome had to end before the age of Jacob-Israel could begin (IV Ezra 6:7–10). Ages were like human beings or fruit. They became "ripe" or "grew old" before they passed away (II Bar 70:3; IV Ezra 14:10; 6:20; 12:25; II Bar 4:11; II Cor 5:17).[21] Barnabas said, "The righteous man both walks in this world (*en toutǭ tǭ kosmǭ*) and expects (*ekdechetai*) the holy age (*ton hagion aiōna*)" (Barn 10:11). Since the world to come was to be an administration (*oikoumenē*) during which

[18] Nor a "transcendent future," as Grässer, p. 210, holds.
[19] Westcott, p. 42.
[20] See further Eliade, pp. 80–81, 126–27, 134–35. [21] CC, pp. 15–16.

the Messiah would reign, it follows that that age would be subject to the Messiah or Son, not to the angels. The task of the angels was to minister to those who were about to inherit salvation in the age to come. The Son, on the contrary, was to rule. "Somewhere someone" (*pou tis*) seems to be a rhetorical form used to avoid explicit reference. It does not mean the author did not know where to find the source, because he quoted it accurately and generally seemed well-versed in the Psalms.

6. "Man" and "son of man" in Ps 8 have the same meaning and refer to the nature of the species *homo sapiens*. Commentators generally have overlooked the fact that the main point of the author's discussion up to this point in Hebrews has been about the Son and that the title "Son of man" was used in the gospels as another name for the Messiah. Therefore, instead of using this passage to understand the meaning of the title "Son of man" commentators have discussed the meaning of the incarnation[22] and its importance to the nature of man. Montefiore[23] insisted, ". . . our writer does not here apply 'the Son of Man' in Psalm 8:4 to Jesus at all." In so doing, Montefiore has simply overlooked some important facts: (1) This quotation was listed together with other Old Testament passages that the author used to describe the nature of the Son, who was Jesus. (2) Ps 2 pictured the king as a Son who would dash the nations into pieces so that they would bow before him and kiss his feet. Ps 110 describes a king as a Son who would shatter opposing kings. His enemies would become a footstool for his feet. Both of these Psalms about sons who were kings were identified with Jesus. In the same context the author quoted Ps 8 about the Son of man, under whose feet God would put all things (8:6). Although he used a Psalm eulogizing the nature of man, he employed it to describe Jesus, the Son, in royal terms. For the author, the term Son of man, like Son, heir, and first-born, seems to have been a title for the Messiah. This possibility will be considered more carefully at the end of the chapter.

7. "For a short time" renders the Greek *brachu* in Hebrews, which is the same word as that which occurs in the LXX Ps 8:6 and renders the Hebrew *mᵉʿaṭ*. In the Psalm, both the Hebrew and Greek mean "a little bit," referring to the status of man (see II Sam 16:1). The context of Hebrews, however, is dealing with "little" in terms of time (as in LXX Isa 57:17) rather than status, so the same word as used in the LXX must here be translated "for a short time." "You have made him lower" (*ēlattōsas*) means "you have reduced him in rank," since the context deals with the Son's status in comparison to that of the angels. The word "angels," like the reference to the Son of man and God's putting all things under his feet, attracted the author's attention to Ps 8. All three of these points were important to his argument. "Angels" (*aggelous*) is the reading of the LXX and concurs with the Targum (*mal'ᵃkayā*). Dahood is probably correct in rendering the Hebrew *'ᵉlōhīm*, "the gods,"[24] rather than "God," as the RSV translates it (Ps 8:5). In rela-

[22] For example, see Turner, p. 3, and Westcott, pp. 43, 60 and 69.
[23] Montefiore, p. 57. [24] Dahood, I, 48, 51.

tionship to Heb 1:6 it is evident from studying the variants of the LXX, MT, and 4Q texts of Deut 32:43 that "gods," "sons of God," and "angels of God" were used interchangeably in some contexts, so that the variants "gods" and "angels" introduce nothing startling in Ps 8:5. The variant "gods" would not have been acceptable to the author of Hebrews, even if it had been available to him. He was contrasting the Son to the angels, and the LXX passage was one he was able to use to support his argument. Since the author of Hebrews was discussing a Son who was a king, it was also important that he be one who "was crowned with glory and honor." This is consistent with his claim that the Son was exalted (1:3), worshiped (1:6), anointed (1:9), that he held the staff of the kingdom (1:8), and sat down at the Lord's right hand (1:3, 13).

8. God's putting "all things under" the Son's "feet" is also consistent with the author's use of Pss 110 and 2 to show that the Son's enemies would become his footstool and prostrate themselves before him to kiss his feet. Paul and the author of Ephesians (1:20–22) also combined Ps 8 with Ps 110 to describe Jesus's activity as Son. Paul said that Jesus would finally deliver the kingdom to God, after destroying every rule, authority, and power, but "it is necessary for him to rule until he puts all his enemies under his feet (Ps 110:1) . . . for [God] has put all things under his feet (Ps 8:6)" (I Cor. 15:25–27). Paul continued to explain that "all things" did not include God who had put all things under the Son's feet, but that when all of this had been accomplished, the Son himself would be subject to God (I Cor 15:27–28). The relationship of the Son to God is reasonably clear. The Son was to be the king who overthrew all his enemies with God's help; then he would rule from his throne while his enemies were suppressed. When he became the victorious king who ruled all other political forces, he would still be subordinate to God. He would sit on God's throne at God's right hand, but he would not be God himself. The author of Hebrews, in all probability, also excluded God from the "all things," even though he emphasized that nothing was omitted of the things that were made subordinate to him. In dealing with Ps 8, Philo said God made everything subject to man that was under the moon, which included all mortal beings that moved in the water, air, or on land, but he did not make the heavenly beings subject to man (*Op.* 28. 84). The author of Hebrews, like the New Testament authors generally, was no longer interested in Ps 8 in relationship to the nature of man as such, but interested only in Jesus, the Son of man, who was king and messiah, and as such was destined to rule "all things," since God had "established" him "heir" of all (1:2; see also Eph 1:22; I Peter 3:22). Since he was then at the right hand of God in the heavens, even the heavenly beings, like angels, were subject to him. The authors of Ephesians (1:20–22) and I Peter (3:22) claimed that, with the ascension, Jesus had already been exalted above all powers, but the author of Hebrews, like Paul (I Cor 15:25–28), admitted that there was no evidence to show that, at that point, "all things" had been "made subject" to Jesus.

9. With vs. 9 it is first clear that the author was speaking of Jesus the

Son, rather than of man in general. It was Jesus, the Son of man, who was temporarily reduced in rank. It does not say specifically that this reduction involved the incarnation, as many scholars assume, but that is possible. The passage here deals only with his "suffering of death," which in itself was enough depreciation to constitute a reduction in rank. His "tasting death" was probably understood in atonement theology. That means that his death benefited all covenanters because it canceled many sins that had accumulated in the debit column of the treasury of merits.

Summary.—The whole unit, 1:5–2:9, deals with the superiority of the Son over the angels. The author argued his case with the strong support of an admirable collection of Old Testament passages. He was not the only one to collect such passages. There were many florilegia dealing with the Messiah and some of these overlapped, as the following comparisons show:

Hebrews 1:5–2:9	*Midrash on Ps 2:9*	*4Q Florilegium*	*I Cor 15:25–27*	*Eph 1:22*
Ps 110:1	Ps 2:7	II Sam 7:10–14	Ps 110:1	Ps 110:1
Ps 2:7	Exod 4:22	Exod 15:17–18	Ps 8:6	Ps 8:6
II Sam 7:14	Isa 52:13	Amos 9:11		
LXX Deut 32:43	Isa 42:1	Ps 1:1		
Ps 104:4	Ps 110:1	Isa 8:11		
Ps 45:6–7	Dan 7:13–14	Ezek 37:23(?)		
Ps 102:25–27	Ps 2:7–8	Ps 2:1		
Ps 110:1		Dan 12:10		
Ps 8:4–6		Dan 11:32		

Referring to the Midrash collection R. Yudan said, "All these comforting [passages] are in the decree of the King, the King of kings, who will perform them for the messianic king (*l^emelek hammašîaḥ*)" (Midr. Ps 2:9). Like the author of Hebrews, R. Yudan understood the Son referred to in Ps 110 to be the same as the Son described in Ps 2 and also the Son of man, which Hebrews related to Ps 8 but which R. Yudan related to Dan 7. Both R. Yudan and the author of Hebrews believed that the titles "Son" and "Son of man" could be applied to the Messiah. 4Q Florilegium related II Sam 7:14 to Ps 2:1 and other passages dealing with David and his son, in somewhat the same way as Hebrews did, although 4Q Florilegium stressed the importance of David's son as the Messiah, whereas Hebrews, using the same texts, did not mention David's name at all. Paul and the author of Ephesians, as well as the author of Hebrews, related both Pss 110:1 and 8:6 to Jesus the Messiah and considered both "Son" and "Son of man" to be messianic titles. The author of Hebrews stylistically related Pss 2, 8, and 110 more closely to each other than the other passages he quoted by beginning his discussion with a quotation from Ps 110 followed by another from Ps 2 and concluding it with a requotation from Ps 110, followed by another from Ps 8. The nature of the Messiah related to these Psalms is vividly described by still another zealous Jew's poem based on Ps 2:8–9 (Ps of Sol 17:23–28):

23 "Observe, Lord, and raise up for them their king, the son of David, at the time in which you see, O God, that he may rule over Israel your servant.
24 Arm him well that he may shatter unrighteous rulers;
25 Cleanse Jerusalem from nations that trample [her] down to destruction;
26 [that he may] expel sinners from [the] inheritance (*klēronomias;* LXX *klēronomian*),
in wisdom [and] in righteousness,
shatter (*ektripsai;* LXX *ektripseis*) the pride of the sinner like a potter's
vessel (*hōs skeuē kerameōs*).
with a rod of iron (*en hrabdǭ sidera*) break to pieces (*syntripsai;* LXX *syntripseis*)
all their substance,
27 destroy the lawless Gentiles with the word of his mouth.
[Let] Gentiles flee from his presence, at his rebuke, and [let him] chastise sinners for the thoughts of their heart.
28 Then he will gather together a holy people, whom he will lead in righteousness, and he will judge the tribes of the people that have been sanctified by the Lord, his God."

Vanhoye has shown the well-balanced structure of 2:1–4 as an *a fortiori* argument by a chart similar to the following:[25]

. . . . *became steadfast* (2:3)
we (2:1) . . . . *to us* (2:2)
to the things that were heard (2:1) *by those who heard* (2:3)
through angels (2:2) . . . . . *through the Lord* (2:3)
was spoken (2:3) . . . . *was spoken* (2:3)
word (2:2) . . . . *salvation* (2:3)
steadfast (2:2) . . . .
transgression (2:2) *having neglected* (2:3)
just recompense (2:2) . *escape* (2:3)
how shall we (2:3)

The author's choice of scripture comes mostly from the Psalms. Of the eight references quoted in this section, six are from Psalms, with only one each from the Pentateuch and the former prophets. This may reflect his liturgical interest, or it may simply mean that the material the author needed happened to be in the Psalms. In a way that is characteristic of the author, he framed 1:5–14 with an inclusion, but his borders are not perfectly sharp. One section seems to shade over into the other and prepares the readers for the shift in subject matter. For example, his introduction includes his first mention of Ps 110, which is basic to the section that follows. If it were quoted as the first quotation in vs. 5 rather than in vs. 3, it

[25] Vanhoye, p. 76. used Greek throughout.

would form a perfect inclusion with its requotation in vs. 13, but the author did not plan it that way. He formed his inclusion with his introductory question "To which of the angels has he ever said" (1:5, 13). Within the inclusion in 1:5–14, there is also a smaller literary form. A chiasm is formed by the organization of contrasts: (5) Son, (6) angels, (7) angels, and (8–12) Son. The theological argument of this section was interrupted by the ethical exhortation (2:1–4) that was not necessary to the discussion, but it was evidently important to the author to relate his doctrine to the needs of his readers, because he follows his doctrine with exhortation throughout the document. In some ways the argument proceeds from 1:5 to 2:9 with an exhortatory intrusion, and in other ways, 1:5–14 forms its own literary unit, framed by an inclusion and including the magic number of seven quotations.[26] To this the reference to Ps 8, together with the exhortation, seems like an appendage. Nonetheless, the subject matter (Son, angels, exaltation, and suppression of enemies underfoot) is coherent throughout 1:5–2:9, which forms the beginning argument in defense of the Son. The nature of the Son, presented in this section, and his relationship to the Son of man is an important item that has been generally overlooked by commentators. It will be given still further attention at the end of this chapter.

The Son and the believers

10. "All things" (*panta*), found also in vss. 11, 16, and 17, refers to Ps 8:6, quoted in 2:8. These are all the things that are to be put under the Son's feet (2:8), which are also the things of which God established the Son heir (1:2). If he is heir of all things and all things have been put under his feet, it would be saying very little more to claim that all things were for and through him, but that is not what it says. The subject here is God and not the Son. God is the one who perfects the Son who is the "pioneer of their salvation." The word "perfect" (*teleiōsai*) was important to the author's vocabulary. In its verbal form it occurs in Hebrews fourteen times; as an adverb (*teleiōs*), once; as an adjective (*teleios*), twice; and as a noun (*teleiotēs*, *teleiōsis*, or *teleiōtēs*), three times. Depending on its context, this verb means to perfect, accomplish, fulfill, complete, or become mature. In a religious context, it usually describes a person who was fully cleansed from sin, qualified for full membership in a religious order, or one who observed rigorously all the rules required by the group. Other terms that are closely allied to the word "perfect" are "sanctified" and "worthy."[27] A sanctified person is one who has been cleansed from all defilement. A person judged worthy of full admission into a sect was considered "perfect." To make Jesus fully qualified

[26] This is the exact number of quotations in the collection in Midrash on Ps 2:9, and Heb 7 is also organized into seven divisions. The author of Hebrews may have used a florilegium of seven passages on the Son, to which he added the eighth, Ps 8.

[27] See H. Ch. Peuch, "Gnostic Gospels and Related Documents," *New Testament Apocrypha,* ed. E. Hennecke, re-ed. W. Schneemelcher, tr. R. McWilson (Philadelphia, 1963) I, 263, 328; Acts of Peter 26; Hippolytus *On Daniel* 4:60; *Recog.* II.viii; III.xxxvii et al.

as "the pioneer of their salvation," the training required involved passing "through sufferings." The author assumed that his readers were informed about the nature of these sufferings, because he did not describe them in detail. The extent of this suffering was also mentioned, but not described in vs. 9, the "suffering of death." The Son was the "pioneer," who after his "suffering of death" was "crowned with glory and honor" (2:9) and was well-qualified to lead "many [other] sons to glory."

11. "He who sanctifies," in this context, is the Son. The word "sanctify" (*hagiazein*—Hebrew *qiddēš*) means to cleanse, make holy, or separate from defiled things. For example, when David was attracted to Bathsheba, she was bathing to cleanse herself from her menstrual defilement (*mitqaddešet miṭṭum'ātā*), or "sanctifying" herself. On the Day of Atonement, there were occasions when the high priest was required to "sanctify" (*qiddēš*) his hands and his feet (Yoma 3:2, 4, 6), meaning he washed them. At Mount Sinai, Moses was directed to "sanctify" the people (*qiddaštām*) and have them wash their garments (Exod 19:10). When Job's sons attended a drinking party, Job "sanctified them," meaning he rose up early the next morning and provided the proper offerings necessary to atone for sins they might have committed (Job 1:5). The people who were cleansed, sanctified, or atoned were called saints (*qᵉdōšīm* or *hagioi*). The term "saint" or "sanctified one" could refer especially to a person who was very carefully observant of all holiness rules, or it could be used quite generally to refer to any convenanter, either a Jew or a Christian. For instance, Paul used the term in a general sense. Whatever the degree of rigidity by which the author of Hebrews understood and used this term, "he who sanctifies" Christians was Jesus, just as Moses was the one who sanctified the people of Israel at the foot of Mount Sinai. "Those who are sanctified" were the Christians, the new "holy people." As in vs. 10, the "all" used here was an intentional repetition of the "all" quoted in vs. 8 from Ps 8:7. "From one" probably means from one father, namely Abraham.[28] This seems to imply that the Christians in which the author was interested were Jewish rather than Gentile Christians, since they, like Jesus, were sons of Abraham. Jesus was the Son and the "one who sanctifies," and Christians were the "many sons" and "those who are sanctified." This constitutes a religious family, "from one [father]." Since religion and family origin were very closely associated in Israel, when sects developed in Judaism—each one posing as the redeeming remnant of Israel—celibate, communistic brotherhoods also developed. These sects, like the Essenes, were composed of very serious, devout Jews who tried to keep every jot and tittle of the law. In order to do so, they had to avoid all types of defilement. Since menstrual and seminal discharges were defiling, and since women of child-bearing age were ritually defiled half of the time, avoidance of all contact with women became necessary; therefore celibate brotherhoods were formed of men of the same convictions and devotion. Since celibates could not father children to care for them physically and materially

[28] Michel, p. 80, insists that both the one who sanctifies and the one from which both originate is God. This makes no sense.

in their old age, it was necessary for these men to form unions that would meet these needs by pooling their resources and taking care of one another as was necessary. These rigid covenanters isolated themselves from the rest of the world, including their own families, who might be defiled and serve food not completely approved.[29] When the mother and blood brothers of Jesus came to see him, and he was told of their presence, he responded, "Who is my mother, and who are my brothers?" Then stretching out his hand to his disciples, he said, "Here are my mother and my brothers" (Matt 12:46–49)! This new social brotherhood provided for its members' needs that which a family normally supplied. Therefore the members called one another "brother." The term "brothers" occurs 217 times in the New Testament, outside of Hebrews, when the term refers to other members of the same covenant rather than to blood brothers. Not all of these "brothers" were celibate, communistic members of rigid brotherhoods. Like the term "saints," sometimes the term "brothers" was used quite generally and inclusively, so it is not certain that the term "brothers" here refers to such a rigid monastic group as some brotherhoods were, but there are other indications in the document that point in that direction. In any event, the "sanctified ones" are the same as the "brothers."

12. The proof text the author used to justify "brothers" was legitimate. The brothers mentioned in LXX Ps 21:23 were not blood brothers but the sons of Jacob or Israel (LXX Ps 21:24). The author of the Psalm, of course, was not Jesus, as the argument suggests, but biblical interpreters in New Testament times, both Jewish and Christian, frequently applied Old Testament passages to whatever subject they chose, especially the Messiah. The LXX word for "announce" is *diēgēsomai,* but the Hebrews variant is *apaggelō.* These words being synonymous, the author may have used a text with the variant he accepted. If he had choices, he may have preferred *apaggelō* to *diēgēsomai* because of its proximity in form to *aggelos,* which had received a lot of attention up to that point in the discussion. The "congregation" was the community composed of sons (2:10), sanctified ones, or brothers (2:11). The pioneer of their salvation would lead many sons to glory by proclaiming the good news or announcing the Lord's name to the brothers.

13. The quotation in the first line is exactly the same Greek as that found in the LXX Isa 8:17 and also II Sam 22:3. *A priori* the author could have used either passage. Vaughan and Michel[30] prefer the II Sam 22:3 passage. Two points in its favor are: (1) II Sam 22:3 is supposed to be a quotation from David, and according to Hebrews this passage is supposed to have been said by Jesus; and (2) the author seemed to prefer Psalms, and therefore would be more likely to quote from a psalm of David than from one of the prophets. Against these are the fact that the author has made no attempt, direct or indirect, to identify Jesus with the son of David, and therefore would not have been likely here to affirm a Davidic messianism by choosing a passage that was once attributed to David, rather than another

[29] CC, pp. 238–81. [30] Vaughan, p. 46; Michel, p. 81.

that said the same thing. Although the author seemed to prefer Psalms, the fact that the second half of vs. 13 is a continuation of the Isaiah passage makes it virtually certain that this first line also came from Isaiah.

The Greek translated "confident of him" (*pepoithōs ep' autǭ*) might also be rendered "persuaded" or "convinced in him." The Hebrew of Isa 8:17 is *w^eqiwwētī lō:* "but I will hope in him." Isaiah had contrasted himself to the house of Jacob from whom the Lord had turned his face. Even though the Lord rejected the house of Jacob, Isaiah would hope in him (8:17). The subject of the sentence in Isa 8:17 was Isaiah. The author of Hebrews changed the subject to Jesus and left the object the same, a practice that was customary to the author of Hebrews and to other Christian and Jewish interpreters of that day. The one in whom both Isaiah and Jesus had confidence was God, whose name was to be announced to the "brothers, in the midst of the congregation." The object, God, was one of the points that related LXX Ps 21:23 to Isa 8:17, but the main attraction of the Isaiah passage to the Psalm was contained in the word "children," quoted in the next verse, which could be identified with "brothers" of Heb 2:12, as well as the "sons" of vs. 10 and the sanctified ones of vs. 11.

"I and the children whom God has given me" in its Old Testament context referred to Isaiah himself, and his children, Shearjashub (Isa 7:3) and Mahershalalhashbaz (Isa 8:3), who were given prophetic names to indicate how the Lord would treat Israel. They were both given as signs. In his customary fashion, however, the author of Hebrews took the "I" to mean Jesus and "the children" to be his followers or "brothers." God had given them; they were God's sons (2:10); they had been sanctified (2:11). Therefore Jesus was "not ashamed to call them brothers" (2:11).

14. The expression "flesh and blood" is a customary Jewish and Christian idiom meaning human nature, especially as distinct from divine nature (Matt 16:17; I Cor 15:50; Gal 1:16; Eph 6:12; Nazir 9:5; Sotah 8:1). Jews who rejected the yoke of Heaven were ruled by a king of flesh and blood (TSotah 14:4; TBK 7:5). The idiom used by the author of Hebrews, however, was "blood and flesh." This was the blood and flesh which Jesus shared equally with the children, and may not have referred specifically to human nature at all. The expression may have taken human nature for granted, but meant to specify that among the human beings that existed on earth, Jesus was of the same "blood and flesh" as other children of Abraham; they were all fellow Israelites and belonged to the same family tree (see Deut 17:15).

There was evidently a strong Jewish and Christian belief that the devil was in control of death. Resh Laqish said Satan, the evil inclination, and the angel of death are identical (BB 16a). According to the Wisdom of Solomon, "God did not make death" (1:13). Death entered the world by means of the envy of the devil (*phthonǭ de diabolou*) (2:24). Paul also said of all the rules, authorities, and powers that God would put under Jesus' feet, that "the last enemy incapacitated (*katargeitai*) is death" (I Cor 15:26). Paul held that the sin of Adam caused death, so that death ruled from Adam to

Moses (Rom 5:12–21). Sin and death were closely related; it was sin that caused death. Death and life were terms not always used to mean just physical existence or lack of existence. In some contexts, life meant existence under the covenant, whereas death was the existence of those outside. A person who committed a sin unto death was expelled from the community, excommunicated from "life," and turned over to "death."[31] Since Jesus' sacrifice was considered enough to cancel all of the sins Israel had accumulated, Israel had become reconciled to God through the death of God's Son (Rom 5:10); this means the Son incapacitated (*katargēsē*) "the devil" "who controls death."[32] At the same time that Jesus incapacitated (*katargēsantos*) death, he also brought life and immortality to light through the gospel (I Tim 1:10; see also I Cor 2:6). The religious death caused by sin was the death which Jesus would "incapacitate." Covenanters would continue to face physical death after that, but since the sting of death is sin, and the sin has been canceled, Christians could be confident that they would later be raised into "life" (I Cor 15:56).

15. Israel reckoned sins as debts for which God was the creditor. When the account became overdrawn, the situation was analogous to that of an Israelite who was not able to repay a debt that he owed his fellow Israelite. He would have to work it out at half wages until the debt was repaid. This made him a slave to his brother until the Sabbath year when all debts were canceled.[33] Righteousness is immortal (Wis 1:15), but sin causes slavery and death. Those who were under a heavy burden because of the debt of sin which they could not pay back, were constantly in "fear of death" and were under bondage to the devil. The situation seemed hopeless. The Jew who owed money to his brother and could not pay it back in money could only hope for someone else to redeem him by paying his debt, or he would have to work it out completely or at least until the Sabbath year. These were his only means of "release." From the national and religious point of view, Jesus became the redeemer. He released all those who were depressed and enslaved in every possible way. Life under such a bondage of sin as this, II Baruch said, is the most bitter existence possible (21:13). Since Jesus provided the necessary offering for atonement, the whole picture has changed. He released covenanters from their fear of death so that they might all be made alive. The sin of man caused slavery and death. The death of Jesus provided the necessary sin offering to cancel the debt of sin (I Cor 15:20–22). Then those who had been enslaved could be set free; those who had been defeated by the devil would now be victorious (I Cor 15:52–57).

16. The word translated "prefer" (*epilambanetai*) means to seize, lay hold of, attack, come up to, reach, or obtain. It is a slight variant from *antilambanetai,* with the same meanings essentially, in the following LXX quotation:

[31] CC, pp. 110–49.
[32] For Paul the true Israel for whom this was effective was composed of those who had faith in Christ.
[33] See further CC, pp. 9–18.

8 "But you, Israel, my son Jacob, whom I chose (*exelexamēn*—Hebrew *b^eḥartīka*).
[the] seed of Abraham, whom I loved,
9 whom I took (*antelabomēn*—Hebrew *heḥ^ezaqtīka*, "laid hold of") from the boundaries of the earth . . ." (Isa 41:8–9).

The author must have had a LXX text which had some variants. He shows no sign of wanting to vary the meaning from its Old Testament context. As he used the compound word "take," he meant, as did the LXX translator by his form of the compound, to "take" by choosing, to take one thing in preference to another. The angels have not been mentioned since vs. 9, but they continue to be involved in the comparison with the Son. Here, however, the claim is made that Jesus was not only greater than the angels, but that the Israelites were also given preference over angels. Paul was also of the same opinion. He claimed that the saints were destined to judge angels (I Cor 6:3). In the Isaiah passage, the subject was God who did the choosing, loving, and taking. As before, the author changed the subject to Jesus who chose (took) the seed of Abraham rather than angels, but the object remains the same. It is Israel, Jacob, or the children of Abraham who were the chosen, the brothers, and the sons of whom the Son was not ashamed. Westcott was in error in denying this. He held that the author meant the "true seed, those who are children of faith, and not of 'the seed of Abraham.'"[34] Westcott had been influenced by Paul's judgment at this point and transferred Paul's theology to the author of Hebrews without any justification. The author of Hebrews held that Jesus and the sons of Abraham were "all from one" (2:11) father, namely Abraham. He shared equally with the children of Israel in blood and flesh; he belonged to the same basic ancestry. This strongly suggests that the author of Hebrews and the community for whom he prepared this document were all members of some branch of Jewish Christianity.

17. It was not enough that Jesus be of the same faith or point of view as "the brothers." He had "to be made like" them "in every way"—blood and flesh, family, and heritage. Jews would never consider an alien as their high priest. They were very careful to see that he belonged to the correct family, preferably Zadok's line. They objected to the Hasmoneans who were only Levites but assumed the position reserved for the sons of Zadok (Gen R. 97; 99:2).

Although Levites were priests in Israel's early history, Ezekiel decreed that they should be given a subordinate rank because of their behavior before the captivity. Nehemiah enforced Ezekiel's command. By the Maccabean period Levites were clearly understood to be subordinate to the sons of Zadok and were not even classed as priests by some convenanters (1QS 1:18–21; 2:2, 5, 11, 20–21). John Hyrcanus broke with the Pharisees because the Pharisees did not think he should hold the office of high priest. They seemed more concerned about the proper requirements for the high priesthood than for the ruler. Pharisees were willing for John Hyrcanus

[34] Westcott, p. 55; so also Michel, pp. 86–87.

to rule even though he had no basis for tracing his ancestry to David's line at all (*Ant.* XIII. 288–97). Hasmoneans were of priestly stock, at least, even though not of Zadok's line. They were frequently on the defensive about their ancestral qualifications for the positions they held. The author of Hebrews had a similar problem. Christians claimed that Jesus was a descendant of David, and on that basis could qualify as a messiah, but not as a high priest. He was not even a Levite. Since the author wanted to present Jesus as a priest and king, he had to justify his claim by some forced logic, similar to that used by the Hasmoneans to justify their position. This involved ignoring his Davidic ancestry, using proof texts to show that he had a different biblical basis for being considered a royal priest, and claiming for him every possible messianic attribute that did not specifically say he was a son of David. The author of Hebrews also made all the priestly claims he could for Jesus without saying he was a son of Zadok. To begin with, he was a son of Abraham, a true Jew. Jesus did belong to the general family. Therefore, to that extent, he had the necessary qualifications to offer sacrifice for "the sins of the people." Just being of the right family does not guarantee that the high priest would be "merciful and faithful," but the author was convinced that Jesus was, and that because of his priestly work the sins of Israel "might be expiated."

The translation "[regarding] divine services," literally "the things pertaining to God" (*ta pros ton theon*), is also used to refer to the offering Paul brought to Jerusalem from the nations (Rom 15:17). Aaron was commissioned to be the spokesman for Moses. He was to be a mouth for Moses and Moses was to be for Aaron "the things pertaining to God" (Exod 4:16). Moses' father-in-law told Moses that he could not bear the duties of judging the people alone; he must delegate authority. Moses should be to the people "the things pertaining to God" and he should carry their words to God (Exod 18:19). Moses complained that the people were rebellious and stubborn. While he was still alive they embittered "the things pertaining to God" (Deut 31:27). "The things pertaining to God" were evidently offerings, oracles, worship services, or other religious or divine objects and services.

18. Mekilta *Baḥodesh* 10:1–87 is a lengthy dissertation on the merits of sufferings which were considered "chastenings" (*yissurīn*). Suffering, more than prosperity, was an indication of forgiveness; it would bring a man into the world to come; it was a means of atonement, even more effective than sacrifices. Therefore sufferings were precious. Since any type of suffering was effective for releasing Israel from sin, then of course the voluntary suffering of the Messiah was the most effective of all. This was why it was important for the author to make a point of showing that Jesus was of the right blood and flesh, the seed of Abraham, so that the sacrifice that he had already made would certainly be effective. Since he had been "tempted" or tested, his sacrifice would be beneficial to others "who [were] being tempted" or made to suffer the same fate. This does not mean

that he just set a good example, but that his suffering canceled Israel's debt of sin.

Summary.—Whereas 1:5 – 2:9 concentrated directly on points where the Son could be compared favorably to the angels, for 2:10–18 this was only a background issue. This section directed its attention to the believers or followers of Jesus in relationship to him. The word "all" quoted in 2:8 was repeated here (2:10, 11, 17) to relate this passage to that preceding. Terms like "sufferings/suffered" and "brothers," near both the beginning and the end, have a literary purpose in forming an inclusion of this paragraph. Some of the catchwords used frequently in this section are: son (1:2, 5, 8; 2:6, 10), all (1:2, 3, 11, 14; 2:8, 9, 10, 11, 15, 17), sins (1:3; 2:17), angels (1:5, 6, 7, 13; 2:5, 7, 9, 16), inherit (1:4, 14), name (1:4; 2:12), and death (2:9, 14, 15).

The relationship of the Son to the followers of Jesus is well defined: They, like the Son, are sons; like him they are exalted to glory; he and they are from one father, Abraham; he claims them proudly as brothers; they share the same blood and flesh; he has chosen ("taken") the children of Abraham, and he has been made like them in every way. Since he was closely identified with the children of Israel, his suffering would certainly be effective in canceling the heavy debt of sin recorded against Israel. They would be able to benefit from the merits he accumulated through his sacrifice. This is a strong argument to justify the Jewish Christian position. It makes no gesture to offer deliverance to the Gentiles.

Although the comparison with angels was not the major point of this section, the subject was introduced near the end (2:16) to assure the reader that the comparison of the Son to the angels was still in force. The return to angels at this point might also have been intended to direct the reader back to the beginning of the whole discussion in 1:5, which introduced the comparison of the Son with the angels. Verses 17 and 18 also helped prepare the reader for the topic that would follow. All this indicates that a major section is completed at the end of this chapter. This section has been directed to an exaltation of the Son, primarily in comparison with the angels, but in the process it disclosed the author's understanding of Christology in relationship to the Son, the Son of man, and the first-born. This topic will receive special attention, because its understanding is basic to a proper comprehension of the rest of the document.

The Son as a Son of Man

a. The Son of Man in Hebrews

When the author of Hebrews described the superior attributes of the Son, he drew on Old Testament passages that described a mighty king. Such enthronement Psalms as Ps 2, which identified the son as a king on Mount Zion who would break the enemy nations into pieces and rule over them with power, and Ps 110, which described the son as a king who sat at God's right hand while God made his enemies his footstool, supported this description. The author also used passages from II Sam and Ps 45. II Sam 7:14 originally described Solomon as God's son when he ruled the United Kingdom from Jerusalem. Ps 45 was addressed to an anointed king (Ps 45:7) who was urged to gird on his sword in glory and ride forth victoriously (Ps 45:3–4). His enemies were destined to fall before his sharp arrows (45:6). From his divine throne he would rule justly (Ps 45:6). The Son of God was to be a king like Solomon for whom God would make his enemies a footstool (Ps 110:1). The author of Hebrews identified the Son of God with the Son of man for whom God had put all things under his feet (Ps 8:6).[35] Since the author also identified Jesus with the king referred to in these expressions, it seems that he understood the expressions "Son of God" and "Son of man" to have the same meaning and to describe a messiah or king, but these are not the conclusions reached by most scholars.

b. Scholarly reaction to Heb 2:6

Commentators generally have done little to draw attention to the term "Son of man" as it appears in Heb 2:6. Some have just ignored it. Others specifically insist that it has no messianic significance. It is simply an accidental term that happened to be in Ps 8 in parallelism with "man." It has no further significance for the author of Hebrews.[36] Some acknowledged it to be a messianic title, or at least identified with Jesus in some way, but they did not make any attempt to say how.[37] Michel erroneously noted that Ps 8 was not used by the rabbis to refer to the Messiah.[38] Laubach held that, for the author, Ps 8 was used to call attention to Jesus as "the man," i.e. the true man, the second from Adam. He noticed, however, that there was a striking resemblance between the subjection element in Ps 8 and that of Ps 110, but he did not indicate what that meant.[39]

Major studies on the Son of Man have given no more attention to Heb 2:6 than commentators have. Jeremias did no more than mention its occurrence in Heb 2:6.[40] Higgins noted that "Son of Man Christology cannot claim to be prominent in Hebrews like that of the Son of God (1:8; 4:14; 6:6; 7:3; 10:29), for it occurs but once, and then only in this

[35] In a larger context of conditions under which the Messiah, the son of David, or redemption would come, Dan 7:13 was quoted by the rabbis, identifying the son of man with the Messiah (San. 98a).

[36] Moffatt, p. 23; Stuart, p. 69; Westcott, pp. 42–43; Windisch, p. 20.

[37] Kuss, pp. 40–41; Spicq, II, 31.

[38] Michel, pp. 70–71.

[39] Laubach, *Der Brief an die Hebräer* (Wuppertal, 1967), p. 62.

[40] Jeremias, I, 265.

quotation from Ps 8."[41] He understood the author of Hebrews to have used this Psalm to show that "the promise of sovereignty held out to man has been fulfilled in Jesus."[42] Bultmann completely ignored Heb 2:6 in his discussion of the Son of Man.[43]

Cullmann said, in reference to Heb 2:6, "Hebrews applies the psalm [Ps 8] to Jesus as the Son of man. The author's interpretation of the citation indicates that he apparently had quite precise information about the Son of Man doctrine."[44] Cullmann was correct on this point, but he did not pursue the matter. The doctrine of the Son of Man which the author of Hebrews presented was quite different from that which Cullmann sets forth. Cullmann made no attempt to tell what this precise information was. Like most scholars,[45] Cullmann made a clear distinction between the "political Messiah who would defeat the enemies of Israel in an earthly war and establish a political kingdom" and "the supernatural, heavenly 'Son of Man.'" Cullmann insisted, "He is a heavenly ruler, not an earthly king."[46] In keeping with this sharp distinction made between the Messiah and the Son of Man, Vielhauer separated the titles so completely as to claim that Jesus never used the term "Son of Man," and that the heavenly Son of Man concept was not at all related to the concept of the Kingdom of God.[47] Proudman went so far as to claim that the Son of man in Daniel was an angel.[48]

It was only in adverse response to Vielhauer that some scholars have tried to close the gap that they had previously developed between the Messiah and the Son of man. Marshall argued: "Furthermore, it is wrong to assert that the Son of man was not in some sense a messianic figure; the author of the Similitudes of Enoch made the identification, and it is hard to see why Jesus could not have made the same identification."[49] His logic was as follows: "So far as the interpretation of the vision is concerned, the Son of man is the representative or symbol of the saints of the Most High (Dan 7:18, 22, 27). If he is their representative, he is most naturally thought of as their head, in which case we should probably see a 'messianic' reference here."[50] Spelled out more precisely,

[41] A. J. B. Higgins, *Jesus and the Son of Man* (Philadelphia, 1964), p. 146.

[42] Ibid.

[43] Bultmann, I, 5, 7, 9, 26–37, 40, 42–44, 47, 49, 51–53, 79–80, 124, 172.

[44] O. Cullmann, *The Christology of the New Testament,* trs. S. C. Guthrie and C. A. M. Hall (Philadelphia, 1957), p. 188.

[45] Jeremias, I, 274–75; H. Teeple, "The Origin of the Son of Man Christology," JBL 84 (1965), 213–50; Bultmann, I, 49, et al.

[46] Cullmann, *Christology,* p. 142.

[47] P. Vielhauer, "Gottesreich und Menschensohn in der Verkündigung Jesu," *Aufsätze zum Neuen Testament. Theologische Bücherei* 31 (München, 1965), 55–140.

[48] C. L. J. Proudman, "Remarks on the 'Son of man,'" CJT 12 (1966), 128–31.

[49] I. H. Marshall, "The Synoptic Son of Man Sayings in Recent Discussion," NTS 12 (1965–66), 347.

[50] Ibid., p. 336. See also A. Caquot, "Les Quatre Bêtes et le 'Fils d'Homme,'" *Semitica* 17 (1967), 37–71, and L.-M. Orrieux, "Le Problème du fils de l'Homme dans la Littérature Apocalyptique," LumVie 12, No. 62 (1963), 9–31.

the "messianic reference" would imply that the son of man in Daniel was a king, and that the one "like a son of man" was a person "like" a king, with all the political implications normally associated with the messiah figure. Such an understanding of the Son of man as this would be completely consistent with the Son of man described in Heb 2:6.

In reaction to a position similar to Vielhauer's, Walker said: ". . . it would be very difficult to deduce from these passages that Matthew makes any distinction between the Kingdom of the Son of Man and the Kingdom of Heaven."[51] It has become more and more difficult for scholars to admit that Jesus was called king, Son of God, and messiah—all of which are royal designations—and at the same time claim that his other title, Son of man, was in no way related to any nationalistic, political movement or aspiration. In addition to emphasizing the heavenly aspect of the vision enthroning the Son of man, scholars have identified the term, Son of man, with "man" in Philip 2:7. This opens up many distracting possibilities. Once removed from the context involving power, glory, and a kingdom, the Son of man meaning man can then be identified with the suffering servant of Isaiah and the new Adam. Once the humbling aspect is raised, the dominion aspect can be dismissed, and the Son of man is safely removed from political anxiety.

Tödt objected to the methodology employed by these scholars. He said, "Christological doctrine has been developed in Protestantism mainly with regard to the concepts expressed in Philip 2. The synoptic texts were interpreted to conform to this passage. Accordingly, the synoptic statements could not be understood otherwise than in the predetermined way; the one who has preached on earth could only be seen as the transcendent person, the pre-existent Son of God, or the heavenly Son of man, and Jesus' acceptance of earthly restrictions could only be understood as humiliation."[52]

Tödt's analysis did not persuade scholars suddenly to stop understanding the Son of man in a predetermined way. Formesyn approved of Tödt's thesis,[53] but Black strongly objected to Tödt's minimizing of the Isaianic influences in the passion sayings.[54] Penetrating studies like those of Tödt and Marshall indicate, however, that some scholars are searching for a more adequate interpretation of the data related to the Son of man. These may be willing to consider a fresh approach which takes Heb 2:6 into account. With that expectation, the following analysis of relevant literature will compare the Son of man in Daniel and Enoch to the royal figure in Heb 2:6.

[51] W. O. Walker, Jr., "The Kingdom of the Son of Man and the Kingdom of the Father in Matthew," CBQ 30 (1968), 577. See also E. Bammel, "Erwägungen zur Eschatologie Jesu," StEv III (1964), 3–32.

[52] H. E. Tödt, *The Son of Man in the Synoptic Tradition* (Philadelphia, 1964), p. 296.

[53] R. E. C. Formesyn, "Was There a Pronominal Connection for the Self Designation?" *Novum Testamentum* 8 (1966), 1–35.

[54] M. Black, "The 'Son of Man' Passion Sayings in the Gospel Tradition," ZNTW 60 (1969), 1–8.

c. The Son of Man in Daniel and Enoch

The term "son of man" seems to have been used in the Old Testament to mean simply "man." For instance, Ezekiel was frequently addressed by the Lord as son of man: "Son of man, stand upon your feet" (Ezek 2:1) or "Son of man, I am sending you to the children of Israel" (Ezek 2:3). The most likely meaning of "son of man" in these passages seems to be simply "man."[55] In Daniel, however, the "son of man" probably has a different significance.[56] *In a vision,* Daniel saw one like a son of man come with the clouds of heaven up to the Ancient of Days. To this being who was like a son of man (*bar 'enāš*) was given dominion, glory, and a kingdom. All peoples, nations, and languages were to serve him. His dominion and kingdom were to continue forever (Dan 7:13–14). At the same time the saints of the Most High were given the kingdom, dominion, and the greatness of the kingdoms under the whole heaven; their kingdom and dominion was to be forever, and all other dominions were destined to serve them (Dan 7:27). The saints of the Most High were the people of Israel who inherited Palestine after the Syrian kingdom crumbled. The Book of Daniel, written after the rededication of the temple and the restoration of worship at Jerusalem, was composed in terms of sabbatical release.[57] Jeremiah had promised that the jews were to be in captivity for seventy years. That time had long since passed, but the author of Daniel took that to mean seventy weeks of years, which could be manipulated so as to coincide perfectly with the Maccabean victory.[58] Seven weeks of years were spent in Babylon; sixty-two weeks of years elapsed during the time from the return to Jerusalem until a certain covenant was made. This totals as follows: sixty-two plus seven equals sixty-nine—only one more week of years until there would be seventy weeks of years—time for the tenth jubilee! One-half week of years later the temple was defiled and sacrifice was discontinued (Dan 9:24–27). Before the second half-week of years was over, the temple had been cleansed (Dan 7:25; 8:14; 9:27; 12:7). This means that the author of the Book of Daniel interpreted the Maccabean victory in sabbatical terms. The jubilee of ten weeks of years was the time when the "captivity" was over, "slaves"

[55] Another possibility is that "son of man" was the self-designation of Ezekiel by which he described his office as a messenger-prophet or eschatological prophet. In any event, it is not the same as the meaning in Daniel, which must be judged by its own context. For the possible relationship of Jesus' use of Son of man to Ezekiel's, see E. Schweitzer, "The Son of Man Again," NTS 10 (1963–64), 256–61.

[56] Although even in Dan 8:17 and 10:16 *ben 'ādām* and *b^enē 'ādām* have a generic meaning.

[57] See further CC, pp. 9–18, or "Sabbatical Eschatology," *Christian News from Israel* 18 (1967), 49–56.

[58] This manipulation involved assigning sixty-two weeks of years to the period from the return to Jerusalem until a certain covenant was made, with little concern for mathematical accuracy.

were set free, and the land was restored to the "original owners," as at jubilee. This was a nationalistic interpretation of sabbatical justice. In this context, when the Maccabees were recovering the promised land from the Syrians, and Jews received a new national freedom, Daniel saw a vision during which the saints of the Most High received dominion and the kingdom, and a being like a "son of man" also received dominion, glory, and a kingdom. This being seems to have been like a king who ruled over a territory at the same time his people were citizens of the territory. Since the saints of the Most High were evidently the Jews after the temple had been cleansed and worship restored, the being like a "son of man" was probably Judas, the Maccabee, who had received the dominion, glory, and the beginning of a kingdom.[59]

In Daniel's vision the being like a "son of man" came with the clouds of heaven (Dan 7:13). In Jewish and Christian literature, dreams and visions were frequently employed as literary devices to communicate messages dramatically. Thus the four beasts included in the same vision (Dan 7:1–8) *symbolized* four nations that controlled the Jews after the Babylonian captivity. It would be a mistake to assume that all four nations came up out of the sea, literally (Dan 7:3), or that all other details be understood literally. The same would be true of the visions of Ezekiel and Zechariah. When the seventy disciples returned joyfully telling of their success, Jesus said, "I saw Satan fall like lightning from heaven" (Luke

[59] Although many scholars, such as Manson, hold to an identification of the son of man with the saints of the Most High in Daniel, this has been difficult to defend. Jeremias, p. 274, agreed that the son of man was a "corporate entity," but he explained that this was so in the sense that "for oriental thought the king or the priest represents his people or his community." In other words, Jeremias really claimed that the son of man was a king or priest, who was corporate only in the sense that other kings and priests are. Cullmann, *Christology*, p. 140, also insisted that "the apocalyptic writer [Daniel 7] identifies the son of Man as the 'saints of the Most High.'" In explaining the relationship of the four beasts to the son of man, he said, ". . . the vision contains a certain inconsistency: the beasts are interpreted as kings, as *representatives* [italics his], of the world empires, but the 'man' is the nation of the saints itself." He was correct in noting that one would have to maintain an inconsistency in the vision not to see the son of man also as a representative. Jeremias did understand the son of man as a representative, and the author of Dan 7 probably did too. Although Cullmann said the son of man was not a representative figure, as the beasts were, on the next page (p. 141) he said, "But we must by no means forget that the idea of the Son of Man at its ultimate source also includes the idea that the figure of *the* Man represents all men." That interpretation would probably have come as a surprise to the author of Daniel. While insisting on understanding the son of man in Daniel as a corporate personality, Cullmann admitted that later Jewish literature, such as Enoch and IV Ezra, which depended on Daniel, understood the son of man as an individual (p. 140). When dealing with Jesus, Cullmann said, "Of course Jesus thinks primarily of an individual redeeming figure as do IV Ezra and Enoch, but we must not forget that for Jewish thought the individual interpretation does not *exclude* the collective one" (p. 156). Caquot, *Semitica* 17 (1967), 37–71, faces the same type of confusion, but others, like Orrieux, LumVie 12, No. 62 (1963), 9–31, and M. Cambe, "Le Fils de l'Homme dans les Evangiles Synoptiques," ibid., pp. 32–64, claim the son of man in Daniel is messianic and not collective.

10:18)—a dramatic way of saying that they were winning and Satan was losing. In the same way, Daniel's vision dramatized a being like a "son of man" coming with the clouds of heaven (Dan 7:13). This did not mean that he had wings or was angelic. It meant that the vision attempted to communicate the belief that the being was divinely appointed.[60] The appearance of the Lord in a cloud was nothing new:[61] The Lord appeared in a cloud of glory when Moses was given the ten commandments for Israel (Exod 19:16–25; Deut 5:4, 22–27; see also 1:33). There was always a cloud of smoke over the tabernacle to indicate the Lord's presence and glory (Num 9:15–23). It was from the cloud that the Lord spoke to Peter, James, and John on the Mount of Transfiguration, saying, "This is my beloved Son, with whom I am well pleased" (Matt 17:1–5). The fact that these events took place in relationship to clouds does not mean that Moses, Jesus, Peter, James, and John were heavenly beings, but that the Lord was present when these important events took place, and that he approved them. Daniel, by relating *a vision,* attempted to say something like that. Just as the time sequence was interpreted in such a way as to show that Jeremiah's prophecy was fulfilled and the people received the benefits of the jubilee when the land was restored and they were delivered from the hand of the oppressing Syrians, so God's approval of the Maccabean victory was shown by a vision of the Ancient of Days giving the dominion, glory, and a kingdom both to one like a "son of man" and to the people of the saints of the Most High.[62]

The being "like a son of man" would seem to be the leader in charge of the Jewish saints who recovered control of the temple, cleansed it, and renewed sacrifice. The leader at that time was Judas the Maccabee, one who gave the initial impetus to the rebellion that finally succeeded in overthrowing the Syrians and restoring the United Kingdom to Israel free from foreign rule and taxation. Complete national liberty was not achieved until Simon's rule when the taxation was removed and Simon was appointed high priest (*Wars* I. 53; I Macc 13:39–42). Aristobulus I was the first Hasmonean to declare himself king (*Wars* I. 117), but earlier Hasmoneans, among their own people, were exalted higher than their official

[60] Likewise, the four nations coming up out of the sea may have dramatized the author's conviction that they owed their origin to the dragon of the great deep, Tiamat.

[61] A. Feuillet, "Le Fils d l'Homme de Daniel et la Tradition Biblique," RB 60 (1963), 187, observed that the cloud frequently accompanies theophanies, but whenever angels are present, the cloud is absent (cf. Dan 8:15; 9:21; 10:5–16).

[62] T. W. Manson, "The Son of Man in Daniel, Enoch, and the Gospels," BJRL 32 (1950), 171–93. assuming that the son of man in Daniel 7 was a corporate personality signifying the saints of the Most High, or the covenant community, concluded that in the New Testament it also sometimes applies to the new elect, of whom Jesus was the head, rather than just to Jesus alone. Overlooking the Midrash on Ps 2:9, he said, "There seems to be no evidence that in Rabbinical circles Son of Man was used as a name for the Messiah" (p. 175). Just because both the saints and the son of man were given the same kingdom does not mean they are identical. This is the normal relationship of a king and his people to their country.

titles acknowledged. Simon, for instance, was called by the Hebrew name, "the prince of the people of God" (Greek *asaramel,* a transliteration for *sar 'am 'ēl*).[63] Judas, the leader when the temple was cleansed, was neither high priest nor king, officially, but he was highly respected by contemporary and later Jews. He was one *like* a son of man.

The suggestion that Judas was the leader whom the author of Daniel had in mind when he described him favorably as one like a son of man implies that the author was favorable to the Maccabees and their movement, as the calculation of the sabbatical chronology would suggest; but that has not been the view most widely accepted among scholars. Many, such as Charles[64] and Montgomery,[65] have understood the author of Daniel to have been in support of the Hasidim but depreciative of the Hasmoneans. The chief basis for their conclusion is their identification of the "little help" given to the Jews in their crisis during the Maccabean Revolt (Dan 11:34). Montgomery said, "The writer is not a Maccabean but an Asidaean, for he looks for help to God alone."[66] This is not a fair distinction to make between the Maccabean movement and that of the Hasidim. The pro-Hasmoneans also believed that Abraham, Joseph, Phineas, Joshua, Caleb, David, Elijah, Hananiah, Azariah, Mishael, and Daniel were glorified and blessed because of their faithfulness, obedience to God, zeal for the law, witness, mercy, and innocence—not because of their military skill (I Macc 2:51–60). The author of I Macc quoted Judas as saying, "Victory in battle does not depend on the size of an army, but rather on the strength that comes from Heaven. . . . He himself will shatter them before us" (3:19, 21; see also 4:8–10, 30–33; 7:36–38). In comparable holy war theology, the poet echoed the following confessions (1QM 11:1–12):

"For yours is the battle, and with the strength of your hand . . . (1)
For yours is the battle, for the Philistines you subdued many times
through your holy name . . . (2–3);
Yours is the battle, and from you is the might, and it is not
ours . . . (4–5).
For it is in your strength and in the power of your great valor . . . (6)
For from of old we have confessed the power of your hand against
the Kittim . . ." (12).

The Hasidim were not opposed to war in principle. At the outset they joined forces with the Hasmoneans in their defense of the law (I Macc 2:42–48). They were willing to fight to restore purified worship in the temple and law observance among the people. Once the temple had been

[63] As S. Tedesche and S. Zeitlin, *The First Book of Maccabees* (New York, 1950), p. 44, correctly suggested in relation to I Macc 14:27. The initial alpha probably indicates a prosthetic aleph since the definite article *ha* would not have been present in this combination.

[64] R. H. Charles, *A Critical and Exegetical Commentary on the Book of Daniel* (Oxford, 1929), pp. 309–13.

[65] J. A. Montgomery, *A Critical and Exegetical Commentary on the Book of Daniel* (New York, 1927), pp. 458–59.

[66] Ibid.

cleansed and a candidate from the tribe of Aaron, Alcimus, had been appointed high priest, they were prepared to make peace with the Seleucids and part company with Judas on this point (I Macc 7:4–14). There is no further report in I Macc of the activities of the Hasidim after Alcimus slew sixty Hasidim in one day (I Macc 7:15–18), but Judas was reported to have avenged their deaths (7:15–50). Enoch 90:6–12, on which Charles[67] drew for support of his position, gives no clearer picture of the Hasidim after Alcimus' slaughter than does I Macc. In II Macc 14:6, however, the Hasidim are reported as "those whom Judas the Maccabee leads" (*hōn aphēgeitai Ioudas ho Makkabaios*). There is not nearly as much evidence for the antipathy between the Hasmoneans and the Hasidim as scholars have implied. The latter were initially part of the Maccabean rebellion; their only rift with the Hasmoneans was over the matter of Alcimus, and after Alcimus slaughtered several of the Hasidim, Judas avenged their deaths. For all we can learn from the sources, the Hasidim may have returned to support the Hasmoneans after Alcimus' betrayal, but this is also a conjecture. There certainly is not enough evidence to support the opposite conclusion, that the antipathy continued, and that the author of Daniel was one of their party who opposed the Hasmoneans.

According to Charles, the Hasmoneans were the ones who offered a little help[68] and were joined by flatterers who followed the Hasmoneans out of fear (Dan 11:34–35).[69] Montgomery said those were "adherents of doubtful character" who joined Judas' group.[70] No doubt Judas had supporters of both descriptions, but that does not mean they were the ones mentioned in Dan 11:34–35.

It is not easy to untangle these puzzles when the allusions are not specific. Once conclusions are reached, however, it is possible to interpret the reports in such a way as to make the conclusions seem reasonable, even if they are wrong. In this realm of conjecture, previous attempts have not been so successful as to rule out other attempts for consideration. The following interpretation will suggest a hypothesis that is not conclusive, but is different from those accepted up to this point. A point in its favor is that it at least takes into account the evidence that the whole Book of Daniel is centered around the Maccabean victory over the Syrians.

In dealing with the crucial passage, Dan 11:29–35, scholars are generally agreed that the reference to the ships of "the Kittim" coming against "him," forcing "him" to withdraw (11:30), refers to the confrontation of the Roman envoy ("the Kittim") under the leadership of Popilius with Antiochus IV Epiphanes ("him") after he had conquered Egypt (Livy 45:12, 1–6). This aroused the anger of Antiochus, which he expressed by taking action against the holy covenant, profaning the temple, and

[67] Charles, *Commentary*, pp. 309–10.

[68] N. W. Porteus, *Daniel* (London, 1965), p. 168, says the "little help" came, not from the Maccabees, but from the martyrs—as if they could be distinguished from those who died in the Maccabean Revolt.

[69] Charles, *Commentary*, p. 310.

[70] Montgomery, *Commentary*, p. 459.

removing the continual burnt offering. This is a description of his plundering the temple at Jerusalem (Dan 11:30–31; I Macc 1:20–53). The abomination that makes desolate which he is reported to have set up (11:31) is the same as that reported in I Macc 1:54. His attempts to seduce with flattery those who violate the covenant (11:32) were successful attempts made to persuade Jews to worship idols and profane the Sabbath (I Macc 1:42), withhold offerings, profane festivals, pollute the sanctuary and the saints, sacrifice pork, and leave sons uncircumcised (I Macc 1:45–47). This was done under threat of death and promise of reward (I Macc 1:50, 57; 2:15–18). "But the people who know their God shall stand firm and act!" (Dan 11:32). Among this group were the instructors of the people (*maśkīlē ʿam*) who instructed and exhorted the many (*lārabbīm*) to hold fast to their faith even though they should fall by the sword, flame, captivity, and plunder (Dan 11:33). Those who held fast faced precisely these consequences. Those who owned scriptures were killed. Mothers who circumcised their sons were put to death with their babies hanging around their necks. Some died rather than eat food not approved by their dietary laws (I Macc 2:57–63). Those who held fast had to live in secret places as refugees (I Macc 1:53).

The Hasmoneans were the main leaders in the whole movement for freedom from heathen oppression and maintenance of their laws. If they were not themselves considered some of the instructors (*maśkīlīm*) who stumbled (*yikkāšᵉlū*) (Dan 11:35) so as to purify and make (the community) white, they were working alongside religious teachers for the same cause.[71] Although there was some conflict among the ranks, those who were not pro-Seleucids were in basic unity. It was not as if one party was for Judas and the other for God. Some were compromisers with the Seleucids, and others were loyal, rigorous, law-abiding Jews. The whole patriotic group, of which the Hasidim and the Hasmoneans were parts, were amazingly successful in fighting the Seleucids on their own, but they did receive some help. The question is, from whom? Most scholars say, "From the Hasmoneans," but there were very few Jews who would have considered that help "little," least of all an author who composed a whole book that interpreted the Maccabean Revolt in terms of God's foreordained and scheduled plan. Not until after the temple had been cleansed, and victory seemed assured, did Judas make an agreement with Rome in which both countries agreed to support one another in international business and war (I Macc 8:1–32). This "little help" was not really minor, either. Without it the Seleucids may never have been repelled, but it was from the outside, and understandably small in comparison to the force of the Jews themselves and their God. Those who joined themselves with flattery to those who provided the little help may have been the opportunists who profiteered by dealing with the Romans as

[71] In Hebrew there seems to be a play on words "the instructors stumbled" (*maśkīlīm yikkāšᵉlū*), but the LXX read *dianoēthēsontai*, apparently rendering *yaśkīlū* "will instruct," which also makes sense.

they had dealt earlier with the Seleucids. The author of Daniel may have been suspicious of the consequences of transferring loyalty from Syria to Rome. There was in Judaism an ancient tradition of warning against foreign alliances. The anxiety was justified. The Rome which provided a "little help" later controlled the entire nation.

This does not prove that the author of Daniel was pro-Hasmonean, but it shows that Daniel can be understood from that point of view at least as reasonably as from the anti-Hasmonean viewpoint. This allows for the possibility that Judas was the one described as being "like a son of man" who was divinely appointed to his role of leadership. To him was given the dominion and glory and a kingdom (Dan 7:14). His was the rule that followed the rule of Antiochus IV Epiphanes, the last remnant of the fourth beast, over the saints of the Most High after the temple had been cleansed and sacrifice restored (Dan 7:23–27). Although he was not officially a king, he was "*like* a son of man," which may have meant that he was *like* a king. The likelihood that this was so will become greater when the role of the son of man is examined in Enoch and the gospels.

In Enoch, the son of man was one who removed kings from their thrones, and upon whom the kingdom was bestowed (46:4–5). He was named before the Lord of Spirits, the Head of Days (48:2), and it was in his name that the righteous would be saved (48:7; 50:3). At the time when the son of man was named, the kings and mighty ones who possessed the land would be downcast because they would be given over in anguish to the son of man who was also the elect one and the anointed of the Lord of Spirits (48:8–10; 62:6). The glory of this elect one was to be forever, and he would judge the secret things (49:2–4; 61:9). Like other good kings, he would judge righteously (50:4). Like other kings, he would sit on his throne of glory (51:3; 55:4; 61:8; 62:2) and be recognized by the kings and mighty ones (62:1–2) who would prostrate themselves before him and plead for mercy; but that son of man would punish them with the sword because they had oppressed the Lord's elect. The righteous and elect, however, would feast together with that son of man and be clothed in garments of glory (62:1 – 63:120). These would be the ones who trusted in the Lord of Spirits. Their lot would be one of joy whenever the son of man sat on his glorious throne from which he would pass judgment, and his authority would be strong before the Lord of Spirits (69:24–29). He would have such authority that he could slay sinners by the word of his mouth. This might mean that, like other kings, he could order someone killed and his decree would be carried out, or it might mean that when he cursed them they dropped dead.

The picture in Enoch is very much like that in Daniel. The son of man was a king destined to rule from his throne. When he ruled, the saints of the Most High or the ones elected by the Lord of Spirits would also be in a position of favor. The powerful king who exercised political authority and military might over his enemies is very similar to the Son in Hebrews who was also called the Son of man.

d. The Son of Man in the New Testament

Freed[72] noticed correctly that in the Fourth Gospel "Son of man" is used synonymously with Jesus, Son of God, Son, and the first personal pronoun spoken by Jesus. Further, he noted that there is no separate son of man christology in that document. Ford[73] further concluded that the title "Son of man" was used with the same meaning as the title "Son of God" in all four gospels. For example, when Jesus asked who men said the son of man was and followed by asking who Peter thought Jesus was, Peter said, "You are the Messiah, the Son of the living God" (Matt 16:13–16). Here the subject matter was the same: Jesus, the Messiah, the Son of man, and the Son of the living God. In John, Jesus was identified with the Son of God who was to be glorified (John 11:4) and the Son of man who was to be glorified (John 13:31). Ford's explanation of these facts in terms of euphemism, however, is not very important for this discussion, and her unsupported agreement with Feuillet that "there seems to be a great deal of originality in Jesus' use of the title 'Son of man,'"[74] contradicts the available evidence. In the Book of Daniel and the Book of Enoch, the Son of man was portrayed as a king who would sit on his throne and rule the people of Israel while judging their enemies. The same was true of the son of man in the New Testament. In Ps 110, it was a king who would sit at God's right hand as God's son. In Stephen's vision, Jesus, as the Son of man, was seen standing at God's right hand (Acts 7:55–56). The Son of man or the one like a son of man in the New Testament was one who would wear a gold crown (Rev 14:14) and sit on his glorious throne (Matt 19:28; 25:31) as other kings do. He would come into his kingdom in glory, as other kings come into their kingdoms. When he did, he would reward his friends and punish his enemies just as other kings do (Matt 16:27–28; Mark 8:38; Luke 9:26). Like other kings he had the authority to judge (John 5:27) and pardon (Matt 9:6; Mark 2:10; Luke 5:24). When Jesus, as the Son of man, would sit on his glorious throne, as other kings do, the apostles were promised that they also would sit on twelve thrones judging the twelve tribes of Israel (Matt 19:28). There seems very little basis for forcing a spiritual interpretation either on the thrones for the twelve apostles over the twelve tribes, or on the throne of glory on which the Son of man would sit as a king over all twelve tribes of Israel. The Son of man described was a king, just as the son of man in Daniel, Enoch, and Hebrews. Jesus, as the Son of man, was destined to sit on his glorious throne with all the nations gathered before him just as the son of man in Enoch, and as *king* he would judge the nations, just as the son of man in Enoch, who was a king, had done (Matt 25:31–33). So closely identified with the being like a "son of

[72] E. D. Freed, "The Son of Man in the Fourth Gospel," JBL 86 (1967), 402–9.

[73] J. M. Ford, "'The Son of Man'—a Euphemism?" JBL 87 (1968), 257–66.

[74] Ibid., p. 64.

man" in Daniel was the Son of man in the gospels that he was described by a quotation from Daniel 7:13–14 (Matt 24:30; Mark 13:26; Luke 21:27).

In the Gospel of John, like the Gospel of Matthew, where the Son of man was identified with Jesus as the Son of God, Nathaniel confessed:

"Rabbi, you are the Son of God;
you are the king of Israel" (John 1:49).

In this couplet, the Son of God means the same as the king of Israel who elsewhere was called the Son of man or the Messiah—all designations suitable for one who would rule over the Kingdom of God or Palestine.[75]

When the Son of man is understood to be a king, the passages referring to the betrayal of one who pretended to be the Son of man make better sense (Matt 20:18; 26:2, 24, 45; Mark 9:31; 10:33; 14:21, 41; Luke 9:44, 22:22), and the irony of a Son of man, destined to rule from a throne of glory, becomes evident when Jesus claimed that the Son of man had nowhere to lay his head (Matt 8:20; Luke 9:58).

Many[76] have avoided the political associations of the Son of man concept by claiming him to be a corporate personality or a heavenly figure, but the Son of man described in Hebrews was a king who ruled over a nation and had such evident might that kings of other nations would be subject to him. In so doing, the author identified the Son of God with the Son

[75] For the basis for identifying the Kingdom of God with Palestine, see CC, pp. 42–90. Although that was not his major thesis, Marshall, NTS 12 (1965–66), 335–36, opposed Vielhauer's claim that the Kingdom of God and the Son of man were mutually irreconcilable concepts. He called attention to such terms as "dominion," "kingdom," "throne," and "crown" used in association with the Son of man. M. Black, "The Son of Man Problem in Recent Research and Debate," BJRL 45 (1962–63), 310, also opposed Vielhauer on that point. H. M. Teeple, "The Origin of the Son of Man Christology," JBL 84 (1965), 238, who thought the Son of man was a personification of Israel, said, ". . . the Son of man Messiah is really as nationalistic as the Son of David. . . . The Son of man of the Similitudes will destroy the gentile kings and exalt the Jewish saints even more thoroughly than the Son of David."

[76] To cite only a few examples, C. K. Barrett, *The Gospel According to St. John* (London, 1967), 60, said ". . . in the synoptic gospels 'Son of God' draws attention to Christ's obedience to God and 'Son of man' means a heavenly being." Bultmann, I, 49, said, "However, the predominant title in the earliest Church, by the teaching of the synoptic tradition, was 'Son of Man,' which comes out of the apocalyptic hope and means a supra-mundane, pre-existent being who at the end of time will come down from heaven to hold judgment and bring salvation." E. Sjöberg, *Der Menschensohn im Äthiopischen Henochbuch* (Lund, 1946), p. 50, called the son of man "der ganz besondere himmlische Mensch." See also pp. 58–59; 141–43; 193–94. Teeple, JBL 84 (1965), 219, said ". . . for the pre-existent, heavenly Son of Man was utterly incompatible with a human type of Messiah born on earth." He further noted, "In Daniel the figure is not the Messiah but the nation of Israel personified . . ." (p. 243). This latter view was in agreement with E. Schweitzer, NTS 10 (1963–64), 122. That understanding was made popular by T. W. Manson, *The Teaching of Jesus* (Cambridge, 1951), 311–36, and "The Son of Man in Daniel, Enoch and the Gospels," BJRL 32 (1949–50), 171–93. For articles surveying other scholarly views on the Son of man, see Black, BJRL 45 (1962–63), 305–15, and I. H. Marshall, NTS 12 (1965–66), 327–51.

of man and Jesus as the gospels did.[77] The political nature of the Son of man described in Hebrews was in agreement with that of the figure described in Daniel, Enoch, and the gospels. This understanding of the Son is basic to a true comprehension of Hebrews, and Hebrews was faithful to the Near Eastern understanding of the Son of man and the Son of God as a political king over a given kingdom.

This insight does not negate all theological attributes previously associated with the Son of man, such as pre-existence, but it means that these concepts must be interpreted in a way that would be fitting for a Near Eastern king of New Testament times.

[77] For the relationship between a king and a son of God, see Mowinckel, I, 48–49, 54, 60, 62–63, 125. Mowinckel also discussed the theology related to kingship in the ancient Near East.

III. SUPERIORITY OVER MOSES
(3:1–4:16)

Son rather than servant

3 [1] Therefore, holy brothers, sharers in [the] heavenly calling, direct [your] attention to Jesus, the apostle and high priest of our confession, [2] [who] was faithful to the one who made him, just as was
also Moses in his house. [3] For he [Jesus] is worthy of as much more
glory than Moses as the builder has more glory than the house he
built. [4] (For every house is built by someone, and the one who has
built all things is God.) [5] Now Moses was faithful in all his house
as a servant to testify to the things to be spoken later; [6] but Christ,
on the other hand, [was faithful] over his house as a Son, whose
house we are if we hold fast the confidence and boasting of hope.

Moses failed to lead the people into their rest

[7] Therefore, just as the Holy Spirit says:

> "Today, if you hear his voice, [8] do not harden your hearts as in
> the rebellion, on the day of testing in the wilderness, [9] where
> your fathers tested [me] severely and saw my works [10] forty
> years. Therefore, I became indignant with that generation,
> and I said, 'They always go astray in heart; they have not
> learned my ways.' [11] So I swore in my anger, ['May such and
> such curses come upon me] if they enter into my rest!' "

[12] Be careful, brothers, lest there be in any of you an evil heart
of unbelief [shown] in turning away from the living God; [13] but
exhort one another every day, while it is still called today lest any
of you become hardened by [the] deceitfulness of sin. [14] For we
have become sharers of Christ, if indeed we hold fast the initial
doctrine until the end, [15] while it is said,

> Today, if you hear his voice,
> do not harden your hearts as in the rebellion.

[16] For who [were the ones who], after they had heard, rebelled?
But were they not all those who went out from Egypt through [the

leadership of] Moses? 17 And against whom did he become indignant for forty years? Was it not against those sinners whose limbs
fell in the wilderness? 18 And to whom did he swear that they
would not enter into his rest, except those who disobeyed? 19 And
we see that they were not able to enter because of [their] unbelief.

New opportunity available for rest

4 1 The promise of entering into his rest is left [unfulfilled]. Let
us be afraid, therefore, lest any of you seem to fall behind; 2 for the
gospel has been preached to us as well as to them, but the message
of the report did not help them, since it was not united by faith, in
those who heard. 3 For we who believe enter into the rest, just as
he said,

"As I swore in my anger,
['May such and such curses come upon me]
if they enter into my rest,'"

namely, [from] the works [that] took place from the foundation of
the world.
4 For somewhere he said the following concerning the seventh day:

"And God rested on the seventh day from all his works,"

5 and again in this [passage]:

["May such and such curses come upon me]
if they enter into my rest."

6 Since, then, it is left for some to enter into it, and the earlier ones,
having received the gospel, did not enter because of [their] disobedience, 7 he again appoints a certain day, today, saying through
David, after such a long time [had transpired], as was quoted
before:

Today if you hear his voice,
do not harden your hearts.

8 For if Joshua had given them rest, he would not have spoken of
another day than this. 9 Therefore there remains a sabbath for the
people of God, 10 for whoever enters into his rest also rests from
his work himself, just as God [rested] from his own [works].
11 Then let us strive to enter into that rest so that no one may fall
because of the same sort of disobedience.

12 For the word of God is living and active,
sharper than any two-edged sword,
penetrating until [there is] a division of soul and spirit,

both joints and marrow;
[it is] critical of designs and intentions of the mind;
13 there is nothing created [that passes] unnoticed before him,
but all things are naked and laid bare before his eyes
—regarding which our word [applies].

Jesus the High Priest

14 Since, then, we have a great high priest [who] has gone through
the heavens, Jesus the Son of God, let us hold fast the confession.
15 For we do not have a high priest [who is] unable to sympathize
with our weaknesses, but [one who] has been tested in everything,
in ways similar [to ours, yet he is] without sin. 16 Then let us approach the throne of grace with boldness, so that we might receive
mercy and find grace for timely support.

Comment

Son rather than servant

3:1. "Therefore" (*hothen*), literally, "from which," meaning that the following arguments could be deduced from the conclusions reached above. This is the connective term that relates the preceding arguments to the discussion which follows. "Holy brothers" is an affectionate address to the recipients (see 2:12, 17). The term "holy" originally was used to describe those who had kept themselves levitically undefiled so that they dared to enter areas where the Lord's presence was expected to dwell. These were such people as the priests who ministered at the altar and soldiers who kept themselves undefiled so that the Lord would be present with them in battle and fight for them (I Sam 21:5; 1QM 7). After the temple had been destroyed in 586 B.C., priests no longer had a holy place where the Lord would dwell. Laymen, then, had to take upon themselves the purity rules that were previously observed by the priests. So that the Lord would be with them in Babylon, they tried to establish a "priesthood of all believers." This meant isolating believers from unbelievers, both physically and socially, so that the believers would not become defiled by touching unbelievers who did not observe levitical purity. This led to the formation of isolated groups or sects who had standards of admission, special initiation instruction and practices, and testing procedures for maintaining perfection within the group and its community dwellings. These sects continued even after the temple was rebuilt, partly from habit, and partly because they questioned the purity practices of the priests in the temple. Because some of these groups were celibate, the community itself replaced the family, and the members cared for each other in cases of illness and old age. In this newly adopted religious family, the members were called "brothers," and they were "holy," rigorously observing all purity rules (see COMMENT on 2:12, 17). Not all groups were equally strict, and some who mingled with Gentiles, like Pauline Christians, still referred to members of their group as "brothers," "holy" or "saints." In addition to being members of the same sect as the author, the members were sons of Abraham, as were also the author and Jesus (2:16–17). Stuart was correct in noting that "when the ancient prophets called the whole Jewish nation *qᵉdōšîm* (*hagioi*), or *'am qādōš* (*laos hagios*), they did not mean to assert that every individual among them was *spiritually* sanctified."[1] The name was sometimes used quite generally, simply to mean fellow convenanters, strict or not, but the author of Hebrews used terms usually associated with narrow, sectarian members in relationship to the recipients to raise the question about the rigidity of the membership. In rigorous sects, brothers were expected to be holy, but the author did not take that for granted. The fact that he used the adjective "holy" may have been intended to be descriptive of their nature.

"Sharers in [the] heavenly calling" were members of the group. This is another way of saying "brothers." "The heavenly calling" (*klēseōs epouraniou*) was the same as the "calling from God" (*klēsis tou theou*) (Rom 11:29).[2] A person who was called to segregate himself from the Gentiles and become a covenanter, a member of God's holy people, joined the community. This means that one who had been called was one who had been initiated into the sect and had become a brother and holy. Therefore Paul could say, "Those whom he has previously set apart, these also he called, and those whom he called, these also he justified, and those whom he justified, these also he glorified" (Rom 8:30). The calling of God, or the "heavenly calling," was a distinguishing event which involved membership responsibilities. So members were urged to walk worthily of their calling (Eph 4:1), to be worthy of their calling (II Thess 1:11), to consider their calling (I Cor 1:26), or to confirm their calling (II Peter 1:10). Recipients of this document were reminded of their calling when they were urged to "direct" their "attention to Jesus."

The meaning of the term "apostle" was considered in relationship to 1:2–3. An apostle was an agent or an ambassador, who, within the limits of his assignment, had the same authority as the one who sent him. He was legally identical to his master. He had the power of attorney. Many of the New Testament documents describe the office Jesus held and his relationship to God in terms of apostolic Christology, but this is the only place in the New Testament where he was directly called an apostle. It is also consistent with the other descriptions given about Jesus in Hebrews (see 1:2–3; 2:9, 17).

Further on in the document the author defended his basis for calling Jesus a "high priest," but here, as in 2:17, the label was given only as a

[1] Stuart, p. 87.

[2] *Contra* Montefiore, p. 71, who said this was "not primarily in the sense that God calls from heaven, but inasmuch as Christians are called to heaven."

preparatory statement, intended to condition the reader for the more elaborate attention that would follow. The "confession" was the doctrinal beliefs or creed to which the members subscribed. The author of Hebrews was much concerned that the readers hold fast to an orthodox theology. This theology involved a belief that Jesus was the Son, first-born, Son of man, Messiah, high priest, and apostle of God, but it did not claim that he was "very God of very God."

2. "Faithful" (*pistos*) is a quotation from Num 12:7 (Hebrew *ne'emān*). This is also the word that described Samuel, whom the Lord promised to raise up as a "faithful priest" (I Sam 2:35).[3] The Hebrew *ne'emān* means "trusted," "trustworthy," "worthy," or "faithful." In later Judaism it was rendered by the Greek *axios* (worthy or trustworthy) or *pistos* and used as a technical term to describe those who could be trusted to keep the rules and practices necessary for membership in the sect. The Essene who was qualified for membership was considered "worthy" (*axios*). In rabbinic literature the person who was *ne'emān* (trustworthy) was distinguished from the person less careful about Pentateuchal rules (*'am hā'āreṣ*) because he could be trusted to fulfill all the dietary, purity, tithing, and heave-offering regulations that his order demanded. According to Matthew, Jesus sent the twelve out without gold, silver, or copper in their belts, no bags, no sandals, and with only one tunic each. They were told: "And whatever town or village you enter, find out one who is worthy (*axios*) in it, and stay with him until you depart. As you enter the house, salute it. And if the house is 'worthy' (*axia*), let your peace come upon it; but if it is not 'worthy' let your peace return to you" (Matt 10:11–13). These were rules similar to those observed by the full members of the Essene sect in order to be sure that no member might mistakenly eat improper food or defile himself in some other way in a house that was not holy, worthy, or trustworthy.[4] Pseudo-Clement described a proselyte of the Jews as "an altogether worthy person" (*Hom.* XIII.vii). The traveling Christians who were sent out worthily (*axiōs*) of God, took no food from the Gentiles (III John 6–7). The author, who has shown other signs of interest in careful law observance, may have understood this kind of faithfulness or trustworthiness in relationship to Moses, and all the more so to Jesus.

"The one who made him" means God who made Jesus. The question is whether this refers to God's creation of Jesus or to his making him "the apostle and high priest." The latter seems more likely. It is consistent with 1:2 and has the support of the RSV, which rendered *poiēsanti* in 3:2 "appointed,"[5] the same word it used in 1:2 for *ethēken*.

Moses was traditionally praised in superlatives in Judaism. Although Philo said that only God was faithful (*pistos*) (*LA* III.lxxii), he acknowledged that Moses was faithful in the sense that he trusted God (*LA*

[3] H. P. Smith, *A Critical and Exegetical Commentary on the Books of Samuel* (New York, 1909), p. 23.
[4] CC, pp. 248–49, 274.
[5] Following Westcott, p. 75, and Moffatt, p. 42.

III.lxxxi). His laws were so excellent that they omitted nothing needful. Through all the years of plenty and famine, not even the smallest part of Moses' laws had changed, and they would continue as long as the heaven and the universe existed, according to Philo (*Mos.* II.iii [12–16]). Samaritans called Moses the great prophet (Memar Marqah 2 §10), the good apostle (Memar Marqah 2 §12), the servant of the Lord, deliverer, savior, chosen one, man of God, and righteous one (Memar Marqah 5 §§3–4). According to Pseudo-Clement, Peter refused to believe anything derogatory about Moses. He insisted that Moses was not a murderer and that he did not learn from an idolatrous priest. Since he had been called a faithful steward, these other allegations are false (*Hom.* II.lii).

The text on which the author commented (Num 12:7) in both Hebrew and Greek is, "in all my house he is faithful." The author changed the pronoun from "my" to "his" to suit his context and probably omitted "all." The best texts (P[13]B Ambr; W) omitted it, but several later texts, probably influenced by the Old Testament, included it. When Miriam and Aaron criticized Moses because he had married a Cushite woman, the Lord defended Moses by contrasting him to other prophets. To other prophets, the Lord spoke in dreams and visions, but to his servant, Moses, the Lord spoke "mouth to mouth" (Num 12:1–8). The author quoted the scripture to show that Moses was "trustworthy" or faithful in the Lord's house and also to affirm that Jesus was also "faithful to the one who made him." Moses was introduced to be compared to Jesus, not to be equated with him. Just as he had earlier argued that Jesus was superior to the angels, the author next set out to show that he was superior to Moses.

3. It became evident in vs. 2 that the Hebrew word *ne'ᵉmān* carried both the meanings "worthy" (*axios*) and "faithful" (*pistos*). Jesus was held to be "faithful" in vs. 2; in vs. 3 he was also called "worthy" (*ēxiōtai*). Not only was Jesus worthy in the sense that Moses was, he was worthy of still "more glory than Moses." The word "house" in the Old Testament sometimes referred to the temple, sometimes to a family or dynasty, sometimes to all Israel. Zadok was called a "faithful priest" (*kōhēn ne'ᵉmān*) for whom the Lord would build a "faithful house" (*bāyit ne'ᵉmān*) (I Sam 2:35). Later sectarians interpreted "faithful house" to mean "The priests, the Levites, and the sons of Zadok" (CDC 3:21–4:1). The house to which Moses was related was probably the house of Israel. Moses was part of that house whereas Jesus was identified with its builder. This does not mean that Jesus was God, but that he was God's apostle, and since from the legal standpoint a man's apostle is like the man himself, Jesus should be related to the builder rather than to the house. As the apostle of the builder, of course, he had "more glory than Moses," who belonged to the house. This was not a completely fair contrast, because Moses was also considered an apostle.

4. Verse 4 is a parenthetical statement to clarify vs. 3. Hanson thinks vs. 4 is an inauthentic and incorrect parenthetical addition. By deleting it, he holds that "the one who built the house" was the pre-incarnate

Jesus.[6] It certainly is parenthetical in nature, but not necessarily inauthentic or incorrect. It is consistent with the rest of Hebrews which acknowledges that "the one who has built all things is God." This was done, however, through Jesus, whom God "established heir of all, through whom he also made the ages" (1:2). Jesus was not God, the Creator, but he was the apostle of the Creator. Paul also insisted that God was the source of everything: "I planted, Apollo watered, but God gave the growth" (I Cor 3:6). Hanson confused *legal* identity with *physical* identity and deleted vs. 4 to reach his conclusion.

5. The "house" in which "Moses was faithful" was probably the house of Israel. Targ. Num 12:17 has *'amī* ("my people") for "my house." Since Jesus was high priest, however, and since there are other indications of sectarian interpretations in Hebrews, the author seems also to have intended "house" to mean "temple." Some sectarians, such as those governed by the Rule of the Community, considered themselves more than just a group of Israelites. They comprised a "temple in Aaron" (*qōdeš b*^{e}*āh*^{a}*rōn*) and "a house of truth in Israel" (*bēt hā'*^{e}*met b*^{e}*yiśrā'ēl*) (1QS 5:6), or a "holy house for Israel and a foundation of a holy of holies for Aaron" (1QS 8:5–6; see also 9:6). Those who belong to this community are "holy men who walk in perfection" (1QS 9:8). The author of 1QpHab 12:3–4 interpreted "Lebanon" (Hab 2:17) to mean "the council of the community" (*'*^{a}*ṣat hayyāḥad*). Rabbis identified Lebanon with the temple in Jerusalem (see Mekilta *Amalek* 2:3–4; Sifré Deut 1:7, 66b; Lam R. 1:5 §31, 14d).[7] This means that the author of that document considered the council of the community to be a pure or "trustworthy" house, a temple. Paul reminded Christians at Corinth that they constituted a temple of God and that God's Spirit dwelt in their midst, just as the Lord dwelt in the midst of his people in the tent of meeting in the wilderness or in the temple at Jerusalem (I Cor 3:16–17; II Cor 6:16; see also Eph 2:18–22). I Tim 3:15 defined the "house of God" as the "church of the living God." I Peter 2:5 described a "spiritual house" in a context of priests, sacrifices, and a cornerstone—all of which seems to be the imagery of a temple.[8] The author of Hebrews evidently intended some such meaning by his use of "house," because he later (vs. 6) identified the house with himself and the recipients of the document. This implies that he belonged to a group that tried to keep its entire membership free from any type of defilement. *A priori* that group might have been as liberal as the Corinthians and still have called itself a temple. The author of Hebrews, however, employed many terms that in sectarian contexts had technical meanings, and he was very much concerned for strict law observance. These characteristics suggest that he belonged to a rigorous

[6] Hanson, pp. 394–98.

[7] See further G. Vermès, *Scripture and Tradition in Judaism* (Leiden, 1961), pp. 28–39.

[8] See further on this whole subject B. Gärtner, *The Temple and the Community in Qumran and the New Testament*, Cambridge, 1965.

law-abiding order of Christianity. This will become more evident as the document is examined further.

The Greek word for "servant" is *therapōn,* which "according to general usage differs from *doulos* and *oiketēs,* being a more honorable appellation; e.g., the correlate of *doulos* and *oiketēs* is *despotēs;* but *therapōn* is related to *patēr, kyrios,* or *basileus.*"[9] Although subservient to a better and more respectable master, a *therapōn* was a "servant," nonetheless, and this was precisely the point the author of Hebrews could use to disparage Moses and exalt Jesus. According to John 8:33–35, even sons of Abraham who have sinned are slaves of sin and as slaves would not remain in the house forever, but the Son would continue forever. Paul also contrasted the slaves of the elemental spirits of the universe to the sons who could call God, "Abba! Father," and be heirs of the whole estate (Gal 4:1–7). To follow this analogy, Moses, as a servant, could never be heir of the house, but Jesus had been established heir over everything (1:2). Moses, as a servant, could be sold whenever his Master chose, but Jesus, as a Son and heir, was in a controlling, administrative position. Moses, as a servant, filled a very utilitarian role. He prepared the law which attested "to the things" that would be "spoken later." These things were not intended to be spoken during Moses' time but during the ministry of Christ.

Not all covenanters would have concurred with the author's depreciative appraisal of Moses in comparison to Jesus. Samaritans claimed that no prophet had arisen or would arise who could compare with the prophet Moses (Memar Marqah 4 §1). It was Moses whom the Lord set over all his possession (Memar Marqah 4 §1). Moses was both the servant of God and the son of the house of God (Memar Marqah 4 §1). Moses was the great prophet whom the Lord chose for his apostleship (Memar Marqah 6 §7); he was the apostle of the True One, the faithful one of God's house (Memar Marqah 6 §3).

In his efforts to exalt the Son, the author of Hebrews selected Moses and the angels, all of whom had been highly exalted in Samaritan and Jewish circles, and argued that they were inferior in comparison with Jesus.

6. By New Testament times, many years of life in the diaspora had taught Jews to get along without the temple. At some point in their tradition, it became the accepted view that ten adult males constituted a quorum or *minyan.* The earliest hint of such a belief is recorded in the story of Abraham's intercession for Lot. Abraham asked if the Lord would save the city for fifty just men. The Lord agreed to the terms. In case fifty could not be found, Abraham reduced the number by fives and tens until he reached the number ten. After that, he stopped trying to find a group that would qualify (Gen 18:23–33). He seemed to know that five were not enough for a congregation. This interpretation of the story, relating it to communal prayer, may have arisen in Babylon

[9] Stuart, p. 95.

after the fall of the temple in 586 B.C. Ordinarily the temple was considered the house of God, the place where he made his name dwell (I Kings 8:29). After the temple was destroyed, however, other adjustments had to be made. Prophets assured the Jews that the Lord would be present with them in Babylon without the temple. In trying to create an alternative to the temple, prayers were made in groups. Later, at least, ten or more adult males were necessary to form such a group, and the area as well as the individuals was required to be levitically undefiled. If these conditions were met, Jews believed that the Lord would be present. Since the Lord's presence was there, the community itself was treated like a temple. It was with such an understanding as this that the author of Hebrews, when speaking of the house of God over which Jesus was the Son and heir, said "whose house we are," but this was not unconditionally so. Jesus was the apostle and high priest (3:1) and the members comprised the temple or "house" in which he officiated. But the recipients would be God's "house" only if they held "fast the confidence and boasting of hope." This was an exhortation which the author echoed again and again. He was concerned about the confession which the believers accepted as doctrine. He was afraid that they might waver from its teaching or become discouraged and lose hope in the promises it contained.

Summary.—Heb 3:1–6 is the opening section of a larger unit, 3:1–4:16. At the beginning of the inclusion, "heavenly," "high priest," and "confession" occurs in the first verse. In 4:14, the words "high priest," "heaven," and "confession" occur again, framing the section in between. 4:15–16 extend beyond the final part of the inclusion, completing the sense of the unit. This is customary for the author's use of inclusions. Chapter 3, like ch. 2, begins with an exhortation, but both are also similar in shifting quickly from exhortation to introduction of more doctrinal subjects. The first two chapters concentrated on the angels in comparison with the Son. These next two chapters contain an equally well-reasoned comparison of the office and work of Moses to the office and work of Christ. They also deal more with the wilderness experience and the children of Israel in comparison with the opportunities available for the followers of Jesus than was evident in the comparison of the two groups in the first two chapters. 3:1–6 shows still further evidence of the author's rigorous concern for the observance of the law and his understanding of the believers as a holy, ritually pure group that should be kept as free from defilement as the priests should keep the temple, or God's house. Just as the community itself was considered to be a temple, so Jesus must be understood as the apostle and high priest in charge of this temple. His relationship to God is that of an agent or ambassador to communicate and mediate between God and the believers. Believers should be confident of this and not give up hope in God's fulfillment of his promises.

Moses failed to lead the people into their rest

7. "Therefore" (*dio*) seems to be the beginning of the sentence "do not harden your hearts" (3:8) rather than "Be careful, brothers, . . ." (3:12), which seems to be its own introduction to the commentary that follows the Old Testament quotation. Vaughan objects to both possibilities and concludes that "therefore" begins "*a suppressed* imperative to be supplied mentally from the general sense of the quotation."[10] Vaughan's objection is that the speaker in 9–11 is in the first person and is God. But this really creates no problem. Ancient exegetes frequently changed subject and applied a quotation to someone other than that originally intended, and furthermore the "just as" indicates that the author was speaking to his generation in the same way and in the same words as the Holy Spirit. Since both the Holy Spirit and God were thought to be the source of all scripture, there is no difficulty in shifting subjects from the Holy Spirit to God and vice versa when discussing scripture. (See 9:8; 10:15; also Acts 28:25; I Clem 13:1; 16:2.)

To "hear" in Hebraic thought often implied obedience. When Moses read the book of the covenant to the people, the Israelites responded, "That which the Lord has spoken, we will do and we will obey (*na'ᵃśeh wᵉnišmā'*)"—literally, "we will do and we will hear" (Exod 24:7). Those who really heard were those who paid attention carefully and accepted that which they had heard. That much force, however, is not intended here. If the people obeyed, of course they would not harden their hearts, so the meaning is "hear."

8. If they did not obey, they would "harden" their "hearts." In Hebrew thought, the heart was the source of thinking, willing, and deciding. A frequently occurring expression, "hardening hearts" (Exod 4:21; 7:3; 9:12; 10:1, 20, 27; 11:10; 14:4, 8; Deut 2:30; 10:16; II Kings 17:14; II Chron 30:8; Isa 63:17), meant "becoming stubborn," "refusing to listen," "paying no attention." The words rendered "the rebellion" (*tǭ parapikrasmǭ*) and "of testing" (*tou peirasmou*) were both proper names, Meribah and Massah, in Hebrew. There was an important play on words in Hebrew, however, because Meribah (*mᵉrībāh*) means "conflict" or "rebellion," and Massah (*massāh*) means "tempting" or "testing." The LXX translator chose to interpret these words rather than transliterate them, and the author of Hebrews simply quoted the LXX.

"Me" does not occur in the best texts and was added to concur with one text of the LXX and because the sense requires it. The LXX Ps 94:9 (MT and English 95:9) reads

"Where your fathers tested [me]
they put [me] to the test and saw my works."

[10] Vaughan, p. 63.

Some Latin and Syriac texts of Heb 3:9 read the same as the LXX; other Syriac as well as the mass of later Greek manuscripts add to this the word "me." "Severely" is the translation given for *en dokimasia,* literally "in a testing," on the assumption that this reflects an original infinitive absolute in a Hebrew text. Instead of "in a testing" (severely), some later texts have "they tested" or "they tested me" in agreement with the LXX. It seems likely that the author of Hebrews used a LXX text no longer extant that omitted the "me" but rendered quite literally a Hebrew text with a stronger force than the MT.

10. The LXX and the MT both relate the clause "and [they] saw my works" with the fathers' testing in the previous line. This meant that the fathers tested, even though they saw the works. Then the Psalm reads "I was indignant with that generation for forty years." The author of Hebrews changed the sense when he gave forty years as the length of time that they saw his works. The Hebrew word *'āqōṭ* (with a waw consecutive borrowed from the preceding verb) means "I loathed." The Greek word *prosōchthisa* is a little softer. It means, "I was burdened," "laden with grief," "weighed down," "exhausted," or "indignant." R. Eliezer took the verb from the root *nqṭ* (to contract or hold) rather than from *qwṭ* (to loathe) and so he said, "The days of the Messiah will last forty years, as it is said, 'For forty years I will contract with that generation' " (San. 99a). The best texts read "this" (*tautē*) for "that" (*ekeinē*) generation, which is probably the correct reading. Some later scribes probably changed it to conform to the LXX. It has been changed in this English translation for the sake of clarity.

The word rendered "go astray" means to slide off an inclined plane. The picture is that of a raised road or highway in which one might get off the road and slide into a ditch. Those who had "learned" the Lord's "ways" should, of course, stay on them and not wander off the track into unmapped areas. The Lord's patience was exhausted with the wilderness generation because they were always going "astray in heart." That was to distinguish between their wilderness wanderings and their character wanderings. The wandering that went with aimless nomadic life was used here in a metaphorical sense to describe those who did not follow the Lord's directions or commandments.

11. Oaths, vows, curses, and blessings were all very serious expressions in Hebrew thought. Ancient Israelites, as well as Jews and Christians of New Testament times, believed that the Lord would fulfill all blessings and curses that had been uttered, if the conditions associated with them took place. Thus, when Isaac blessed Jacob by mistake, he could not take back his blessing and give it instead to Esau (Gen 27:1–37), nor could Balak change the destiny of Israel once Balaam had pronounced a blessing on that nation (Num 23). If an oath was administered by someone else, the person administering the oath listed the curses and the conditions under which they would be received. For example, the woman suspected of adultery was brought before the priest, who made

her drink the water of bitterness, and as he administered the oath he warned her that if she had been unfaithful to her husband she would suffer a miscarriage, but if she had been faithful her pregnancy would be undisturbed. The woman answered, "Amen, amen," meaning that she accepted the conditions under which the curses would apply (Num 5:16–28). If she received the curses that had been pronounced, it was believed that she had been unfaithful. A self-administered oath was one that Ruth took, speaking to Naomi: "Thus may the Lord do and thus may he add, if [even] death separates me from you" (Ruth 1:17; see also I Sam 3:17; II Sam 3:35; II Kings 6:31). The curses here were only summarized rather than specified. Self-administered oaths usually were understood to have the following parts: (1) the holy being or object by whom the oath was invoked; (2) the curses to be received if the following conditions were not fulfilled; and (3) the conditions under which the curses would be effective. Sometimes oath-takers intentionally omitted a negative or mispronounced the sacred object involved, so fearful were they of the destructive effects of oaths. For example:

(1) *"Qonam!* (i.e., Qorban, the gift for the altar)
(2) may my wife [never] be useful to me,
(3) if I have eaten today" (Sheb. 3:4; see also Ned. 3:2–5).

No. 1 indicates the sacred object by which the oath was taken; no. 2 is the adverse situation that will occur to the oath-taker if no. 3 is not the case. The oath-taker wanted to affirm very strongly that he had not eaten that day. If he had eaten he would be willing to be deprived of satisfaction received from his wife. Although he was sure he had not eaten, he protected himself by mispronouncing the name of the sacred object by which the oath was taken and omitted the negative, without which the conditions of the oath make no sense. Frequently oath-takers omitted the entire list of curses and/or the sacred object by which the oath was taken. They said only, ". . . if I do such and such," and the divine name or sacred object, followed by a list of curses, was understood. Matt 15:5 quotes Jesus scolding the Pharisees: "But you say, 'Whoever says to his father or mother, "Gift! (i.e., Qorban!) [unmentioned curses understood], if from me you receive benefit," he will not honor his father or his mother.'" The Pharisees were so fearful that Israel might receive the curses understood that they permitted the oath-taker to break the commandment rather than to allow the oath to be broken and the curses received.[11] In this case the oath was that the oath-taker would neglect his parents in their old age. Under such a fearful concept of oath-taking as this, the abbreviated oath in Ps 95 was composed.

Ps 95:11 said only, "As I swore in my anger, 'if they enter into my rest.'" RSV rendered Ps 95:11 thus: "Therefore I swore in my anger that they should not enter my rest." This communicates the basic message

[11] "Some Vow and Oath Formulas in the New Testament," HTR 58 (1965), 319–26.

involved by replacing the oath formula with an indirect quotation. The initial understanding was that the Lord took an oath by listing some unmentioned curses that he volunteered to accept if the oath was broken.

In Num 14:23, 29–30, the Lord swore that those who rebelled would not enter into the land, meaning the inheritance, the promised land. According to Ps 95:11, the Lord took an oath that they would not enter into his "rest," which meant exactly the same. In Deut 29:9, the Israelites were reminded that they had not yet come to the "rest and inheritance" which the Lord would give them, but after they crossed the Jordan and entered the land and the Lord had given them rest from their enemies, then they should offer sacrifice to the Lord (Deut 12:10–11; see also Deut 3:20; 25:19; Josh 1:15; 22:4). Later the Lord "gave to Israel all the land which he swore to give to their fathers" (Josh 21:43), "and the Lord gave them rest on every side . . . not one of all their enemies had withstood them" (Josh 21:44). This meant that "not one of all the good promises which the Lord made to the house of Israel had failed" (Josh 21:45). It was possible to live on the land without rest from the enemies, but it was not possible to have rest without the acquisition of the land of Canaan. The rabbis understood that this was the case. "R. Judah says 'If Israel had been virtuous, in three days they would have entered the land, as it is said, "And the ark of the covenant of the Lord goes before them, a journey of three days, to spy out for them a rest" (Num 10:33)—and there is no rest but the land of Israel, as it is said, "For you have not entered into rest until now, into the inheritance which the Lord your God gives you" (Deut 12:9)'" (Sifré Deut 1:2, 65b, §2).

The word "rest" belonged to the terminology associated with sabbath rest. Just as there was one day of rest in every seven, so there was also one year of rest in every seven. In the seventh year, Israelites who had allowed themselves to be enslaved by their Israelite brothers to pay back the money they had borrowed were released to "return home," and on jubilee years, those who had sold their property because of indebtedness had their property returned to them or to their posterity. In this same thought form, the Lord announced that the Hebrews could return to Palestine. Their period of "servitude" was over; they were allowed to return "home"; and their land was to be restored. This was their jubilee, but when they tested the Lord in the wilderness, he withheld the fulfillment of his promise. He swore that he would not let them enter the promised land while that generation was alive; they would not enter into his rest. In another context, the Lord promised Moses that his "presence" would go before them and give the people "rest" (Exod 33:7–14). When David had conquered the promised land, the Lord gave him "rest" from all his enemies (II Sam 7:1).

Scholars have admitted that the rest mentioned in the Old Testament involved possession and settlement in the land of Canaan and that the author of Hebrews used the very same terminology, but they have not been willing to acknowledge that he belonged to the same religious environment in which these terms were used with their Old Testament meanings and that he therefore meant the same by them as Jewish writers of the time meant. Turner, for instance, on the one hand, insisted that the word "rest" in Ps 95 does not speak "exclusively of future rest in heaven. . . . But the texts cited above clearly prove that the settlement in the land of the promised inheritance is itself the rest spoken of."[12] But on the other hand, when it came to Hebrews, for no internal reason, Turner suggested that we "consider the land of Canaan is a *type* [italics mine] of heaven . . ."[13] In his judgment, "His rest, that is God's rest in heaven of which that in the promised land was a *type* [italics mine] . . ."[14] and "The author certainly employs the word *rest* here to denote the heavenly inheritance."[15] Westcott similarly said, "The rest was primarily Canaan (Deut 12:9–10), and then that divine kingdom and order of which the earthly Canaan was an imperfect type."[16]

Although Moffatt interpreted the aspirations of Hebrews as being heavenly in other contexts, he made no effort to venture an interpretation different from those of the rabbis he quoted.[17] Michel quoted Käsemann's view that the rest of God, according to Hebrews, was nothing other than the heavenly *kosmos* itself. Michel, himself, identified it correctly with the *oikoumenē* and *polis mellousa* which he mistakenly understood as the *jenseitigen Ruhe Gottes* (otherworldly rest of God). He offered an existential hope, however, by suggesting that we might begin here and now to participate in a share of the promised rest.[18] The Old Testament and rabbinical references with which these scholars were familiar made it difficult, even arbitrary, to suggest that the author of Hebrews had a different meaning in mind when he used the same terms as the others. The text here is consistent with other affirmations made in Hebrews in showing that the author expected the promised heritage of the land of Canaan under the rule of the Messiah to be fulfilled for Jesus and his followers.

12. Like the author of the legalistic sections in Matthew, Hebrews demands perfection in character of *all* members of the community. The exclusive terms like "holy brothers" (3:1), which might have been used rather generally and loosely but might also have been intended definitively, are here clearly understood as the latter. References to the brothers in sacred, undefiled terms, comparing them to a temple, were not intended to be broad generalizations. There must not be "an evil heart of unbelief" in any one of the brothers. The author required even more rigorous law observance than Matthew (Matt 5:17–48; 7:13–14). Matthew at least allowed opportunity for repentance before the member was excommunicated (18:15–17). This was not the case in Hebrews (6:4–6; 12:16–17) and the work of others of the same conviction (*Vis.* II 2:4–8; *Mand.* IV 3:1–3,

[12] Turner, p. 56. [13] Ibid., p. 57. [14] Ibid., p. 60. [15] Ibid., p. 61.
[16] Westcott, p. 82.
[17] Moffatt, pp. 45–56.
[18] Michel, pp. 1–2, 104.

7; *Dial.* 44:4; *Strom.* III.62:2; Irenaeus *Heresies* IV.42:4), who allowed no repentance.

The psalmist warned his readers not to let their hearts become hardened as in the rebellion (Ps 95:8; Num 14:22–23). Using the same words, the author of Hebrews warned his audience in relationship to their hearts. They should watch that no single one of them had "an evil heart of unbelief," which would be exhibited by "turning away from the living God." While commenting on the word "hearts" from Ps 95, the author of Hebrews supplemented the text with references from Numbers, reminding the readers of those who turned back from following the Lord (Num 14:43). He also alluded to an "evil" congregation (Num 14:27) and the Lord's oath, "As I 'live'" (Num 14:21, 28).

13. The word translated "one another" is *heautous,* literally, "yourselves," but in context this means that they should encourage or "exhort" one another. The rigorousness of the author is again evident. They should exhort "every day" to be sure that there was *no* sin among *any* of the brothers. This was the same kind of advice offered by Matt 18:15–17. The urgency of the situation was emphasized on the basis of the word "today" quoted from the Psalm. The time was short. They were obliged to act properly while they still had the chance not utilized by their fathers. The words "become hardened," also from the Psalm, were used by the author of Hebrews to warn the readers against the repetition of the sin of their fathers in the wilderness. If they should "become hardened by the deceitfulness of sin," that would be the same as having "an evil heart of unbelief" and "turning away from the living God." If that happened, they could expect the same fate as the exodus generation.

14. Verse 14 is a summarizing sentence that refers the reader to the beginning of the chapter and picks up words from there on. Those who had become "sharers of Christ" were the same "holy brothers" who were "sharers of [the] heavenly calling" (3:1); those encouraged to "hold fast the initial doctrine until the end" were the same ones who would belong to God's "house," if they would "hold fast the confidence and boasting of hope" (3:6). They were also the ones warned to "be careful" (3:12).

The word rendered "doctrine" (*hypostasis*) is translated "confidence" by the RSV, which also translated a quite different Greek word (*parrēsia*) by the same English word. The RSV probably identified the two meanings because of their proximity in use in 3:6 and 3:14, but the author used different terms. Whereas *parrēsia* refers to the boldness which characterizes one who is sure of himself in a situation which would usually make one tremble, *hypostasis* refers to the reality, essence, or nature of something, or the groundwork or basis of hope. Those who held "fast the initial doctrine" were those who did not give up the creed or confession which they were taught at the beginning of their catechism.

15. "While it is said" refers to scripture. The quotation given is a repetition of Ps 95:8, quoted before in vss. 7 and 8. It was repeated here because the author intended to comment on it directly.

16. Vaughan has offered an attractive translation that is different from the one given here.[19] By only omitting the accent on *tines,* which would then mean "some" rather than "who?", this verse would read, "For some, after they had heard, rebelled; but not all those who went out from Egypt [did so]." This would take into account Joshua and Caleb who did not rebel. In further support of this translation is the strong word used for "but" (*all'*). When interpreted as a question, this "but" is almost unnecessary. The only problem with this translation is that it does not cohere well with the required translation of the next two verses. Each verse contains *tisi,* the dative of the same pronoun. It does not seem likely that the author would have used the same ambiguous pronoun in one case indefinitely and in the other interrogatively, but maybe he did.

If *tines* is to be understood interrogatively, then the *all'* was used hyperbolically, as in Matt 3:5, 6 and John 3:26. The author correctly identifies the word "rebellion" of Ps 95 with the activity of the Israelites described in Deut 1 and Num 14. Instead of entering the promised land as the Lord had directed, "those who went out from Egypt" first sent spies to search out the land to see whether or not it was likely that the Lord could fulfill his promise. This was the testing (Heb 3:9) that they did against the Lord, and "after they had heard" the evil report of the spies, they "rebelled" (Num 14:9) and made plans to go back to Egypt (Num 14:4).

17. Again the author correctly identified the ones involved in the exodus from Egypt as those who had made the Lord indignant (mentioned in Ps 95). After they had rebelled and complained against the Lord and against Moses, the spies who brought back the evil report died from a plague (Num 14:37), and the Lord threatened to destroy all those who came out from Egypt and to disinherit them altogether (Num 14:11–12), but after Moses' intercession, he modified his threat by exempting the children and teen-agers, under the age of twenty years. The author of Hebrews wove words and phrases from the Numbers passage into his interpretation of Ps 95. Moses asked the Lord to forgive the sin of the people (Num 14:19; see also 14:40–41), so the author called the people "those sinners." The Lord promised: "Your limbs will fall in this wilderness" (Num 14:29), so the author referred to the exodus generation as those "whose limbs fell in the wilderness."

18. The oath mentioned in Ps 95 that God would not let these people enter into his rest refers to Num 14:30: ["May these unmentioned curses come upon me] if you enter the land upon which I raised my hand [in oath] that you would dwell in it." That was the oath the Lord took against the exodus generation which the psalmist interpreted as meaning "they would not enter into his rest." This clearly refers to life in the promised land, but Stuart said, "But what was the *rest* in question? Is it quiet possession of the Land of Canaan? No, says the apostle. Believers *now* enter the rest (vs. 3), i.e. the same kind of rest as was anciently proffered.

[19] Vaughan, p. 71.

Moreover, God calls it *katapausin mou,* MY *rest,* i.e. (adds he) such rest as God enjoyed, after he had completed the creation of the world; consequently spiritual, heavenly rest."[20] The text does not justify such interpretations as this.

The disobedience about which the author spoke came after the Lord had sworn that they would not enter the land. They then confessed their sin and said they would repent and enter the land. Moses told them not to, because the Lord would not be with them, but they "disobeyed" and tried to take the hill country, so the Canaanites and Amalekites defeated them (Num 14:39–45).

19. After the spies brought back the evil report and the people complained and made plans to go back to Egypt, the Lord, in his anger, asked Moses, "How long will they not believe in me?" (Num 14:11), and he threatened to destroy them. It was on this basis that the author of Hebrews concluded that the exodus generation was "not able to enter because of [their] unbelief."

Summary.—Following the comparison of Jesus as apostle and high priest with Moses (3:1–6), the rest of chapter three (7–19) deals with the negative half of a comparison of the punishment inflicted upon the exodus generation with the opportunities still available to the believers of the author's time. It was primarily based on Ps 95, which the author first quoted at length, then interpreted on the basis of the account of the rebellion of the exodus generation reported in Deut 1 and Num 14. Verse 14 was a summarizing sentence that tied together all that had been said in chapter three up to that point, but it did not mark the end of the section, 3:15–19 being a further development of the same subject, using the same text. Because the topic was discussed at length, the author summarized briefly at 3:14 and reintroduced his text at 3:15 so that the reader could keep the author's main point in mind. This is typical of the excellent style of the author.

New opportunity available for rest

4:1. The reason why the "promise" was "left unfulfilled" was explained in chapter three. The exodus generation was disobedient, sinful, rebellious, and lacking in faith. Now for the first time the contemporary believers are brought into the picture. Since it was not fulfilled for the exodus generation, it "is left unfulfilled." Therefore, the Christians for whom the author was writing were strongly urged to be careful, even fearful, lest any single one of them should fall behind. The verb "to fall behind" (*hysterēkenai*) pictures someone in a company marching together with others who march faster than he can. He cannot keep up, so he falls behind. That means he will not reach his destination at the same time the others do. He will fail in his mission. Metaphorically speaking, falling behind in religious matters

[20] Stuart, p. 104.

means not being able to fulfill all of the demands or commandments, being negligent, failing to qualify or measure up. Anyone who had an evil heart of unbelief (3:12) would *fall behind,* which means the same as turning away from the living God (3:12). Hence the warning "be careful" (3:12), "be afraid."

2. The "gospel" was related to the sabbath and jubilee releases. For the Israelite who had not been able to repay his fellow Israelite the money he had borrowed, there were only two options: (a) If it was a reasonably small loan, he might work it off at half wages. (b) If it was a sizable loan, he might have to turn over his estate to the creditor. In either case, he was considered a captive or a slave to his brother, but not forever. Whenever the sabbath year came around all the Jews or Israelites were set free from their obligations to their brothers who were their creditors, and whenever the jubilee year occurred all land that had been surrendered for indebtedness was restored to the family to which it had originally belonged.

Israel's theological concepts, vocabulary, and logic were generally transferred from ordinary customs and practices in business, law courts, and society. So the concepts related to sabbath and jubilee releases were applied to national eschatological hopes. The Jews who were removed from Canaan, their inheritance, into Babylon were called captives (*šᵉbūyīm*) (Isa 52:2; 61:1; 11Q Melchizedek 4), because they were taken away from their land; but they were not all slaves, in the usual sense, because when the opportunity came for them to return, many preferred Babylon. Within a hundred and fifty years Jews like Nehemiah had worked themselves into top positions in the government, and the Jewish community in Babylon continued to be a very strong and effective branch of Judaism. So long as they were not permitted to return to a free country under the rule of a Davidic king, however, Babylonian Jews called themselves "captives," who were paying double for all their sins (Isa 40:1; Jer 16:18; cf. Deut 15:18), working off their debt of sin in half wages.

Hebrews frequently used words like "captives" metaphorically. For instance, after Rehoboam succeeded Solomon, he went to Shechem to be made king and to introduce himself to the northern community. When asked to reduce the "yoke" that had been placed upon them by Solomon, Rehoboam replied, "My father chastened you with whips, but I will chasten you with scorpions" (I Kings 12:11). The "yoke" consisted of heavy taxation and demands for labor and military service. The chastening would involve still more oppressive treatment, but probably not with whips or scorpions, literally. Likewise the "slaves" in Egypt may not all have made bricks with their own hands (Exod 1:8–14). They had enough respect and credit to borrow silver and gold from their neighboring Egyptians (Exod 11:2; 12:35–36) and they left with cattle, flocks, and herds (Exod 12:38). Moses was an Israelite who had held an influential position with Pharaoh (Exod 11:3). That may have been a distinct exception, but if it had been, it seems strange that uneducated and uncultured slaves would have had the audacity to challenge his authority (Num 12:1–8;

16:1–30), or that seventy of them could qualify to assist him in his administration (Num 11:16–17). Israelites who were called slaves and captives in these situations were certainly not slaves like the Negroes were in the United States or like prisoners of war in concentration camps. However the oppression was expressed to them, the main point seemed to be that they were away from their inheritance and not allowed to return home.*

The gospel was the announcement of the good news that the term of service was up (see Lev 26:13). The sabbath or jubilee year had arrived. The captives were to be set free, and the land was to be restored to the "original owners," the "true" heirs. To the exodus community, the gospel was that they were free to leave Egypt and return and have rest on the promised land.

The author said that "the gospel" had "been preached to" him and his contemporary Christians just as it had been to the exodus generation. There is no indication that he was comparing two different gospels related to different promises. It was the one "promise of entering into his rest" that was "left" unfulfilled, simply because the exodus generation lacked the faith and obedience to claim it. Therefore it was still "left" for the author's generation—the same "promise of entering into his rest."

"The message of the report" (*ho logos tēs akoēs*) may have been the good news that they could return to the promised land, but it was more likely the report (*dābār;* LXX *hrēma*) that the spies brought back (Num 13:26). They told the congregation that the land flowed with milk and honey and produced fruit like that which they brought to show them, but they also told them how strong and mighty the people were who lived there (Num 13:26–29). As a result Caleb and Joshua said they should go up at once and take it (Num 13:30), but the others said it was impossible. This was the evil report which prevented the exodus generation from "entering into his rest." "The message of the report did not help them." The reason the author of Hebrews gave is obvious and based on the Old Testament—the people did not have faith (3:19). The exact wording of the text is not very clear. There is textual witness for each of the following readings:

(a) *mē synkekerasmenos tę̄ pistei tois akousasin*
(it) "not being united by/with faith to/in those who heard"
(b) *mē synkekerasmenous tę̄ pistei tois akousasin*
(they) "not being united in/with faith to those who heard"
(c) *mē synkekerasmenous tę̄ pistei tōn akousantōn*
(they) "not being united by faith of those who heard"
(d) *mē synkekerasmenous tę̄ pistei tois akoustheisin*
(they) "not being united in faith to the things that were heard."

* After the Soviet Union demanded repayment for the money she had invested in the education of professional Jews before releasing them to move to Israel, many Israeli newspapers referred to this action as twentieth-century slavery and the economically prosperous Jews in Russia as "slaves." For example, see *Yediōt 'Aḥarōnōt,* August 23, 1972, p. 25.

There is strong textual witness for only the first two readings. The differences in the readings are mainly in the identification of subjects and objects. In (a) the word was not united to the people who heard. In (b) the people who heard were not united in faith to those who had (previously) heard. In (c) the people who heard were not united to the faith of those who heard. In (d) the people who received the report were not united in faith to the things heard. RSV, following reading (a) has a simple translation: "it did not meet with faith in the hearers." A phrase like this naturally gave rise to variants, but fortunately the differences in meaning are not very great.[21]

3–4. The Greek *houtōs* ("thus") is rendered "the following" in vs. 4. The author's step-by-step logic is choice. Having shown that the exodus generation did not enter into God's rest, he deduced that the promise was left unfulfilled in his day. Since his generation had received the gospel as the exodus generation had, they had just as good an opportunity to enjoy its fulfillment in his day as the Israelites did after they left Egypt. So he concluded that "we who believe" might "enter into the rest," because God took an oath that they [the exodus generation] would not enter into his rest. "Namely" is a possible translation for *kaitoi* and is the sense the context requires.[22] "From the foundation of the world" means from the very beginning. "The works" mentioned are the acts of God involved in creation itself, which took place during the first six days before the sabbath day of rest. Up to this point the author has always meant peaceful and quiet, independent existence on the promised land under the rule of her own king, when he used the term "rest." Here he relates the rest in the inheritance to God's rest from his labors after creation. He thus also relates God's works in Egypt and the wilderness to those which took place "from the foundation of the world." This was to confirm the enduring dimension of God's promise. It also provided a basis for understanding national "rest" in sabbatical terms (see Isa 58:13–14). The point to be understood may be that, since God's behavior is a prototype for Israel's, Israel can then be confident that she also will receive rest after her "works" (see *Hom.* 17:10). The words "the works" are quoted from Gen 2:2 which was anticipated in vs. 3 and quoted in full in vs. 4.

5–6. Verse 5 is only a repetition of part of the passage quoted in vs. 3. The quotation stands on both sides of the reference to God's rest, so that the reader will know that the author wanted to relate the two rests closely together. This relates God's oath concerning his promised rest to Israel to his own rest. Verse 6 is a repetitious elaboration on vss. 1 and 2. His criticism of "the earlier ones" for their "disobedience" in vs. 6 and for their lack of faith in vs. 2 referred to specific acts related to the same basic event reported in Num 14.

7. Once his logic moved from showing that the promise was unfulfilled, and his own generation was one of the ones for whom it might be fulfilled, the author needed a text to show that it would happen in his day and no

[21] See further Westcott, p. 110.
[22] For other examples of this meaning for *kaitoi* see Stuart, p. 110.

other. Such a text was conveniently available in Ps 95: "Today," which the author, in *pesher* logic, interpreted to mean his own day. First, however, he acknowledged that this promise was recorded in the Psalms of David written many years after the exodus, but the author applied this to his readers: "Do not harden your hearts."

8. Joshua in Hebrew is the same as Jesus in Greek. The Joshua discussed here was Moses' successor who finally succeeded in leading the second wilderness generation into the promised land. The author insisted, however, that the first Joshua had not "given them [i.e. the first generation] rest." This has opened the door for extensive spiritualization on the part of scholars. If Joshua's conquest was not understood as *rest,* then the author must have had in mind something non-political, non-material. Windisch said, "The earthly Canaan had for Hebrews absolutely no meaning . . . [Joshua] is here not a type but a contrast."[23] Stuart said, "'Hence,' he [the author of Hebrews] concludes, 'it is evident, since the rest which is spoken of is not of a temporal nature, but of a spiritual enduring nature, that there remains a rest for the people of God, i.e. believers.'"[24] The spiritual conclusions Stuart gave were his own. The author made no mention of a spiritual nature as over against a temporal nature in this context. Spicq concluded that 4:4–5 was added "to prove that the rest is no longer Canaan but heaven, not an object of pure human hope, but a reality of divine experience."[25] He admitted that the rest about which the author of Hebrews spoke in the Old Testament was to take place on the promised land where the elect would enter, inherit salvation, and have access to the temple,[26] but Spicq insisted that, for Christians, rest is the ultimate celestial blessedness in heaven to be enjoyed at the end of the road.[27] Like Stuart, Moffatt transferred his own assumptions to the author of Hebrews: "He [the author] simply assumes (a) that God's promise of *katapausis* is spiritual . . . (b) as a corollary of this, he assumes that it is eschatological."[28] Schröger said the author must not mean Canaan as "rest." Therefore he must intend a deeper meaning for the term.[29] Grässer noted the Old Testament instances in which "rest" was associated with the promised land and admitted that this prompted the notion "that Hebrews accepted these Old Testament ideas, but his transposition to a heavenly-otherworldly rest places him much closer in relationship to religious-philosophical speculations of clear apocalyptic-gnostic and Alexandrian provenance."[30] The Greek philosophical thought, which others have also used to explain Hebrews, is misleading, and the normal interpretation by Grässer deserves more careful consideration. Bruce rejected a millennial interpretation as "the importation into the epistle of a concept which in fact is alien to it,"[31] but he then proceeded to import his own alien concept. Realizing the close relationship the author of Hebrews placed between rest and the entrance

[23] Windisch, p. 34, and Williamson, pp. 395–97. [24] Stuart, p. 104.
[25] Spicq, II, 82. [26] Ibid., 102. [27] Ibid., 102–5.
[28] Moffatt, p. 53. [29] Schröger, pp. 114–15. [30] Grässer, p. 106.
[31] Bruce, p. 75.

into Canaan, Bruce defensively said, "The meaning of 'rest' was not *exhausted* [italics mine] by the earthly Canaan as a goal of the people of God today."[32] On the basis that Joshua had not given the people rest, Bruce made a contrast between the "temporal 'rest' " and the "true rest,"[33] which he imported as being non-temporal. Although he admitted uncertainty about the real nature of this rest, he affirmed: "one way or another, this blissful rest in unbroken fellowship with God is the goal to which His people are urged to press forward."[34]

Hebrews did not make the sharp distinction between spiritual and national-political-material that modern scholars make. They understood God's will and blessings in terms that affected their national, social, economic, and personal lives. They understood religion in very practical terms. That which seemed best in their society seemed God's will. At that time, in their judgment, that which seemed best for them was peace and prosperity in the land of Canaan under the rule of a Davidic king, so this was considered God's will. Israel needed a Sabbath, so God must need a Sabbath (Gen 2:2), and he rested in Zion (Isa 66:1, Ps 132:14), the way Israel hoped to do.

This may seem anthropomorphic to Americans in the twentieth century, but even we, in our apparent sophistication, have not transcended some anthropomorphic ways of understanding God's will. The only way we have changed is the character we ascribe to God because of our own understanding of what is best for human beings in society. In trying to understand the views of an author of long ago, however, it is important to try to understand the values and thought forms of his day rather than transposing our own twentieth-century values to him.

This seems like an easy way to dismiss other scholars who have seemed to import a non-national meaning for the rest the author said was still awaiting fulfillment, but an easy dismissal is not intended, for there really is a problem here. The author spoke of the rest available to his readers as being the same as that offered to the exodus generation. Initially this rest was clearly related to settlement and peace in Canaan. It was reported in Josh 21:43–45 that Joshua did lead the Israelites into the promised rest. That would seem to have been the fulfillment, but the author of Hebrews denied that Joshua had given them rest. It is in trying to understand why the rest Joshua gave did not meet the qualifications that scholars have introduced something not related to the land. Some conjectural interpretation is necessary, but care should be taken to stay within the author's concepts in so doing.

The author of Hebrews was a good student of the Old Testament. He interpreted Ps 95 in relationship to Num 14 because he knew that they dealt with the same subject. He assumed that David wrote Psalm 95 (4:7), and David was not even born until many years after Joshua died. If David could write in his day that they had not entered the promised rest, then surely the rest Joshua had given was not adequate. Furthermore, as

[32] Bruce, p. 72 [33] Ibid., p. 77. [34] Ibid., p. 79.

the author of Hebrews said that "after such a long time [had transpired]" (4:7) as elapsed between Moses and David, and David was still wishing the people of his day would hear the Lord's voice (Ps 95:7), then obviously there was no rest in David's day either. That does not mean that the author looked for a non-national, non-material rest in heaven. It just meant that, according to the scriptures, the rest had not been given as late as David's time. They were probably expecting a rest that was basically of the same nature as Israelites had anticipated all along, yet one that was to be more prosperous, more peaceful, more luxurious, and in a position of higher dignity among the nations than had been known by any Israelite or Jewish kingdom up to the author's time. In all probability he also expected that when such a "rest" really came, it would never end (Dan 7:14; Gen R. 65:23; Exod R. 15:21, 31; 50:5). That was the promise given to the Son of man in Dan 7. All independent control the Israelites had of the promised land was of short duration. With the rise of Herod the Great, even the most recent Hasmonean dynasty crumbled, and after Archaelaus was deposed in A.D. 6/7, Roman governors were introduced and Jews lost all semblance of self-rule. This did not mean that all Jews stopped hoping and believing that the Romans could be overthrown and their own nation restored. Many believed, lived, and fought to bring this about. It was in this milieu that the author wrote. It seems likely that he hoped to see in his own day the permanent fulfillment of the promise.

9. Following this line of reasoning, then, the author concluded that "there remains a sabbath-keeping for the people of God." There were probably many Jews and Christians who had given up hope. So many plans and hopes had failed! The promise must have been withdrawn or fulfilled long ago, they thought. The author of Hebrews denied these possibilities and urged his people to maintain their confidence and hope.

10. Earlier the author had related God's work in creation to his work in Egypt and in the wilderness experience. Both had involved doubting, tempting, grumbling, disobeying, and rebelling. This certainly was not rest. Whenever they received their rest all of this should stop, because the person who enters into rest also rests from the works of this nature just as God rested from his own works.

11. The author took frequent opportunities to exhort his readers to hold fast to their confidence, keep all the laws, and be careful not to go astray. The exodus generation who doubted and rebelled obviously had no rest or confidence. Therefore Christians of the author's day must prepare themselves for the rest by giving up all grumbling, lack of confidence and faith, lest they "fall because of the same sort of disobedience." "To fall because of" (*pesę en . . .*) pictures someone handicapped by being blindfolded or distracted in some way, in this case by disobedience. Since the Christians of the author's day knew how the exodus generation fell, they should avoid the same mistake of being disobedient.

The author of Hebrews was not the only one to compare his own generation with that which came out of Egypt. Paul also told of the fathers who all went under the cloud, through the sea, were all baptized into Moses, drank of the same spiritual drink and ate the same spiritual food. Nonetheless, God was displeased with most of them (only Caleb and Joshua were excepted), and dispersed them in the wilderness. That should be an example from which Corinthian Christians should learn, said Paul. They must not be idolators, immoral, or grumblers who test the Lord, because if they are they will receive the same punishment (I Cor 10:1–10). Just as the author of Hebrews understood that Ps 95 was written as prophecy to be applied to his own generation, Paul said the account of the wilderness was written down for the instruction of covenanters of his day, "on whom the end of the ages has come" (I Cor 10:11). By this Paul meant that the captivity was over; jubilee was about to be sounded; covenanters were about to receive the promise made to Abraham and his posterity; the good news had been announced; if Christians believed properly, they would have the opportunity to enter into his promised rest. Details of Paul's eschatological expectations are ambiguous, but his dependence upon sabbatical concepts is clear.

12. Soul (*psychē*) and spirit (*pneuma*) are very closely related. Sometimes they are used synonymously, and both are rendered by the Latin *anima.* Both are used in contrast to *sōma,* "body." *Psychē* comes from the verb *psychō,* "to breathe," "make cool or cold," as a breeze does. *Pneuma* also means wind, air, breath. Paul contrasted between the first Adam, who was a "living soul" (*psychēn zōsan*) and the last Adam who was a *pneuma zōopoioun,* a "life-giving spirit." In religious circles, *psychē* was sometimes identified with secular life, which a person surrendered for "life" (*zōē*) in a communal order under the covenant. Spirit (*pneuma*) was related more closely to *zōē* (religious life) than to *psychē* (secular life). The author of this poem may have wanted to distinguish between the spirit (*psychē*) which constituted physical breath that keeps animate beings alive, and the holy breath or spirit (*pneuma*) that provided religious life with its necessary basis. Philo said "spirit is the essence of the soul" and "he names the soul of man, 'spirit'" (*QDPIS* 80–84; see also Wis 15:11). The point of the author's affirmation was to show that the Word of God could make divisions and distinctions that are impossible for human beings. To separate between "soul and spirit" was as difficult as distinguishing between "designs and intentions of the mind." "Joints and marrow" can be humanly separated, but the author wanted to show that there was no area out of God's reach, physical, spiritual (in the sense of being alive), and intentional or moral. An early pastoral benediction prayed that God would keep the recipient of the blessing sound in spirit, soul, and body (I Thess 5:23), which involved every aspect of life. The poem in 4:12–13 intends the same complete inclusiveness in the terms expressed. A similar eulogy of the Word is:

> "For the swiftness of the Word is inexpressible
> and like his expression is his swiftness and his sharpness."
>
> (Odes of Sol 12:5.)

Pseudo-Phocylides said the word was a tool, "sharper than iron" (124). The Lord's servant's mouth was "like a sharp sword" (Isa 49:2). Clement says, "Let us notice how near he is, and that nothing escapes him of our thoughts or of the devices which we undertake" (I Clem 21:3). "For he is a searcher of designs and intentions" (I Clem 21:9). II Baruch said the Most High would "carefully scrutinize the deep thoughts (*cogitationes*)" (83:3).

13. The word *tetrachēlismena* is rendered "laid bare." It comes from the noun *trachēlos,* "neck," but the image is not perfectly clear. It may intend to show a person who has left his neck unguarded in wrestling so that his opponent was able to get a "half nelson" on him, or it may indicate a person without armor to cover his throat. Some have suggested that it referred to baring the neck of a sacrificial animal for slaughter.[35] Whatever the exact image, the general meaning is clear. It refers to a person who is defenseless and at the mercy of his opponent. The author of this unit expressed vividly and beautifully the thoroughness of God's scrutiny. No part of any human being can escape his examination.

Michel has correctly called attention to the poetic nature of 4:12–13.[36] Line two (see translation) supplements line one, showing how "living and active" the word of God is, and the successive lines further supplement, expand, and conclude the description of the omniscience of the word. The unknown author of the poem had prepared a composition that was useful for the author of Hebrews to illustrate his strong attempt to urge his recipients to see that no single one of them disobeyed God in any way. They had to be extremely careful because the consequences would be at least as disastrous for them as for the exodus generation. Furthermore they were sure that no sin would go unnoticed. There was no way they could escape deserved punishment.

The most difficult part of these verses to understand and translate is the last part of vs. 13, *pros hon hēmin ho logos.* Michel rendered this as part of the poem, but it seems more likely to be a midrashic commentary on the poem which the author added. The following three examples will show that such additions are typical of the author:

(a) Following a discussion which called attention to Moses' position as only a servant "in his house" (3:1–5), the author of Hebrews pointed to "Christ as a son over his house," and then commented:

—"whose house we are" (*hou oikos esmen hēmeis*) (3:6).

(b) In contrast to the temple priests of the family of Aaron, the author spoke of Christ, who "was declared by God a high priest according to the order of Melchizedek," and then commented:

—"concerning which (*peri hou*) our message is extensive and difficult to interpret" (5:10–11).

(c) Claiming the superiority of Christ's priesthood over that of the temple priests, the author said, ". . . but he [became a priest] with

[35] Windisch, pp. 36–37.
[36] Michel, p. 114.

oath-taking, through the one who said to him: "The Lord has sworn and will not change his mind; you are a priest for the age." Then he commented:

—"just so much more (*kata tosouto*) has Jesus become a surety of an even better covenant" (7:21–22).

In all three instances the connecting word ("whose," "concerning," or "just so much more") refers to a quotation from the Old Testament scripture in just the same way as the phrase in 4:13 refers to the poem just quoted. This suggests that the phrase in 4:13 should also be considered a commentary to the poem and not a part of the poem itself, as Michel considered it; but that does not solve all of the problems of translation. Translators have regularly had difficulty with this passage and have reached different conclusions: The KJV rendered the passage, ". . . with whom we have to reckon" and the RSV, ". . . with whom we have to do." The differences are slight, and Davidson,[37] Moffatt,[38] and Turner[39] have translations agreeing with one or the other. Some variants are: Delitzsch, "to whom we have to give account,"[40] Stuart, "before whom, in whose power, or at whose disposal is our account,"[41] and Spicq, *"c'est de ce sujet dont nous parlons."*[42] Moffatt[43] and others deal more with the meaning of the word *logos* than with the meaning of the whole passage or its relationship to the context. Delitzsch[44] was correct in saying that the *pros hon* of 4:13 could bear the same meaning as the *peri hou* of 5:11. This is apparently a *pros* used with the meaning of "in reference to" as in 1:7, 8.

The real problem is supplying missing verbs and understanding antecedents for the relative pronoun *hon*. Except for 4:13, the only other use of *pros* together with *hon* also follows a poem. This poem differs from that quoted in 4:12–13 in that it is a paraphrase of scripture as well as being a poem:

"By faith Abraham offered Isaac, being tested,
(and) the one who received the promises offered [his] only born."

The Hebrews comment is:

—"[with reference] to whom (*pros hon*) it was said, 'In Isaac
your seed shall be called' " (Heb 11:17–18).

The use of *pros hon* immediately after the quoted poem and referring back to it is exactly like the small comment immediately following the poem in 4:13. That the poem in 11:17 may have been composed by someone other than the author of Hebrews is suggested by one of the quotations of scripture taken directly from the MT rather than the LXX, which

[37] Davidson, p. 97.
[38] Moffatt, p. 54.
[39] Turner, p. 64.
[40] Delitzsch, I, 216.
[41] Stuart, p. 117.
[42] Spicq, II, 91.
[43] Moffatt, pp. 54–55.
[44] Delitzsch, I, 216.

Hebrews normally follows. The Hebrew *y^eḥīd^ekā* (Gen 22:2), "your only one," would normally be rendered by the Greek *monogenēs* rather than the LXX *agapētos,* "beloved." The use of the *pros* plus the accusative after a verb that indicated saying rather than the usual Greek use of the dative case is typical of the author of Hebrews. Of the nineteen usages of *pros* in this document, ten are used in this very manner. This suggests a Semitism, reflecting the use of a *lamed* as a dative indicator. Other usages of *pros* in Hebrews point in the same direction, reflecting a *lamed* used to indicate a direct object, or possession, purpose, or reference.[45] Of the nineteen usages, only two carry the meaning of "against" or "toward."[46]

Even if it were clearly ascertained that this difficult passage is a literal translation of some Semitic original, there still remain only uncertain conjectures as to the true meaning of the text. There seemed to be some regularity in the way the author used *pros,* which might help in proposing the conjectures. The only other use in Hebrews of the expression *pros hon* follows a poem, just as in 4:13. This may indicate that the expressions were similar in meaning, but it is far from certain. The clause *pros hon elalēthē* (11:18) means "[with reference] to whom it was said." The corresponding passage in 4:13 has no verb: *pros hon hēmin ho logos.* If the same verb were supplied to 4:13 that occurs in 11:18, the passage would read: "with reference to which the word [was spoken] for us" or "to us, for whom the word was spoken." In an exhortation to the readers, the author employed a poem (4:12–13) as a warning and concluded the poem with a brief, approving comment, "which word is for us," "which word [applies] to us," or some such general comment. Another possibility is that it should be understood just as a similar comment which reads "concerning which our message is extensive" (*peri hou polus hēmin ho logos*) (5:11). In this case, *hēmin ho logos* is the subject. If 4:13 were similarly rendered, the result would be something like this: "with reference to which (*pros hon*) our message (*hēmin ho logos*) [applies]." This would mean that the admonition given in 4:1–11 applies to an understanding of God's scrutinizing word. This translation would support Spicq's translation, *"c'est de ce sujet dont nous parlons."*[47]

The meaning of "which word applies to us" does not differ very much practically from that of "with reference to which our message applies." Both are intended to relate the message of the author to the poem he quoted, and the entire message was intended to be taken seriously by the readers.

Summary.—Given the presuppositions that were accepted in Christianity and Judaism in New Testament times, the author of Hebrews was an

[45] See *Gesenius' Hebrew Grammar,* §114, f–p, 117n; 119c; 121f; 129; 143c.

[46] Heb. 12:4; 13:13. One of these occurs in the thirteenth chapter, which is a postscript added later by a different author. See H. Kosmala, *Hebräer-Essener-Christen* (Leiden, 1959), p. 408, and Moffatt, p. 224.

[47] Spicq, II, 91.

excellent logician and artist in the use of scripture. Although the entire document (1:1 – 12:29) was based on Ps 110, it was proper to utilize other scriptures to support the main point, and, as here, to develop a separate text by itself that would later contribute to the major point. Heb 4:1–13 is a small midrash by itself, based on Ps 95:7–11 and supported by Num 14 and a small poem which the author quoted in 4:12–13a to strengthen his argument. He wanted to show his readers the opportunities that were available to the exodus generation, their faulty reaction, and the consequences they received as a result. He did this in order to remind his readers that they had even better chances for success than the exodus generation, but just as great chances for failure. One reason why he used Ps 95 as his principal text rather than Num 14 or Deut 1 may have been his conviction that the law had been superseded; another may have been the fact that he believed David wrote the Psalm and that this late authorship would dispel all arguments to the effect that the promise had already been received. Had he used only the Hexateuch, this important point might have been overlooked. His step-by-step logic from the premise that the promise is still pending to his exhortation and warning against disobedience was supported by a poem on the thoroughness of God's examining omniscience. This reminder of God's inescapable judgment was the kind of message which should be applied to the author and the readers of the document.

Chapters one and two included the introduction and a comparison of the superiority of the Son to the angels and his relationship to his believers. Chapter three showed how Moses failed to lead the people to receive the promised rest. Chapter four argued cogently that the rest was now available to his generation. Each of these sections has concluded with a brief introduction to the subject that would follow. At the conclusion of this chapter also, the author prepared the reader for the next major doctrinal subject, Jesus the great high priest. Jesus had earlier been called a faithful high priest (2:17) and the apostle and high priest of our confession (3:1). The conclusion of chapter four will prepare the reader still further to read the discussion of Jesus' priestly qualities in the chapter that immediately follows, and these will be considered even more extensively in chapter seven.

Jesus the High Priest

14. The highest ranking priest in Judaism was normally called the "high priest," in Hebrew *kōhēn haggādōl,* "the great priest," usually rendered *archiereus,* "the ruling priest," in Greek. The first of the Hasmoneans to be given an official title was Simon, who was called "the great high priest, general, and ruler of the Jews" (*archiereōs megalou kai stratēgou kai hēgoumenou*) (I Macc 13:42). The author of Hebrews may have been influenced by this title when he called Jesus "a great high priest." There are many other indications that the author of Hebrews was influenced by the literature and theological beliefs related to the Maccabean period and that the Hasmonean priestly rulers influenced his Christology.

The affirmation that Jesus had "gone through the heavens" expressed belief in his ascension, but it was couched in terms of sacrifice in the temple. Most people who lived at the time of the author understood the world in which they lived as it appeared to the naked eye. Since they had no modern telescopes and nuclear-powered rockets, their knowledge of heaven was limited. It seemed to them that heaven was just above the treetops and the hills. God was somewhere in the sky and was always covered with a cloud so that human beings could not see him clearly. His presence was made known when clouds came down and settled around mountains. Smoke and clouds were very similar to the naked eye, so it seemed that the smoke that went up from a bonfire formed a pillar which would both let God come down to earth and let human beings send things, like incense and offerings, up to God. They evidently thought of several heavens, something like floors in an apartment building, but they were described more in terms of tent roofs than concrete floors. Like their goat- or camel-hair tents that could be rolled up, heaven was described as a scroll that God could spread out (Isa 40:12; 45:12; 48:13) or roll up (Isa 34:4). It was also called a *rāqīa'*—"something spread out" (Gen 1:6). Whenever God wanted to create a new heaven, all he had to do was roll up the old one and spread out a new one. Since Jesus' crucifixion was interpreted by the author in terms of a sacrifice on the altar, and since animal sacrifices were cooked or burned completely so that their odor could be sent up through the column of smoke to God in the heavens, it seemed reasonable to conclude that Jesus, too, ascended into heaven, or through the various heavens, up to the very throne of God.

"Son of God" was a name ordinarily given to kings, but Philo said the high priest was not a man but a divine word (*logos theios*), whose father was God (*Fuga* 108). The author of Hebrews, however, clearly related the attributes of the Son in royal terms; thus he here was thinking of Jesus as both priest and king. The words "hold fast" and "confession" were both important words to the author. Jesus was previously called the "high priest of our confession" (3:1); therefore it seemed reasonable for the author and readers to "hold fast" to the "confession." The author also told the readers to hold fast to the "initial doctrine" (3:14; see also 10:23). Both admonitions probably have the same meaning—that they should know the entire doctrine of the sect and be disciplined to practice it unfailingly. Bornkamm has suggested that the confession is that Jesus is the Son of God, and that the baptismal confession mentioned in 3:1; 4:14; and 10:23 is as follows:[48]

> "Who, being a reflection of the glory and stamp of his nature,
> bearing everything by the word of his power,
> when he had made a purification for [his] sins,
> sat down at the right hand of the Majesty in exaltation" (1:3).

This is interesting, but not convincing. Jesus was certainly important to the

[48] G. Bornkamm, *Studien zu Antike und Christentum* (München, 1959), II, 188–203.

confession, but the limit and entire content of the creed are not known. It was extensive enough, however, to include rules which were difficult to observe.

15. The word *peirazein,* "to test," can mean to put to trial by torturing, to seduce, attempt, or experiment. In the Old Testament it usually refers to the testing that the Israelites put the Lord through when they doubted him. The testing "in everything" probably referred to hardships Jesus faced, including the crucifixion. They were the same kind of tests which later Christians had to face. Just as Jesus had been made like the brothers in everything (*kata panta tois adelphois homoiōthēnai*) (2:17), so he was also "tested in everything, in ways similar [to ours]" (*kata panta kath' homoiotēta*). The difference was that he was "without sin." When the high priest functioned on the Day of Atonement, very careful efforts were made to keep him from being defiled in any way, so that he could be free from defilement. He also offered a bull for a sin offering for himself and his family so that he could be absolved from every other type of sin against God before he ministered in behalf of the people. This meant that he was legally free from sin on the Day of Atonement. Philo claimed even more for him. He said that, in his judgment (*tǭ nǭ*), the high priest was the child of incorruptible parents and free from any kind of defilement, since God was his father (*Fuga* 109–10). Philo said further that when the high priest entered the holy of holies, he became more than a man, but not yet God, retaining both mortality and immortality, created and uncreated essence. As such he was the mediator between man and God until he returned from the holy of holies and would again become flesh and blood (*Som.* II. 231–32). Philo claimed that this half-divine nature made it possible for the high priest to be free from sin and defilement. If he had not been sound, he would not have been permitted to serve (*Spec.* I. 293). He was really immune to sin (*ametochos hamartēmatōn*). If he ever slipped, the sin would never be anything that could not be cleansed, and it would be something imposed upon him by the nation (*Spec.* I. 230).

The double negative, "we do not have . . . un-," is a good example of *litotes.* It means, "we *do* have a high priest who *is* able." This type of speech is frequent in Semitic style. For example, "Do not lead us into temptation" (Matt 6:12) means "lead us away from temptation" or "deliver us from evil" (Matt 6:13). "Cast me not away from thy presence, and take not thy holy Spirit from me" (Ps 51:11) means "Keep me in thy presence, and give me thy holy Spirit."

Jesus was not the only leader of antiquity claimed to be "without sin." Philo said the high priest was free from any kind of defilement, and the author of Ps of Sol 17:41 said of the anticipated son of David, who would crush the Gentiles and lead Israel in peace and prosperity,

> "And he will be clean from sin (*katharos apo hamartias*) so as to rule a great people."

If the high priest and the Messiah were both expected to be sinless, then it seems a reasonable claim for the author, who insisted that Jesus was both king and priest, to call Jesus one who was "without sin." This does not necessarily mean that he had never committed a moral offense in his life. Since the author presented Jesus as a high priest, he may have understood his crucifixion as an offering on the Day of Atonement to cleanse his own sins as well as those of the faithful, all of whom would have been made sinless or perfect (see also COMMENT on 1:3; 7:28; 9:14).

16. The term "approach" (*proserchōmetha*) is used in a priestly-temple context, picturing the high priest on the Day of Atonement approaching the altar in the holy of holies. Only the high priest could come this close to the altar. Other priests might enter the holy place; undefiled male Jews were admitted into a court just beyond. Farther still from the altar was the women's court, and the very farthest in the temple precincts was the court of the Gentiles. When a Gentile male was converted and became a proselyte, he was allowed to come closer to the holy of holies, but each class was expected to stay within its prescribed limits. Only the high priest was allowed to "approach" or come near the "throne of grace." The "throne of grace" was another name for the throne of God, which either was the altar itself or was on the altar. The high priest was the representative and mediator for the people. It was through him that they were able to approach God (7:25). The law was never able permanently to fulfill the needs of those who approach by means of the same sacrifices every year (10:1), but because of the sacrifice of Jesus, Christians may confidently approach the altar (10:22). Those who approached the altar did so with a gift which the priest offered in their behalf. His approaching "the throne of grace" with the believer's offering constituted the believer's approach. When Jesus, as high priest, entered the holy of holies, he not only was the priest who approached "the throne of grace" with an offering for the believers, but he was himself the offering. The smoke which carried the fragrance of the offering to God, carried Jesus himself as the offering "through the heavens." This sin offering was sufficient to cancel all of the sins that had kept the children of Israel removed from and unreconciled to God. Since the offering had already "gone through the heavens," believers were reconciled, no longer kept at a distance, but invited to "approach the throne of grace with boldness." Those who did so would benefit from the offering themselves, which means they would "receive mercy and find grace." They would have their sins forgiven and might even have some merits on hand "for timely support." Since this opportunity was available, of course, the author urged his readers to take advantage of all the benefits available to them. The Greek for "timely support" is *eukairon boētheian,* sometimes translated "time of need." It is literally "timely help" or "timely assistance." In the context of a Day of Atonement gift and the judgment associated with it, the author probably thought that all the support a covenanter could muster was necessary to make his case favorable at that particular time.

The Greek word rendered "boldness" is *parrēsia,* literally, "saying everything." It refers to the freedom of citizens to speak and sometimes has the force of "outspokenness." In Hebrews it can mean the unquestioned right to approach God (3:6, 4:16; 10:19) or the openness with which they should confess their faith.[49]

Delitzsch had noticed the euphonious chiasm in the concluding line:[50]

hina labōmen eleos	*so that we might receive mercy*
kai charin heurōmen	*and grace we might find*

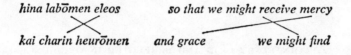

Summary.—The words "high priest," "heavens," and "confession" form the concluding parts of an inclusion which refers the reader back to 3:1, where their counterparts occur. Heb 4:15–16 are further elaborations of this conclusion and preparation of the reader for the content of ch. 5.

The importance of the priesthood, the temple, and the treasury of merits to the Jewish doctrine of atonement provides the basis for the author's Christology and understanding of the role of Jesus. Jews and Christians of New Testament times thought of heaven in terms of temple surroundings (see further COMMENT at the end of ch. 9). Josephus said the holy of holies was like heaven (*Ant.* III. 123). Just as the high priest passed through the veil into the holy of holies which was like heaven, so Jesus as "a great high priest has gone through the heavens." Since it was sin and defilement that kept others from the holy of holies, and since Jesus' sacrifice canceled all of these, believers no longer were required to keep at a distance from holy things, lest some defilement take place. Instead of being afraid of touching something sacred, believers should be afraid of falling behind (4:1), but they should "approach the throne of grace with boldness." It was only in this way that they might receive the benefits tabulated to the credit of Israel in the treasury of merits by the sacrifice of Jesus.

[49] See W. C. Van Unnik, "The Christian's Freedom of Speech in the NT," BJRL 44 (1962), 466–88.

[50] Delitzsch, II, 223.

IV. JESUS THE HIGH PRIEST
(5:1–10:39)

Appointed by God and perfected in obedience

5 1 For every high priest selected from men is appointed [over]
divine things in behalf of men, so that he might offer gifts and sacrifices for sins 2 being able to bear gently with the ignorant and way-
ward [sinners], since he himself is also clothed in weakness, 3 and
because of it, is obligated to offer [sacrifices] for his own sins as well
as those of the people.
4 Now no one takes the honor for himself but is invited by God,
just as Aaron also was. 5 Thus also the Christ did not exalt himself
to become high priest, but [was appointed by] the One who said to
him,

"You are my Son. Today I have begotten you."

6 Just as it also says in another [place],

"You are a priest for the age according to the
order of Melchizedek,"

7 who, in the days of his flesh, offered prayers and supplications to
the One who was able to save him from death, with a loud cry and
tears, and from his anxiety, was heeded. 8 Although he was a Son,
he learned obedience from the things he suffered; 9 and, having
been made perfect, he became a source of eternal salvation for all
those who obey him; 10 he was declared by God a high priest according to the order of Melchizedek.

Exhortation

11 Concerning which our message is extensive and difficult to interpret, since you have become dull of hearing. 12 For, because of
the time [that has elapsed], you ought to be teachers [yourselves],
but [instead] you again need someone to teach you the simple

principles of the beginning of God's words; you have become [in-
fants who] need milk—not strong food. 13 For everyone who enjoys
milk is unskilled in the word of righteousness, for he is an infant,
14 but strong food is for the "perfect"—those who, because they
have their perceptions trained, have [the ability] to discern good
and evil.

6 1 Therefore, leaving the word of the beginning [teachings] of
Christ, let us carry on to perfection, not laying again a foundation
of repentance from dead works, faith in God, 2 teaching of ablutions, laying on of hands, resurrection of [the] dead ones, and judgment of [the] age 3 —and we will do this if God is willing. 4 For
(6 after they have fallen by the wayside) it is impossible (6 to renew
again for repentance) those who have once been enlightened, tasted
the heavenly gift, become sharers of the Holy Spirit, 5 and tasted
the good word of God and the miracles of the coming age,
6 [thereby] crucifying and making a public example of the Son of
God for themselves. 7 For land that drinks the rain which comes
upon it many times and produces vegetation [that is] useful to
those for whom it is also cultivated, receives blessings from God;
8 but when it bears thorns and thistles, it is worthless and nearly
a curse. Its end is burning.

9 But concerning you, beloved, we are convinced about the better
things belonging to salvation, even though we speak thus; 10 for
God is not unjust [so as] to forget your work and the love which
you have demonstrated for his name, having ministered to the
saints as you still do, 11 but we want each of you to show forth the
same zeal toward the fulfillment of hope until [the] end, 12 so that
you may not become dull, but [rather] imitators of those who inherit the promises through faith and long suffering.

The promises of God

13 For when God made a promise to Abraham, since he had no one
else greater [by whom] to swear, he swore by himself, 14 saying,
"[May the following unexpressed curses come upon me] if I do not
surely bless you and multiply you"; 15 and thus, after he had suffered patiently, [Abraham] received the promise. 16 For men swear
by someone [or something] greater [than themselves], and every ar-

gument [is brought to an] end by the confirmation of an oath.
17 So when God wanted very much to show the heirs of the promise the unchangeableness of his will, he imposed an oath [on him-
self], 18 so that through two unchangeable things in which it would
be impossible for God to falsify, we who have recourse [in the oath
and promise] may have a strong encouragement to seize the hope
set before us, 19 which we have as a secure and steadfast anchor of
the soul, and one that is entering into the innermost [area which is
behind] the curtain, 20 where Jesus entered [as] a forerunner in our
behalf, since he is a high priest for the age according to the order of
Melchizedek.

Melchizedek superior to the Levites

Melchizedek and Abraham

7 1 For this Melchizedek, king of Salem . . . priest of the Most
High God, who met Abraham returning from smiting . . . the kings,
and blessed him; 2 and to him Abraham apportioned a tenth of all.

First [Melchizedek] is interpreted "king of righteousness," and
then [second] also king of Salem, which is "king of peace."

> 3 Without father, without mother, without genealogy,
> having neither beginning of days nor end of life,
> but resembling the son of God,
> he remains a priest continually.

4 See how great he is! To him the patriarch Abraham gave a tenth
of [his] choice [acquisitions]. 5 Now, even the sons of Levi, on the
one hand, receiving the priesthood, have a commandment according to law to collect [the] tithe [from] the people, that is, their
brothers, even though [these] have come from the loins of Abraham; 6 on the other hand, the one who does not have a genealogy
from them collected the tithe from Abraham, and blessed the one
who had the promises. 7 Incontestably, the lesser is blessed by the
greater, 8 and here, on the one hand, mortal men receive tithes, but
there, on the other hand, it attested that "he lives." 9 One might
even [extend the figure to] say [that] Levi, who receives tithes, was
[himself] tithed through Abraham, 10 for he was still in the loins
of his father when Melchizedek met him.

The imperfect priesthood and law

11 If perfection had been through the levitical priesthood (for the
people were governed by it), what need would there still be for
another priest to arise according to the order of Melchizedek and
not to be declared according to the order of Aaron? 12 For when
the priesthood is changed, there is necessarily a change of law as
well, 13 for the one about whom these things are said belonged to
a different tribe, from which no one ministered at the altar. 14 For
it is clear that our Lord arose from Judah, regarding which tribe
Moses said nothing about priests, 15 and it is still more abundantly
clear [that] if another priest arises according to the likeness of
Melchizedek, 16 [he is one] who did not come into existence according to the law of a fleshly commandment but according to the
power of an indestructible life. 17 For it is attested, "You are a
priest for the age according to the order of Melchizedek." 18 For,
on the one hand, a previously functioning commandment is removed because of its weakness and uselessness 19 (for the law
perfected nothing), but on the other hand, [there is the] beginning
of a better hope through which we come near to God.

The perfect priest

20 And just as much as it was not without oath-taking (for they are
priests [who] became [such] without oath-taking, 21 but he [be-
came a priest] with oath-taking, through the one who said to him:
"The Lord has sworn and will not change his mind; you are a priest
for the age)," 22 just so much more has Jesus become a surety of an
even better covenant. 23 Now those are numerous, since they became priests because [their predecessors] were prevented by death
from continuing [in office], 24 but he [is one] because he remains
"for the age"[and therefore] has the priesthood without change.
25 Therefore he is also able to save those who approach God through
him for the entire [age], since he always lives to make intercession
in their behalf. 26 For such a one also became high priest for us,

holy, guileless, undefiled,
separated from sinners,
and become higher than the heavens,

27 who does not have the daily necessity, as the high priests do, first

to offer sacrifices for their own sins, then those of the people, for he did this once for all, having offered himself. 28 For the law establishes men [as] high priests [who] have weakness, but the word of the oath which [came] after the law [establishes] a Son made [him] perfect for the age.

Old and New Worship

The old cult

THE EARTHLY MINISTRY

8 1 Most important of the things said [is that] we have such a high priest [as this] who sat down at the right hand of the throne of Majesty in the heavens,

2 a minister of the holy things
and of the true tent
which the Lord set up—not man.

3 For every high priest is established for the purpose of offering gifts and sacrifices; therefore it is necessary for this one also to have something that he might offer. 4 If, then, he had been on earth, he would not have been a priest, since there [already] are those who offer the gifts according to the law, 5 who serve [as] a pattern and shadow of the heavenly things, just as Moses was advised when he was about to finish the tent: "See," he said, "[that] you do everything according to the pattern which was shown to you on the mountain." 6 But now he has acquired as much a more excellent ministry [than the previous one] as he is also a mediator of a better covenant, which has been made into law on the basis of better promises.

THE FIRST COVENANT

7 For if that first [covenant] had been faultless, a place for a second would not have been sought. 8 For [he is] blaming them [when] he says:

> " 'Behold the days are coming,' says [the] Lord, 'and I will conclude upon the house of Israel and upon the House of Judah a new covenant—9 not like the covenant which I made with their fathers on [the] day when I took them by

their hand to lead them from [the] land of Egypt, because
they did not remain in my covenant, and [so] I ignored
them,' says [the] Lord— 10 'rather, this is the covenant
which I will make with the house of Israel after those days,'
says [the] Lord, '[I will] put my laws into their minds, and I
will be their God and they will be my people. 11 And they
will not teach, each one his fellow citizen and each one his
brother, saying, "Know the Lord"; because they will all
know me, from the least to the greatest of them, 12 for I
will deal mercifully with their unrighteous acts, and I will
no longer remember their sins.' "

13 In using the word "new," he made the first [covenant] obsolete. Now that which is becoming obsolete and aging is almost gone.

TEMPLE FUNCTIONS

9 1 Now, on the one hand, even the first [tent] had the proper
things for worship and an earthly sanctuary, 2 for the first tent,
which is called "[the] holy," was prepared in which there were the
lampstand, the table, and the setting forth of loaves. 3 On the other
hand, beyond the second curtain is a tent called "[the] holy of
holies," 4 which has a gold altar and the ark of the covenant, completely covered with gold, in which there is a gold jar, containing
the manna, the rod of Aaron that budded, and the tablets of the
covenant. 5 Above it are cherubim of glory overshadowing the
mercy seat (concerning which things, this is not the proper time to
speak).

6 These things having been thus prepared, into the first tent the
priests enter continually while performing the ritualistic services,
7 but into the second [tent] only the high priest enters, [and then
only] once during the year, [and even then] not without blood
which he offers in behalf of his own [sins] and the unintentional
[sins] of the people. 8 The Holy Spirit makes it clear [that] the way
of the holy [precincts] is not yet visible while the first tent still
stands. 9 This [tent] is a parable for the present time, according to
which both gifts and sacrifices are offered [which are] not able to
perfect the worshiper according to [his] conscience; 10 only being
concerned with foods and drinks and various ablutions—proper
[observances] of the flesh [imposed] until the time of correction.

The new cult

CHRIST'S SACRIFICE

11 But Christ, having become a high priest of the good things
that have happened, through the greater and more perfect tent
not made with hands (that is, not of this creation), 12 and not
through blood of goats and bulls, but through his own blood,
entered once for all into the holy [precincts], having found eternal
redemption. 13 For if the blood of goats and bulls and ashes of a
heifer, sprinkling those who are defiled, sanctifies [them] for the
cleansing of the flesh, 14 how much more the blood of Christ,
who through [the] eternal spirit offered himself blameless to God,
will cleanse our conscience from dead works for the purpose of
worshiping [the] living God.

THE BLOODY COVENANT

15 And, because of this, he is [the] mediator of a new covenant,
so that, since a death has occurred for the purpose of redemption
from the transgressions in the first covenant, those who are called
might receive the promise of the eternal inheritance. 16 For wherever there is a will, it is necessary for death to be suffered by the
one who made the will, 17 for a will is secure [only] with reference
to the dead, since it is never valid when the one who made the
will is alive. 18 From this [it is evident that] not even the first
covenant was renewed without blood, 19 for when every commandment had been spoken according to the law by Moses to all the
people, [Moses], after he took the blood of the bulls and the goats
with water and crimson wool and hyssop, sprinkled both the book
itself and all the people, 20 saying, "This [is] the blood of the
covenant which God has commanded you." 21 And he likewise
sprinkled the tent and all the liturgical vessels with the blood,
22 and nearly everything is cleansed with blood, according to the
law, and without [the] pouring out of blood, forgiveness does not
occur. 23 Therefore, on the one hand, it was necessary [that] the
symbols of the things in the heavens be cleansed by means of
these, but, on the other hand, that the heavenly things themselves
[be cleansed] by means of better sacrifices than these.

THE HEAVENLY MINISTRY

24 For Christ did not enter into the holy [precincts] made with
hands, antitypes of the true [precincts], but into heaven itself, now
to appear before God in our behalf, 25 and not in order that he
might offer himself many times, just as the high priest enters into
the holy [precincts] every year with the blood of another, 26 since
[then] it would have been necessary for him to suffer many times
from the foundation of the world, but now he has appeared once
at the end of the ages for [the] removal of sin through his sacrifice. 27 Now, however much is laid up for men, [they have but]
once to die, and after this [is] judgment; 28 so also the Christ,
having been offered once "to bear [the] sins of [the] many," will
next appear without sin to those who await him for salvation.

Better mediator of forgiveness

10 1 For the law, having a shadow of the good things to come,
not the image itself of the things, every year, by means of the
same [kinds of] sacrifices which they offer continually, is never able
to perfect those who sacrifice. 2 Otherwise, [the sacrifices] would
have stopped being offered, would they not? Because the worshipers, once they have been cleansed, have no longer any consciousness
of sins, 3 but [as it is they are being offered] every year with [the]
same remembrance of sins, 4 for the blood of bulls and goats is not
able to remove sins. 5 Therefore, coming into the world, he says:

> "Sacrifice and offering you did not desire. A body you furnished
> me; 6 in whole burnt offerings and sin offerings you took no
> pleasure."
>
> 7 Then I said: "Behold, I have come. In a division of [the]
> book it is written concerning me: '[I have come] to do your
> will, O God.' "

8 Above it says, "sacrifices and offerings," both "whole burnt
offerings and sin offerings, you did not desire nor delight [in
them]," which things are offered according to the law. 9 "Then,"
it said, "Behold, I have come to do your will." He removes the
first in order that he might establish the second. 10 In which will
we are being sanctified through the offering of [the] body of Jesus

Christ, once for all. 11 On the one hand, every priest stands every
day ministering and offering the same [kinds of] sacrifices many
times; these are never able to remove sins; 12 but he, on the other
hand, having offered one sacrifice on behalf of sins, "sat down at
the right hand of God" to perpetuity 13 [and] continues to wait
"until his enemies are placed [as] a footstool for his feet." 14 For
by means of one offering he perfected to perpetuity those who are
being sanctified. 15 The Holy Spirit also witnesses for us, following
the saying,

> 16 "This is the covenant which I will covenant [to them] after
> those days, says the Lord, After [I] have placed my laws on
> their hearts and on their minds I will write them; 17 and their
> sins [and their lawlessness acts] I will no longer remember."

18 Wherever [there is] forgiveness of these, [there is] no longer an
offering for sins.

Exhortation

Exhortation

19 Therefore, brothers, since we have [the] boldness [necessary]
for entering the holy [precincts] by means of the blood of Jesus,
20 which way he inaugurated for us [that is] new and living, through
the curtain, that is, his flesh, 21 and [since we have] "a great priest
over the house of God," 22 let us approach [the altar] with a true
heart in fullness of faith, [our] hearts sprinkled [clean] from evil
conscience and [our] body washed with clean water, [and] 23 let
us hold fast unmoved the confession of hope, for the one who has
promised is faithful. 24 Let us consider [how we] might stimulate
one another for love and good works, 25 not giving up meeting
together (as some have been doing), but encouraging [one an-
other], even the more so since you see the day drawing near.

Consequences of failure

26 For when we sin deliberately, after receiving the knowledge of
the truth, there is no longer left a sacrifice for sins, 27 but [the]
expectation of judgment and [the] burning of fire about to consume the opponents is something dreadful.

> 28 Anyone [who] has rejected the law of Moses will
> die without mercy

on the [testimony] of two or three witnesses;
29 how much worse punishment,
do you think, will he deserve, who (1) trampled
upon the Son of God,
(2) considered the blood of the covenant in
which he was sanctified, defiled,
and (3) depreciated the spirit of grace?
30 For we know the one who said, "Vengeance is mine; I will pay
back" and again, "The Lord will judge his people." 31 Falling into
the hands of [the] living God is dreadful.

Memory

32 Remember the earlier days in which, after you had become enlightened, you endured a great trial of sufferings, 33 sometimes
being exhibited both for insults and tribulations, and other times
becoming sharers of those who were thus upset; 34 for you suffered
with those in bonds, and you accepted with joy the confiscation of
your possessions, knowing that you yourselves have a better possession [that is] lasting. 35 Therefore do not cast off your boldness
which holds a great reward.

Brevity of waiting time

36 For you must have endurance so that, after you have done the
will of God, you may obtain the promise,
37 for still "how little, how little—the coming one will come and
not delay, 38 but my righteous one will live by faith, and if he
shrinks back, my soul does not take pleasure in him."
39 But we are not [in favor] of shrinking back for destruction,
but of faith for [the] acquisition of a soul.

COMMENT

APPOINTED BY GOD AND PERFECTED IN OBEDIENCE

5:1. The word rendered "offer" (*prospherē*) occurs 19 times in Hebrews. It is a term commonly used in the LXX in relationship to various kinds of sacrifices. It literally means to "bring toward," meaning to bring toward the altar. "Divine things," literally "the things related to God" (*ta pros ton theon*), are the sacrifices that are brought to the altar to be given to God as well as the services and the sacred precincts in and around the temple. The "gifts and sacrifices" offered for sins were the sin and guilt offerings. These were specified or determined by the priests. If a person of a certain financial ability committed a certain sin, he was obligated to offer a certain sacrifice so that the sin might be removed.

2. "To bear gently" (*metriopathein*) means "to moderate one's feelings," to empathize or sympathize. Josephus used this term to describe the generous and restrained attitude of Titus and Vespasian toward the Jews after the wars with the Jews were over (*Ant.* XII. 128). Philo used it and its cognates to describe Abraham's self-controlled grief at the death of Sarah (*Abr.* XLIV. 257) and Jacob's patience when afflicted (*Ios.* V. 26). Not all sins could be removed. "If a man said, 'I will sin and repent, and sin again and repent,' he will be given no chance to repent. [If he said], 'I will sin and the Day of Atonement will effect atonement,' then the Day of Atonement effects no atonement. For transgressions between man and God, the Day of Atonement effects atonement, but for the transgressions that are between man and his fellow, the Day of Atonement effects atonement only if he has appeased his fellow" (Yoma 8:8–9). Because the high priest was not authorized to atone for the sins of intent and malice, the author of Hebrews limited his gentle bearing to those who commit sins of ignorance and waywardness. These could be forgiven, and the high priest had an understandingly kind attitude toward those who made these mistakes, because "he himself" was "also clothed in weakness" and committed the same kind of misdemeanors.

3. Here as elsewhere, the author of Hebrews has shown his familiarity with Jewish customs and Old Testament scripture. The high priest was required on the Day of Atonement to offer a calf as an offering for his own sins and those of his family before he offered only a goat for the sins of all Israel (Lev 9:7–17; 16:6–19; Yoma 4:2–5:7).

4. Still considering the office of the high priest generally, the author noted that "no one takes the honor for himself." God calls men to that office, just as he commanded Moses, "Then bring near to you Aaron your brother, and his sons with him, from among the people of Israel, to serve me as priests" (Exod 28:1; see also Num 3:10; *Ant.* III. 188–92).

5–6. The qualifications that applied to any high priest applied just as well to Christ, and there are two Old Testament scripture passages to prove it. The first passage, quoted earlier (1:5), proved that Jesus was the Son, and as such, the Christ or the Messiah (Ps 2:7); the other passage showed that the Messiah was also a priest, "according to the order of Melchizedek" (Ps 110:4). These two Psalms were basic to the author for establishing the Sonship of Jesus (1:5–13).

At least from the time of Saul and Samuel, it had been customary for the high priest and the king to be different people, and some scholars trace the division of the priestly and administrative offices much earlier, even before there was a kingdom. From the time of Absalom's revolt on, the king was expected to be a son of David, and the high priest a descendant from Zadok. There were exceptional instances when the king also offered sacrifice. For instance, Saul offered sacrifice after Samuel delayed in coming to fulfill this function (I Sam 13:2–10). When the ark of the covenant was brought to Jerusalem, David danced before the Lord and offered burnt offerings and peace offerings (II Sam 6:14–18), but this may only mean that David had the priests offer these sacrifices. The same may be true of Solomon, who offered many burnt offerings on the altars of various high places before the temple was built (I Kings 3:3–4). By the time of the Hasmoneans, moreover, the normal expectation was that the nation would be restored with two leaders—a king from the line of David and a priest from the line of Aaron, or preferably Zadok.[1] In actuality, however, the Hasmoneans, who were levitical priests of the line of Aaron, but descended through Joarib, were neither sons of David nor of Zadok (Gen R. 97; 99:2). Nevertheless, they proved themselves capable of winning the war against the Syrians; so they gradually took over the roles both of priests and of kings. Of the first generation of Hasmoneans, only Simon was given an official rank. According to I Macc 14:41, "The Jews and the priests approved Simon's being leader and high priest for the age (*eis ton aiōna*) until a trustworthy prophet arose." The prophet was expected to announce the true anointed high priest from Zadok's line and the anointed king from David's line. Many Jews continued to think of the Hasmonean dynasty as a temporary measure, and the Hasmoneans had to begin with this understanding, but the pro-Hasmoneans called Simon also "prince of the people of God" (I Macc 14:27) as well as the anointed high priest. Although never anointed king, Josephus said of Simon's son John Hyrcanus I, "He was the only one to hold three offices [at once], rule of the nation, high priesthood, and prophecy" (*Wars* I.68). Hyrcanus' oldest son, Aristobulus I, was the first to assume the crown and openly claim to be both high priest and king (*Wars* I.70). By that time, many Jews accepted the Hasmonean rule as legitimate, but others still looked for another prophet and two messiahs, one of Zadok's line and one of David's. It was with this in mind that the restriction was placed on Simon's position.

The expression "for the age" meant the age or generation during which Simon lived. *Eis ton aiōna* is usually translated "forever," but in this instance, at least, it did not mean "forever," because a limit was set for the condition of his rule. When a faithful or trustworthy (*pistos*) prophet arose, Simon would stop being leader and high priest. An "age" was ordinarily considered temporally to be a period of about fifty years, a jubilee, or a generation in length, but this was not followed rigidly. Ages followed each other in temporal sequence; when an administration or time of fortune changed, the age changed, regardless of the length of time that had elapsed. The "age to come" would begin when the

[1] Zech 6:9–13; T. Reuben 6:7–12; T. Sim 5:4–6; T. Levi 8:1–17; T. Judah 21:1–5, 25; T. Iss 5:6–8; T. Naph 5:3–6; 6:6; T. Jos 19:11–12; 1QS 9:11; CDC 14:19. Num R. 4. 18:16 interpreted the two sons of oil (Zech 4:14) as Aaron and David. One would receive the priesthood and the other the kingdom.

current evil age ended (see COMMENT on 1:2). It was usually identified either with the messianic age which would come at "the end of days," when "this age" would be over, or it would be the age of peace that would follow the messianic age. Rabbis expected that the Messiah would come at the end of the age of oppression. He would drive out the oppressors and establish peace on the land. The sabbath age of rest, the renewal of the world, or the age to come would follow (San. 97a–b). The Messiah would not come without "birth pangs"—wars, hardships, oppression. Simon's rule came during the "birth pangs," and he ruled until there were signs of peace and "rest." He was anointed high priest and called prince of the people of God. Among his supporters, he was probably considered a messiah who had come at the "end of days" to restore Israel to her independence and permit the Jewish people to enter into their promised "rest."[2] His grandson was certainly accepted, at least publicly, as the anointed king, and later rabbis referred to the entire Hasmonean government as a kingdom (*mlkwt hšmwn'y*) (RH 18b). Simon was a high priest, as was his son and grandson, but the purists, like those reflected in the Habakkuk Commentary, could never be satisfied with a ruler who was not from David's line and a high priest that was not a son of Zadok.

According to Gen 14:18, Melchizedek was called "priest of the Most High God"; according to Ps 110, the enthroned person who would sit at the Lord's right hand was a "priest for the age according to the order of Melchizedek." There is quite a firm tradition that the Hasmoneans were to be identified with both of these passages. Rabbis called John Hyrcanus, "John, high priest of the Most High God" (*ywḥnn khn gdwl l'l 'lywn*) (RH 18b). Josephus also referred to John Hyrcanus as "high priest of the Most High God" (*archiereōs theou hypsistou*) (*Ant.* XVI. 163). According to Jub 32:1, Levi, from whom the Hasmoneans descended, dreamed that he had been ordained (*ordinatus*) priest of the Most High God, he and his sons, continuously for the age (*usque in saecula*). In I Macc 14:41 Simon was called a "priest for the age" with the apparent intention of identifying him with the hero (*kōhēn le'ōlām*) in that enthronement Psalm (Ps 110). This would be especially applicable since the one described in that Psalm may not have been called "king," but his activity was described as that of a king, and, like Simon, he was called "a priest for the age." Initially, Dahood's translation, "His legitimate king, my lord" (Ps 110:4), may have been correct,[3] but the tradition that identified Ps 110 with Gen 14 did not understand it that way. Hasmoneans were identified with both Ps 110 and Gen 14, which would have required Ps 110:4 to be rendered ". . . Melchizedek." Whether this was understood by the author of I Maccabees is not certain. That pro-Hasmonean author did not quote the pertinent line. It would have served his purposes to have Simon accepted as the Lord's legitimate king or to have had his priesthood

[2] CC, pp. 9–18.
[3] Dahood, III, 112–18.

justified on the basis of Melchizedek. The author of Hebrews, however, left no uncertainty. The Psalm that he related to Jesus was also attached to Gen 14 (Heb 7). Because the Hasmoneans did not fit the traditional expectation, they had to defend their position continuously. This was accomplished partly through the subtlety of the author of I Maccabees. He did not call Simon a king, but he quoted from an enthronement Psalm intended for a king and describing the activity of a king. An anti-Hasmonean did not feel the same way about the Hasmoneans. He called their leadership "iniquity in the holy of holies" (*impietatem ab sancto sanctitatis*) (Assump. Mos. 6:1; see also *Ant.* XIII. 372–76).

Similar conditions existed during the period when the author of Hebrews lived. Jesus was understood to have been a son of David, a messiah, and a royal pretender, but not a priest. The author wanted to interpret Jesus' role in terms of a priesthood and his death as a priestly sacrifice. Therefore he had to support his position rather defensively on the basis of scripture. He used two enthronement Psalms, one which called its hero "messiah" and "son," and the other that called him a priest. On the basis of these, he could offer an interpretation that was not traditional for Jesus, but one that was patterned somewhat according to the leadership of the Hasmoneans, who assumed both priestly and royal functions.[4]

Ps 110 and Ps 2 were quoted earlier to show that Jesus was to be a powerful king, since he was God's son (1:5, 13). Heb 5:6, however, was the first time the author justified Jesus' priesthood on the basis of Melchizedek's order.

7. Following Brandenburger[5] *eisakoustheis apo tēs eulabeias* is rendered "from his anxiety, was heeded." RSV renders the same Greek "he was heard for his godly fear." Without noting the relationship of this passage to Ps 116[114] and the balance of "from his anxiety" and "from death," this would be a reasonable translation; but in New Testament Greek *apo* with the genitive more frequently means "from" than "because of," and the allusion to the Psalm seems likely. Brandenburger was not the first, but he has presented a recent and cogent argument for interpreting this

[4] The "Davidic descent" of Jesus was not even "implied," as F. F. Bruce, "The Kerygma of Hebrews," *Interpretation* 23 (1969), 5, holds. Just as the Hasmoneans functioned even though they were not of the prescribed stock, so the author of Hebrews interpreted Jesus' role as if David and Zadok were not legitimate lines. Like the author of I Maccabees, who did not even discuss the legitimacy of the sons of Zadok as over against the Hasmoneans, so the author of Hebrews did not even mention a two-messiah doctrine. Bruce, ibid., p. 7, strains to show that, although not a Levite, Jesus fulfilled Israel's expectation as reflected in the Twelve Patriarchs, CDC, 1QS, 4Q Testimonia, Zechariah, and others.

[5] E. Brandenburger, "Text and Vorlagen von Hebr. V 7–10," *Novum Testamentum* 11 (1969), 190–224. Earlier arguments relating Heb 5:7 to Ps 116 are F. Bleek, *Der Brief an die Hebräer* (Berlin, 1840), p. 73; B. Weiss, *Kritisch exegetisches Handbuch über den Brief an die Hebräer* (Göttingen, 1888), 136a; E. Riggenbach, *Der Brief an die Hebräer* (Leipzig, 1922), 132A, 49; Schröger, pp. 120–22; and A. Ströbel, "Die Psalmengrundlage der Gethsemane-Parallel Hebr. 5:7 ff.," ZNTW 45 (1954), 252–66.

verse in relationship to LXX Ps 114[MT 116], which clarifies an otherwise difficult passage.

The worshiper in Ps 116 expected that the Lord would heed the voice of his prayer (Ps 116:1). He was encompassed by the snares of death (Ps 116:3), the pangs of Sheol; he suffered distress and anguish (Ps 116:3) The Lord responded and delivered his soul from death, his eyes from tears, his feet from stumbling (Ps 116:8).

Against this background, in an original thanksgiving hymn of the community, Heb 5:7 was composed as a praise to God as "the One who was able to save him" (i.e., Jesus) "from death." God had heeded the "loud cry and tears" of Jesus as, "in the days of his flesh," he "offered prayers and supplications" to God. God, then, "delivered him from death . . . and from his anxiety." Brandenburger's claim that this was originally composed as a confession to which the author of Hebrews had access is convincing. The confessional nature of this verse is suggested by the beginning attribution, "who . . . offered," which is similar to Philip 2:6, "Who, being in the form of God, did not consider . . ." and Col 1:15, "Who is an image of the invisible God." This is one of the few allusions to the life of Jesus in Hebrews (see also 7:14 and 13:12). These few are all used without clarifying historical events, but as bases for theological interpretations of doctrines.[6] The association of 5:7 with Ps 116 even makes the allusion to Gethsemane less important. The creed might have been written simply on the basis of Jesus' suffering, without any familiarity with the Gethsemane story itself, but it seems more likely that this also was a part of the suffering intended in the creed.[7]

8–9. Verses 8 and 9 evidently constitute a second confession which associated Jesus with the suffering servant of II Isaiah, as Brandenburger suggested. The liturgy confessed that Jesus "was a son," i.e. a king, who by his suffering had "been made perfect," and therefore became a source of eternal salvation for all those who obey him (*Spec.* I. 252). The "eternal salvation" mentioned in Isa 45:17 is provided to Israel by her Savior, Jehovah. The Lord promised to do this "for the sake of my servant Jacob, and Israel my chosen" (Isa 45:4). The servant Jacob was a man of sorrows and acquainted with grief (Isa 53:3); the Lord laid on him the iniquity of all Israel (Isa 53:6); it was the Lord's will to bruise him and put him to grief (Isa 53:10); he bore the sin of Israel, making intercession for the transgressors (Isa 53:12). For the author of II Isaiah, the servant constituted the generations of Jews that were cut off from Palestine and removed to, or born in, Babylon where the members suffered to perform enough merits to balance the books so that the rest of Israel, the second and third generations in Babylon,

[6] See E. Grässer, "Der historische Jesus im Hebräerbrief," ZNTW 56 (1965), 63–91.

[7] Among those who put a good deal of emphasis on Gethsemane in the interpretation of 5:7 are T. Lescow, "Jesus in Gethemane bei Lukas und im Hebräerbrief," ZNTW 58 (1967), 215–39; Ströbel, ZNTW 45 (1954), 252–66; Montefiore, pp. 97–98; and Vaughan, pp. 94–95.

might return to the promised land, "the land of life." The Jews who died in Babylon before the return became the cause of eternal salvation (Isa 45:17) for their posterity.[8]

For the author of Hebrews, however, Jesus, the Son and high priest, who had suffered like the servant in Babylon, "became a source of eternal salvation for all those who obey him." Just as Isa 45:4 claimed that the Lord would call the servant Jacob by name, so the author of Hebrews said that God had declared Jesus to be "a high priest according to the order of Melchizedek" (vs. 10).

10. Brandenburger correctly believed that there were two creeds in Heb 5:7–10, the first, 5:7, and the second, 5:8–10. It seems more likely that the second creed included only vss. 8 and 9. Heb 5:10 probably is an editorial comment made by the author of Hebrews, who put these two confessions together with the preceding Old Testament quotations, and concluded by using another Old Testament quotation from the main text of his message, Ps 110. He had already quoted this Psalm in 1:3, 13, and 5:6, and suitably quoted it again in 5:10, before moving doctrinally into the more specific discussion of this Psalm in 7:1 – 10:39.

Rabbis were not agreed upon the true meaning of Ps 110:4. R. Simon ben Gamaliel related it to Zech 4:14. The two olive trees, then, were the Messiah and Aaron, and the most beloved was the Messiah, because R. Gamaliel understood that he was the priest of the age, according to the order of Melchizedek (Yalqut HaMakiri on Ps 110; see also ARN 34). R. Joshua ben Korcha claimed that Ps 110:4 applied both to Abraham and to Moses, since both were kings and priests (Yalqut HaMakiri Ps 110:4). R. Berekiah said in the name of R. Isaac that the four craftsmen of Zech 2:3 were Elijah, the Messiah, Melchizedek, and the military messiah (Song of Songs R. 2.13.4).

The most important pre-Christian identification of Melchizedek with the Messiah was found on one of the scrolls of Cave 11 at Qumran. This document revealed the anticipation of a jubilee at the end of days for the "captives" (*l^{e}'aḥ^{a}]rīt hayyāmīm 'al š^{e}būyīm*), who were the sons of light and belonged to the lot of the heritage of Melchizedek (*minnaḥ^{a}lat Malkī ṣedeq; g]ōrāl Mal[kī] ṣedeq*). Melchizedek was expected to come to proclaim release to those captives (*ūq^{e}rā' lāhēmāh d^{e}rōr*) and atonement for their sins. This would happen in the year of the last jubilee (*bišnat hayyōbēl hā'aḥ^{a}[r]ōn*), which was the appointed time of favor for Melchizedek (*š^{e}nat hārāṣōn l^{e}Malkīṣedeq*). At that time God would judge his people and chasten those who showed favoritism to the wicked ones that belonged to the lot of Belial. When Melchizedek arose he would punish them on the day of vindication in the last days. This would

[8] The identification of the servant in Isaiah with the Jews who died in Babylon before an opportunity was available to return removes many difficulties prevalent in other theories. It allows for the servant both to be Jacob and to have a ministry for Israel. It is contingent on the identification of Palestine with the "land of life." For the views of other scholars and the defense of the land of life as Palestine, see CC, pp. 123–31.

fulfill the prophecy of II Isaiah, who foresaw one proclaiming good news and announcing peace to Zion. The herald of good news was not only the figure Melchizedek, but he was also the one who had been anointed by the spirit (*hamm^{e}baśśēr hū[' m^{e}]šîaḥ hārū[aḥ]*).

The Jewish author of this document identified Melchizedek with the Messiah, who was a warrior king destined to vindicate the chosen people against their enemies and free them from "bondage" to foreign powers. This function of Melchizedek compares very well with the king described in Ps 110, the Hasmoneans, and also the Son and high priest described in Hebrews, who was said to belong to the order of Melchizedek.

Without calling him a high priest or Melchizedek, the rabbis said that when the son of David came, people would lay an iron beam on his neck, so heavy that he would bow from its weight. He would weep and cry, "Lord of the age, how great is my strength; how strong is my life's spirit; and how strong are my limbs? Am I not flesh and blood? . . . My strength is as dry as a potsherd (Ps 22:16)." Then God replied, "Ephraim, my just Messiah, long ago you have taken it upon yourself, since the six days of creation. Now let your pain be as my pain, for since the day, since Nebuchadnezzer the wicked one, came up and destroyed my house and burned my temple and led my children into exile among the nations of the world, I have not returned to my throne" (PR 36, 162a).

Summary.—Heb 5:1–10 is a unit introducing the reader to Jesus, the high priest. It is marked by an inclusion using the key word, "high priest" (5:1, 10). Since this is a preamble or introduction to the main thesis of the document, the author's summarizing sentences use words that are significant to that section. These are "perfect" (5:9; 7:28), "salvation" (5:9; 9:28), and "Melchizedek" (5:10; 7:1). Before beginning that dissertation, however, the author interrupted his argument with further exhortations.

This unit was well organized. It began by listing qualities of high priests in general, and it followed with a presentation of the qualifications that shows that Jesus fitted these qualifications very well. The author supported his claims by using two of his basic quotations from the Psalms, followed by two small confessions of faith, which were probably well known in Christian circles of that time. He then concluded with a summarizing sentence that related all of this to his major text, Ps 110. At the end of the exhortation, he reintroduced this summary (6:20) before returning to the thesis introduced here.

Exhortation

5:11. "Concerning which" (*peri hou*), like the *pros hon* of 4:12, refers to that which was just said. Jesus was declared a high priest according to the order of Melchizedek (5:10). Even though the "message is extensive and difficult to interpret," the author did interpret it extensively in chapter seven, but first he interrupted his thesis for an exhortation to the readers who seem to "have become dull of hearing."

12. For many sects of Judaism and Christianity, there was a certain length of time allowed for moving from one degree of initiation to another. The first step was baptism, which probably required an initial training; then a more extensive and thorough training was required before full admission. There were unbaptized novices, baptized trainees, and full members. I John 2:12–17 referred to these degrees as "children" (*teknia* or *paidia*), "young men" (*neaniskoi*), and "fathers" (*pateres*). The "young men" needed the most exhortation, so that they would hold fast to the severe training required to become "fathers." Paul classified the new initiates as "infants" (*nēpioi*) (I Cor 3:1) and the advanced members as "perfect" (*teleioi*) (I Cor 2:6). The Essenes required one year of training before baptism and two more before becoming full members; the Community of the Rule required the same length of time. An early sect of Christians in Egypt, whose instructions for training and receiving members has been preserved, normally trained prospective members for three years; then the catechumens were baptized and received at once into full membership. If a catechumen (*katechoumenos*) was extremely zealous (*spoudaios*), however, he was allowed to advance more rapidly.[9] The Clementine Christians also baptized catechumens and received them into membership at once, but they required only a three-month training period. Hillel admitted members within sixty days. Shammai required thirty days for the first step and a year for the second.[10] No time is indicated for the training required for the readers of Hebrews, but, in the author's judgment, they were slow learners and had already taken a longer time than was customary. Had they been zealous, they could now have become "teachers," which was probably the same status as that which I John called "fathers." The ones Hebrews depreciatively called "infants" probably belonged to the same class as those I John referred to affectionately as "children," the difference being that the author of Hebrews addressed those who should no longer have been "infants." The author used the word "food" metaphorically to refer to teaching or doctrine. Those who continued mulling over elementary subjects were not yet weaned, academically.

13. The word rendered "unskilled" (*apeiros*) describes a person who lacks experience, is untried, or ignorant (see LXX Zech 11:15; Wis 13:18). The Shepherd of Hermas listed among the most important deeds a Christian should always do, "words of righteousness" (*hrēmata dikaiosynēs*) (*Mand.* 8:9). Hebrews considered those not weaned who did not even know what "the word of righteousness" (*logos dikaiosynēs*) was. They were unlearned, "unskilled," in this area.

14. The term "perfect" held a wide range of meanings, one of which described a person who was chronologically mature, no longer a minor,

[9] CC, p. 289. [10] Ibid., pp. 285–93.

an adult,[11] or a married person (*teleioi hoi gegamēkotes*).[12] "Perfect" also described a full member of a sect in good standing. Only those who walked perfectly (*wlhthlk lpnym tmym*) were admitted into the sect of the Rule (1QS 1:8). Although Paul spoke simply to the Corinthians, he said that he imparted wisdom to the "perfect" (*teleiois*) (I Cor 2:6). Paul compared the knowledge that was partial (*ek merous*) with that which was perfect (*teleion*) in the same way that he compared being an infant (*nēpios*) with being a grown man (*anēr*) (I Cor 13:10–11). He encouraged the Corinthians not to be children (*paidia*) in their thinking but to be "perfect" (*teleioi*) (I Cor 14:20). Those who had reached the stage of "perfect" manhood (*andra teleion*), religiously, were no longer "infants" (*nēpioi*) who could be carried about with every wind of doctrine (Eph 4:13–14). Paul considered it his task to make the word of God fully known, allowing even the Gentiles to know "the riches of the glory of this mystery," "teaching every man in all wisdom" so that every man might be "perfect" (*teleion*) in Christ (Col 1:25–28). Paul prayed that the Colossians might stand "perfect" (*teleioi*) and fully assured in all the will of God (Col 4:12). The concept of being grown-up in relationship to physical age and stature was used metaphorically to describe religious growth. The same was true of the expression "to discern good and evil." In New Testament times, "knowing good and evil" meant, first of all, having sexual intercourse, which usually came with adulthood, marriage, and other mature responsibilities. Thus when Adam and Eve ate of the tree of the knowledge of good and evil, Eve became pregnant and Adam had to work for a living.[13] When the children of Israel came to Kadesh-barnea, the Lord commanded them to go in and take the land (Deut 1:21). When they balked, the Lord swore, "Not one of these men of this evil generation shall see the good land which I swore to give to your fathers, . . ." (Deut 1:34–35). The promise to the future generation was as follows: "Moreover your little ones (*ṭapkem*) who you said would become a prey, and your sons (*b*ᵉ*nēkem*) who this day have no knowledge of good and evil (*ṭōb wārā'*), shall go in there, and to them I will give it, and they shall possess it" (Deut 1:39). According to Num 14:29–30 the same curse that Deut placed on the men who knew "good and evil" was placed on those "from twenty years old and upward." This is consistent with the description of the young man by the Rule of the Community (1QS 1:10–11): "He is fully twenty years of age when he knows good and evil." The "little one" was a child who had not passed his Bar Mitzwa—under thirteen years of age; the "son" was a Bar Mitzwa—between thirteen and twenty years of age; and the "man who knew good and evil" was twenty years of age or more.[14] Like the person who was "perfect," he was old enough to marry, pay taxes, provide sacrifices for the temple, bear arms, and in other ways

[11] Plato *Leges* 929c; Xenophon *Institutio Cyri* I.2.4, 12, 14; *Oxyrhynchus Papyrus* 485:30.

[12] Pausanias *Grammaticus,* Fragment 306.

[13] CC, pp. 174–76. [14] Ibid., pp. 181–82.

assume adult responsibilities. Since the one who had had sexual intercourse was expected to be married and an adult, the term "knowing good and evil" came to be an expression applied to adults or the age of adulthood.

The author of Hebrews was using these terms of human development metaphorically to describe the readers' development in faith. Knowing "good and evil" was the same as being "perfect" or having "their perceptions" adequately "trained."

6:1. "The beginning [teachings] of Christ" can be understood either as Christ's initial teachings (subjective genitive), or the beginning teachings *about* Christ (objective genitive). In favor of the subjective genitive is the reference to the salvation which had its beginning when it was spoken through the Lord (2:3). The things which Christ originally taught were undoubtedly important to early Christians,[15] but not as something to consider only elementary. The context suggests that these teachings are the earliest Christian teachings to which catechumens were exposed, and therefore would be the beginning teachings about Christ. "Let us carry on" (*pherōmetha*) literally means, "let us be carried" or "let us carry ourselves" along.

"Dead works" referred to the life Christians had lived before they were baptized into the community. "Dead" described those people who were outside of the covenant, living as other pagans. When a person entered the covenant, he passed from death to life, repented of the works he did as a pagan, and was baptized to cleanse him from this defilement. Once inside the covenant, he was alive and presumably did no more "dead works." After the fall of Jerusalem, IV Ezra reasoned that Israel's punishment must have come because of Adam's sin which every person repeated who married. Only those who practiced abstinence would shine like the stars. Others had faces blacker than darkness (7:125). "For how does it profit us if we are promised an immortal time (*immortale tempus*) since we really have done dead works" (*mortalia opera*).[16] According to IV Ezra, all those who married, like Adam and Eve, were expelled from the covenant, which is the same as the garden of Eden, where they could eat of the tree of "life." Once expelled, they were "dead," and all the works that they did were "dead works." Terms like "dead" and "alive" were used metaphorically not only by the rigid, monastic orders of Christianity; the frequency with which the author of Hebrews used terms that were common to communal sects tends to relate him in some way to such a group. "Faith in God," of course, was a basic belief for all Jews and Christians. The author insisted that without faith it is impossible to please God (11:6).

2. Commentators have objected to any suggestion that teaching of ablutions (*baptismōn didachēs*) could possibly refer to the levitical ablutions practiced by Jews. Stuart asked, "But what has the apostle to do here with

[15] For an impressive defense of "tou Christou" understood as a subjective genitive, see J. C. Adams, "Exegesis of Hebrews 6:1 f.," NTS 13 (1966–67), 378–85.

[16] CC, pp. 110–49.

Jewish ceremonial rites, as the first elements of *Christian doctrine?*" His answer is, "Plainly nothing; so that this exegesis cannot be admitted."[17] Turner explained just as defensively, "I can see no probability that the author intended any union of such merely external washings with fundamental principles of Christianity."[18] More recently, Montefiore also refused to entertain the possibility that this meant Old Testament ablutions, but, observing the plural, deduced that "it must refer to second baptisms for those first baptized by John (Acts 19:5–6)."[19] Michel left the question unanswered,[20] but Moffatt thought that ablutions probably continued among some groups of Christians, even though others objected to them.[21] Moffatt was right on this score. Justin's attack on these practices would have been unnecessary if they had not existed (*Apol.* I. 62). Members of the Clementine sect, who had already been baptized, were still obligated to keep other purity rules, eating only with those who had been baptized, eating only food approved by dietary laws, washing after intercourse, refraining from intercourse during a woman's menstrual period, and, for women, observing the law of purification.[22] To be sure, there was only one baptism for admission into the community, but among Jewish Christians, at least, continual observance of levitical laws was basic to their code of ethics. The author of Hebrews and his original readers seem to have belonged to some such group. "Laying on of hands" was a practice sometimes associated with the reception of the Holy Spirit for new initiates (Acts 8:17–19). The doctrine of the "resurrection of [the] dead ones" was prominent in Judaism as early as Maccabean times. It seemed a reasonable extension of Deuteronomic justice. Pious Jews, who were willing to fight and die so that the nation might live and so that other Jews would receive the promise to live on the promised land, believed that those who died in the faith would be raised, after the land was freed from foreigners, and allowed to receive their reward of living on the same land under the conditions for which they fought and died. This was not a belief that they would never again cease breathing and become corpses, but that they could finish out their years on the only land where "life" was possible—Palestine. After the death of Christ, early Christians believed that Jesus had himself been raised, taken into heaven, and that he would return to the promised land. At that time, the ones who had "died in Christ" (i.e. as Christians) would be raised to be with him on the promised land. When he had failed to return after many years, several varying interpretations were given. One of these was reported by Eusebius (*HE* X.iv.11–12, who understood Constantine's victory and the establishment of Christianity as the religion of the state, as the "resurrection of the dead." In praise to Jesus, he said, "the only unique One, the all-good Son of the all-good Father," for whom the Father "saved us,

[17] Stuart, p. 139.
[18] Turner, p. 71.
[19] Montefiore, p. 106.
[20] Michel, pp. 145–46.
[21] Moffatt, p. 75.
[22] *Hom.* VIII.viii; XI.xxviii, xxx, xxxii; *Recog.* I.xix, liv; II.lxxii; VI.xi; VII.xxix.

when we were not only sick or afflicted by terrible sores and wounds already decayed, but we were also lying among the dead; . . . [this he did when we] were not just half dead (*hēmithnētas*), but even in tombs and graves, completely loathsome and stinking, raising [us] up (*analabōn*); as of old, so also now."[23]

"Judgment of [the] age" (*krimatos aiōniou*) is a court term. To judge means to divide, separate, or decide. The judge separates the guilty from the innocent; he decides which of the accused deserve release and which deserve punishment. In Jewish sabbatical eschatology, covenanters believed that God would hold a court session in which the Gentiles and Israel might offer their complaints against each other. At that time, which would be the end of the evil age when the Gentiles ruled, Israel would be vindicated and released, freed from guilt as at jubilee. From that time on, Israel would rule. That would be the age to come, the new age (see *Hom.* XX.ii). "The judgment of the age" was the turning point in Israel's history. The division would be made between the innocent convenanters and the guilty heathen. Early Jews and Christians were able to face oppression and death for their behavior without denying their traditional heritage because they were confident that this judgment would take place. Jesus promised that, at the end of the age (Matt 24:3), the Son of man would enter into his glory, which would be his position as king over the promised land. Then all nations would be gathered before him to learn how he would treat them. Those who helped him or any of his supporters to bring him into this position of power would inherit the kingdom, which meant entering into "life of the age" (Matt 25:31–46). Those who resisted him or did nothing to help him went away into punishment "of the age" (Matt 25:31–46) or were cast into outer darkness (Matt 25:14–30). Uncooperative cities, like Chorazin and Bethsaida, would receive worse punishment than Tyre and Sidon, the pagan cities, or Sodom, which God destroyed (Matt 11:20–24). Belief in this doctrine was elementary to the Christians to whom the author of Hebrews wrote.

3. The fear of resisting God was offset, then as today, by stating what would happen in the future "if God is willing." The Hebrew *'im yirṣeh 'ᵃdōnāy*, the Arabic *'inša 'allā*, the Latin *deo volente* (d.v.), and the German *Gott willig* are all frequent in Jewish, Moslem, and Christian usage. James cautioned his readers against saying, "Today or tomorrow we will go into such and such a town and spend a year there and trade and get gain," since no one knows about tomorrow (James 4:13–14). "Instead you ought to say, 'If the Lord wills, we shall live and we shall do this or that'" (James 4:15). To do otherwise would be arrogant (James 4:16). Paul told the Corinthians, "For I hope to remain with you some time, if the Lord permits" (I Cor 16:7).

4. "Once" (*hapax*) was an important word to the author. The high priest entered the holy of holies *once* a year (9:7); Jesus offered himself as a sacrifice *once* (9:26, 28); men die but *once* (9:27); if worshipers had *once*

[23] CC, pp. 321–26.

been cleansed, they would no longer have a consciousness of sin (10:2). The author quoted the Old Testament promise that the Lord would shake heaven and earth *once* more (12:26); this "once more" indicated to the author the removal of the things that could be shaken so that the things that could not be shaken might remain (12:27). This was not only true of Hebrews, however. I Peter 3:18 said Christ died for our sins *once,* and Jude told his readers about the faith which was *once* delivered to the saints (3), and he reminded them that they had *once* been informed (5). The author of Hebrews also used a more emphatic word for "once" (*ephapax*) several times (7:27; 9:12; 10:10; see also I Cor 15:6). His emphasis in 6:4 is for the readers who had "once been enlightened."[24]

Enlightenment is a term frequently used for instruction. Thus the teachers are "those who make shine" (*maśkilīm*) (Dan 12:3), and the covenanters are called "children of light" (*b^enē 'ōr*) in some of the Dead Sea scrolls (1QM and 1QS). Justin Martyr said baptism is called illumination because those who learn these things are illuminated in their minds (*Apol.* I.61; see also I.65 and *Dial.* 122). The author encouraged the readers to remember the earlier days just after they had become enlightened (*phōtisthentas*). "Enlightenment" probably meant the catechism required for baptism. Therefore Justin could identify the two, and the Syriac text of 6:4 could read "those who have once descended for baptism" (*hānōn daḥdā z^eban l^ema'mūdītā n^eḥetū*) for "those who have once been enlightened."

"The heavenly gift" may have been the common meal, sometimes called the holy meal (*sanctus*) (*Recog.* III.lxvii), to which sectarians were admitted as a final step of initiation.[25] Also associated with membership initiation was the reception of the Holy Spirit, which occurred either at baptism or later, perhaps when new members had the hands of full members laid upon them. At that time they became "sharers of the Holy Spirit." In some groups, like the Essenes and the sect governed by the Rule of the Community (1QS), members also shared all material possessions with one another (Acts 4:32–37).

5. When dealing with the heavenly gift (vs. 4), that which was tasted was probably the communal meal, but "tasted" is used metaphorically in vs. 5 to mean "sampled" or "had been introduced to," as Josephus used the term in reference to those who had once tasted (*hapax geusamenois*) (*Wars* I.158) the Essene philosophy (see also Ps 34:8; 119:103; Job 34:3; I Peter 2:3; Matt 16:28). "The good word of God" (*kalon . . . theou hrēma*) refers to God's favorable promise. In the Old Testament this sometimes refers to the promise that God would give the Israelites the land of Canaan. After the Lord had given the Hebrews rest on every side, the claim was made that not one word fell from all the good word(s) (*haddābār haṭṭōb*) which the Lord had spoken to the house of Israel (Josh 21:44–45). Every good word which the Lord had spoken had come to pass

[24] See A. Winter, *APAX EPHAPAX im Hebräerbrief,* Rome, 1960.

[25] CC, pp. 285–92; Spicq, II, 150. Williamson summarized the differing views of many scholars on the meaning of "heavenly gift."

for Israel (Josh 23:14–15). Jeremiah said that after the Jews had served their seventy-year sentence in Babylon, the Lord would fulfill his good word (*dᵉbārī haṭṭōb*) to return them to Judah (Jer 29:10; also 33:14). The author of Hebrews probably had the same "good word" in mind, which the readers had only "tasted" (*geusamenous*). They were just on the verge of receiving the promised heritage. If they only would hold out and not make the same mistakes that the exodus generation had made, they might receive it in full. The sacrifice and ascension of Jesus constituted just a foretaste that the promise would soon be fulfilled.

When II Isaiah announced the good news that the Jews in Babylon would be released to return to Zion, he told of the miracles that would be performed to enable every faithful Jew to return. These would be the kind of miracles performed in the wilderness to sustain the Israelites until they entered their promised land (Isa 35:5–10; 43:15–20; 44:3–4; 49:1–13; *et passim*). They were a foretaste of the good things to come. Since miracles accompanied the Israelites between Egypt and the entrance into the promised land, and since they were promised to the Jews between Babylon and the promised land, Jews of New Testament times assumed that miracles would accompany the new entrance into the promised land. "The coming age" (*mellontos aiōnos*) was the same as "the world to come" (2:5). This was the time when "the good word of God" would be received in full. The miracles (*dynameis*) had been performed in the midst of the readers. They had "tasted" them, but like "the good word of God," the age to come had not fully come.

6. Although the proximity of the promise which the author gave was very encouraging, it was conditional. Those who "have fallen by the wayside," after they have been initiated into the community and received its benefits, are then guilty and cannot be pardoned. It is impossible (6:6) "to renew again for repentance." This is consistent with the author's doctrine of repentance and atonement.

In addition to "foreclosures" and consequent "releases" on sabbath and jubilee years, Israel's doctrine of forgiveness and reconciliation with God was related to the Day of Atonement. On that day an Israelite could be forgiven his sins against God, but only on the following conditions: (a) that he repent of his sins; (b) that he be reconciled with his fellow Israelite against whom he had sinned; and (c) that he bring the proper sin and guilt offerings to the altar on the Day of Atonement to pay for his sins against God. Against this doctrine, the instruction of Jesus makes sense: "So if you are offering your gift at the altar, and there remember that your brother has something against you, leave your gift there before the altar and go; first be reconciled to your brother, and then come and offer your gift" (Matt 5:23–24). The gift would have had no atoning effect unless the covenanter was first reconciled to his brother. Paul understood that Jesus was the sin offering made for Israel's sins on the Day of Atonement. Like Micah, Paul knew that God could not be appeased with "thousands of rams, with ten thousands of rivers of oil" (Micah 6:7). Since Israel could not provide a gift large enough to meet the required conditions, God took the initiative: he it was who "through Christ reconciled us to himself and gave us the ministry (*diakonia*) of reconciliation; that is, God was in Christ (i.e. in the body of Christ, the church), reconciling the world to himself, not counting their trespasses against them, and entrusting to us the reckoning (*logos*) of reconciliation" (II Cor 5:18–19). The sin offering that God required, according to Paul, was met by the sacrifice of Christ. Christians were still left to meet the other two requirements: (a) repentance and (b) reconciliation with one another. Therefore, Paul said Christians were given the ministry of reconciliation. It was because the Colossians had been made alive by God's grace when he forgave their accumulated debt of sin that Colossians were required to forgive one another and be patient with each other (Col 3:13). This was necessary to make atonement complete. Paul rejoiced in his own sufferings in behalf of the Colossians by which he filled up that which was lacking of the tribulations of Christ (Col 1:24–25). The author of Hebrews, however, argued that Jesus' offering of himself once for all (*ephapax*) (7:22–28) was adequate. Since this was true, the merits which were added by that sacrifice could be used once, but no more. Once a Christian had been forgiven, there were no further sacrifices possible to build up the treasury of merits upon which one might draw. Therefore there could be no further backsliding followed by forgiveness. Since the sacrifice of Christ was enough to cover all the sins committed before belief, no further sacrifice was available for additional sinfulness (6:1–12).[26] Therefore the author made no attempt to suggest that the readers relearn the doctrine, if it had been forgotten. They were not given a chance to start all over again. "After they have fallen by the wayside," those who had once accepted the responsibility of covenanters had utilized the benefits of Christ's sacrifice. They could not again crucify Jesus and make "a public example of the Son of God for themselves."[27]

The author of Hebrews was not the only sectarian who believed there was a limit to forgiveness. The Shepherd of Hermas held that sins committed before baptism would be forgiven, but that there would be no second forgiveness (*Mand.* IV.iii; see also *Vis.* II.ii and *Sim.* VI.ii). For Gentiles the opportunity for repentance would continue until the last day, but for the saints, forgiveness had reached its limit (*Vis.* II.ii; *Mand.* IV.iii). Those baptized should always thereafter live in purity (*Mand.* IV.iii; XII.iii; *Sim.* V.vii). If they erred in this way, they would be cast out of the society of the righteous and condemned to eternal death (*Mand.* XII.iii; *Sim.* VI.ii; VII; VIII.vi, viii; IX.xiii, xiv, xvii, xviii). Being condemned to "death" meant excommunication from the society where alone "life" was possible. The Johannine sect counseled that if one of the brothers saw another sin, he could pray and God would give him "life," which probably meant that his sin would be forgiven and he could be retained within the

[26] CC, pp. 226–40.

[27] For a defensive attempt to soften and justify the meaning of the author's clear statement, see Spicq, II, 167–78. Also, but with less distortion, Bruce, pp. 122–25.

community (I John 5:16–17). This would be true, however, only if it was a sin "not to death" (*hamartia ou pros thanaton*). Sins that were "to death" (*pros thanaton*) could not be forgiven by intercessory prayer (I John 5:16–17). This probably meant that the unforgiven sectarian was excommunicated from the covenantal community where "life" was possible. The sect of St. Matthew had special rules by which a sinner was invited to repent of his sin, but if he refused even after he was tried before the church, he was treated as a Gentile and a tax collector (Matt 18:15–17). This meant he was excommunicated.

Many sectarians believed blasphemy against God or sacred rites was a sin for which there was no forgiveness. According to Matt 12:31–32, a person who said a word against the Holy Spirit could not be forgiven either in this age or in the age to come (see also Gospel of Thomas 88:26–30). The rule of the later church followed Matthew and decreed: "Those who blaspheme the spirit of grace and despise the gift from it, *after grace* [italics mine], for them there will be no forgiveness, neither in this age nor in the age to come" (*Apos. Cons.* 6:18). The sect of the Rule decreed: "Whoever swears (*yzkyr*) by the Name which is honored over every name . . . either for fear of persecution or for any other reason whatever, shall be separated [from the community] and not allowed to return again" (1QS 6:27 – 7:2; see also 7:16–17, 21–24). The Zadokites ruled as follows: "[Let him not] swear either by *Aleph* and *Lamed* (*'El, 'Elōhīm*) or by *Aleph* and *Daleth* (*'Adōnāy*), except for oaths of enrollment [which are taken] with the curses of the covenant. If he swears by the curses of the covenant before the judges and then transgresses, he is guilty; and [even] if he confesses and repents, they will not forgive him" (CDC 15:1–4).

Josephus held that Essenes caught in grievous sins (*ep' axiochreois hamartēmasan*) were cast out of the community and usually died horrible deaths, because they were bound by oath to abstain from eating food not prepared under Essene supervision. They were forced to eat grass and famish with hunger until physical death (*Wars* II.viii.143–44). Early sectarians lived in such closely segregated communities that excommunication was called "death" and sometimes really meant physical death as well as religious death. Those who remained within the community had to be forgiven. If no further forgiveness was possible, they had to be extremely careful not to sin.[28] According to the Sybil, God's wrath would come down from heaven upon his people to exact just retribution. In advance he would send a savior so that the saints would have a chance to repent. This meant that they could repent up until then, but afterward it would be too late (*kai metanoian echēt' apo nun, kai mēketi mēden*) (*SO* 1:165–68). II Baruch said that after the appointed time, there would be no duration of the hours, change of ways, place for prayer, sending of petitions, receiving knowledge, giving love, place for repentance of the soul, supplication for offenses, intercession of the fathers, prayer of the prophets, or help of the righteous (85:12). The author of Hebrews demanded the same kind of rigid

[28] CC, pp. 229–33.

ethics of his readers that other sectarians expected.[29] He warned them that they should not have an evil heart of unbelief nor allow themselves to become hardened by the deceitfulness of sin. As a consequence no one of the members would dare to sin (3:13; see also Aboth 5:18; Yoma 87a; San. 107b).

7–8. As an analogy to the person who once accepted the responsibilities of membership in the community and then became apostate, the author of Hebrews compared the good condition of the land as God originally created it with the cursed condition under which Adam had to cultivate it after he had sinned. The pertinent verses are these:

"And the land produced vegetation, plants producing
seed after their kind and
fruit-bearing trees whose seed was in the fruit,
after their kind.
And God saw that it was good (Gen 1:12).
"Cursed be the ground because of you
with toil you shall eat of it all the days of
your life,
thorns and thistles it will produce for you (Gen 3:17–18).

The land, which is blessed abundantly and has received a good deal of rain, is expected to produce "vegetation." When this happened, God was pleased, for the result was good. The land did not deserve credit for all that it had produced, because it could not have done so if it had not drunk "the rain which comes upon it many times." But if, after it had received so much rain as this, it produced only "thorns and thistles," then something had happened to the land. Between Gen 1:12 and 3:18, God had cursed the ground. Land that produces weeds is later burned off to destroy the weeds, so the end of such land is "burning."

Analogous to this is the member who becomes apostate. He cannot return and repent. He has to remain faithful all of the time if he expects to receive the reward of the faithful. Just as Adam was expelled from the garden where "life" was possible, the member was excommunicated from the community where "life" was possible. For neither Adam nor the member of the sect to which the author belonged was there a second chance. "The Lord placed the cherubim with a flaming sword which turned every way, to guard the way to the tree of life" (Gen 3:24). Ben Sirach's analogy is not so harsh: "He who washes after [contact with] a dead body and touches it again, what did he gain by bathing? So a man [who] fasts for his sins and does the same again, who will listen to his prayer?" (Sir 34[31]:25–26; see also JTaan. I. 63d, 64a).

9. This is the author's first note of affection for his readers. It is the only time he called them "beloved." Although he was basically severe and de-

[29] There is no textual or traditional support for Spicq's (I, 57–58) view that the impossibility was only because of the apostate's unwillingness to repent. Like Esau, he could not return even if he wept to show his earnest desires.

manding, the author also knew how to mingle his warnings with assurance and encouragement, and on this one occasion he seemed tender.

10. "Work and love" do not belong in separate categories, as if one involved activity and the other feeling. In biblical times, when "love" was used in a contractual framework, it referred to responsibility under contract. Therefore sectarians were commanded to love all the sons of light and hate all the sons of darkness (1QS 1:9–10). The sons of light were the members who had brought into the community all of their knowledge, ability, and wealth to share in common with other sectarians (1QS 1:11–12). A man should be either loved or hated according to his spirit, which meant either accepted or rejected from the community "according to the cleanness of his hands" (1QS 9:15–16). These segregated sectarians were warned that love for the world meant enmity with God (James 4:4). Those who loved the world had no love for the Father (I John 2:15). People either chose to love darkness and therefore became sons of darkness or they chose light and became sons of light (I John 2:9–11, 19). Those who joined the sect passed from death to life because they loved the brothers (I John 3:14). Those who joined the group accepted the responsibilities of membership which involved loving one another. In communal groups this meant sharing materially and caring for one another in very practical ways. Those who continued in love provided hospitality for traveling sectarians (Heb 13:2). Because of Philemon's love, Paul could impose sanctions on him and demand that he release Onesimus (Philem 9). Members of covenant communities could be commanded to love. This was not a new custom of New Testament times. Joshua encouraged the Hebrews to love the Lord their God (Josh 23:11). Deuteronomy commanded them to love the Lord their God with all their heart, soul, and might (Deut 6:5), and also instructed them to keep the Lord's charge, his statutes, his ordinances, and his commandments always (Deut 11:1), which apparently meant the same as loving God (see also Ps 31:24[23]). Israelites were not to take vengeance against other covenanters (Lev 19:18) but they were to love even the stranger who sojourned in their land (Lev 19:33–34). The Lord commanded Hosea to go love a woman (Hosea 3:1). In response Hosea bought a woman for fifteen shekels of silver and a homer and a lethech of barley, and made her dwell with him under his jurisdiction (Hosea 3:2–3). No mention was made of any affection in relationship to this act of redemption, and that is part of the point. In the same way Israel could count on the Lord to fulfill his covenant to "love" Israel, even though his feelings toward her were sometimes negative. He would act according to his obligation to love. In the same way Hosea loved the woman as he had been commanded, by providing for her needs. The commandment to love the neighbor as oneself summarized other commandments relating to the neighbor. The corner of the field and part of the fruit crop must be left for him; his property must not be stolen; and he must not be cheated in business or overworked. He must be paid his wages day by day, and he must not be abused or injured. He must be judged fairly. All of this is involved in "loving" the neighbor (Lev 19:9–18). Christians were

reminded that the greatest love required giving up one's "life" (*psychē*) for his friends (John 15:12–13). They were told that they, like Jesus, should lay down their lives (*psychai*) for their brothers. This probably meant giving up existence in the world, such as job, family, and position, to join the sect where the new member shared all his possessions with other members of the sect, just as Jesus had done before them (see II Cor 8:9). This meant following Jesus' example *before* the crucifixion.[30] It meant loving the neighbor as oneself. By losing his secular existence (*psychē*) he found his life (*zōē*) and became one of the *beloved*.

Because wives had no right to own property or control money, they had no substance to share or with which to be loving; Paul commanded them to be subject to their husbands, who, in turn, were commanded to love their wives (Col 3:18–19; Eph 5:25, 28, 33). These admonitions did not apply to the feelings wives and husbands should have toward one another, but rather to the treatment that should be expected of them.

God loved the world and gave his Son (John 3:16). He loved the Son and gave all things into his hand (John 3:35). God's love was poured into the hearts of believers through the Holy Spirit which God gave them. (Rom 5:5). The Son of God loved covenanters and gave himself for them (Gal 2:20; Eph 5:2). Numerous other biblical references show that love was very closely related to work, serving, giving, being responsible, and providing. Some lovers were nations with whom there were treaties guaranteeing support in time of war. Of course it was possible to have fond feelings toward the one loved, but the importance of "love" in early Christian communities was its relationship to "work," which could be "demonstrated for his name."[31]

The specific way in which the readers demonstrated love for his name was in ministering "to the saints." Particularly in celibate communities, ministering to saints was very important. In the ancient Near East there was no social security program or pension plan to care for people in their old age. The main insurance a person had against neglect and starvation in his old age was the provision he could expect from his children. Therefore children were commanded to honor their parents, which command involved provision for old age (Exod 20:12; Mekilta *Baḥodesh* 8:1–3; *Decal.* XXIII. 116–18). Members of a monastic order, deprived of children, would be neglected in their old age and during periods of illness if the community had not made other plans to fulfill the needs otherwise met by members of the family. By pooling their funds and agreeing to work to care for each other, members could live to a comfortable and prosperous old age (*Hyp.* XI. 4–5; *Prob.* IX. 86–87; see also *Ant.* XVIII.20–22; *Wars* II.122; and *Philos.* IX.iv.19). This was part of the "work and love" that was called ministering to the saints. Another aspect was hospitality shown to visiting saints.

[30] For an examination of Jesus' relationship to wealth and communal, celibate groups, see "Jesus and the Upper Class," *Novum Testamentum* 8 (1964), 195–209.

[31] CC, pp. 293–308.

According to Philo, no Essene called his house his own in the sense that he was free to exclude other Essenes, but the door was open to visitors from other places who shared his convictions (*Prob.* ix. 85). This means that those who could be trusted to keep the same tithing, heave offering, dietary, and purity regulations could make demands on their hospitality. Josephus said that Essene customs permitted them to travel without taking any provisions except weapons as protection against brigands, but that in every city an appointed person was responsible for providing visiting Essenes with clothing and other necessities (*Wars* II. 125). Hippolytus added that the person assigned to care for traveling Essenes did so from a fund provided for that purpose (*Philos.* IX.iv.20).[32] Early Christians observed some of the same practices. According to Matthew the twelve were sent out without gold, silver, or copper in their belts, no bags, no sandals, and with only one tunic each. They were told: "And whatever town or village you enter, find out one who is worthy (*axios*) in it, and stay with him until you depart. As you enter the house, salute it, for if the house is 'worthy,' let your peace come upon it; but if it is not 'worthy' let your peace return to you" (Matt 10:11–13). It was in view of this kind of hospitality program that disciples were assured that they could ask, seek, and knock, and be sure that their needs would be met (Matt 7:7). It was the traveling missionaries who depended upon the hospitality of other sectarians who were taught to pray, "Give us today our daily bread" (Matt 6:11). It was itinerant disciples who were told not to lay up for themselves treasures on earth (Matt 6:19). Those saints who were not itinerant, who kept supplies on hand to provide for the traveling missionaries, had to lay up treasures on earth, however, or the whole program would have broken down. This provision was called "love" or ministering to the saints. This kind of ministry could not be taken for granted. Diotrephes was scolded because he not only turned away strangers who came asking for hospitality, but he prevented others from receiving them as guests (III John 9–10). This did not mean that the community was required to accept all guests, but the ones Diotrephes turned away were those who had been sent out under approved levitical standards (*axiōs tou theou*) (III John 5–6). They were so careful in their habits that they refused to eat food offered by Gentiles. Therefore sectarians were obligated to provide for them (III John 7–8).[33]

In addition to caring for the sick and elderly and providing hospitality for traveling sectarians, a third way of ministering to the saints involved providing financial support to those in Jerusalem who were dependent upon contributions from the diaspora for their livelihood (Rom 15:25; II Cor 8:4; 9:1). The readers to whom the author of Hebrews wrote were meritorious in one or more of these respects. Therefore they were assured that the better things of the salvation that was coming would be theirs (6:9).

11. The Greek term rendered "fulfillment" is *plērophorian* which comes from the verb *plērophorein,* meaning "to bring in full, to fulfill, or to satisfy"; but Vaughan is correct in his insistence that there is nothing in the

[32] CC, pp. 246–48.
[33] CC, pp. 275–82.

derivation to suggest conviction or assurance, as the RSV translates it.[34] Furthermore "full assurance of hope" (RSV) does not make much sense. People do not become convinced or assured of a hope. If they hope, they have some assurance. But those who had tasted the heavenly gift, shared in the Holy Spirit, and tasted the miracles of the coming age (6:4–5) might be zealous toward the "fulfillment" or satisfaction of the "hope" that the good word of God would be completely realized (6:4–5). The author's reassurance carries with it his more important message of stressing the serious nature of their religious task. The believers must "show forth" "zeal" to the "end."

12. Verse 12 is a connective sentence, preparing the reader for the next topic of discussion, the promise given to Abraham and the basis for the hope discussed above.

Summary.—The author began this literary unit by accusing his readers of being "dull" and formed an inclusion by urging at the close that they not let themselves "become dull." In between were accusations and assurances, all organized into a pattern. The author accused the readers of staying in kindergarten and listed the concepts related to elementary religious development. He compared this depreciatively with milk for unweaned infants, and urged them to grow up. Like Paul he encouraged them to put away childish things (I Cor 13:11–12). In addition to his analogy of milk and solid food, he compared them to the land that produces weeds and thistles, deserving only to be burned. The entire unit was exhortative. It began with accusation and urgency and concluded with reassurance and urgency. The promise was great; the opportunity was endless; it would be foolish to become lackadaisical, as the readers seemed to be doing. The inclusion was followed by a typical statement introducing the reader to the topic to follow which included the following catchwords to be discussed in the next section: "promise" (6:13), "heirs" (6:17), "hope" (6:18).

The promises of God

13. The occasion for this "promise" followed Abraham's willingness to offer his only son, Isaac, to God as a sacrifice. God prevented the execution of his intent, and at that time "swore by himself" (Gen 22:16) that he would bless Abraham and multiply his seed. For the oath formula see the COMMENT on 3:11.

14–15. The quotation is from LXX Gen 22:17, with no significant variants except that the quotation stops with "multiply." The author has changed the object from "your seed" to "you." The promise came to Abraham "after he had suffered patiently" (*makrothymēsas*) in his willingness to sacrifice Isaac. The emotional torture which Abraham suffered has been eulogized extensively, both in Jewish and in Christian literature. This suffering was considered meritorious enough to have motivated God

[34] Vaughan, p. 112.

to offer the promise and oath on which an important element of Jewish and Christian faith is based. That which Abraham "received" (*epetychen*), achieved, obtained, or acquired was the "promise"—not its fulfillment, which the author claimed was still pending in his day.

16–17. The Greek word for "imposed" is *emesiteusen,* which means to act the part of a mediator. Josephus told of an occasion when the Israelites took an oath, invoking God as the mediator (*mesitēn*) (*Ant.* IV. 133). In this case, however, God acted as his own mediator.

It was customary in biblical times to assume that God functioned according to the customs and practices that were common to Near Eastern society. When there was an argument, one member of the discussion might take an oath, imposing certain curses upon himself if he were not telling the truth (*Spec.* II. 10). After this there could be little question about his veracity, because it was assumed that God would fulfill the curses upon him if he were lying. So fearful were Near Easterners of the curses that they often left them unexpressed, even though they were understood. Since this was the custom, "when God wanted very much to show the heirs of the promise," namely Abraham's seed (Gen 22:17),[35] "the unchangeableness of his will, he imposed an oath [on himself]." This was intended to convince "the heirs" that they had no need for anxiety about God's intention.

Philo and the author of Hebrews agreed on God's reason for swearing by himself. "For, indeed, concerning the perfect Abraham, he spoke in this manner; 'By myself I have sworn,' says the Lord . . . You see that God swears by no other, for there is nothing better than he, but [he swears] by himself, who is the best of all" (*LA* III. 203; see also III. 204, 207; cf. *Abr.* 273).

18–19. The "two unchangeable things" are the promise and the oath. Philo agrees in his understanding of Gen 22:16–17: "It is good that he confirmed the promise by an oath, and by an oath proper for God" (*LA* III. 203). God's promise itself would be "unchangeable" without the oath, but the two together gave covenanters confidence.

The word translated "have recourse" is *kataphygontes,* literally, "fleeing ones." RSV renders it "have fled for refuge," but that does not clarify the message. This verb, in relationship to an oath, can mean "have recourse" in the sense that the people who flee to an oath are the ones who can gain support from it, count on it, make a legal claim against it. The Christians are the ones who can draw on the promise as affirmed with an oath. This provides a strong motivation to take advantage of "the hope" that this promise would be fulfilled in their days, as the author led them to believe. The quotation varies a little from LXX Lev 16:2. Instead of

[35] Dealing with this heritage, Eusebius referred to the heirs as "heirs of the kingdom" (*tois klēronomois tēs basileias*) (*Demonstration Evangelica* V. 3 [PG 368]), showing the close affinity of the kingdom or the land to the promise in early Christian understanding. Delitzsch, II, 310, mistakenly assumed that all Christians believed that *hā'āreṣ* (Gen 12:7; 24:7) meant the whole earth.

eisporeuesthō, "Let him [not] enter," Hebrews has *eiserchomenēn,* "entering." The LXX has *to hagion esōteron,* "The *holy* innermost place." The author either used a different text or chose to omit this word, but the context requires that the place be understood as the holy of holies. The LXX passage refers to the conduct of Aaron on the Day of Atonement. The author's reason for quoting this passage was in continuation of his previous discussion. The hope for which other generations had expected fulfillment since the promise was first made to Abraham might be fulfilled for the author's generation. There is very little to prevent its fulfillment. Other generations have been prevented by the sinfulness of the people, but for believers of the author's generation, all of these sins had been atoned. Not only did these believers have hope, but they had "a strong encouragement" "as a secure and steadfast anchor of the soul." The word corresponding to "entering" was singular in the LXX and left unchanged by the author of Hebrews. It was not the believers who entered this holy place. It was Aaron in the Old Testament and Jesus in the author's time (the word is feminine, referring to "hope," but signifying Jesus), but it is this "entering" to atone for sins which clears the way for the reception of the promise. Rabbis said God would restore the promised land if all Israel repented for just one day (Song of Songs R. 5 §2, 2). That day would be the Day of Atonement, when each year Israel had a chance to have its debt to God forgiven.

20. Verses 19 and 20 form the tie between the exhortation that began with 5:11 and the doctrinal discussion that was interrupted after 5:10 but picked up again in chapter seven. The atonement made by entering into the innermost area was made when "Jesus entered [as] a forerunner in our behalf." This suggested the way to return to the discussion on Melchizedek for a proper understanding of Ps 110 and Jesus.

Summary.—With 5:11, the author of Hebrews interrupted his exegesis to make an exhortation. At that point he promised to deal with that subject more extensively even though it was "difficult to interpret" (5:11). At the end of his exhortation he was prepared to return to his initial subject, so he summarized his exhortation in a way that tied it very neatly to the subject he had left (5:10) and would continue (7:1). In relationship to the exhortation, he referred to the "two unchangeable things" (6:18) which provided Christians "strong encouragement" (6:18) and "a secure and steadfast anchor of the soul" (6:19). In relationship to the doctrinal discussion, he mentioned Jesus' function as "high priest" who would enter "the innermost [area]" and function for the atonement of the covenanters, under the authority of "the order of Melchizedek" which was "for the age."

The author's custom of using analogies was apparent again in this unit. He first explained the significance of an oath generally and then showed how important this was to God's oath. He explained how this brought about the promise and the assurance it left for fulfillment for Christians.

Melchizedek superior to the Levites

Michel identified seven subheadings in chapter seven which are related to seven Greek words used in the divisions.[36] Vanhoye accepted these subheadings but, on the basis of inclusions, grouped them also under three general headings.[37] The inclusions are as follows: (a) *Melchizedek* and *met* (7:1, 10), (b) *perfection* (7:11) and *perfected* (7:18), and (c) *oath* (7:20, 28). Vanhoye's division will be followed here. This chapter is well organized around the topic of Melchizedek. Like the rest of 1:1–12:29, chapter seven is based on Ps 110, but it is also centered around a little poem that is non-canonical (7:3), and it utilizes another non-canonical poem in conclusion (7:26). The poem in 7:3 seems to have been important to the author. It is echoed in vs. 25, and apparently was used as a proof text in 7:6, 8 and 16.

Melchizedek and Abraham

7:1. Albright read the Hebrew of Gen 14:18 as follows: *ū-malkî-ṣédeq mélek šelôm* <*ōh*> *hôṣî' léḥem wa-yáyin* and translated it: "And Melchizedek, a king allied to him, brought out bread and wine."[38] This analysis and rendering would eliminate the problematic term *šālēm* which was traditionally understood as a place name, as the author of Hebrews confirms in vs. 2 (see below). The Old Testament text quoted is put together from parts of the LXX translation of Gen 14:17–19. "Melchizedek king of Salem" comes from the beginning of Gen 14:18, and "priest of the Most High God," from its conclusion. From 14:17 comes "met," "returning from smiting" and "the kings," but "blessed" comes from 14:19. Instead of the aorist articular infinitive *anastrepsai* of LXX 14:17, Hebrews has the present participle, *hypostrephonti,* for "returning," but the meaning is the same. The author exchanged proper nouns for pronouns, and vice versa, but his report of the account in Genesis was basically fair.

There is some question about the unity of the text of Gen 14, but the author of Hebrews probably did not know that, so he accepted the event as historical. After Chedorlaomer and his allies overpowered the kings of Sodom and Gomorrah, capturing Lot, who also lived there, Abraham followed them to rescue Lot (Gen 14:1–4). When he overtook them, with 318 men, he conquered all those kings, took their possessions as booty, and returned (Gen 14:15–16). Two people were interested in his success: the king of Sodom, who hoped to recover from Chedorlaomer and his allies part of the possessions he had lost, and Melchizedek, who was entitled to share in the loot.[39] Melchizedek blessed Abraham (Gen 14:18–20), after which Abraham paid a tenth of his booty, perhaps as tariff for

[36] Michel, pp. 158–83.

[37] Vanhoye, pp. 125–36.

[38] W. F. Albright, "Abram the Hebrew: A New Archaeological Interpretation," BASOR 163 (1961), 52.

[39] See *Fragments of Philo,* ed. J. R. Harris, p. 72, on Gen 14:18.

crossing his land. After that Melchizedek evidently went his way while Abraham and the king of Sodom took care of their negotiations. The author of Hebrews was not interested in the king of Sodom or his transaction with Abraham, even though it was the more important of the two settlements Abraham made that day. To him, Melchizedek was of primary importance, because he, like Jesus in the author's view, was a priest-king to whom Abraham gave a tenth of all (7:2).

In chapter three, the author used Ps 95 as his basic text to tell of the way the Hebrews forfeited the promise after the exodus from Egypt, but he elaborated on the account with the support of Num 14. In the same way, in chapter seven, although much attention is given to the Genesis account of Melchizedek, the basic text is Ps 110:4: "You are a priest for the age according to the order of Melchizedek."

2. The first half of this verse concludes the author's presentation of the Melchizedek story; the second half begins his exegesis of the text. This starts by interpreting the name *Melchizedek.* This word means literally "my king" (*malkī*) [is] "righteousness" or "justice" (*ṣedeq*). Dahood followed Albright in rendering it "legitimate king,"[40] which is the same as the etymology of Josephus (*basileus dikaios*) (*Ant.* I. 180; *Wars* VI.438) and roughly corresponds to the author of Hebrews' interpretation, "king of righteousness." Philo called Melchizedek both "king of peace" and "righteous king" (*LA* III. 79). The second word for the author to etymologize was *Salem,* which MT pointed *šālēm,* "completed," "paid in full," but the author pointed *šālōm,* "peace." Therefore the "king of Salem" was the "king of peace." Dead Sea scrolls, rabbis, and Josephus follow Ps. 76:2 in identifying Salem with Zion (Ant. I. 180; Wars VI.438; Gen Apoc. 22:13; Targ. Gen 14:18), which seems to contradict Gen 33:18 which in LXX calls Salem "the city of Shechem." This is a literal translation of the MT, *šālem ʿīr šᵉkem,* however, which means Jacob entered, "safe and sound, the city of Shechem." By the time Joshua was written, at least, Jerusalem was known by the name it still holds (Josh 10:1). In John 3:23 Salem was a location near Aenon, where John the Baptist was baptizing, but that only locates it near water somewhere. Eusebius reported that Abraham was admitted "as a guest into the temple of the city called Mount Gerizim (*argarizim*), which being interpreted is 'Mount of the Most High,' and received gifts from Melchizedek, who was king and high priest of God" (Prep. Ev. IX. 17, 491a; also VII. 7–8). This identifies Salem with Mount Gerizim as the place where Melchizedek ruled and officiated as priest. Since Shechem is at the foot of Mount Gerizim, the one who ruled Shechem would officiate on Mount Gerizim, where the temple was. This supports the LXX translation of Gen 33:18.

The author of Hebrews was happy to be able to interpret "Melchizedek, king of Salem" as "king of righteousness" and "king of peace," since the Messiah was expected to rule justly and to establish peace (Isa 9:5–6;

[40] Dahood, III, 117–18. See also J. A. Fitzmyer, "Now this Melchizedek . . . ," CBQ 25 (1963), 311.

32:17; Jer 23:5–6; 33:15; Dan 9:24; Zech 9:1–10; Mal 4:2). This did not mean that he would never have war, but that he would overcome all of his enemies so that the land would have "rest" from its enemies (Josh 21:44).

Melchizedek was not really a very important personage in the history of Israel. He met Abraham once, collected his tariff, and went his way, but the author of Hebrews makes much of the silence. On the basis that if it is not in the scripture, it is not in the world (so *QDPIS* 178; San. 107b), the author reasoned that since nothing was said about Melchizedek's origin, he evidently did not have any. To support this judgment, he used a poem that was already familiar to him and perhaps to his readers as well.

The author of Hebrews was not the only one to attribute messianic significance to Melchizedek. Several Jewish scholars of antiquity identified Melchizedek with the Hasmoneans (see COMMENT on 5:6). The messianic character of Melchizedek is especially clear in one of the Dead Sea scrolls (11Q Melch.). This document disclosed the expectation of a jubilee that would come at the end of days for the captives, the sons of light, who belonged to the heritage of Melchizedek. Melchizedek was to proclaim release to the captives and atonement for their sins. This would be the last jubilee, the appointed time of favor for Melchizedek, when God would judge his people and punish those who favored the lot of Belial. Melchizedek would punish them on the day of vindication in the last days. This would come as a fulfillment of Isa 52:7, 9; 61:1–2 which promised that one would come proclaiming good news and announcing peace to Zion.[41]

3. Michel noted the similarity in poetic structure between 1:3 and 7:3, which he took to be from the same source.[42] If so, it must have been an important source because both were given strategic locations and treated as proof texts. Windisch observed that the terms "without father, without mother, without genealogy," were often applied to deities in Greek literature.[43] One writer described Athene as *amētōr* (motherless) and Hephaistos as *apatō*r (fatherless).[44] On the basis of Gen 20:2, Philo said Sarah was *amētōr* (*Ebr.* 61; *Heres* 62), and reports that other philosophers claim that the virgin Nike was *amētōr* (*Op.* xxxiii. 100). Since this poem was once independent of the rest of the document, it is difficult to know whether it was originally intended to show any relationship to the Old Testament or not. Some of the following are possibilities: "Without genealogy" may echo Isa 53:8: "Who shall declare his generation" (genean)? The expression "resembling the son of God" may reflect the narrative of the fiery furnace. In that story, one like a son of God appeared in the furnace (Dan 3:25).

The greatest significance of this poem for the author was that it gave him still more support for his conviction that Jesus was both king and

[41] See also San. 97b; CC, pp. 9–15.
[42] Michel, p. 114.
[43] Windisch, p. 60.
[44] Pollux, *Onamasticon,* III.26.

priest. The poem said its subject was one "resembling the son of God," which means king, and that "he remains a priest continually" (*eis to diēnekes*). The Greek means "continually," "without interruption," or something like that, depending on the context. In referring to a dynasty, this means the family would never fail to have a male heir to rule.[45] This supported the author's main text, which claimed that Jesus was "a priest for the age" (*eis ton aiōna*) (Ps 110:4). Before the author's time, Simon, the Hasmonean, had been called "leader and high priest for the age" (I Macc 14:41, 47). R. Simeon Ḥasida said the four craftsmen of Zech 2:3 were the Messiah from David's line, the Messiah from Joseph's line, Elijah, and the righteous priest (Suk. 52b). The office of "righteous priest" (*kōhēn ṣedeq*) was probably the same office as the "legitimate teacher" or "teacher of righteousness" (*mwrh ṣdq*), who was also a priest.[46] Throughout his message the author was dependent upon Ps. 110, from which he gained his theological and biblical basis for his claims about Jesus. Since Melchizedek was mentioned there, it was very important to deal with him in great detail.

4–5. "See how great he is" is a rather free translation of the author's figurative *theoreite de pēlikos houtos,* "See how large [is] this one!" The word *pēlikos* occurs only here and in Gal 6:11 in the entire New Testament. Whereas the author paraphrased LXX Gen 14:20 in vs. 2, in vs. 4 he quoted "Abraham gave a tenth." "Choice [acquisitions]" (*akrothiniōn*) refers to the best of a group, the first fruits. Here it deals with the choice parts of the booty he had taken from the kings. "To collect [the] tithe" is the translation given for *apodekatoun,* which can refer either to the person claiming the tithe from another (I Sam 8:15; Neh 10:37) or to the person who pays the tithe (Gen 28:22; Deut 14:21; 26:12; Matt 23:23; Luke (11:12).

Verse 5 is the first half of an *a fortiori* argument, in which "the sons of Levi" are exalted, so that they can be compared unfavorably to Melchizedek and thus exalt Melchizedek even higher. The Levites were subordinate cultic assistants in the judgment of Ezekiel, Nehemiah, and the community governed by 1QS, but here, as in Deut 17:9, 18; 18:1; 24:8; 27:9, the priests are called the levitical priests. Because they were given no inheritance in the land, they were assigned certain privileges to compensate for this (Deut 18). Since the Levites were sons of Jacob, they were also descendants of Abraham. They were authorized by law to collect tithes from "their brothers." This ranked them above the other Israelites.

6. The second part of the comparison deals with Melchizedek who "does not have a genealogy from them," i.e., he does not descend from the Levites. In fact he does not have a genealogy at all, according to the

[45] There are some hints that suggest a Hasmonean subject for the original poem. Judas was never a king, but came like a son of man (Dan 7). Simon was not a king, either. He was priest, however, and called a prince (I Macc 14). He was "like a son of God."

[46] See further "The Priestly Teacher of Righteousness," RQum 6 (1969), 553–58.

verse quoted in 7:3. Nevertheless, he "collected the tithe from Abraham," which implies that he was as much superior to Abraham as the Levites were to the Israelites. Furthermore, Melchizedek "blessed" Abraham, whom the author calls "the one who had the promises" to indicate his importance.

7. There are blessings which the inferior gives to the superior, such as the anonymous woman in the crowd who said to Jesus, "Blessed is the womb that bore you, and the breasts that you sucked" (Luke 11:27), but the great majority of the blessings listed in the scripture are those given by God, Aaron, a father, or someone else in a superior position. It was this kind of blessing about which the author spoke. There is no argument about the matter. "The lesser is blessed by the greater." Since it was already shown that Melchizedek blessed Abraham, the next step was to show that this meant that Melchizedek was superior to Abraham as he did so.

Rabbis did not concur in the author's depreciative evaluation of Abraham in comparison to Melchizedek. They said that as soon as Melchizedek blessed Abraham, Abraham objected that a servant must never be given precedence over his master. At that point, Abraham was given the priesthood. Scriptural proof for that comes from Ps 110:4, which the rabbis claim was written to Abraham: "The Lord said to my Lord, 'Sit at my right hand, until I make your enemies your footstool.'" This is followed by, "The Lord has sworn, and will not change his mind, 'You are a priest for the age after the order of Melchizedek,'" "After the order of Melchizedek" means that because of Melchizedek, Abraham was made a priest forever. They also claimed that the quotation, "He was a priest of the Most High God" (Gen 14:18), meant that Melchizedek was a priest, but not his posterity (Ned. 32b). The author of Jubilees used the statement about tithes in Gen 14:20 to justify tithing in general. This, of course, meant tithes to the priests who were sons of Aaron, Zadok, and Levi. In the Jubilee account, there is a lacuna which covers the section mentioning the name Melchizedek. There is no way of knowing whether this was an intentional omission or not (Jub 13:25–26).

8. The Levites who "receive tithes" were described as "mortal men." This is just a statement of basic knowledge. Levites, like others, died. There would be no purpose in making such a statement if it could not be contrasted with Melchizedek. Of Melchizedek "it is attested that 'he lives.'" When the subject is left undetermined in reference to a statement or testimony, the author regularly means "God," "the scripture," or "the Holy Spirit" says or testifies, but there is no basis in the scripture quoted, or in any of the proof texts from scripture used by the author, which would justify the claim that Melchizedek "lives." The only apparent quotation that might justify this claim is in the little poem quoted in 7:3. There the subject, which the author held to be Melchizedek, was said to have no end "of life" (*zōēs*). That seems to have been used as a proof text to show that Melchizedek "lives" (*zē̜*), just as "without genealogy" was used to prove Melchizedek was not from the genealogy of the

Levites (7:6). If this is the correct analysis of the data, then the author evidently held the poem to have doctrinal status very nearly that of the scripture. If we only had access to the source from which this poem was taken, many points would be clearer.

9–10. The Greek for "one might even [extend the figure to] say [that]" is the little idiom, *hōs epos epein,* which is very common in Greek literature. It softens an expression. It is a mild indirect apology in advance for that which follows. An English equivalent might be, "If I may be allowed the expression."[47] The argument thus introduced was certainly an extended one: Since Abraham paid tithes to Melchizedek, and Levi was one of the descendants of Abraham, therefore Abraham represented Levi in this act, even though Levi had not yet been born! Levi was considered "still in the loins of his father" Abraham "when Melchizedek met" Abraham. Therefore the collector of tithes (Levi) was himself tithed by Melchizedek, who was obviously much greater. Then the point of the *a fortiori* argument is, "If Levi is great, how much more so Melchizedek!"

Summary.—Chapter seven was introduced by a quotation from Ps 110:4 referring to Melchizedek (6:20). The opening unit of that chapter (7:1–10) begins with the catchword "Melchizedek," which was taken from Gen 14. The scriptural passage (Gen 14:17–20) and the poem quoted in 7:3 provide the textual basis for the rest of the unit. The inclusion is formed by the words "Melchizedek . . . met" (7:1, 10). The point of this unit was to show that Jesus was superior to the Levites. The author had already argued that he was superior to the angels and Moses. By showing that Melchizedek was superior to Abraham, he concluded that Jesus was superior to the Levites. His reasons for claiming Melchizedek's superiority were as follows: (a) He received tithes from Abraham, and, by extension, from the Levites; (b) he blessed his inferior, Abraham; and (c) he lives, in contrast to mortal men like the Levites.

The imperfect priesthood and law

11. The word translated "perfection" (*teleiōsis*) occurs in this form only in Luke 1:45 and here. In Luke 1:45, it clearly means "fulfillment" of Israel's expectations. Here, however, it refers rather to the fulfillment of required obligations of the priestly office. The infinitive "to arise" (*anistasthai*) means to arise as one arises from sleep or rises to leave. It also refers to resurrection from the dead. For a "priest to arise" might imply that he had arisen for action. On the basis that God does not allow things that are unnecessary, the author reasoned that "another priest" would not have arisen for action if the existing priesthood had been functioning effectively. The fact that "another priest" has arisen means there was a "need." Therefore there was "no perfection through the levitical priesthood." This argument would only make sense if the "priest to arise according to the order of Melchizedek" came later than the Levites,

[47] So Stuart, p. 167. For numerous examples, see Williamson, pp. 103–6.

and therefore later than Melchizedek himself.[48] According to Hebrews, this was Jesus.

12. For the levitical priesthood the "law" was either Leviticus or, more likely, the entire Pentateuch, which the author subordinated to the Psalms.

13. "The one about whom these things are said," in the author's judgment, was Jesus, who belonged to none of the priestly families—Aaron, Zadok, or Levi. He belonged to one of the twelve tribes, to be sure, but a tribe from which there was no record of anyone ever serving as priest at the altar.

14. "Our Lord" refers to Jesus, as also in 2:3. It was generally expected that the Messiah would belong to the tribe of Judah (Targ. Pseudo-Jonathan Gen 49:9–10; 4Q Patriarchal Blessings 1:4), and Matthew and Luke recorded that Jesus was born in Bethlehem (Matt 2:1–6; Luke 1:32; 2:4–7), but John 7:41 said he was from Galilee. It was also widely accepted that Jesus was from the family of David and that the Messiah should also be a son of David, but the author of Hebrews made no mention of that. He admitted the Judaic origin of Jesus, partly because of tradition, partly because of scriptural prophecy (Gen 49:9–10), and partly because of the Jewish tradition that Melchizedek was from Jerusalem, but he never mentioned the son of David as the Messiah nor Jesus as the son of David. He used messianic prophecies that had usually been applied to the son of David and applied them to Jesus, but without calling Jesus a son of David.[49]

The Greek word for "arose" is *anatetalken,* a different word from that used in vs. 11 to describe the priest to arise. The verb *anatellein* refers to rising as the sun, moon, and stars arise, and is used in this way fifteen times in the Old Testament. It also describes the sprouting or growing of plants, hair, disease, and human bodies sixteen times in the Old Testament. It occurs twenty-five times with a metaphorical usage in the Old Testament, where the imagery reflects the rising or growth of stellar bodies or planets. Babylon (1), wicked ones (2), fortunes (1), ruins (1), new things (2), Israelites (1), judgment (1), vision (1), righteousness (6), faithfulness (1), life (1), light (meaning knowledge or success) (3), and the glory of the Lord (1) were all reported as subjects that would arise or had arisen to prominence or prosperity, and would increase in prominence.

This word was easily applied to a king or expected messiah. So Ezekiel spoke of a "horn" that would arise (*anatelei keras*) (29:21). Balaam foresaw a "star" that would arise (*anatelei astron*) from Jacob who would overpower Moab and Edom (Num 24:17–18). Zechariah described Zerubbabel as an *Anatolē* (shoot, branch, or star) who would arise (*anatelei*) and build the temple in Jerusalem (6:12). Philo said of this man whose name was "Rising," about whom Zechariah spoke, that he is the oldest son (*presbytaton*

[48] Hanson, pp. 398–402, has argued unconvincingly that the author of Hebrews intended Christ to be identified with Melchizedek himself.

[49] Bruce, *Interpretation* 23 (1969), 5, 7, unwittingly assumed Hebrews was dealing with a two-messiah doctrine which involved a son of David messiah. See also Grässer, pp. 73–91.

huion) whom the Father raised up (*aneteile*) and was otherwise called his first-born (*prōtogonon*) (*CL* XIV. 61–63).

In none of the Old Testament usages of the verb *anatellein* was it employed to mean a "descendant" of a certain tribe or family. The importance of this term to the author of Hebrews was that Jesus arose as the Messiah. Even though this meant arising from Judah, in no place in his document did the author of Hebrews explicitly identify Jesus with the son of David, nor did he show any interest in David himself. His only mention of David was in a list of various kinds of leaders (11:32) and in relationship to the Psalms, which he assumed David wrote (4:7). The royal-priestly figure, that he exalted here as the Son, apostle, high priest, first-born, and one from the order of Melchizedek, had attributes very similar to those of the Hasmoneans, who were also royal-priestly figures and some of them anointed high priests and kings, even though they descended neither from the line of Zadok nor from that of David. It may have been with the Hasmoneans in mind that the priest Levi was called "son" (T. Levi 4:2). They were Levites who "arose" from Jerusalem, and later Modein, both in the territory of Judah (I Macc 2:1). The author did not go further and say Jesus descended from the Hasmoneans. In fact, he denied that he came from the same tribe as the Levites or that he had any genealogy at all. Not all early Christians were willing even to agree that Jesus came from Judah. Some held that it was Galilee (John 7:41). The tradition that Jesus was actually born in Bethlehem (Matt 2:1; Luke 2:1–7) may have developed to conform to the normal messianic expectations (John 7:42). Since other Christians developed their own traditions and accounts of the facts dealing with Jesus, there is no certainty that the author of Hebrews did not make a few innovations himself. Without denying other messianic expectations, the author of Hebrews used only as much historical material about Jesus as he needed to present him as a high priest and king like one of the Hasmoneans, though not from the levitical line. Here he used a verb to describe Jesus' appearance that was normally associated with the Messiah and probably alluded to Gen 49:9–10, which was normally applied to the Messiah. He said Jesus came from a different tribe from the Levites, and that made him authorized by the order of Melchizedek. He acknowledged that Jesus was from Judah, but he did not say he descended from David. Had he done so that would have associated Jesus with a two-messiah expectation, which would not allow Jesus to be a high priest since John the Baptist would have been the expected high priest. By using terms just as he did, he could claim as much as he wanted and no more. "Our Lord arose from Judah"; he was the Messiah; he was not from the tribe of Levi but "belonged to a different tribe"; he was a priest according to the order of Melchizedek. "Moses said nothing about priests" from the tribe of Judah. Nonetheless the Hasmoneans had arisen from Judah and had become high priests. Jews in the author's time knew that very well, for the Hasmonean family continued to have a great deal of influence in Palestinian politics until the last of the fortresses had been captured in A.D. 73, and their memory never ceased.

15. T. Levi 8:14 predicted that a new king would arise from Judah who would establish a new priesthood. This reference was probably intended to apply to the Hasmoneans, who were also identified with Melchizedek (see COMMENT on 5:6). Without being of the same family, the author claimed that when "another priest arises" he would be "according to the likeness of [i.e. similar to] Melchizedek." If the author had any subtle reason for changing the usual wording from "order" to "likeness" of Melchizedek, it may mean that the priest that was Jesus would be *like* the Hasmoneans, but not of the same family. Of course he may have used a different word for no other purpose than to vary his literary style.

16. The Levites or sons of Aaron acquired their position "according to the law of a fleshly commandment." The law involved was probably the Pentateuch, which the author had insisted would change (7:12). The offices they had held had been passed down from father to son with no discrimination shown to the quality of the person involved. The term "fleshly" (*sarkinēs*) here refers to physical heritage, but it is also a derogatory term used in early Christian and Jewish ethical dualism. Paul contrasted the desires of the spirit to the desires of the flesh. This was not a contrast of the physical to the spiritual, but a contrast of evil action to good action. The "works of the flesh" were just as spiritual as the "works of the spirit," since they did not concentrate on material aspects. They were listed as follows: "immorality, impurity, licentiousness, idolatry, sorcery, enmity, strife, jealousy, anger, selfishness, dissension, party spirit, envy, drunkenness, carousing, and the like" (Gal 5:19–21). The fruits of the spirit were also spiritual: "love, joy, peace, patience, kindness, goodness, faithfulness, gentleness, self-control" (Gal 5:22–23). The levitical priesthood, then, not only was of physical descent, but it belonged to the classification of "fleshly," which included all things that were ethically bad. The claim that Jesus "came into existence . . . according to the power of an indestructible life" (*zōēs*) may be based on the little verse in 7:3, which claimed that Jesus, like Melchizedek, had neither beginning of days nor end of life (*zōēs*). The term "power" (*dynamis*) also means "miracle" and may have been intended here to describe Jesus' miraculous origin, but that does not mean a virgin birth. The miracle of Jesus, according to the author, was that he was *not* born, and he did not descend from a special family; he was "without father, without mother, without genealogy" (7:3). He was neither conceived nor born, he arose (*anatetalken*); he "came into existence." His whole existence was a miracle. He could not be explained according to family origin. Since he had no end of days (7:3; I Tim 6:16), his life was "indestructible." That would contrast him to the Levites who were mortal (7:8), and came "into existence according to the law of a fleshly commandment."

17. The testimony that Jesus was "a priest for the age according to the order of Melchizedek" was given here as if this were proof that Jesus' origin and existence were miraculous, but the texts came from the poem quoted in 7:3. This may be one more indication that this poem was originally written about the Hasmoneans, who were identified with Melchizedek, because the

author seems to have expected his readers to know that the poem and Melchizedek belong together.

18. According to the author, the people of Israel had been governed by the Levitical priesthood (7:11). It was necessary for the priesthood to be changed (7:12), so the law which established the priesthood would have to be changed too (7:12). This was the "fleshly commandment" (7:16) which had functioned "previously." It was removed because it "perfected nothing" "because of its weakness and uselessness." In a similar way Paul discredited the law, which he described as being "of sin and death" (Rom 8:2); it was "powerless . . . in that it was weak through the flesh" (Rom 8:3). In contrast to this is the "law of the spirit of life in Christ Jesus" (Rom 8:2).

19. Whereas Paul contrasted flesh and spirit when referring to the old and new covenants, the author of Hebrews described the fleshly law or commandment in contrast to the "beginning of a better hope through which we come near to God" (see also 3:6; 6:11, 18; 10:23).

Summary.—This section is limited by the words "perfection" (7:11) and "perfected" (7:19), which form the inclusion. The main point of the unit is that the new priesthood makes the old priesthood obsolete and with it the law which brought it into existence. Both priesthood and law were imperfect. The law was also fleshly, weak, and useless. The reason the reader can be sure about all of this is that a new priest has arisen according to the likeness of Melchizedek. He is not from the same tribe as the Levites. In fact, he has no parents or genealogy. His is a miraculous existence without beginning of days nor end of life. Therefore his life is indestructible. He is the priest who has given us a "beginning of a better hope through which we come near to God." This new priest is "our Lord" who "arose" from Judah. He "came into existence," but was not born.

This tenor is similar to that of the rest of the document which shows Jesus superior to the best of the old covenant. The term "better" occurs twelve times in the document. The fondness of the author for the perfect tense is evident in vss. 13 and 14 as well as the following additional places: 1:4, 13; 2:14; 3:3, 14; 4:2, 4, 14, 15; 7:3; 8:5, 6; 9:18, 26; 10:14; 11:5, 17, 28; 12:2, 3. The conclusion of this unit also prepares the reader for the next division that will be concentrated on the better hope in the new priest.

The perfect priest

20. The construction "just as much as" (7:20) . . . "just so much more" (7:22) (*kath' hoson . . . kata tosouto*) is typically rabbinic and seems to mean about the same as *ka'ᵃšer . . . 'al 'aḥat kamāh wᵉkamāh*.

The sons of Aaron were given the perpetual priesthood when they were originally designated to be the priests (Exod 29:1–9; see further Exod 28–29; Lev 8–9; Sir 45:15). Phineas, the forefather of the Hasmoneans (I Macc 2:54) was also granted the perpetual priesthood, but in neither case was this done with an oath.

21. The word translated "change his mind" is *metamelēthēsetai.* Etymologically it is formed from the preposition "after" and the verb "to care," "be anxious about," "take thought." This word, then, means to have an "after thought" or an "after care," to give the matter a second thought. Since a second thought might reverse the decision, it has come to mean "repent" or "change one's mind." The claim of both Ps 110 and the author is that God made a firm decision about this and he would never give it a second thought. It could not come up for reconsideration. It was like the law of the Medes and the Persians (Dan 6:15). The oath which God took to establish a position was applied to the promise made to Abraham (Gen 22), the rejection of the exodus generation from the promised rest (Ps 95), and the promise that someone would be "a priest for the age according to the order of Melchizedek." In each case the author of Hebrews called attention to the significance of the oath. It is the oath that distinguished the promise made to Jesus from the promises made to the sons of Aaron or Phineas.

22. A "surety" (*eggyos*) is a bond, bail, collateral, or some kind of guarantee that a promise will be fulfilled. In this case, God had made the promise with an oath, and Jesus had become the guarantee that the promise would be fulfilled. A covenant is a formal contract that is made between two parties defining their agreed-upon behavior in relationship to one another. The law and commandment associated with the Levites were weak and useless. They "perfected nothing," but with Jesus as the high "priest for the age" there is assurance that a better covenant would be established between God and his people.

23–24. Another contrasting point between Jesus and the Levites is that they were plural and he was singular. Josephus said there were eighty-three high priests from the time of Aaron until the temple was destroyed in A.D. 70 (*Ant.* XX. 227). This concurs with JYoma I. 1, which says there were between eighty and eighty-five. Some rabbis held that there were more than three hundred high priests during the period of the second temple alone (Yoma 9a). Because they were mortal (7:8), the Levitical priests needed many replacements. Jesus seemed to suit the author's monastic ideal. Just as a monk was required to separate himself from his family and deny it, so the author denied that Jesus had any parents or genealogy. His was a miraculous, indestructible existence. Not only did he not have a genealogy, but like other celibates he had no posterity. It was not a whole tribe that maintained this office down through the generations, like the Levites. He alone held the office. He alone was the surety. There was no danger of corruption in the future, as Malachi said had happened to the Levites. This makes his priesthood much superior. The priest was not mortal. He continued to minister "for the age." Therefore there would be no "change" in his "priesthood."

25. "Those who approach God through him" are the people whom he represented when he offered sacrifice for atonement of sins. Because of his ministry, their sins were forgiven. "The entire [age]" (*eis to panteles*) seems parallel with "for the age" of vs. 24. Both apply to the term of service Jesus would hold as priest. The unbrokenness of this ministry was empha-

sized by the expression "continually" (*eis to diēnekes*) (7:3). Another expression used to describe this tenure is "indestructible" (*akatalytos*) (7:16). None of these expressions carries the force of "forever." "For the age" probably meant for the messianic age when Jesus, as Son and high priest, would rule and officiate.[50]

26. Three of these adjectival words and phrases are nearly identical in meaning, and they all describe the condition required of a high priest when he functioned in the temple. All priests who served in the temple where God's presence was understood to dwell were obligated to keep themselves "holy," which meant "undefiled" by any type of levitical impurity (see II Macc 14:36; 15:34; James 1:27; I Peter 1:4). On the Day of Atonement, the high priest bathed five times and washed his hands and feet ten times (Yoma 3:3). To avoid defilement, the high priest was "separated from sinners" for seven days so that he would not be defiled on the Day of Atonement. He was put on short rations the day before the Day of Atonement to prevent a nocturnal discharge that would have defiled him (Yoma 1:1–8) or to prevent any need for elimination in the holy place. On the Day of Atonement, transgressions against God could be atoned, but only on the condition that the believer first appease his neighbor against whom he had sinned and become reconciled to him (Yoma 8:9). This is probably the condition described as "guileless" (*akakos*), which sometimes means "simple" or "naïve," almost to a fault (Prov 14:15). For a priest this would describe the moral condition necessary for atonement. If a high priest were not "separated from sinners," he would become defiled by them and be incapable of interceding for his people. The priest and the Levite were not free to help the man on the road from Jerusalem to Jericho who was "half dead," because of their fear that he might die and defile them by their contact with a corpse (Luke 10:29–32). The nature of the priestly office is reflected in the appointment of Levi to the priesthood.

> "Therefore, the Most High has heard your prayer so as to separate you from iniquity and that [you] may be to him a son and a servant and minister of his presence" (T. Levi 4:2; see also *Ant.* III. 258).

The claim that Jesus, as high priest, was "higher than the heavens" may have reflected the visual concept of a sacrifice taken up to God in the heavens through the column of smoke that touches heaven (see discussion at the end of chapter nine). It was not a unique claim for one who thought of the heavens as being like a tent roof, just above the treetops and the hills. Enoch's spirit was believed to have ascended into the heavens where he could see the sons of God (Enoch 70:1–4; 71:1), and Isaiah was thought to have been raised to see all of the seven heavens (Assump. Isa 7:1–11, 42; see also 4:10). The structure and content of this verse suggest that it is part of the same poem from which the verse in 7:3 was taken.

27. The author's familiarity with liturgical customs is reflected here. The law instructs that the high priest, on the Day of Atonement, must first offer a bull as a sin offering for himself and his family, and afterward he was to

[50] CC, pp. 15–18.

offer a goat as a sin offering for the sins of the people (Lev 16:6–28; Yoma 4:3–6:3). There is a problem, however, in the claim that high priests do this "daily" (*kath' hēmeran*) whereas the atonement offerings the author described took place only on the Day of Atonement, so far as is generally known. Some possible explanations for this situation are these: (a) The author may have rendered the Aramaic *yōmā'* which literally means "the day," but was used as a technical term for "the Day of Atonement," by *kath' hēmeran,* meaning "daily" (cf. Heb. *yōmām,* "by day"). This would have been caused by a misunderstanding of the Aramaic of some document and a faulty attempt to give the expression sense in Greek. The document may have been one that compared the action of the high priest on the Day of Atonement with that of Jesus. (b) He may have tried to increase the contrast by confusing the high priest's function on the Day of Atonement, which Lev 16 spells out clearly, with the daily sacrifices which were also performed (Lev 6:13, 19–22; Num 28:3–4; Tamid 7:3; Sir 45:14). (c) The author may have meant by "every day," "every day on which he ministered to atone for the people." (d) Daily sacrifices may have been understood as atoning sacrifices. High priests did function on days other than the Day of Atonement (Tamid 7:3; *Wars* V. 231). According to Jub 6:14, Noah's posterity was commanded to supplicate every day both morning and evening with blood, and seek forgiveness, just as Noah sacrificed a kid for atonement (Jub 6:2).[51] Philo said the high priest offered prayers and sacrifices every day (*kath' hekastēn hēmeran*) (*Spec.* III. 131). The solution to this problem is not certain.

Another puzzling question is the meaning of the claim "for this he did once for all." What did he do? Did he "offer sacrifices for [his] own sins" as well as for "those of the people"? *A priori* it would seem that "this" which he did "once for all" was the same as that which the priests did "daily," which the author understood to include *two* offerings. The one offering of Christ was better than the *two* offerings the high priest made every day or every year. This would imply that Jesus' sacrifice also cleansed his "own sins" as well as the sins of the people. Rabbis believed that the suffering associated with death would atone for sins of the individual himself (ARN 39). Furthermore the poem in 1:3, applied to Jesus, said,

> "when he had made a purification for [his] sins,
> sat down at the right hand of the Majesty in exaltation."

This seems to mean that when Jesus was crucified, and therefore sacrificed, then he was exalted. His sacrifice provided the cleansing or sin offering. If the verses in 1:3, 7:3, and 7:26 were all from the same poem originally, the author's interpretation of 7:26 and 7:27 would be expected to be consistent with that of 1:3. This seems to be the most normal interpretation, but it poses some difficulties. The claim in 4:15 is that Jesus was tempted in the way other people are, but still he was without sin. This is usually understood to describe his day-by-day moral conduct. It is in a context, however, that allows a different interpretation. Heb 4:14–15 describes Jesus who had gone

[51] See further Michel, pp. 180–81; Sowers, pp. 69–70.

through the heavens, meaning he had already been sacrificed. His temptations may have been only those associated with his crucifixion, at which time he did not betray his cause by sinning. Without denying this kind of logic, Vaughan said of this interpretation: "To say so would be to contradict the whole language of the Epistle (as well as the Scripture throughout) as to the sinlessness of Christ. In many places a text may be found which, taken by itself and isolated from all others, might seem to be capable of an Arian or Socinian meaning. But confront it with the *tenor* of Scripture, and all is consistency."[52] Vaughan, however, did not demonstrate his general claims and show that the entire epistle and scripture excluded this possibility. In fact, the interpretation Vaughan disparaged is consistent with 1:3 and the expiatory understanding of death according to the rabbis. The only difficulty is with the claim to sinlessness in 4:15, and even that may be understood in reference to the crucifixion alone, and not to Jesus' entire life. It is possible that the deed which Jesus "did once for all" meant only cleansing for the sins "of the people," as most scholars assume, but that is not the only possibility. The fact that Jesus "offered himself" as a sacrifice was very important to the author's understanding of atonement (8:3; 9:14, 26; 10:10–12).

28. The imperfect law which was weak and useless (7:18–19) was the same law which "establishes men [as] priests [who] have weakness." This probably meant the whole Pentateuch. The author assumed that Moses wrote the entire Pentateuch and David wrote all of the Psalms. The sons of Aaron were established priests on the basis of the Pentateuch, which preceded the Psalms by as many years as Moses preceded David. This was the logic by which the author understood the testimony in Ps 95 that the Israelites would not enter into the "rest," to cancel the claim in Joshua that they had done so. Also here, the Psalms take precedence. In the Pentateuch the sons of Aaron and Phineas were promised the eternal priesthood, but in Ps 110 there is an "oath which [came] after the law" which established Melchizedek a priest "for the age." This supersedes the previous promise, in the judgment of the author. Since David also wrote Ps 2, which the author identified with Jesus as well as he identified the priest in Ps 110 with Jesus, the author reasoned that the "oath" in Ps 110 could also apply to the "Son" mentioned in Ps 2:7.

To be consistent with vs. 27, which seems to mean that Jesus' sacrifice of himself was for a cleansing of his own, as well as the people's, sins, it would also be the sacrifice of Jesus which "made [him] perfect for the age." This is consistent with the claim that he was made perfect through suffering (2:10). He learned obedience through the things he suffered, after which he was made perfect (5:8–9). This is in contrast to the offerings of the levitical priests which do not make perfect (9:9; 10:1). Jesus' offering of himself, however, not only made him perfect, but also those who were sanctified (10:14). The relationship of perfection to sacrifice makes it likely that the author understood Jesus' offering to be that which made him as the Son

[52] Vaughan, p. 139.

perfect. This supports the interpretation of 1:3 to mean that Jesus made an offering for his and the other people's sins before he ascended to sit at the right hand of God. It also seems consistent with the rest of chapter seven and the author's doctrine of atonement, but it does not support the concept that Jesus was sinless before his crucifixion.

Summary.—The concluding section of chapter seven was framed as an inclusion by the word "oath," which occurs in vss. 20 and 28. The author argued that the oath made the promise given to the priest in Ps 110, whom he understood to be Jesus, superior to the promises given to the sons of Aaron and Phineas. Also the fact that the Psalms were written after the Pentateuch means that the later promise in the Psalms supersedes the earlier promises made by Moses. The argument that Jesus was without parents or posterity, in contrast to the Levites for whom lineage was important, may support the possibility that the author was not only a very rigid legalist concerned about the ethics of a communal group, but that Jesus represented his monastic ideal of celibacy and denial of family. Verses 25 and 26 seem to be related to the poem quoted in 7:3. Verse 26 may even be a verse of the same poem. Perfection seems to have been acquired by sacrifice, in the author's judgment. Therefore it was Jesus' self-sacrifice that made him perfect. It also cleansed him from sin (1:3), since he offered himself for his own sins as well as for those of the people.

The author's use of scripture here shows that he gave more credence to the Psalms than to the Pentateuch. This may be because the prophets and Psalms contained more material suitable for his eschatological purposes, or it may be that he related the Pentateuch typologically with the old covenant which had been superseded.

Summary of Chapter Seven

Michel holds that chapter seven is divided into seven sub-headings, based on the following seven terms: 1–3, Melchizedek; 4–10, tithing (*dekatē*); 11–14, order (*taxis*); 15–19, law (*nomos*); 20–22, oath-taking (*horkōmosia*); 23–25, "for the age" (*eis ton aiōna*); and 26–28, high priest.[53] This is an attractive division of the chapter, although it makes very small units. It is not so convincing, however, as Vanhoye's three divisions which are all marked by inclusions. The argument moves in an orderly and progressive fashion from a discussion of the relative merits of Melchizedek and Abraham to a depreciative analysis of the Levites who were Abraham's sons, mortal men, imperfect in their function, on the basis of an imperfect law, to an appreciative evaluation of Jesus as the perfect priest, installed by a promise accompanied with an oath, based on a later testimony. This high priest was without parents or posterity; his once-for-all sacrifice cleansed both him and his believers for the age. If the poem in 7:3 which seems to be echoed in 25 and

[53] Michel, pp. 158–83.

used as a proof text in 6, 8, and 16 was part of the same poem quoted in 7:26, then the author may have intended the parts of this poem to serve as an inclusion for the whole chapter. The final verse acts as a summarizing sentence, picking up terms used throughout the chapter: "For the age" (7:28) may be intended to refer the reader to Melchizedek in the opening and concluding verses of the first section (7:1, 10). "Perfect" is the word in vs. 28 that recalls the opening and concluding verses of the second section (7:11, 19). The "oath" mentioned in 28 refers the reader to the beginning of the third section (7:20).

That which was a part of the old covenant also belonged to the new. With Jesus there was a new covenant, a new priesthood, a new sacrifice. Not only was all of this new, but it was better than the old. Angels continued to function in the new covenant as they had in the old, but they were clearly subordinate and inferior to the Son. The servant Moses was replaced by the Son Jesus; in place of the levitical priesthood was the priesthood according to the order of Melchizedek, established by a later promise and confirmed by an oath as a priesthood for the age. The Levites were mortal but Jesus' life was indestructible. Levites were not perfect and they were established by a law that could not perfect anything, but Jesus was a son made perfect for the age by the word of the oath. Not only in chapter seven, but in the previous six chapters as well, Jesus was shown to be superior to anything belonging to the old covenant, and this proof was presented on the basis of Ps 110 around which the whole document (1:1 – 12:29) was oriented. Furthermore, the new which was better than the old also replaced much that was old so that the old became unnecessary.

Old and New Worship

The old cult

THE EARTHLY MINISTRY

8:1. The Greek for "most important" is *kephalaion,* which means literally, "belonging to the head." It sometimes means "first of all" or "in summary" as well as being a reference to the main point. Here it refers not only to the discussion in chapter seven, but to the very beginning of the book. The author's reintroduction of a passage from Ps 110 reminds the reader that this Psalm is the main text of the entire book. "The throne of Majesty in the heavens" is a euphemism for God, similar to "the Majesty in exaltation" (1:3), used also in relationship to Ps 110.

The idea of a throne or a temple in heaven was quite common to Jewish thought in New Testament times. The following message was ostensibly given to Levi: "And then the angel opened for me the gates of heaven and I say the holy One, the Most High (*ton hagion hypsiston*) seated upon the throne, and he said to me, 'Levi, I have given you the blessing of the priesthood until I come and dwell in the midst of Israel'" (T. Levi 5:1–2). The temple in heaven was closely related to that in Jerusalem: "You have said [we should] build a temple on your holy mountain,

an altar in the city of your dwelling,
an imitation (*mimēma*) of the holy tent which you
prepared from the beginning" (Wis 9:8).

According to the rabbis: "*Zebul* is that in which Jerusalem and the temple and an altar are built, and Michael, the great prince (Dan 12:1), stands and offers a gift on it, as it is said: 'I have surely built for you a house of dwelling (*zebul*), a place for you to dwell forever' (I Kings 8:13). And from where do we conclude that it is called 'heaven'? As it is written, 'Look down from heaven and see from your holy and glorious dwelling (*zebul*)' " (Isa 63:15) (Hag. 12b). This also reflects another common custom of believing that God's presence is both in heaven and in the temple. So close was the heavenly Jerusalem to the earthly Jerusalem that R. Joḥanan said, "The Holy One blessed be He said, 'I will not come into heavenly Jerusalem (*Y^erūšālayim šel ma^{ʿa}lāh*) until I come into Jerusalem which is on earth' (*Y^erūšālayim šel maṭṭāh*). How [can I know] there is a heavenly Jerusalem? Is it not written, 'Jerusalem, you are built like a city that is compact together' " (Ta'anith 5a)? By this he meant a heavenly and an earthly Jerusalem compact together. The two Jerusalems were so closely identified that priests who served the temple at Jerusalem were compared to angels of heaven: "And may the Lord give to you [Levi] and your seed greatness and great mercy, and cause you and your seed, from among all flesh, to draw near to him and serve him in his sanctuary as the angels of the presence and the holy ones" (Jub 31:14). "The throne" in the temple was on the altar, where God's presence dwelt. When Jesus as the high priest entered the holy of holies in the heavenly temple, instead of facing the altar while standing or kneeling, he "sat down at the right hand" of God's throne. This was the chief seat of honor (see also 1:3; 8:1; 10:12; 12:2).

2. Prof. W. F. Albright said that the word *dēmiourgos* doubtless formerly belonged to the text as the subject of the second line of this couplet:

"A minister of the holy things
and an intercessor (*dēmiourgos*) of the true tent"

If a synonym for "minister" did not drop out of the text, the word "minister" was understood to apply both to "the holy things" and to "the true tent," both of which are designations of the same place of worship. The word used for "minister" is *leitourgos,* which, in religious contexts, is the office of a priest (1:7; 8:2; 10:11; Num 7:5; Isa 61:6; Jer 33:21; Neh 10:39; *LA* III. 135; *Fuga* 93). The "holy things" are the sacred precincts and objects related to the temple or "the true tent." This verse is based on the LXX version of Num 24:6–7, which is quite different from the MT, reading certain vowel points and consonants differently. The LXX version is as follows:

"As *tents* [MT aloes] *which the Lord set up* [planted],
and as cedars beside waters.
A *man* [MT waters] shall come [flow] from his seed [buckets],
and he [MT his seed] shall rule [be in] many nations [waters]."

The author of Hebrews took the "man" from LXX Num 24:7 and placed it in contrast to "the Lord," mentioned in LXX Num 24:6. The temple that had been in Jerusalem, served by sons of Aaron and Levi, had been made by man. This was in contrast to the high priest from Melchizedek's order, who ministered at "the true tent which the Lord set up." After the fall of Jerusalem, Jews believed that the temple which God had recorded on the palms of his own hands (*d'l ps' d'ydy*) had been taken from his people, just as Paradise was taken from Adam, because of sin. The temple had been shown to Adam, Abraham, and Moses before it was built in the land. Then God preserved both the temple and Paradise to be restored later (II Bar 4:1–7), so the temple the Romans destroyed was not the temple God had made. This was made by men, or, to use another of the author's expressions, it was made with hands (9:11).

3. In a pattern similar to 6:16, the author first explained what the custom was for priests in general. He then applied it to Jesus in particular. If a priest were to fulfill his function of "offering gifts and sacrifices," of course, he must have the necessary gifts to "offer." The same was true of Jesus.

4. Just as the author had argued earlier (7:11) that another priesthood would not have arisen if the old one had been adequate, he reasoned here that there were already priests to "offer the gifts according to the law." Since God creates nothing unnecessarily, it follows that he would not have created a duplicate priesthood. Therefore, his function was not "on earth" as the Levites' ministry was.

5. The temple which the levitical priests served was only a pattern and shadow of the "heavenly" temple. The "pattern" (*hypodeigmati*) and "shadow" (*skia*) are terms that have prompted many scholars to interpret the whole document "To the Hebrews" in terms of Platonic philosophy.[54] In Greek, *skia* was used philosophically and otherwise to describe a silhouette, outline, or reflection, whereas in Hebrew, *ṣēl* figuratively meant "shelter" or "protection." This was the pattern given to Moses on the mountain, which God said Israel was to follow when she built a temple (Exod 25:40). The contrast between the earthly temple in Jerusalem and the heavenly pattern reflects Near Eastern concepts inherited from the Old Testament. Platonic philosophy is one branch of this outlook, but the point of view in Hebrews does not come from the Platonic branch. This can be shown negatively and positively.

Negatively, this is not Platonic because: (a) Plato's ideal world was not a place, like heaven, where anyone could enter—even Jesus. It could only be reached by the intellect. (b) The contrast in Hebrews was temporal. Jesus, at a particular *time,* entered the true tent—a concept thoroughly un-Platonic. It was not a contrast just between an earthly copy and its heavenly reality, but one between a historical time in the past compared with one which was to succeed it.[55]

[54] W. F. Howard, *The Fourth Gospel in Recent Criticism and Interpretation* (London, 1955), p. 115; Manson, pp. 124–26; Moffatt, pp. xxi ff., 107 ff.; V. Taylor, *The Atonement in New Testament Teaching* (London, 1941), pp. 101–2.
[55] See further R. Williamson, "Platonism and Hebrews," SJT 16 (1963), 418–19.

Positively, according to the Old Testament, not only the tabernacle but also the temple at Jerusalem was built according to the plan received from God's hand (Exod 25:40; I Chron 28:19; Wis 9:8; Ps 78:69; Mekilta *Shirata* 10:29–42), was constructed by God's own hands (Exod 15:17), and God made his name to dwell there (I Kings 8:29; Ezek 48:35). While in captivity, after the temple had been destroyed by the Babylonians, Ezekiel was given a vision of the ideal temple which he described in detail so that the temple in Jerusalem might be built according to that plan when the land was restored (Ezek 40–48). Zion was not the only ancient temple for which a heavenly prototype was claimed. The temple built at Lagash was the result of a dream in which the goddess Didaba revealed to the king the plan of that temple.[56] Like Jerusalem (II Bar 4:2–7; Tobit 13:16; Isa 60:11–14; Ezek 40), other cities were built according to heavenly archetypes. This was true of cities such as Sippar, Nineveh, and Assur.[57] Segiriya, the palace fortress in Ceylon, was patterned after the model of the heavenly city Alakamanda.[58]

Plato was not alone in his idea that all earthly things were created after a heavenly archetype. This concept was quite common in the Near East, and the particular form of this concept given by Plato was not that reflected in Hebrews. The author of Hebrews evidently owed his concept to other Near Eastern influences. Platonism belongs to the same general point of view as that shared by the author of Hebrews, but Hebrews was not directly influenced by the Platonic variety of this outlook.[59]

After the temple which had been built according to the pattern given on Mount Sinai was destroyed in A.D. 70, Jews looked forward to the time when the heavenly city and the heavenly temple would appear on earth still more luxurious than before in the position where the archetype formerly stood—Zion (IV Ezra 7:26; 8:52; *SO* 5:420–29). According to Pseudo-Philo, Joshua called the altar built across the Jordan by the two and a half tribes stationed there an "altar made with hands" (*sacrarium manufactum*) (Pseudo-Philo 22:5). Some of the Dead Sea scroll fragments seem to reflect an anticipation of the destruction of the then existing temple and the establishment of one built with God's hands (4Q Florilegium). Flusser compared this to the report that Jesus planned to destroy the temple and build another not made with hands.[60] The expression "made with hands"

[56] Eliade, p. 7; E. Burrows, "Some Cosmological Patterns in Babylonian Religion," in *The Labyrinth,* ed. S. H. Hooke (London, 1935), pp. 65 ff.; C. T. Fritsch, "TO ANTITYPON," in *Studia Biblica et Semitica* dedicated to Th. C. Vriezen (Leiden, 1966), pp. 100–7.

[57] Eliade, p. 8. [58] Ibid., p. 9.

[59] Eliade, pp. 6–10. Williamson, p. 557, said: ". . . although something like the language of Philonic Platonism may be found in 8:5, there is no trace in the verse, or indeed anywhere else in the Epistle, of the fundamental attitudes or conviction which constitutes Platonism either in its original or in its Philonic form. The Writer of Hebrews does not even use his philosophical terminology in anything approaching a rigorously philosophical way."

[60] D. Flusser, "Two Notes on the Midrash on II Sam 7," IEJ 9 (1959), 99–104; see also Y. Yadin, "A Midrash on II Sam 7 and Ps 1–2 [4Q Florilegium],"

(*cheiropoiētos*) frequently referred to idolatry in the LXX, rendering *'elīl* or *'elīlīm.* LXX Daniel rendered these terms "gods" or "idols made with hands"; Stephen described both the temple and the golden calf as objects "made with hands"; and Paul was quoted in relationship to the pagan temples in Athens as saying that the Lord did not dwell in temples made with hands (*cheiropoiētois naois*) (Isa 2:18; 19:1; 31:7; LXX Dan 5:4, 23; 6:27[28]; Acts 7:41, 48; 17:24).[61] Enoch spoke of the temple that had been folded up and carried off. After that, however, the Lord of the sheep provided a new temple (*bēt ḥadīs*) which was bigger, but placed where the old one had formerly stood (Enoch 90:28–29). IV Ezra thought that when the Messiah was revealed the city which had previously been hidden would appear (IV Ezra 7:27, Arabic text). When the Son is revealed, Zion will become visible to all men, prepared and built without hands (*parata et aedificata . . . sine manibus*) (IV Ezra 13:36).[62] Eusebius referred to the Christian church after the liberation by Constantine as the new temple (*HE* X.iv.1–v.14).

Although the author of Hebrews may have expected the heavenly Jerusalem to be restored to earth and the real temple to be one ministered on earth by Christ in behalf of his church, the body of Christ, at the time of the writing the only real temple was in heaven, and it was from there that Jesus functioned as priest. He was not "on earth" to offer gifts according to the law (8:4), serving only "a pattern and shadow of the heavenly things." Scholars have found it difficult to think of Jesus offering sacrifice in heaven. The only offering he was thought to have made was the crucifixion, which was understood to be on earth.[63] The author, however, had a view of heaven that was much like the holy city and the temple where the Lord's presence was and sacrifices were offered. His concept of heaven in relationship to the temple will be examined in greater detail at the end of chapter nine.

The Greek word for "advised" is *kechrēmatistai,* which means "to transact business," "to act under the name of someone," "to advise," or "to warn solemnly." In scripture, this term is nearly always restricted to communications from God through a revelation, admonition, or direction from heaven (Matt 2:12, 22; Luke 2:26; Acts 10:22, *et passim*). Such is also the case here: "Moses was advised" means God advised or warned Moses solemnly to follow the specified "pattern."

6. The main discussion in this unit is the "ministry" of the earthly priests in comparison with that of the true priest who ministers in heaven. The words "minister" (*leitourgos*) and "ministry" (*leitourgias*) form the inclusion for this unit. The ministry under discussion is the function of the priest-

---

IEJ 9 (1959), 93–98; R. Hummel, *Die Auseinandersetzung zwischen Kirche und Judentum* (München, 1963), pp. 106–7; Matt 26:61; 27:40; Mark 14:58; 15:29; John 2:9; Acts 6:14.

[61] Sowers, p. 110, n. 57.

[62] For this whole discussion, see CC, pp. 76–80.

[63] Delitzsch, II, 67–68.

hood. This final verse also introduces the reader to the next topic that deals with the "covenant." The heavenly high priest, Jesus, "is also a mediator of a better covenant." In the author's judgment a new religion brings about a change in every aspect, priesthood, law, and covenant. In every instance, Jesus' religion was considered superior to that which preceded it, and the covenant was "made into law on the basis of better promises" which had been recorded in the later word of God according to the Psalms and prophets and confirmed by oath.

Summary.—This small unit introduced the heavenly nature of Jesus' ministry as over against the earthly ministry of the Levites. This means he has a better temple in heaven than the antitype on earth. From there he continues to offer sacrifices. The contrast between the earthly and the heavenly temple reflects a typical Near Eastern outlook on the relation of earthly objects to heavenly prototypes, but it is not Platonic. A proper understanding of Near Eastern concepts is necessary for a clear understanding of the rest of the document.

THE FIRST COVENANT

7. The author's logic is consistent: He reasoned that something's existence proves its necessity. The fact that there is "a place for a second" covenant proves that the first was not "faultless" (*amemptos*). It was Jeremiah, to be quoted next, who "sought" a new covenant, proving the old one faulty. Jeremiah had promised Judah that she would be taken captive into Babylon because her debt of sin to the Lord was so great that she could never repay it. Like a Jew in debt to his brother, Judah would have to work off her debt at half wages until sabbatical justice had been fulfilled.[64] Afterward the Lord would gather his children from the diaspora and bring them to their homeland in Palestine. The exodus from Babylon would be greater than the exodus from Egypt, and the Lord would make with his redeemed captives a new covenant that would be better than the old one that he made with those Hebrews who had been captive in Egypt (Jer 16:14–18; 23:3–8). The new covenant was to be better than the old one because the people would be enabled to keep it. It would be written on their minds and hearts rather than on tablets of stone. Since Jeremiah's prophecy about the captivity and return had been fulfilled to a satisfactory degree, later Jews expected the new covenant as well. One sect of covenanters believed that its members were the ones the Lord had chosen to be members of the new covenant (CDC 6:19; 8:21; 20:12). According to Paul, at the last supper which Jesus ate with his disciples, he said, "This cup is the new covenant in my blood" (I Cor 11:25). Hebrews also held that with Jesus, the new high priest, was established a new covenant which Jeremiah had promised.

8. The Greek for "blaming" (*memphomenos*) is from the same root as that translated "faultless" in vs. 7. The covenant was not blameless be-

[64] CC, pp. 9–18.

cause Jeremiah blamed Israelites for their inability to keep it. The "house of Israel" included the ten tribes of the Northern Kingdom, sometimes called "Joseph," "Ephraim," or "Samaria." "The house of Judah" included only Judah and Benjamin—two tribes near Jerusalem that comprised an area roughly twenty-five miles square. The two houses together constituted the entire Davidic kingdom. Jeremiah was from "the house of Judah," but he looked forward to a reunification of the United Kingdom. The Greek words for "conclude . . . a . . . covenant" are *syntelesō . . . diathēkēn,* literally, "I will finish," "conclude," "bring to an end," "a covenant" or "contract." The LXX for this is *diathēsomai . . . diathēkēn,* "I will covenant a covenant" or "agree upon an agreement." Here as in many places the author has varied his text from that of the LXX, and there has been no way of knowing whether he had access to a different version of the LXX or whether he just took liberties with the text, changing a word here or there to meet his needs. Because he quoted parts of this passage more than once, it will be possible to examine more closely his methods of using this scripture.

9. "Their fathers" are clearly not the patriarchs, but the Israelites in general who came out of Egypt. The picture of a father holding his small son's hand to keep him from getting lost or hurt is painted of the Lord taking Israel "by their hand to lead them from [the] land of Egypt." "Did not remain in my covenant" means they did not keep their side of the agreement or covenant. The Lord agreed to be their God, but they also agreed to be his people, which meant obeying him, keeping his commandments, trusting him, and treating one another according to his directions. The author earlier complained about the exodus generation. They had evil, unbelieving hearts; they resisted the Lord; they became bitter, unbelieving, and disobedient (3:12–19). The Greek translated "I ignored" is *ēmelēsa,* "I had no care," "I neglected," "I slighted" or "I overlooked," which is the same as the LXX Jer 38:32. The MT Jer 31:32 has *w^{e}ānōkī bā'altī bām,* "and I was a husband to them," "I was a Lord to them," or "I loathed them," "rejected them with loathing."[65] The author used the LXX but he did not follow it exactly. For "says [the] Lord" Hebrews has *legei* meaning "says," which is a synonym for LXX *phēsin,* but as in the change from "contract" to "conclude" in vs. 8, the change was only to a synonym; it did not change the meaning of the sentence.

10. Verse 10 is a direct quote from LXX Jer 38:33 with only three variants:[66] *legei* is given for the LXX *phēsin; epigrapsō* replaced *grapsō* for "I will write"; and for *didous dōsō,* "I will surely give" or "I will surely put" (a Semitism), the author of Hebrews reads only *didous,* "giving" or "putting," rendered here more freely "[I will] put." Quoting the same passage in 10:16, however, the author of Hebrews additionally changed "with the house of Israel" (*tǭ oikǭ Israēl*) to "with them" (*pros autous*) and changed

[65] So Stuart, p. 187.

[66] An important variant between the LXX and MT is the LXX reading "my laws" for "my law."

"in their minds and on their hearts" to "on their hearts and on their minds" in 10:16. Since presumably in both cases the author of Hebrews used the same LXX text and in one case showed variants not in the other, it seems likely that he also took the liberty to make the other minor changes in the text that he used. There is very little likelihood that he used a different text for 8:10 from the one he used in 10:16–17.

Jeremiah seemed to think if all people *knew* the Lord, i.e., knew his commandments and will, then there would be unity under the covenant. In his day, people followed various religious customs and laws. If the Lord would only fix indelibly on their minds the same rules, then the covenant community would function as the Lord planned it.

11. "Fellow citizen" (*ton politēn*) and "brother" (*ton adelphon*) were both synonyms for Jew, Israelite, or covenanter. If the Lord put the laws on their hearts and minds, then they would all have them memorized, so there would be no need to teach them to one another. Another possibility is that they would be new creatures made unable to sin. "From the least to the greatest" is a merismus, a literary form using both extremes as a means of including everything in between. It is the same as saying "all," the word with which the expression stands in apposition.

12. In this Semitic parallel, dealing "mercifully with their . . . sins" means that he "will no longer remember" them.

This passage from Jeremiah (LXX 38[31]:31–34) is even longer than the quotation from Ps 95 in chapter three, which indicates that the author considered this a very important passage, just as he did Ps 95.

13. The short comment that the author made following the quotation was only a summary. The further discussion on the covenant was planned to come later in his discussion.

"In using the word 'new'" is a free translation for *en tǭ legein kainēn,* literally, "in [the act of] saying 'new.'" The author emphasized this word to contrast the new covenant with the old, which he considered obsolete, vanishing, practically worn out.

Summary.—This unit includes only a brief introduction and conclusion to the text quoted from Jeremiah, but the author used these to form an inclusion of the two uses of the word "first" (8:7, 13). The word "first" also is a catchword used to introduce the reader to the subject that follows. The "first" which follows, however, is not the covenant, but the tent (9:1). The following unit is still centered around the old cult.

TEMPLE FUNCTIONS

9:1. The conjectured noun which "the first" modifies is here taken to be "tent." In fact some minor texts (326 *pm*) read "tent" (*skēnē*) here, but that is not the basic reason for the conjecture given. This is the first part of a *men* . . . *de* (on the one hand . . . on the other) construction, and the second part of the construction is taken to refer to "[the] holy of holies," "beyond the second curtain" (9:3). This seems to imply that "the first" refers to the first part of the temple and that "beyond the second curtain" refers to the second "tent." Josephus also described the *hēkāl* which contains the "lampstand, table, and altar of incense" as the "first part" (*prōton meros*) (*Wars* V.216) and the "holy of holies" as the "innermost part" (*endotatō meros*) (*Wars* V.219). The RSV understood this differently, however, and rendered Heb 9:1 as referring to "the first covenant," rather than "the first [tent]," and the second part of the *men . . . de* construction to be continued in Heb 9:11. This would be a very long grammatical construction that would include one *men . . . de* construction (9:6–7) within another (9:1, 11–12). The RSV understanding would show the contrast between the first covenant and the second covenant rather than between the first part and the second part of the temple. Since Hebrews clearly did contrast the covenants, and since Christ's function in the more perfect tent (9:11) is contrasted to the priest's function in the first tent, it is possible that the RSV is correct in understanding this to be a very long *men . . . de* construction which further contrasted the two covenants; but this ignores the structure which the author has designed to show the division of his units. Heb 9:1–10 is enclosed in an inclusion, separating the content of 9:1–10 from the following material. It therefore seems unlikely that he would have intended to hold the two units together by a *men . . . de* construction.

"The proper things" (*dikiōmata*) are the things prescribed as being necessary "for worship." The "earthly sanctuary" (*hagion kosmikon*) was the temple in which the levitical priests functioned on earth (8:4), in contrast to the heavenly temple, where Jesus ministers (8:2, 5; 9:11, 24; 11:16). Josephus and Philo, however, both describe the temple, its contents, and the priestly garments as symbols of the universe (*Ant.* III.180–87; *Wars* IV.324; V.216–18; *Heres* XLI.196–97; XLVI.226), which may be another reason for calling it "earthly."

2–3. The division of the temple into two units or "tents" as Hebrews describes them conforms to the architecture of the temple as closely as the insights of early literature and archaeology can reconstruct. The temple at Arad, Israel, excavated by Prof. Aharoni, was originally constructed in about the tenth century B.C. Its entire size was only about sixty-five feet long and forty-nine feet wide. The largest room was the court (*'ūlām*) which contained a large altar for sacrificing animals, just as Philo (*Mos.* II. 94) described. The next room (the *hēkāl*, "outer tent," or "[the] holy") was only nine feet wide and thirty feet long—about a third as large as the court. The very small room that was connected to this room was the "holy of holies," the *d^{e}bīr*, or the inner tent. It was in the center of the western wall of the "outer tent" and had three steps in the doorway. Inside this "inner tent" were found a pillar (*maṣṣēbāh*) and a small, square, paved altar (*bāmāh*). This early temple was later enlarged, but only to the extent that was admissible by changing to a larger Egyptian cubit from an earlier smaller cubit measure (ca. 18 to ca. 21 inches). There was enough similarity between the measurements of the temple at Arad and Solomon's temple in Jerusalem (II Chron 3–4) for Aharoni to conjecture that there was an intentional attempt to follow the proportions of the tabernacle in the wilderness when building temples (Exod 26:16–30) such as that at Arad, or those at Jerusalem, Shiloh, Bethel, and Dan.[67] Josephus' dimensions of Herod's temple, however, were somewhat different.

The author may have deduced the contents of the respective "tents" from II Chron 4, but the contents are not precisely the same as the ones given in Hebrews. That there were such things as tables, lampstands, and an ark in the Jerusalem temple which Herod built is evident from the picture of the victory procession carved into the Arch of Titus in Rome. These objects were shown as those taken from the temple when Jerusalem was captured in A.D. 70. Other biblical descriptions of the temple are given in Isa 6, Ezek 40:1–45:5 and I Kings 6–7 (see also II Bar 6:7). Josephus described the Herodian temple at length (*Wars* V.184–236). He said the temple (*naos*—both the holy and the holy of holies, but not the court) was sixty by twenty cubits (ca. 35 ft. by 105 ft.; see Ezek 41:2). This was divided into two parts: The holy was forty by twenty cubits (35 ft. by 70 ft.) and the holy of holies (*hagiou de hagion*) was twenty by twenty cubits (35 ft. by 35 ft.). He said that there was a partition between the holy and the holy of holies, and he also said the one was separated from the other by a veil or curtain. Either this partition was a curtain or the partition had a gate or doorway in it that was closed by a curtain. In the first portion (*prōton meros*), the "holy," was kept "a lampstand, a table, and an altar of incense" (*luchnian trapezan thumiatērion*) (*Wars* V.216). Philo concurred in this (*Heres* XLVI.226). The author of Hebrews did not mention an altar of incense, but he said there was a gold altar in the holy of holies, which may be the same piece of furniture with some disagreement about its location.[68] Hebrews and Josephus both said there were "loaves" on the table, and Josephus, following Lev 24:3, said further that the number of loaves was twelve (*Wars* V.217; *Ant.* III.182). The second tent, which both Hebrews and Josephus described as the "holy of holies," contained many important objects according to 9:3 (also II Bar 6:7), but according to Josephus it contained "nothing at all" (*ouden holōs en autǭ*) (*Wars* V.219). The rabbis claim that the ark of the covenant was removed and a stone remained in its place from the time of the early prophets on (Yoma 5:2; Shek. 6:1–2).[69] "The second curtain" separated "[the] holy" from "[the] holy of holies." No mention is made of a first curtain, but there probably was a curtain separating the "holy" from the court where the large altar was constructed for sacrificing animals. Philo said the altar for the burnt offerings was placed in the open air opposite the "tent" (the "holy"), at a distance adequate to allow the

[67] Y. Aharoni, "Arad: Its Inscriptions and Temple," BA 31 (1968), 18–27.

[68] See R. de Langhe, "L'Autel d'Or du Temple de Jerusalem," *Biblica* 40 (1959), 476–94, for a thought-provoking analysis of the function of the altar of incense and its relationship to the altar of gold.

[69] For a careful analysis of Near Eastern temples made before Aharoni's excavation of Arad, see W. F. Albright, *Archaeology and the Religion of Israel* (Baltimore, 1942), pp. 142–55.

ministers to work (*Mos.* II. 94). This fits in perfectly with the design of the temple at Arad, which seems a bit different in design from that described by Josephus. Since Josephus described only the holy and the holy of holies, no attempt will be made to indicate the place of the altar for sacrificing animals in relationship to the rest.

According to Josephus

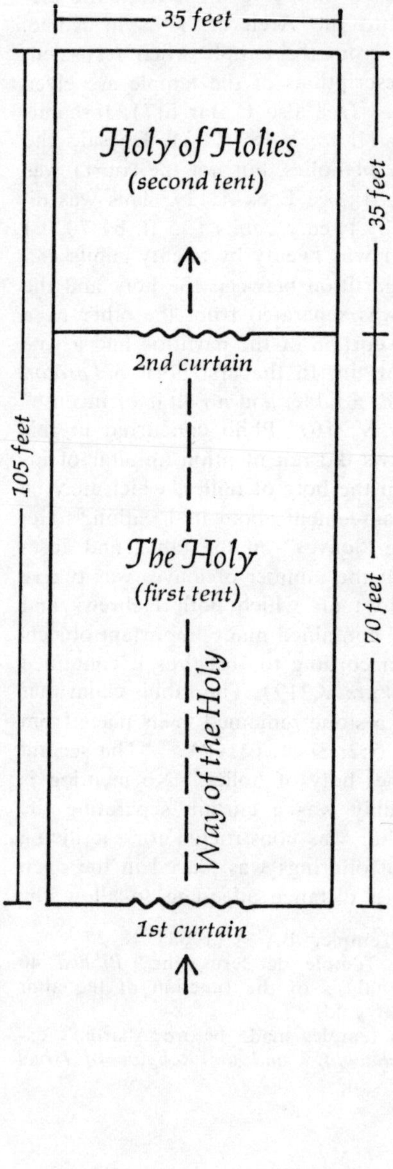

According to Philo and excavations at Arad

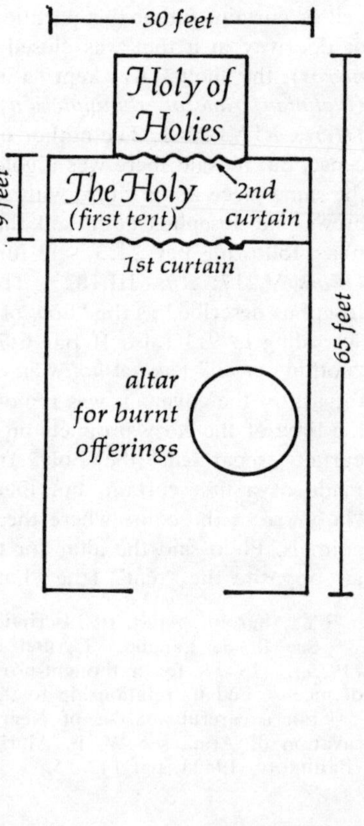

4. The "gold altar" may be the same as the altar of incense which Philo said was in "the holy." Philo agreed that "the ark of the covenant" was kept in the "holy of holies." He also said the ark was covered on the inside and outside "with gold." According to Exod 16:33 and Num 17:25 (MT; RSV 17:10), Moses commanded that Aaron's staff and the jar that contained the omer measure of manna be placed before the ark of the covenant. Hebrews follows the LXX in noting that the "jar" for the "manna" was "gold" (Exod 16:33). Mekilta *Vayassa'* 6:65–70, held that the jar was of earthenware. Rabbis also believed that in the future Elijah would restore to Israel the container of manna, the flask of sprinkling water, and the jar of anointing oil. Some also said "the rod of Aaron" produced ripe almonds and blossoms (*Vayassa'* 6:82–85). Philo called "the tablets of the covenant" "the holy books," but agreed that they were kept in the ark (*Mos.* II. 95).

5. "The cherubim" were Sphinx-like beings with faces of human beings, bodies of animals, and wings like birds. Their description, "of glory," means "of God" (see Exod 25:22; Num 7:89; Ezek 10:19; Rom 1:23). They might be called "divine cherubim." The object rendered "mercy seat" is *hilastērion,* from the verb *hilaskomai* which means "to appease," "propitiate," or "conciliate." This is the word used to render *kappōret* in Exod 25:17, 21. The Hebrew root *kpr* means to cover and is used to describe atonement, which is a covering for sins. That which is called "the mercy seat" is really the cover or lid for the ark, and the Hebrew word meant that. Because this was in the holy of holies where the priest entered to make atonement, the word may have taken on an added significance (I Chron 28:11). It was not just a "cover," but something related to the covering of sins. The LXX translated it as such.[70] Philo said the *hilastērion* was a cover (*epithema*) for the ark which supported the cherubim. He reported that "some say" the cherubim faced each other on top of the cover, but he seems not to have known for certain (*Mos.* II. 97–98).

6. "These things having been thus prepared" refers to the furniture and required objects in the holy and the holy of holies, the proper things for worship (9:1), made ready for priestly function. "The first tent" was "[the] holy" place on the other side of the first curtain from the court where the large altar for burnt offerings was. No laymen were permitted in that holy place, but "priests enter continually" as they perform the various "ritualistic services" required by the law.

7. "*The second* [*tent*]" excludes admission, not only of all laymen, but of all priests except "*the high priest,*" and he used it "[only] once during the year," on the Day of Atonement. This evidently means "one occasion" during the year, rather than one specific entrance. Lev 16:11–16 describes two entrances on the Day of Atonement, one to atone for the high priest and his family and one for the whole people of Israel. Rabbis said the high priest entered the holy of holies four times on the Day of Atonement (Num

[70] So Stuart, p. 195. D. N. Freedman has noted that in Akkadian the cognate apparently means "wipe away," which seems to fit the priestly actions and both traditions. Only Philo seems to be at variance with this.

R. 7:8. 21a; Yoma 5:1 – 7:4). When he entered the holy of holies, he brought "blood," first from the bull (Lev 16:14) and then from the goat (16:15), which he sprinkled ritualistically with his finger seven times before the ark. The ritual prescribed in Lev 16 for the Day of Atonement was supposed to atone for *all* Israel's sins (Lev 16:34), with no distinction made between the intentional and unintentional sins. Rabbis, however, claimed that atonement was not automatic (TYoma 5:6). On that day the Lord forgave only the sins committed against him, and then only if the conditions were right. The covenanter was required first to be reconciled to his brother against whom he had sinned; he had to repent; and he had to bring his sin and guilt offerings to the temple of the Lord (Yoma 8:8–9; see also Matt 5:23–24). "If a man said, 'I will sin and repent, and sin again and repent,' he will be given no chance to repent. [If he said], 'I will sin and the Day of Atonement will effect atonement,' then the Day of Atonement effects no atonement" (Yoma 8:9). This was probably the condition the author of Hebrews had in mind when he wrote about the priest's atonement "of his own [sins] and the unintentional [sins] of the people." It would seem as if the same conditions would also apply to the priest himself. It is not clear from the text itself whether "his own" refers to the noun "[sins]," which is understood, or whether this modifies "unintentional [sins]." If the latter is true, as seems likely, then a better translation is: "in behalf of his own unintentional [sins] and those of the people." This would concur with the assessment of the high priest being able to intercede for the people's sins of ignorance since he himself was clothed in weakness (5:2). Being "guileless" (7:26) may have meant having committed no intentional sins and no sins that had not been reconciled. Philo said the high priest never committed sins that could not be cleansed (*Spec.* I. 230), which meant he never sinned intentionally. Therefore this would not be an issue, but Philo's idealization of the priesthood may not have been representative of general Jewish understanding of that time.

8. When "the Holy Spirit" communicates, according to the author, it usually means that the scripture says (3:7; 10:15), but here there is no scriptural proof text, so it is not certain on what basis "the Holy Spirit makes it clear." "The way of the holy [precincts]" in a temple context probably means the way from the court through the first curtain, to the holy, then through the second curtain, to the holy of holies. Before Christ's sacrifice, laymen had no access to the holy, and while curtains were closed they could not even see the holy. If the curtain was open, they could see the holy but not the holy of holies. "While the first tent" (the holy) was still standing, it provided an obstacle to the vision of those in the court, keeping the holy of holies from being visible. In fact, with the curtains, the entire "way of the holy [precincts]" from the court to the altar was not visible to the layman in the court. Therefore the layman gave his offering, but did not get to see what happened to it. It was shrouded in mystery. The worshiper with a little skepticism about the priests might doubt whether his offering was really sacrificed and offered

properly. "While the first tent still stands" seems to imply that the time might come when the "first tent" would be removed. This reference does not seem to be in a fitting context to mean the first temple that was destroyed in 586 B.C. or the second temple replaced by Herod's temple about 20 B.C. It seems to have no bearing on any destruction of the temple, but rather to the removal of the outer "tent" which kept "the way of the holy [precincts]" from being "visible." Later in the document the author said the sacrifice of Jesus opened a fresh and living way through the curtain (10:19–20). That would mean that the believer would no longer have this "way" closed to him.

9–10. "This," literally "which" (*hētis*), seems to have "tent" (*skēnē*) (vs. 8) as its antecedent, although it might have a general subject, meaning this whole situation or something like that. The basic meaning is very similar in any case. The first tent is considered "a parable" or an analogy "for the present time" and the current situation. The liturgical situation of that time seemed analogous to the first tent which stood in the way and obstructed the view. This was "not able to perfect" the worshiper's *"conscience,"* perhaps because the worshiper went away doubting or wondering whether his gift had really been offered and his sin removed. He was left either to trust where he could not see or to have an imperfected "conscience." If he had no confidence in the priesthood or the efficacy of their sacrifice, he had to rely on the rules that laymen could observe: dietary laws, fasts, and levitical ablutions. This explanation would make rather good sense if the author had not spoken about "drinks" as well as about "foods and various ablutions." There are no general rules in the Pentateuch concerning the drinking of intoxicating liquors or prohibition of drinking any other kind of liquids, that would affect the average layman. Priests refrained from drinking alcoholic beverages in the temple (Lev 10:8–9). Jews refrained from drinking alcoholic beverages as part of the fast on the Day of Atonement (*Mos.* II. 24). There are regulations for priests (Lev 10:9) that prohibit their use of wine or strong drink while they functioned at the tent of meeting, and there are prohibitions against the Nazirite's drinking any kind of juice from grapes. This kind of regulation would apply only to a group of priests who were disgruntled with the administration of the temple in Jerusalem or to some very rigorous group of legalists like the "mourners for Zion" who were sometimes, if not always, under Nazirite vows. The other possibility is that it referred to the fasting and purification associated with the Day of Atonement, i.e. part of the service in which the laymen could participate.

There are many indications in the document that the author and readers were very rigorous legalists, and maybe even a communally oriented group of monks, but the specific nature of the society can only be deduced from the message "To the Hebrews." Therefore the implications involved in these statements must be very tentative and conjectural.

The "proper [observances] of the flesh" are the same as the "proper things for worship" related to "an earthly sanctuary" (9:1). Both "earthly" and "flesh" are negative evaluations of the Pentateuchal rules and the sacrificial system of the levitical priests. "The time of correction" (*kairou diorthōseōs*) is literally, "the time of setting straight" or "making right." This would happen when the "jubilee" arrived, the "captives" were set free and the land was restored to its "original" owners. This would be the end of the evil age and mark a beginning of the age to come when a new administration would be in force, and the believers would find "rest." It is the same as the time of restoration (*apokatastaseōs*) of all that which God had promised (Acts 3:21; see also Mal 3:1; 4:5, 6; Isa 65:17; 66:22).

Summary.—This unit is also framed by an inclusion, marked by the word "proper" (*dikaiōmata*) in both 9:1 and 9:10. In between these verses is a rather accurate and explicit description of the parts of the temple where priests alone were admitted and the ways in which these were used and by whom. Throughout, the author appears critical of the whole system. It was earthly (9:1) and it was "not able to perfect the worshiper according to [his] conscience," so the worshiper was left to his own methods of keeping or becoming sinless "until the time of correction" when this whole system would be replaced by something better and more satisfying.

Chapters eight and nine are organized so as to present a balanced argument of Christ's superiority over the previous system. In a way that is typical of the author, he first explained the normal way of functioning and the basis for judging its validity. Then he followed with an argument showing that Jesus was superior by the very same standards. The remainder of the outline will show that the last three units were intended to negate the present temple and its priestly functions. These next three units will show the wonderful way in which Christ replaces each of them. The argument was presented in a chiastic structure[71]:

1. The old cult	2. The new cult
a) Earthly ministry	a) Christ's sacrifice
b) First covenant	b) The bloody covenant
c) Temple functions	c) The heavenly ministry

The new cult

CHRIST'S SACRIFICE

11. The strongest reading favors "the good things that have happened" (*tōn genomenōn agathōn*) but some good texts (ℵA) have *tōn mellontōn agathōn,* "the good things to come." The more difficult reading is "the good things that have happened," which occurs only here in Hebrews. *Mellō,* on the contrary, is used frequently (1:14; 2:5; 6:5; 8:5; 10:1, 27; 11:8, 20) and is the reading one might expect here. Therefore it would be a normal

[71] As my colleague, Dr. J. T. Clemons, has observed.

correction for later scribes, whereas it is difficult to understand why a later scribe might have made the opposite change.[72] The good things to come would refer to the "time of correction" (9:10) when the promises of God would be fulfilled. "The good things that have happened" probably refer to the crucifixion and the sacrifice of Christ that has been made for believers. The "greater and more perfect tent" is in contrast to the "earthly sanctuary" in which the sons of Aaron conduct their ministry (9:1).[73]

The expression "not made with hands" (*ou cheiropoiētou*) means it is not idolatrous as are frequently the objects "made with hands" (see COMMENT on 8:2–5). Philo said that Moses allowed a temple made with hands (*cheirokmēton*) but permitted only one temple for one God (*Spec.* 66–67). The rabbis said that the Lord built the temple with his own hands (Mekilta *Shirata* 10:29–42), and when he built it again with his two hands, he would again rule from there (ibid., 10:42–43). The main Old Testament testimony for God's having made the sanctuary (*miqdāš*) with his own hands is Exod 15:17, which the rabbis understood to mean the temple at Jerusalem, but before the rabbis reached their conclusions, the Psalmist wrote:

> "He chose the tribe of Judah, Mount Zion which he loved;
> Then he built, like lofty ones, his sanctuary,
> like the land [which] he established for the age (*'ōlām*)
> (Ps 78:68, 69).[74]

Since it was made with God's own hands, it was "not made with [human] hands." The earthly temple was considered by some to be so much like the heavenly temple (JBer. IV.5.8c) that the two were sometimes almost confused, but they were not always considered synonymous. Those who did not approve of the priesthood at Jerusalem and its conduct of liturgical affairs called it a temple made with hands (Acts 7:47–48) and contrasted it to the temple "not made with hands." Some also called the Jerusalem high priest "the wicked priest" (1QpHab). The author of Hebrews was associated with those of this opinion. The statement, "that is, not of this creation," is an interpretative gloss, apparently added by someone who was not familiar with the technical meaning of the expression "not made with hands."

12. According to 9:7, the high priest never entered the holy of holies

[72] So also J. M. Boyer, "Las Variantes *Mellontōn y genomenōn* en Heb 9:11," *Biblica* 32 (1951), 232–36.

[73] A. Vanhoye's suggestion that the greater and more perfect tent is the risen body of Christ ("'Par la Tente plus Grand et plus Parfait' [Heb 9:11]," *Biblica* 46 [1965], 1–28) and J. Swetnam's theory, that it was a eucharist allusion ("'The Greater and More Perfect Tent.' A Contribution to the Discussion of Heb 9:11," *Biblica* 47 [1966], 91–106) both seem far-fetched. See also J. Swetnam, "On the Imagery and Significance of Hebrews 9:9–10," CBQ 28 (1966), 155–73.

[74] D. N. Freedman called attention to this and has tentatively suggested on the basis of this that the whole promised land may have been considered a holy temple made with God's own hands.

without blood, but, of course, the blood he sprinkled on the ark was the "blood of goats and bulls," goats for the people and bulls for the priests. Christ, acting as high priest, offered "his own blood," a much superior offering. Also in contrast to the priests, who entered the holy continually, and the high priest, who entered the holy of holies every Day of Atonement, Christ entered "once for all" (*ephapax*) "into the holy [precincts]" (see also 4:14; 6:20; 9:12, 15, 23–24). Although their many sacrifices did not succeed in satisfying the conscience (9:9), his "once for all" sacrifice successfully "found eternal redemption."

The whole doctrine of redemption was determined in relationship to business ethics. If an Israelite became poor, he might "sell" the use of his property until the jubilee year, but he always did so with the right of redemption. That is, if some kinsman became his redeemer and provided the necessary money, he could buy the property back. Or, if he became more prosperous himself, he might redeem his own property. If he could not redeem it, it was restored to the original family in the jubilee year, in any event. If the property was in a walled city, however, he had only one year to redeem it. After that, the property became unconditionally owned by the purchaser, unless the man who sold it was a Levite. If he was, his land within a walled city could only be kept from him until the next jubilee (Lev 25:25–34). If a person did not have land he might repay his debts by selling his labor to the creditor until his debt was paid (Lev 25:39–55) or until the sabbath year. When the jubilee year arrived, all land was restored to its original owners, and debtors were released from their labor. This was a joyful time, but it sometimes required a long wait. The waiting time was shortened if a man could redeem himself, which was seldom the case. Usually his freedom and his possession of the land depended upon a redeemer who came to his rescue and paid the necessary price for him to gain his freedom or his land. The feeling of gratitude toward a redeemer was natural.

It was in the light of this concept of a redeemer that the Lord was called Israel's redeemer. When the Israelites were in bondage to Pharaoh, the Lord delivered them from there, which meant that he redeemed them (Exod 6:6). After he had redeemed them, the Lord led his redeemed people through the wilderness (Exod 15:13). Likewise after the Jews had become enslaved in Babylon, away from their promised land, the Lord redeemed them and restored them to their land (Isa 43:1; 44:22–23; 48:20; 52:9; 63:9), so the Lord was called the redeemer (Isa 41:14; 43:14; 44:6, 24; 47:4; 48:17; 49:7, 26; 54:5, 8; 59:20; 60:16; 63:16). Since sins were thought of as debts in relationship to a treasury-of-merits theology (Matt 6:12), the Lord who redeemed Israel pardoned her iniquity (Isa 40:2). The high priest (9:11) who obtained forgiveness of sins, by the same token, "found . . . redemption" and shortened the term of service (Matt 24:22).

13. The "ashes of a heifer" were those obtained by burning a red heifer outside of the camp according to a specially prescribed process. The ashes

were used to mix with water, as necessity arose, to be sprinkled on persons who had become defiled by touching a corpse or being in a tent where there was a corpse, or by touching the slain in battle, or a bone from a corpse (Num 19). When this was properly done, it was believed that it would sanctify the "defiled" persons "for the cleansing of the flesh."

14. The main thrust of the *a fortiori* argument comes here. If such weak and primitive methods as those prescribed in the Pentateuch cleansed people from defilement and sin, "how much more the blood of Christ" would "cleanse"! The red heifer had to be without blemish (Num 19:2), so Christ was "blameless." In addition he functioned "through [the] eternal spirit." Therefore, he could be expected not merely to cleanse covenanters from corpse defilement; he could "cleanse" their "conscience" as the earthly tent ministries could not (9:9) from "dead works." These were the deeds done before baptism into the community where alone "life" was possible. Those who joined these exclusive sects separated themselves from the rest of the world, which was considered dead. They repented and were cleansed by baptism from this "dead" life they had once lived. The terms for corpse defilement were applied to non-sectarians to emphasize the difference between the Jews and the Gentiles, the church and the world, the clean and the defiled. The blood of Christ was used both in the way the blood of goats and bulls was used, and in the way the ashes of the red heifer were used. Blood was sprinkled against the ark (Lev 16:14–15), and ashes and water were sprinkled on the unclean. It was more efficacious than both the other methods put together. It "cleansed" the "conscience" so that the redeemed and cleansed person would be completely freed from his former "dead works" and as one who was then alive, he might worship "the living God." The person defiled by corpse uncleanness, who failed to be properly cleansed, would be excommunicated if he dared to enter the tabernacle (Num 19:11–13). Until he was cleansed, he was not free to worship. The author extends the figure to deal with those who have not been cleansed of their "dead works." The cleansing of Christ's blood is necessary for worship.

Summary.—The word "Christ" which appears both in vss. 11 and 14 forms the inclusion that separates this as a unit. The whole unit consists of a comparison of Jesus' sacrifice and cleansing, in an *a fortiori* argument, with the sacrifices offered by the Aaronic priests and the cleansing method employed by using the ashes of the red heifer. The comparison of method was followed throughout, using metaphorically the imagery of sacrifice, cleansing, corpse defilement, and worship in the tabernacle.

Many parallels exist between 9:1–10 and 9:11–14. These are antithetic, as the following chart, adapted from Vanhoye, shows.[75] They also point out the step-by-step logic of the author and his consistent emphasis on the superiority of Christ.

[75] Vanhoye, pp. 150–51.

a. The first tent . . . prepared (1–2)	a. tent not made with hands (11)
b. priests enter continually (6)	b. Christ . . . entered once for all (11–12)
c. not without blood (7)	c. through his own blood (12)
d. gifts and sacrifices (9)	d. offered himself blameless (14)
e. not able to perfect the worshiper according to [his] conscience (9)	e. will cleanse our conscience (14)

THE BLOODY COVENANT

15. "Because of this" refers to Christ's effectiveness in offering sacrifice and cleansing from sin so that the believer might worship the living God (9:11–14). Jesus is understood as "[the] mediator of a new covenant," just as Moses was understood to be the mediator of the law which was ordained by angels (Gal 3:19).

The covenant that the Lord made with his people was an agreement that he would be their God, and they would be his people. This agreement was intended to be in force while both God and the Israelites were very much alive. The new covenant which Jeremiah predicted was intended to be the same kind of agreement. Since Jesus had died, however, and since the author of Hebrews was convinced that Jesus was the "mediator of a new covenant," it strengthened the author's case if he discussed the covenant in terms of a will, since the Greek word *diathēkē* means both "will" and "covenant." The importance of a will is that the persons designated in it "receive" an "inheritance."

"The eternal inheritance" (*tēs aiōniou klēronomias*) or "the inheritance of the age" refers to that possession which was promised to the elect or "those who are called" in the age to come or the age of rest. Those who inherited the promises (6:12, 17) or "the eternal inheritance" had rest on the land (Josh 21:43–45). R. Yoḥanan said that whoever walked four cubits in the land of Israel was promised (*mubṭaḥ*) that he was "a son of the age to come" (Keth. 111a). Those who gathered around Moses were "preserved for life of the age" (Sifré Deut 29:9; 129b §305). Enoch promised that the elect would inherit the land (Enoch 5:7). Dalman correctly acknowledged that Ps 37:11 refers to the possession of the land, but added without evidence, "that the expression is metaphorical in Matt 5:5 there can be no doubt."[76] This was an easy dismissal of a logical assumption—that the same land referred to in Ps 37:11 was also intended by the author who quoted Ps 37:11 in Matt 5:5. In the age to come the elect were promised that they would receive the land of Israel for an inheritance.

[76] G. H. Dalman, *The Words of Jesus,* tr. D. M. Kay (Edinburgh, 1902), I, 126.

This would be their "inheritance of the age" or the "eternal inheritance." The close relationship between being "called" and being heirs is also reflected in Rom 8:17–30. "Those who are called" are the elect, who have been justified and glorified. They are "sharers in [the] heavenly calling" (3:1), and the ones whose names are mentioned in the "new covenant" (will).

16. The author regularly used analogies in his exposition, and he also regularly explained the full meaning of a term in its normal usage before he applied it to Jesus and his ministry. Since he intended to point up the significance of a *diathēkē* as a "will," he explained the normal conditions of a will. The person who made a will designated in it what should happen to his possessions in the event of his death. Therefore the will would have no effect on anyone until or unless the "one who made the will" died.

17. This verse is somewhat redundant and somewhat a further elaboration on 16. The will is secure or valid only "with reference to the dead." Whatever the one who made the will stipulated would apply after his death. The will would not be opened until the one who made the will was dead. After death wills are administered according to the conditions set forth by the dead while they were still living. But, even though a will was made out when the person was alive, "it is never valid when the one who made the will is alive."

18. The Greek word rendered "inaugurated" (*egkekainistai*) can also mean "renewed" or "dedicated." "Renewed" or "inaugurated" seems a better word in this context, referring to Sinai. The ceremony usually called the covenant renewal, however, did not refer to blood (Josh 24).[77] "The first covenant" referred to the covenant associated with the decalogue (Exod 24) which was first "inaugurated" and later "renewed" after Moses broke the tablets because the people's idolatry (Exod 32:15–19) had broken the covenant and dissolved the relationship. Afterward Moses went back up on the mountain and cut two more tablets of stone; the decalogue was given again; and the Lord made a covenant with the people again (Exod 34:1–10). There is no reference to sprinkling blood in this renewal, but since it was a covenant made in relationship to the same people, the same Lord, and the same decalogue, the author may have supposed that it was made with the same ceremony the second time (Exod 34) as was described at first (Exod 24). Therefore it could be called "the first covenant" which "was renewed" and "not without blood."[78] By the author's time the first covenant had already been "renewed."

19. This verse returns to the main covenantal theme with the verbal tie

[77] G. E. Mendenhall, *Law and Covenant in Israel and the Ancient Near East* (Pittsburgh, 1955), p. 40, insists that there was a new covenant formed in the time of Joshua rather than a renewal of a previously existing covenant.

[78] J. Swetnam, "A Suggested Interpretation of Hebrews 9:15," CBQ 27 (1965), 373–90, has made a good case for the consistency of the author's argument. He held that the animals sacrificed for the Sinai covenant really put the covenant in force. In the same way, the new will was made effective by Jesus' death.

to Heb 9:7, "not without blood." Just as 9:15–17 showed that Christ's testament was valid from the standpoint of a last will and testament, so here the author shows that Jesus' covenant was made in the proper form to be considered favorably in relationship to the first covenant of the Israelites with Jehovah.

The author of Hebrews correctly reported the actions of Moses in relation to the people: "Now Moses came and told the people all the words of Jehovah and all the ordinances, and all the people answered with one voice" (Exod 24:3). After this, Moses took the blood from the sacrifices (which Hebrews said was from "bulls and goats").[79] He sprinkled it upon the altar and upon the people (Exod 24:5–8). The author of Hebrews expanded the event to include not only blood, but "water and crimson wool and hyssop," which were not a part of the covenant ceremony at all but belonged to the ceremony used (together with blood from a bird) to cleanse a leper (Lev 14:6–7), and they were mixed with the red heifer's corpse and burned to provide the ashes necessary for cleansing a covenanter from corpse defilement (Num 19:6). The author also expanded the report to include not only the altar and "the people," but also "the book itself," which was probably understood to mean the two tablets on which the decalogue was engraved.

20. The quotation from Exod 24:8 was paraphrased by Jesus when he instituted the new covenant according to Matt 26:28. The author of Hebrews changed from "Behold" (LXX Exod 24:8) to "This [is]," possibly to agree with the eucharistic words of Jesus (Matt 26:28), and "Lord" to "God" to avoid confusing the subject with Jesus.[80]

21. Although the scripture does not confirm this claim, Josephus told of cleansing the priests, their vestments, the tabernacle, and its vessels, not only with oil (so Exod 40), but also with the blood of bulls and goats (*Ant.* III. 206). Since the author has associated the covenant so closely with sacrifice, the temple, and atonement, he may have mingled his report of the sprinkling associated with the covenant ceremony with the atonement ceremony and also the dedication of the tabernacle. He may have reasoned that the tabernacle was dedicated at the same time Moses brought the tablets down from the mountain and placed them in the ark in the tabernacle. Therefore the blood used for the covenant ceremony was also used for sprinkling the rest of the liturgical objects.

22. Not "everything" was "cleansed with blood." Some things were cleansed with water (Lev 15:10 et al.) and some by fire (Num 31:22–23), but "nearly everything" was "cleansed with blood." This is part of the author's inclusive speech: "every commandment . . . all the people . . .

[79] The author of Hebrews may possibly have taken this from Josephus, but it is more likely that Hebrews and Josephus depended upon a common source (*Ant.* III. 206). For an interesting discussion on this text, see Swetnam, CBQ 27 (1965), 373–90.

[80] So K. J. Thomas, "The Old Testament Citations in Hebrews," NTS 11 (1964–65), 313.

all the people (19) . . . all the liturgical vessels . . . nearly everything." In dealing with punishment for murder, Philo said, "Blood is cleansed with blood" (*Spec.* III. 150). Rabbis insisted that atonement could be made only with blood (Zeb. 6a; Men. 91b; Yoma 5a). Together with the covenant the Lord made with Noah, he commanded that Noah's posterity continue daily sacrifice before the altar with blood to obtain forgiveness (Jub 6:1–14). The author of Hebrews, accordingly, reflected quite a general opinion when he said, "without [the] pouring out of blood, forgiveness does not occur."

23. "The symbols" (*hypodeigmata*) referred to the things associated with the temple made with hands. They are under the administration of the inadequate priesthood, the first covenant, and the law. "These" (things) are only a pattern and shadow of the heavenly things (8:5) or "the things in the heavens." Earthly things that are only "symbols" have to "be cleansed by means of these" formulae prescribed in the Pentateuch, but, in the author's judgment, "the heavenly things themselves" also had to be cleansed. The only difference between "the heavenly things" and "the symbols" is that the former must be cleansed "by means of better sacrifices than these" employed by the Aaronic priesthood. The author thought of heaven in earthly, and especially temple, terms. He assumed that heaven would involve sinning and cleansing from sin just as earth does. His concept of heaven that makes such a deduction reasonable will be considered at the end of this chapter.

Summary.—This unit dealt with the necessity of death for the terms of a will to be effective for the heirs, and the effectiveness of blood in cleansing. Jesus superbly met both qualifications. His death made the new covenant effective, and his sacrificial blood cleansed not only the earthly symbols but even the heavenly things. So Jesus is without question the mediator of a new covenant. The heirs will receive their eternal inheritance and be redeemed from their transgressions. The author justified all of this by giving the rules and customs by which ordinary wills are executed, and reviewing how cleansing is ordinarily obtained under the Pentateuchal laws.

THE HEAVENLY MINISTRY

24. "The holy [precincts] made with hands" are the sacred areas in the temple at Jerusalem which the author considered nothing more than mere "antitypes of the true [precincts]."[81] Not all Jews considered these areas to be idolatrous. Josephus said the holy of holies was like heaven (*Ant.* III. 123), and Philo, commenting on LXX Lev 16:17, said when the high priest entered the holy of holies he was neither God nor man but God's minister. He had contact both with the mortal and the immortal, until he came

[81] See COMMENT on 8:1–7 for a discussion of the temple made with hands.

out again to the realm of flesh and blood. The author of Hebrews rather contrasted heaven to the temple. Jesus the great high priest went through the heavens (4:14), not merely the holy of holies which seemed to some to be like heaven, but was really only a symbol, an antitype. The Aaronic high priest entered "the holy [precincts] made with hands," but Jesus entered "into heaven itself." It is in heaven that Jesus appears "before God in our behalf." The best the high priest could do was to send incense and fragrant smoke up to heaven in an attempt to placate God, but Jesus was an apostle, an ambassador, who could himself come directly before God to intercede in behalf of the believers.

25. Jesus' offering is much superior to the animal sacrifices presented by the Aaronic high priests. He offers "himself," not "every year" nor every day (7:27).

26. If Jesus had not had a better offering to present—"himself"—he would have had to suffer "many times from the foundation of the world." This is a contrary-to-fact conditional statement, with ellipsis of "if it were different" or "otherwise." Christ's having "appeared" (*pephanerōtai*) in the perfect tense reflects the same concept rabbis anticipated in the future, when they promised that the Messiah would be revealed (*yitgalē*) (Targ. Jer 30:21; Zech 3:8; 6:12). According to the Palestinian targum, the "king Messiah is to be revealed" (*'tyd d'ytgly mlk' mšyḥa'*) at the end of days (Gen 35:21). The expression "the end of days" or "the end of the ages" means the end of the days or the ages of "captivity" under foreign rule before the national jubilee when the land would be restored to the "original owners" and the "captives" would be liberated to return to Palestine and live on the land of the promise (11:9)[82] It is the same period referred to as "the last of these days" (1:2) when God spoke to us through a Son (1:2; see also T. Benj. 11:3; T. Levi 10:2). For many Jews of New Testament times, the Messiah, who was to rule "at the end of the ages" and the beginning of the messianic age, was expected to be the son of David, who would rule from Jerusalem in the new age that would begin when "the ages" came to an end. The author of Hebrews, however, did not describe a Davidic messiah at all, but one who was an apostle and high priest, who would both rule and offer sacrifice the way the Hasmoneans did.

"At the end of the ages" Jesus "appeared" but "once" (*hapax*), a term the author repeated many times (6:4; 9:7, 26, 27, 28; 10:2; 12:26, 27). The purpose of his appearing was priestly. He offered "his sacrifice" for the "removal of sin."[83]

27. In a way that would be consistent with a treasury of merits theology, the author seemed to think of every event, both good and bad, as that which was "laid up for men" in treasuries or account books. No one would know in advance how much his account held. But "however much" it

[82] CC, pp. 9–18.

[83] For a thought-provoking discussion on the relationship between revelation and sacrifice, see J. Swetnam, "Sacrifice and Revelation in the Epistle to the Hebrews: Observations and Surmises on Hebrews 7:26," CBQ 30 (1968), 227–34.

was, there was one thing that was certain: there was only one occasion for death. That was the same for all men, including Jesus, whose self-sacrifice could be made but once. "After this [is] judgment." Rabbis understood that after death every covenanter would appear before the great tribunal of God and face judgment. Then the books would be opened and all his deeds would be used either for him or against him. R. Eliezer b. Jacob said a person who performed one good deed acquired for himself one defense attorney and the one who performed one transgression acquired for himself one accusing attorney. After death, all of these attorneys would stand and plead for or accuse the person standing in judgment (Aboth 4:11). Akabya b. Mahalaleel said, "And before whom are you about to give account and reckoning?" "Before the King of kings, the Holy One, blessed be He" (Aboth 3:1).

28. The Hebrew text of Isa 53:11 contains the clause "and he will bear [the] sin of the many." LXX Isa 53:12 had ". . . sins of [the] many he bore (*anēnegken*)." The author of Hebrews varied this slightly to fit his sentence structure: ". . . of [the] many to bear [the] sins," changing the word order and the finite verb to an infinitive, but not changing the basic meaning of the passage. The servant in Isaiah was a personification of the Jews who were taken from Palestine to Babylon, where they had to pay double for the sins of Israel until Cyrus captured Babylon and Jews were allowed to return. Those who had died in Babylon by then were the ones praised by later generations as having borne the iniquities of "[the] many."[84] "The many" is a technical term used in the Dead Sea scrolls to mean the whole community (see 1QS 6:1, 8, 9, 11, 13, 16; Dan 11:33; 12:3). In Isaiah it referred to the Jews who would be permitted to return, the ones who benefited from the sacrifice and suffering of the Jews who died in Babylon. The author of Hebrews identified Jesus as the servant who bore "[the] sins of [the] many" by offering himself as an atoning sacrifice. The Greek for "will next appear" is *ek deuterou . . . ophthēsetai,* literally "from a second . . . will be seen." "Those who await him" are those who have held fast to the hope (3:6; 6:11, 18) and now have a still better hope by which they might draw near to God (7:19). The "salvation" they expect is the fulfillment of the promise, the long expected "rest," the restoration of the land, and peace and prosperity while dwelling there. Jesus will appear "without sin" because he was made a cleansing for sin (1:3) when he offered himself as a sacrifice for his own and the people's sins (7:27). He learned obedience and was made perfect through his suffering sacrifice (5:7–8), so he has passed through the heavens and has been exalted to the right hand of God "without sin" (4:14–15).

Summary.—The word "Christ" in the beginning and concluding verses acts as an inclusion to make these verses a separate unit. The close parallels be-

[84] For a justification of this interpretation see CC, pp. 123–31, and COMMENT on 5:7–8.

tween unit (1) (9:11–14) and unit (3) (9:24–28) also form a larger type of inclusion, enclosing units (1), (2), and (3). This also reflects the author's skill in effective repetition. The word "Christ" in 9:11 as well as 9:28 shows that this word ties together two inclusions, a larger and a smaller unit. Vanhoye called attention to the following comparisons:[85]

Unit 1	*Unit 3*
a. not made with hands (11)	a. not . . . made with hands (24)
b. once for all into the holy [precincts] (12)	b. into heaven itself . . . once (24–26)
c. offered himself blameless to God (14)	c. appear before God (24)
d. the blood of Christ . . . will cleanse our conscience (14)	d. Christ . . . bear [the] sins of [the] many (28)
e. having found eternal redemption (12)	e. for [the] removal of sin (26)

Words like "renewal" (*anakainizein*) (6:6) *egkekainistai* (9:18), "many times" (*pollakis*) (6:7; 9:25, 26; 10:11), "symbols" (*hypodiegmata*) (9:23), "example" (*paradeigmatizontas*) (6:6), and "made with hands" (*cheiropoiētos*) (9:11, 24) are terms which belong to the ages at the end of which Christ appeared. Words that belong to the coming age are "once" (*hapax* or *ephapax*) (6:4; 9:7, 26, 27, 28; 10:2; 12:26, 27), "eternal" (salvation, 5:9; judgment, 6:2; redemption, 9:12; spirit, 9:14; inheritance, 9:15; covenant, 13:20), "heaven," "heavens," or "heavenly" (1:10; 4:14; 7:26; 8:1; 9:23, 24; 11:12; 12:23, 25, 26 and "true" (*alēthinos*) (tent, 8:2; things or precincts, 9:24; heart, 10:22).

This last unit (9:24–28) seems to summarize more than just chapter nine. There are here catchwords that refer to material in chapters six, seven, and eight, as well; and the emphasis here seems to sharpen the contrast between the priests, temples, sacrifices, cleansings, and liturgical practices of the old covenant and those of the new covenant. Although this appears to be a summarizing paragraph, it is not a final summary. The topic that continues in chapter ten is an extension of arguments presented in chapter nine, showing the superiority of Christ's offering to that of the high priests of Aaron.

The comparison of the earthly temple with the heavenly has misled many scholars into thinking that Hebrews was basically Platonic in outlook.[86] Because the author's concepts of heaven and the Lord's presence are important to a proper understanding of the author's message, a more careful investigation will be made of that subject.

[85] Vanhoye, p. 157.

[86] For objections to that interpretation, see Williamson, SJT 16 (1963), 418–19; A. Feuillet, "Les points de vue nouveaux dans l'eschatologie de l'Épître aux Hébreux," StEv III (1964), 369–87; and Fritsch, "TO ANTITYPON," in *Studia Biblica et Semitica*, pp. 100–7.

Heaven, the presence, and the temple

The real presence of the Lord was made apparent in the fire that burned at the tent of meeting in the wilderness,[87] the smoke on Mount Sinai, or the fire on the altar in the temple. At night the fire was most visible and during the day the smoke or "cloud" was most visible (Num 9:15–16). This was the pillar of cloud that moved before the Hebrews and stood behind them as they escaped from Egypt (Exod 14:19–20). When the surface was damp and cold, the smoke settled around the camp like smog, and the people kept the camp stationary. When the weather cleared, the smoke went up directly and the people then were free to move the camp. They understood the rising of the smoke to be the command of the Lord to move camp (Num 9:17–23). When the smoke went straight up, to the naked eye it appeared to reach heaven where the Lord dwelt. At that time, they dared to move, because the Lord could come down through the smoke and be with them. When the Lord wanted to speak to his people, he came down from heaven through the pillar of smoke and made his real presence known (Num 11:17, 25; 12:5). Since the pillar of cloud or smoke was the bridge that joined earth to heaven, it was therefore the means by which the Lord could be present on earth. For this reason, the fire on the altar was considered to be very holy, and the altar was reserved only for the high priest. Both the altar and the fire on the altar were thought to be close to heaven.

When the temple was dedicated in Jerusalem, Solomon is reported to have offered a long prayer (I Kings 8). He acknowledged that heaven and the highest heaven could not contain God (I Kings 8:27), but he prayed that God would constantly watch the temple where he had promised that his name should dwell (I Kings 8:29). From then on prayers were directed to the temple in the belief that God's presence was there, just as in heaven. God's presence was assured when the temple was filled with the smoke of the glory of God (Rev 15:8). Rabbis said that in the messianic age the Lord would again protect Israel with a cloud of smoke over Mount Zion (Exod R. 50:5). Since this was so, covenanters spoke of "seeing God," when they meant that they would worship in the temple (Isa 6:1; Ps 24:3–6; Matt 5:8). Amos said he saw God upon the altar (*'al hammizbēaḥ*) (Amos 9:1), and Hezekiah addressed God in prayer as "the Lord of Armies, the God of Israel, whose presence dwells high above the cherubim [in the temple]" (Targ. Isa 37:15). The smoke which connected earth to heaven was sometimes spoken of in terms of a pillar and at other times as a sort of tube. According to Targ. Ps. Jon. Gen 2:6, "The cloud of majesty came down from the throne of majesty and filled itself with water from the ocean, and then rose up from the earth and gave rain to water *the whole face of the ground.*" This seems to

[87] The Lord went with the people (Exod 33:16) through the wilderness to give them "rest" in the promised land (Exod 33:14–15); likewise, the ark of the covenant went before them and the cloud overshadowed them (Num 10:33–34).

be the description of a tornado which looks like a cloud in the shape of a funnel which could "draw up" water from the ocean. After the tornado, the rain that followed would have convinced early Near Easterners of the relationship of the "funnel cloud," the rain, and God's activity. Commenting on the story of Jacob's ladder, Bar Qappara said, "And the top of it [the ladder] reached heaven" (Gen 26:12)—[This refers to] the sacrifices, the odor of which went up to heaven" (Gen R. 135b §68:12). Other rabbis compared the ladder to Mount Horeb, whose top reached heaven because the scripture says "the mountain burned with fire up to the heart of heaven" (Deut 4:11; Gen R. 135a §68:12). When Manoah first confronted the man of God who announced Manoah's wife's impending pregnancy, Manoah slaughtered a kid as a sacrifice (Judg 13:1–19). When the fire burned, the man of God ascended with the flame toward heaven (Judg 13:20), as if the smoke were some kind of conveyance. It was through this conveyance that the offerings made on the altar reached heaven as a pleasing odor to the Lord (Lev 1:17 *et passim*). The smoke united earth with heaven; therefore, the smoke that filled the temple made the temple a place where the Lord might dwell. The close relationship between God and the temple prompted worshipers to describe heaven in the holiest terms that they knew—the holy city, Jerusalem, and the temple at Mount Zion. Josephus said that the innermost sanctuary, which was accessible only to the high priest, "was dedicated to God (just) as Heaven (was)" (*hōs ouranos aneito tǭ theǭ*) (*Ant.* III. 123).

The service of the Levites in the sanctuary was compared to the service of the angels of the presence and the holy ones in heaven (Jub 31:14). Israelites knew more about the function of the Levites than about angels, but they conjectured from the Levites that the angels were God's messengers, doing the kind of errand work that Levites did at the temple. Like the Levites, they formed a militia (Matt 13:41; 16:27; 25:31; 26:53; Mark 8:38; Luke 2:13; Rev 12:7) and a choir to sing and blow trumpets (Rev 5:11; 8:2, 6, 7, 8, 12; 9:1, 13–14; 10:7; 11:15); they were in the temple in heaven (Rev 14:15, 17, 18; 15:6; 16:1); they distributed incense (Rev 8:3–5); and they stood before or around God, the throne, or the altar, which seemed to be at the same place (Rev 5:2, 11; 7:11; 8:2, 3; Enoch 14:22–23; 71:8–9; T. Levi 5:1; Ascension of Isaiah 7:14, 19, 24, 31, 33, 35, 36; 8:8–9, 16). Like the Levites, angels were ministers (Ps 104:4; Hag. 12b; II Enoch 4:1 – 5:2) who petitioned, interceded, and prayed for others (Enoch 39:5). As in the temple, there was an altar in heaven (Rev 6:9) before the throne (Rev 8:3–5) or before God (Rev 9:13), and there were cherubim in the temple (Rev 14:17–18; Enoch 14:11, 20; 71:7). When the seer saw the holy city, the heavenly Jerusalem, coming down from the heaven, a voice said, "Behold, the dwelling of God is with men" (Rev 21:2–3). This heavenly Jerusalem was like an idealized earthly Jerusalem, having high walls, twelve gates, and streets of pure gold (Rev 21:10–21). God's throne in heaven was evidently located in the temple, in the position of the altar, perhaps on the mercy seat between the cherubim (Enoch 71:8–9; T. Levi 5:1), or maybe the cherubim formed the throne. Just as the Lord appeared in the fire on the altar or at the tent of meeting, so God's presence in heaven was surrounded by fire (Enoch 14:19–23; 71:5–10). The four beasts and the twenty-four elders brought incense and lyres and worshiped the Lamb who was between the elders and the beasts and the throne (Rev 5:6–10), just as Levites and priests brought incense and worshiped before the altar in the temple with song and music. The picture of peoples coming from every nation together with angels, the four beasts, and the twenty-four elders, worshiping while dressed in white garments and carrying palm branches in their hands, evidently refers to the throne in heaven, but it was patterned after scenes in Jerusalem on great feast days when Jews from the diaspora gathered to worship at the temple. The priests always wore white to symbolize their ritual purity, so heaven was pictured in the same way (Rev 7:9–12). Those dressed in white were pure and, like priests, served the Lord day and night before his throne in his temple. He would shelter them with his presence, just as his presence hovered over the temple in Jerusalem (Rev 7:13–16; Enoch 14:20). As in Jerusalem, there was a golden altar for incense in heaven, where angels, like priests, offered prayers by burning incense before the throne (Rev 8:1–5; 9:13; Enoch 14:18–19; 71:1). In God's temple in heaven, like that at Jerusalem, there was the ark of the covenant (Rev 11:19). Just as the Lamb was before the throne in heaven, so the Lamb stood on Mount Zion together with all the gathered saints, and there were voices of angels singing with lyres before the throne and before the four beasts and the twenty-four elders, just as in the temple scenes in heaven (Rev 14:1–5). Closely associated with this scene in Jerusalem, angels came out of the temple on Zion and out of the temple in heaven (Rev 14:13, 15, 17) and from the altar (Rev 14:18). In the temple of the tent of witness in heaven, angels wore white, like priests at Jerusalem, and when they burned incense the temple filled with smoke, like the temple at Jerusalem (Rev 15:5–8; Isa 6:4). The bowls of wrath which the angels poured were like the bowls of incense Levites poured in the temple (Rev 15:7 – 16:20). The scenes describing Rome's fall were mingled with heavenly temple scenes and angels (Rev 18:1, 4, 21), with the multitude in heaven together with the four beasts and the twenty-four elders and the throne (Rev 19:1–8). The four beasts described in the temple in heaven may have been like the four beasts or the cherubim Ezekiel described as being part of the furniture and decoration of the temple vision (Ezek 1:4–26; 10:9–22) or the Seraphim described by Isaiah in the temple at Jerusalem (Isa 6:2–7). The throne itself may have been a chariot pulled by heavenly beasts.

Although it seems to us that the ancient Near Easterners examined the most holy places they knew and described God or heaven in these terms, to them it seemed the other way around. Human beings merely imitated the activity of the gods and built structures after divine patterns. Ural-Altaic peoples, for instance, thought earthly mountains had archetypes in the heavens, and in Egypt, fields were named after celestial fields which were known before their earthly counterparts.[88] This was especially true of temples which had heavenly prototypes. Not only the temple at Jerusalem, but the temple at Lagash was also constructed according to a plan that was divinely revealed.[89] Cities such as Jerusalem, Sippar, Nineveh, and Asshur were built according to heavenly patterns.[90] When a wilderness area was cultivated or civilized, it was believed to be a new creation, repeating God's creation of chaos into cosmos.[91]

Sacred places were constructed on mountains in an effort to get close to heaven where God dwelt. These high places were considered the center of the world. Thus Mount Gerizim and Zion were both called the navel of the land (Judg 9:37; Jub 4:26), implying that each was the cord that bound earth to heaven. Samaritans claimed that Gerizim was the holiest of mountains, the place of the True One's presence, the house of God, the gate of heaven (Memar Marqah 2 §10), the place of the glory of the Lord, the dwelling place of angels, and the place of blessings. This mountain is so high that the waters of the flood did not reach it (Memar Marqah 3 §4). Zion was called the holy mountain (Isa 31:4–5), the city of our God, the joy of the earth; his holy mountain (Ps 48:1–2), the highest of the mountains (Isa 2:2), the place over which the Lord hovers and from which he fights (Isa 31:4–5). Javanese pilgrims approaching the temple of Barobudur ascend from the earthly plane to the "pure region."[92] A Babylonian temple was called the "Link between Heaven and Earth."[93] Primeval man dreamed of building towers from which he could reach heaven (Gen 11:1–4). Heaven was just above the mountains and the treetops. To the naked eye, heaven seemed like a tent roof that could be lowered (Mekilta *Baḥodesh* 4:47–50) or rolled up like a scroll and replaced with a new one when God so chose (Isa 34:4; 42:5; 44:24; 45:12; 48:13; 51:6, 13; 64:1; 65:17; 66:22; Zech 12:1; *Recog.* 2:68; 3:14). With this cosmology, it was not a strain on reason to conceive of ladders reaching up to heaven (Gen 28:12) or a messenger of God taken up through a column of smoke in the presence of Manoah and his wife (Judg 13:20) or a man like Elijah taken up in a chariot of fire (II Kings 2:1, 11). By this logic, the imagination could fill in the unseen details, picturing God just above human traffic, sitting on a great throne, smelling the fragrance of the incense sent through the column of smoke to please him.

The ancient Near Eastern mentality that visualized a column of smoke as a means of communication between earth and heaven, temples as the link between earth and heaven, temples as places where the Lord's presence dwelt

[88] Eliade, p. 6. Sumerians used the term *giš-zar* to describe the mystic prototype that existed in heaven before its earthly counterpart was created. So W. F. Albright, "The Supposed Babylonian Derivation of the Logos," JBL 39 (1920), 150–51.

[89] Eliade, p. 7.

[90] Eliade, p. 8.

[91] Eliade, p. 10.

[92] Eliade, p. 15.

[93] Eliade, p. 14.

and where heavenly angels hovered (Memar Marqah 2 §10, 3 §2), clarifies some otherwise difficult passages in the New Testament. Four of these are: (a) the heavenly Jerusalem in Heb 12:22; (b) the Father's house in John 14:2; (c) the relationship of Jesus to the Levites and angels in Hebrews (5:1–5; 7:4–8:5); and (d) the reference to sacrifice in heaven in Hebrews (8:3–4). These will be considered in order.

a. *Heavenly Jerusalem.*—Since ancient Near Easterners considered places where communication with God was possible to be very close and very similar to heaven, it is no longer necessary to spiritualize "Zion, even [the] city of [the] living God" (Heb 12:22), as many scholars have done,[94] just because it is also called "heavenly Jerusalem" (Heb 12:22). This is a reasonable and respectable ascription for a city that contains the temple which links earth to heaven. At this point it was believed possible for God himself to be present. This was the place of worship for "a church of first-born [people], enrolled in heaven" (Heb 12:23), who had "tasted the heavenly gift" (Heb 6:4). This was "the city which had the foundations, whose builder and constructor was God" (Heb 11:10). This city, for which the patriarchs looked, was the capital city of "the land of the promise" (Heb 11:9). The patriarchs left Haran and journeyed toward Palestine. They could have returned either to Ur of the Chaldees or to Haran if they had not wanted a better fatherland, "that is a heavenly [one]" (Heb 11:14–16). In this fatherland, this "land of promise," this "heavenly" land, God "prepared for them a city" (Heb 11:16), which was "Zion, even [the] city of [the] living God, heavenly Jerusalem" (Heb 12:22).

b. *The Father's House.*—The temple at Jerusalem was frequently called "the house" or "the house of the Lord." In that temple were quarters where young priests stayed (*Wars* V. 220–221; Mid. 1:8–9). Some of these may have been for the overnight accommodations of priests who served in shifts. This may have been the imagery intended by Jesus when he assured his disciples that his "Father's house" had many places to stay (*monai*) (John 14:2). Just as the earthly temple, which was called the Lord's house, had hospitality provisions for visiting priests, so also the heavenly archetype would have many such places to stay. This means Jesus would be prepared to receive the disciples to himself (John 14:2–3).

c. *The Levites and angels.*—Since the high priest was considered more than human while he was in the holy of holies (*Som.* II. 231–32), and since the holy of holies was thought to be like heaven (*Ant.* III. 123) because it was dedicated to God and was the place where God had chosen to dwell (I Kings 8:29), the comparison of Jesus with the angels as well as the Levites makes good sense. Jesus was compared as a high priest with Levites who were subordinate to the high priests. In the heavenly archetype, the situation was the same. As high priest in heaven, he was also compared to the angels, who ministered in heaven just as the Levites ministered on earth. Enoch pictured the angels as holy messengers who were like the Levites in that they were not admitted into the holy of holies (Enoch 14:12).

[94] Bruce, pp. 374–75; Windisch, p. 113.

Of course a high priest was higher in status than a Levite, and by the same token, the heavenly high priest was higher than the angels who have the same status in heaven. Jesus was pictured as a high priest because the high priest was the mediator for the people, and as such was higher in status than other people, especially when he was in the holy of holies. This did not keep the high priest from being human. In fact, Jews dared to pelt him with citrus fruit if he failed to function properly, even in the temple (*Ant.* XIII. 372), but still this was considered a heavenly place in the heavenly city, and by some, a temple not made with hands (Exod 15:17; Ps 78:69; Mekilta *Shirata* 10:29–42). Therefore when Jesus became high priest in heaven, it was natural to assume that he would have subordinate assistants there just as a high priest had in Jerusalem. Accordingly the angels were considered by the author of Hebrews to be clearly subordinate to the son who was high priest in heaven.

d. *Sacrifices in heaven.*—Since the heavenly archetype functions just as its earthly imitation, it seemed reasonable for the heavenly high priest to offer sacrifices in heaven (Heb 8:3–4). These sacrifices, of course, must be better than their earthly counterparts, but their function is to cleanse "the heavenly things" (Heb 9:23).[95] Scholars have had trouble with these passages, because Christ's "once for all" sacrifice on earth was thought to make all other sacrifices unnecessary. It also seems a little surprising to think of heaven as a place where there would be sin and defilement that needed cleansing. The author of Hebrews found no difficulty with this, however. For him, heaven and the holy of holies were very close together. God's presence and his angels were in both. From the holy of holies the smoke carried the incense from the sacrifices directly to heaven, where there were also a holy of holies, sacrifices, and angels. When Jesus, as the heavenly high priest, passed through the curtain into the holy of holies, which was like heaven, he not only offered a sacrifice, but he was himself the sacrifice (Heb 9:12). Just as other sacrifices were taken to heaven through the pillar of fire and smoke, and just as the man of God went up through the column of smoke to heaven before the eyes of Manoah and his wife (Judg 13:20), so also Jesus was the sacrifice that "went through the heavens" (Heb 4:14) with the column of smoke in the holy of holies. Such imagery is consistent with the Near Eastern concept of the relationship of heaven to earth, columns of smoke and fire, temples and high places, heavenly archetypes and earthly counterparts, and the specially holy places that link heaven to earth.

A better understanding of the Near Easterner's concept of heaven in relationship to the temple is important for understanding the imagery related to the temple, the priesthood, and heaven, particularly in Hebrews and the Book of Revelation.

[95] W. L. Moran, "The Creation of Man in Atrahasis I 192–248," BASOR 200 (1970), 50, quoted the following poem attributed to the god Enki:

"On the new-moon, seventh and fifteenth days
A purification let me institute—a bath.
The leader-god let them slaughter, then
Let the gods purify themselves by immersion."

Better mediator of forgiveness

10:1. The Jerusalem priests were earlier reported as serving only as "a pattern and shadow of the heavenly things" (8:5). This pattern and shadow was the temple made with hands, and not the heavenly temple itself. In the only other use of the word "shadow" (*skian,* 8:5) the author seems to have the same temple in mind. Here the author says the law has (*echōn*) "a shadow of the good things to come," which would seem to be the heavenly things mentioned in 8:5. "The image" (*eikon*) does not seem to be in the same category as shadow (8:4–5), symbol (8:4–5; 9:23), and antitype (9:24). The image is the real object which casts the shadow that the law has. The same is true of "the things" (*tōn pragmatōn*) of which the law has not the "image itself." "The things" are evidently heavenly things (8:5). The author would agree with Paul that "the law" was not completely out of the picture, but it has limitations. It was not against "the promises of God" (Gal 3:21); rather "the law was our schoolmaster" (*paidagogos*) which would lead us "to Christ" (Gal 3:24), but it was not able to give life (Gal 3:21). Or, as the author of Hebrews put it, "The law is never able to perfect those who sacrifice." The author used the word "perfect" in close association with sacrifice, as if a sacrifice that successfully removes sin also perfects or makes perfect. Thus Jesus became "perfect" through the suffering of his sacrifice (2:10); he learned obedience and was made "perfect" through his sacrifice (5:7–9); he was made "perfect" for the age because he had offered himself (7:27–28). The Aaronic priests were inadequate, however, since their gifts and sacrifices did not "perfect" the consciences (9:9). If the sin offering was effective, both the priest and the people affected by the service should be "without sin" (4:14–15; 9:28). "Continually" (*eis to diēnekes*) means at regularly scheduled intervals, without interruption. "The same [kinds of] sacrifices" "every year" are the goats for the people and the bulls for the high priests.

2. "Otherwise" is a free translation of *epei,* "since," "because," or "when," that recognizes its use here in an elliptical contrary-to-fact condition (cf. 9:26). The rhetorical question emphasizes the point that sacrifices would not be continued if there was no need for them: i.e., if they were completely effectual they would not need to be repeated. This is just a repetition and elaboration of 9:9. There the author said directly that the Aaronic priests offered sacrifices that were not able to perfect the consciences of the worshipers. Here he reasoned that the continuation of sacrifice proves this. If they had really "been cleansed" "once," then their guilt would be removed and they would "have no longer any consciousness of sins." The author of Jubilees did not feel that way about the Day of Atonement. He said this day was established so that Hebrews could remember the sins they had committed against Joseph and grieve for them as they should. They also should grieve for their own sins which they had committed that year and have them cleansed (34:18–19). This seems more reasonable, but it did not

convince the author of Hebrews. With his severe demand for sinless ethics, he evidently assumed that if the Day of Atonement had really been effective, Israel would be free from her sins and the kingdom would have come. Once Israel's sin was removed, of course, she would continue to be sinless. Why should she want to sin again? Sin should be cleansed and forgotten.

The idea of a sinless Kingdom of God was not a unique idea of the author's however. John and Jesus both preached repentance in preparation for the kingdom. The argument Jesus had with the Pharisees was not that Jesus was more liberal and willing to have a sinful kingdom whereas the Pharisees would exclude tax collectors and sinners. They argued about the ethic required before the kingdom came. Jesus said it should be like that of a fisherman bringing in the net. He first included all that came into his net; then he selected the good fish that had scales and fins and discarded the rest (Matt 13:47–48). He also used the analogy of the farmer who found weeds in his field. He let them grow until harvest; then he burned the weeds and gathered the wheat into his granary (Matt 13:24–30). The generosity ceased when harvest came or the net was drawn in. Only good wheat and good fish were kept. According to the seer, the redeemed would all be celibate (Rev 14:3–4) and those who enter the holy city are those who have washed their robes (Rev 22:14). In the same way, there was evidently a very wide belief among Jews that the Kingdom of God was only for the righteous. The author of Hebrews subscribed to this sinless ethic. He urged his readers not to sin at all and he criticized the effectiveness of the priestly methods for canceling sin. They just had not worked.

3–4. "Every year" the same kinds of offerings were offered in the same way "with [the] same remembrance of sins." After all these years of experimenting with this method, it was clear to the author that the method was ineffective. Blood is necessary for forgiveness of sins (9:22), but "the blood of bulls and goats" used on the Day of Atonement was "not able to remove sins."

5. The text quoted is Ps 39[40]:7–9, according to the LXX with some variants. Some LXX texts read with the MT *ōtia* "an ear." The author followed the texts (BSA) which read *sōma* "body," because that suited his purpose, if he knew the other reading. The Pentateuch commanded that sacrifices be offered, but the Psalm, which came later, claimed that the Lord "did not desire sacrifice and offering," therefore the law was out of date, just as Ps 95 took precedence over the statement that Joshua led the people into their promised "rest," the promise of a priesthood "for the age" in Ps 110 took precedence over the promises in Numbers and Exodus, and the new covenant promised in Jeremiah made the old covenant recorded in the Pentateuch obsolete. In the author's judgment the Pentateuch was obsolete, out of date, almost gone (8:13). He used later Psalms and prophecies to supersede the Pentateuch. As Hebrews used the text, the "body" "furnished" was the body of Jesus which was given as a sacrifice to replace the "sacrifice and offering" which the Aaronic priests had been offering.

6. "Whole burnt offerings" were offerings of animals that were completely

burned, not just roasted and eaten by the worshipers and priests. For "sin offerings" the author followed the LXX and read "concerning sin" (*peri hamartias*) as a translation of the Hebrew *ḥᵃṭā'āh* (sin), which seems to be a copying error for *ḥaṭṭā't* (sin offering). In a listing of various kinds of offerings, a "sin offering" should be expected which is an offering concerning sin. For the LXX *ętēsas,* "you requested," the author of Hebrews has *eudokēsas,* "you took pleasure in."

7. The LXX reads, "I wanted (*eboulēthēn*) to do your will, O my God." Hebrews omitted the pronoun "my" and the verb "I wanted." By omitting this verb, the finite verb understood to accompany the infinitive would be "I have come." This suited the author's needs, because he was emphasizing Jesus' coming into the world (10:5) to replace the sacrifices prescribed in the Pentateuch. Yeb. 77a interpreted this Psalm to refer to David who had come.

8. The author's dependence upon the LXX is apparent. He understood "sacrifices and offerings" to be exactly the same as "whole burnt offerings and sin offerings." The Hebrew for offering is *minḥāh,* usually a grain offering. A sin offering is some type of animal or bird. The author's step-by-step logic is so consistent that it can be predicted. He did not omit a single point. First, he gave his version of the Psalm which contradicts the Pentateuch. Then he called attention to that fact. The next step was to show how Jesus fitted the picture perfectly.

9. "The first" which he (the Lord or the Holy Spirit) "removes" is "the law" (vs. 8) which he repudiated in the Psalm, thus making the law invalid. He did this "in order that he might establish the second," which is not the Psalm, but the testimony in the Psalm that, according to the author, Jesus had come to do God's will.

10. The "will" which the author interpreted midrashically was God's will mentioned in the Psalm he quoted. "Sanctified" means "holy," "cleansed from sin," "ritually pure." The author used the word "perfect" to describe the condition of the believer for whom atonement had been made through sacrifice. He seems to use the word "sanctified" here to mean "made perfect," because those who "are being sanctified" are those who are the recipients of the benefits of Christ's sacrifice.

11. This verse repeats much of 10:1–4: "every day"/"every year" (1); "offering"/"they offer" (1); "the same sacrifices"/"the same [kinds of] sacrifices" (1); "never able to remove sins"/"not able to remove sins" (4).

12–13. Verse 12 also repeats some of the same words as 10:1, but with a contrasting significance: instead of "the same [kinds of] sacrifices" (10:1), vs. 12 has "one sacrifice"; instead of meaningless sacrifices being offered "continually" (*eis to diēnekes*) (10:1), Jesus, as God's Son, "sat down at the right hand of God to perpetuity" (*eis to diēnekes*). This does not mean he is continually sitting down, but that he will never be removed from his position of honor at God's "right hand." Since the author's main text was Ps 110, it was necessary for him to remind the reader from time to time that all of his arguments return to support that one text. At the beginning the author introduced the Son as one who "sat down at the right hand of the Majesty" (1:3), and the Lord promised to make his enemies his "footstool" (1:13). Later the Son was introduced as the high priest who would sit "down at the right hand of the throne of Majesty" (8:1). Here the Son was shown to be an offering for sins (also 10:18). Since Jesus had offered himself as the one perfect sacrifice and had gone through the heavens, the first part of the promise in the Psalm had been fulfilled. He had then only to wait "until his enemies are placed [as] a footstool for his feet." Jesus' waiting is comparable to that of those who await him for salvation" (9:28). The author was confident that this would happen shortly.

14. In a summary fashion the author here repeated terms used before: "offering" (see 10:1, 5, 10, 11, 18) is a central word for this unit. Jesus "perfected" the worshiper as the Aaronic priests could not (9:9; 10:1), but here the worshipers are called "sanctified" (2:11; 10:10) "to perpetuity" (10:1, 12).

15. The author regularly acknowledged that "the Holy Spirit" or God was responsible for the composition of the scriptures, even though he attributed the Pentateuch to Moses and the Psalms to David.

16–17. For the variants between the author's use of Jer 31[38]:33–34 here and in 8:10, see COMMENT on 8:10. This variation demonstrates the author's willingness to paraphrase a text. The author's return to the Jeremiah passage had two purposes: (a) It further emphasized the author's point that effective sacrifice, based on an effective covenant and law, would remove all consciousness of sin, sanctify the people completely, and make all further sacrifice unnecessary. His logic above had shown how he came to this conclusion. Now he could clinch his argument with the text that promised that the new covenant which God would provide was going to achieve precisely that. (b) It was a good text on which the author could base his exhortation which was to follow. The sinlessness which Jeremiah promised was the very sinlessness the author demanded.

18. "These" refers to the sins and lawless acts mentioned just above. With the new covenant comes the promise of "forgiveness." When sins have been forgiven, there is "no longer" any need for a Day of Atonement or any kind of sacrifices to remove sin. This concludes the argument with which the discussion began (10:1–2).

Summary.—The main topic of this unit was offerings or sacrifices, and the inclusion was composed of the words "offer"/"offering" (10:1–18). Given the author's presuppositions, his logic is watertight. He assumed that sinlessness was both possible and the will of God. God's will would certainly be realized. The sacrifices prescribed by the law had not been effective. Therefore God must have a different plan. That plan is not found in the Pentateuch, but in the Psalms and the prophets. These prohibit the sacrifices prescribed by the Pentateuch and promise a new covenant that will remove sins effectively and permanently. This required the sacrifice of a body instead of the levitical offerings. This has been provided once for all by Jesus, who has been exalted into the heavens where he is seated at the right hand of God. The new covenant is now in effect; those who believe and are sanctified or made perfect by Jesus' sacrifice have been effectively and permanently cleansed from sin, which means that the levitical offerings are no longer needed. Neither is the law which prescribed them. Although the concept of a new covenant is found in other New Testament literature (Luke 22:20; I Cor 11:25; II Cor 3:6), it is nowhere so prominent as in Hebrews (7:22; 8:6–10; 9:4–20; 10:16–29; 12:24).

This provides the conclusion to the doctrinal portion of a very important argument presented by the author (7:1–10:18). Jesus is the true high priest after the order of Melchizedek; he belongs to a superior priesthood, has a superior sacrifice, functions in a superior temple, offers a more effective forgiveness, and introduces a superior covenant. For none of these is a son of David theology important. The author regularly related his theological deductions to the ethical demands of Christians. Therefore, this whole discussion would not be complete without the exhortation that follows (10:19–39).

EXHORTATION

Exhortation

19. The word translated "boldness" is *parrēsia* (from *pas* and *rēsis*), which means freedom of speech, the right to speak openly. It was used more widely to mean "without fear," "freedom of action," "outspokenness," or "power" (see COMMENT on 4:16). Nadab and Abihu were consumed with fire while offering incense (Lev 10:2). On the Day of Atonement, when the high priest entered the holy of holies to offer incense, he did not prolong his prayer, lest all Israel become terrified (Yoma 5:1). When Zechariah entered the holy of holies to offer incense, he was slow in returning and the people were astonished (Luke 1:21). Christians, however, "by means of the blood of Jesus," had no need to fear "the holy [precincts]" but entered with "boldness." It was a privilege and an honor to have any position in the Lord's house. Only the high priest entered the holy of holies, and only priests entered the room adjacent to it, and then only under conditions of levitical purity. No one could stand in his holy place who did not have clean hands and a pure heart (Ps 24:3–4). The Levite was glad for even such a humble position as a doorkeeper in the Lord's house (Ps 84:11).[96] Priests loved dwelling in the Lord's house (Ps 26:8). Some priests were so fortunate as to have tenure there, to dwell there all the days of their lives, to behold the beauty of the Lord and to inquire in his sanctuary (Ps 27:4). One was confident that goodness and mercy would follow him all the days of his life, and he would dwell in the house of the Lord as long as his days lasted (Ps 23:6).

A person would have to have that kind of position of authority to "have

[96] See "The Courts of the Lord," VT 6 (1966), 231.

[the] boldness [necessary] for entering the holy [precincts]." This "boldness" is an attitude one might expect in a religion centered around a chosen or an elect people, which considers itself superior to others in the Lord's eyes. Jews in Babylon were promised that they could return to Israel, but not in haste or flight. Instead of being refugees, they would be exalted and prosperous (Isa 52:12–13). The author of Hebrews called attention to the "boldness" that came as a privilege to Christians because of their status (3:6; 4:16; 10:19, 35). The phrase "[necessary] for entering" is a rather free translation of *eis to eisodon,* literally, "to the entrance." "By means of the blood of Jesus" (*en tǭ haimati Iēsou*) is rendered as a dative of means, assuming the *en* to be a Semitism, reflecting the Hebrew *b*[e], "in," "with," "by means of," "through," "on account of," or "on the condition."

20. The "way" mentioned here is the same as that in 9:8, "the way of the holy [precincts]." This is the path through the holy into the holy of holies. The word rendered "inaugurated" is *enekainisen,* "made new," "innovated," or "newly dedicated." This is a pregnant word in Jewish and Christian eschatology. When Saul was made king, Samuel and the people went to Gilgal to establish anew the kingdom (*ūn*[e]*ḥaddēš šām hamm*[e]*lūkāh*) (I Sam 11:14–15). When II Isaiah promised that the Lord would do something new (*ḥ*[a]*dāšāh*) he meant that the Lord would reestablish the promised land (Isa 43:19; also PR 84a; 31:146b). Rabbis were convinced that the Lord would renew the age (*lḥdt' 'lm'*) for the righteous (Targ. Jer 23:23; Targ. Deut 32:23; see also Tanḥuma *Noah* 12, 19a). Baruch promised that Zion would be renewed (*lmtḥdtw*) (II Bar 32:4). That which Jesus "inaugurated" was a new access to "the holy [precincts]" which was also associated with the new age. "New" (*prosphaton*) is a word that means "freshly slaughtered" and has taken on the broader meaning of "fresh," "new," or "recent" (see Num 6:3; Deut 24:5[7]; 32:17; Ps 81:9; Acts 18:2). "New and living" meant something associated with the new age, under the new covenant, where "life" was possible. "The curtain" was that which separated the holy from the holy of holies. There was also a curtain that separated the holy from the court. There is a rather complex metaphorical imagery used here. Since Jesus was both the high priest and the offering, he both brought the gift for the people's cleansing into the holy of holies where the Lord was present and was himself the gift through which the people were cleansed. "The way" which went "through the curtain" into the holy of holies was the gift which Jesus offered, "his flesh." Another less likely interpretation would be to consider "the curtain" to be "the curtain of his flesh" (*tēs sarkos*) through which the believer must go to enter the holy of holies. The allegorical interpretation, "that is, his flesh," seems like a later gloss, similar to the gloss "that is, not of this creation" in 9:11.

21. "A great priest over the house of God" is used as if it were a quotation from scripture, but there is no Old Testament passage that qualifies it as it is. There is a reference to "the great priest" (*ho hiereus*

ho megas) in Lev 21:10 who was instructed not to go out of the sanctuary (*ek tōn hagiōn*), but no mention is made of the house of God. A closer parallel is the reference to "Jesus . . . the great priest" (*tou hiereōs tou megalou*) who was associated with the royal messiah, *Anatolē* (Rising). The latter would build "the house of the Lord" (*ton oikon kyriou*) (Zech 6:11–12). The author of Hebrews, however, shows no interest in a two-messiah doctrine or a son-of-David messiah. For that reason he seems to have taken the parts of this messianic passage that could apply to a messiah who was also a high priest and applied them to Jesus.

22. The Psalmist said no one could stand in the Lord's holy place if he did not have clean hands and a pure heart (Ps 24:3–4). The author of Hebrews was even more demanding. Those who would "approach [the altar]" must have their "hearts sprinkled [clean] from evil conscience" and their whole bodies "washed with clean water." His imagery is consistent with this sacrificial and liturgical context, but realistically, how should the Christian who wanted to have his heart sprinkled go about it? The author had an answer.

23. Having one's heart sprinkled meant that Christians should "hold fast unmoved the confession of hope" (cf. *bebaiōs kai aklinōs* in *Som.* II. 278). The "hope" was the anticipation that the promise given to Abraham would be fulfilled in the days of the readers because of Jesus' sacrifice. The author had earlier urged his readers to hold fast to the end (3:6, 14). God was "the one who has promised," and it was necessary to remind the readers again and again that he was "faithful" (6:10–12, 17–18), so that they would "hold fast . . . the confession of hope."

24. The problem of holding fast to the hope was apparently a difficult one. The enthusiasm was waning. If the hope was to be maintained at all, some very practical efforts would have to be made to keep it alive. The author suggested that the Christians should make a concerted effort to show concern for each other's emotional, religious, social, and material needs, by stimulating "one another for love and good works" (see also COMMENT on 6:10). The community that kept itself busy caring for one another would have less time and inclination to become discouraged and grumble, as the exodus generation had done.

25. Some, who had lost hope, had given up regular attendance at congregational meetings. This was a certain way to lose the promise. Meeting together provided an opportunity for members to encourage one another, stimulate one another, and help each other to keep from becoming discouraged. This is in agreement with the counsel of R. Hillel: "Do not separate [yourself] from the congregation" (Aboth 2:5; see also *Vis.* III. vi. 2).

The longing for "the day" when the enemy would be driven from the land, taxation removed, and Israel given a position of status among the nations under the leadership of her own king was a common Christian and Jewish eschatological expectation. "The day" was sometimes called "the day of the Lord" (Acts 2:20; I Thess 5:2; II Thess 2:2; II Peter 3:10), "that day" (Matt 7:22; Mark 13:32; Luke 10:12; 17:31; I Thess 5:4; II Thess 1:10, 18; 4:8), "the day of God" (II Peter 3:12), "the day (or days) of the Son of man" (Luke 17:26, 30; John 8:56), "the day of Christ (Jesus Christ or Lord Jesus)" (I Cor 1:8; 5:5; II Cor 1:14; Phil 1:6, 10; 2:16), "the great day" (Jude 6; Rev 6:17; 16:14), and "the day of judgment" (Matt 10:15; 11:22, 24; 12:36; II Peter 2:9; 3:7; I John 4:17; Rom 2:16). In order to keep up their hope, it was necessary for Christians to remind one another that the time of waiting was just about over; "the day" was "drawing near" (see also Rom 13:12; Philip 4:5; James 5:8; I Peter 4:7).

Summary.—On the basis of the doctrinal teachings given, the author encouraged the readers to apply these insights to their own behavior. Given a new access to the holy of holies, they must take it and draw near to this formerly forbidden area. Like priests of antiquity, however, they must observe all of the necessary priestly rules for purity in so doing. To have pure hearts meant to hold fast to the hope, stimulate one another, keep up regular attendance at congregational gatherings and express their love and good works for one another. This they could do with the confidence that God is faithful and the time of waiting was about over. This unit is a summary exhortation, similar to 4:14–16:

a. "Since, then, we have a great high priest,	a. "Therefore . . . since we have . . . a great priest (10:19, 21)
b. [who] has gone through the heavens, (4:14)	b. . . . for entering the holy [precincts] . . . which way he inaugurated for us [that is] new and living, through the curtain (10:19, 20)
c. . . . Jesus the Son of God (4:14)	c. . . . by means of the blood of Jesus (10:19),
d. let us hold fast the confession (4:14).	d. let us hold fast unmoved the confession of hope (10:23);
e. Then let us approach the throne of grace with boldness" (4:16).	e. let us approach [the altar] with a true heart in fullness of faith (10:22); therefore, brothers, since we have [the] boldness [necessary] for entering the holy [precincts] . . ." (10:19).[97]

[97] Comparison made earlier by C. Spicq and W. Nauch, "Zum Aufbau des Hebräerbriefs," *Judentum, Urchristentum-Kirche,* ed. W. Eltester (Berlin, 1960), pp. 203–4.

There is also a close parallel between the following two passages:

"which we have as a secure and steadfast anchor of the soul, and one that is entering into the innermost [area which is behind] the curtain, where Jesus entered [as] a forerunner in our behalf, since he is a high priest for the age according to the order of Melchizedek" (6:19–20).	"Therefore, brothers, since we have [the] boldness [necessary] for entering the holy [precincts] by means of the blood of Jesus, which way he inaugurated for us [that is] new and living, through the curtain, that is, his flesh" (10:19–20; cf. also 9:8 and 10:20).

Consequences of failure

26. The author here reviewed a point he had made earlier (see COMMENT on 6:4–6) and planned to repeat again (12:17). The once-for-all nature of Christ's sacrifice is like a two-edged sword. On the one hand, it is so effective that it does not need to be repeated (7:27), but, on the other hand, it cannot be repeated, even if needed. There is no second repentance (6:4–8). It was customary in Israelite law to distinguish between the punishment inflicted upon a person who sinned unwittingly and one who sinned "deliberately." Hebrews made the same distinction. The word "truth" is from Isa 26:10 and there refers to the Lord's commandments. Similarly for Hebrews, those who had been instructed in "the knowledge of truth," took their membership vows, and were baptized, were at that time forgiven for all the sins they had committed earlier unwittingly, because they had not received "the knowledge of the truth." The "sacrifice" of Christ was adequate to cover all of those unwitting sins, but that was all it would cover. The sacrifice was completed. It could not be done over. Anyone who committed the kind of sin that would require excommunication after admission could not be readmitted. He had exhausted all the merits of Christ's suffering to cover his sins for the first admission.[98]

27. Isa 26:11 comes from a context dealing with the righteous and the unrighteous in the land. After the Lord's commandments had been established in the land, the inhabitants were obligated to learn righteousness. There would be an end to those who were impious and did not learn righteousness, or, knowing, did not act according to "the truth." They were to be removed so that they could no longer see the glory of the Lord. The Lord's hand had been raised, but the impious did not realize it, but when they would find out they would be ashamed. The Lord's zeal would take over an uninstructed people, and "fire" would "consume the opponents" (LXX Isa 26:9–11). The author of Hebrews was also dealing

[98] Cf. 6:4–8; 10:26–31; 12:15–17. For Williamson's argument that the author considered only apostasy unpardonable, see Williamson, pp. 250–51, 261.

with the righteous and the impious, but they were members of a group, all of whom had learned the truth; the impious turned against the truth they had learned, so they could expect the judgment which Isaiah promised would come upon the impious who did not learn righteousness. Since Isaiah had promised it, Christians must live in the "expectation of judgment" that was promised, and the author assured his readers that this would be "something dreadful."

A similar threat was made by II Bar 48:39–40, also based on Isa 26:10:

> "Because of this, a fire will devour their plans,
> and in flame the concerns of their hearts will be tested;
> for the Judge will come and will not delay,
> because each of the inhabitants of the land knew
> [*sciebat*] when he was committing iniquity."

28. The author had previously disparaged "the law of Moses" as being inadequate, based on inadequate promises and covenant. Now he uses this evaluation as the first half of an *a fortiori* argument. Even that weak law could put a person to death without any hesitation, "on the [testimony] of two or three witnesses" (Deut 17:6).

29. Since the Torah could be that severe, the author reasoned, apostate Christians should receive a "much worse punishment." The word translated "defiled" is *koinos,* "common," and is usually associated with unclean things covenanters should not touch or eat. Thus Peter refused to eat food that was "common or unclean" (Acts 10:14). That which was not holy was "common." Rabbis said there could be no forgiveness for anyone who profaned holy things, despised the set feasts, nullified the covenant of Abraham, or revealed secret meanings of the Torah which were not according to the *halakah* (Aboth 3:11; see I Macc 1:15). This was the same kind of blasphemous attitude that the author of Hebrews abhorred, defiling the sacred, depreciating that which they had once praised, rejecting the new covenant into which they had once been admitted. Such people deserved more than excommunication. They would receive a "much worse punishment" from God.

30–31. Like Paul (Rom 12:19), the author quoted from a text that is no longer extant. MT has "Vengeance is mine and recompense"; the Samaritan text reads "for the day of vengeance and recompense"; and the LXX has "In a day of vengeance, I will pay back." The author quoted the first part of the MT clause and the last part of the LXX saying, but, since Paul used the same formula, it is quite likely that there already existed a text just like the one quoted here. "Vengeance" is that which is inflicted upon the enemy as punishment, in which process the allies are vindicated. The word "judge" can mean to decide the person judged is guilty and punish him, or to judge him to be innocent and vindicate him. In the Deuteronomic context the Lord's "people" were to be vindicated, but the author used the term in the negative sense (as in Enoch 38:3). Those of the Lord's people who become apostate will be judged and punished or paid back. "Falling into the hands of [the] living God" means being caught by "the living God" after sinning. This is like Adam being found after he had eaten the forbidden fruit (Gen 3:9–20). Bruce was embarrassed by the author's stern, unforgiving attitude and assumed he probably took for granted God's merciful and forgiving nature.[99] The author, however, is clear. Those who reject their faith do not receive God's mercy, but his wrath.

Summary.—The word "dreadful" in 10:27 and 31 marks the inclusion for this unit, and it also sets the tenor for the whole passage, which is generally threatening. The author quoted Old Testament passages which include severe warnings of punishment. His strongest argument was an *a fortiori* argument comparing the punishment dispensed by the law of Moses which was inferior to the still more severe punishment that would come to those who accepted the faith and then turned their backs to it. The author's exegesis of Isa 26:10–11 was very similar to that of II Bar 48:39–40. The previous section consisted of exhortations; this unit gave the consequences for those who did not heed the exhortations.

Memory

32. "The earlier days" (*tas prōteron hēmeras*), "The first days," "the former days," after they "had become enlightened" were the days just after their admission into the community. Their enlightenment was their catechetical training prior to baptism (see COMMENT on 6:4).

33. "Sometimes . . . other times" (*touto . . . touto*). The Greek word for "upset" (*anastrephomenōn*) means to turn upside down, revolve, turn back, or busy oneself in. Those who were thus turned around were upset, perhaps in a very rigorous way.

34. The Greek word for "confiscation" is *harpagēn,* which usually means "plunder," "booty," or "robbery." "A better possession [that is] lasting" is literally, "a better and lasting possession."

35. For the meaning of "boldness," see the COMMENT on 10:9 and 4:16.

Summary.—After warning the readers of the terrible punishment that God would inflict upon those who did not hold fast to the faith, but rather left it and even despised it, as some members of their group had already done, the author reminded them of "the good old days" when their faith was strong and stable. After they had received the instruction necessary for admission to the community, they were required to endure a great deal of suffering. This was of two kinds: (a) "Sometimes" they had been publicly "exhibited" and embarrassed by being afflicted both with "insults" and physical injury; (b) "other times" they shared the reputation associated with those who had been "thus upset." When others were

[99] Bruce, pp. 263–64.

"in bonds," members of the community who were not in prison visited them (see Matt 25:36, 43) and in other ways "suffered with" them. This probably was not an easy thing to do, because it exposed those not in prison as being part of the same movement and put them in danger of the same kind of punishment.

A third point to their credit was that they "accepted with joy the confiscation" of their "possessions." This probably refers to one of the following inconveniences: (a) The plunder and confiscation of their property and possessions by the government or some outsiders. This might mean that individuals within the group had suffered financial loss in this way, or it might mean that a community which lived together, communally, had been attacked and its possessions taken. The word *harpagēn* first suggests something like this. If this kind of plunder motivated the brothers to accept the misfortune "with joy," then the members were trained to rejoice in their sufferings with the understanding that God would reward them generously in the future and wreak vengeance upon those who confiscated their property. Since non-resistant suffering was encouraged by the Sermon on the Mount, Romans 12–13, James, and I Peter, it would not be surprising if the group to which this document was addressed also enjoyed hardship unjustly caused by an enemy. The fact that the confiscation was classed along with insults and physical injury also supports the likelihood that this referred to plunder by those outside the community. The other possibility is: (b) Other sectarian groups, such as the Essenes and the community governed by 1QS, who were known for their strict discipline, observance of ritual ablutions, and other practices necessary for holiness, strained every muscle to avoid defiling their community, which 1QS, like Hebrews, called "the many." Essenes and members of the community governed by 1QS were also celibate and communal. The very last step required for admission into these groups involved giving up their personal property (1QS 6:22–23), which might be considered having it "confiscated" by the community. This also meant they gave up all financial responsibility for their families and all physical contact with them, since their families did not observe the same rules with the same strictness. Nonetheless, many did this, believing the new family to be better than the old anxiety of the world (Acts of Thomas 144–46). In other words, this was the kind of deprivation which the instructed could not only tolerate, but even accept "with joy." Since Hebrews reflects many attitudes and practices observed specially by rigorous, even monastic, groups, this communal economics is a real possibility. Because surrendering their goods was associated with the last step of their initiation, it would have happened in the "earlier days, after" they "had become enlightened," or trained in the doctrines of the sect. Both of these interpretations are possibilities, but neither draws conclusive evidence strong enough to exclude the other.

The reference to "boldness" (10:35) refers the reader to the original topic sentence of this discussion (10:19). The two terms constitute an inclusion to remind the reader of the beginning and conclusive limits of the topic. In between were personal words, divided into three distinct categories; exhortation, warnings and threats, and an appeal to return to the earlier days when their character was better.

Brevity of waiting time

36. Over and over again the author encouraged his readers to endure so that they might receive "the promise." This was his central motivation and ethical requirement.

37. The text quoted from Isaiah was 26:20. Isaiah urged the people to hide themselves for a little while (*kimeʿaṭ regaʿ; mikron hoson hoson*) until the wrath would pass over. The wrath came when God visited his people to punish them for their iniquity (Isa 26:20–21). The people's fortunes were believed to reflect God's attitude toward them. If they suffered, God was angry; if they prospered, God was pleased with them. The author of Hebrews lived under the same belief. He used this passage to encourage his people to endure the wrath they now faced, because it would soon pass away when God came to visit them with blessing, fulfilling his promise to them.

38. With a slight variation, the author of Hebrews masterfully spliced a passage from Habakkuk to the one from Isaiah, as if they initially constituted one Old Testament quotation. The Hebrew infinitive absolute, "for he will surely come" (*kī bōʾ yābōʾ*) was literally translated by the LXX, "because coming, he will come" (*hoti erchomenos hēxei*) (Hab 2:3). The author of Hebrews omitted just one syllable (*ti*) to change the meaning to suit his needs: "because coming, he will come" (LXX Hab 2:3) became "the coming one will come" (*ho erchomenos hēxei*). This type of change is typical of *pesher* exegesis. In Habakkuk, that which would come was the vision (Hab 2:3), but in Hebrews, "the coming one" would be the Lord or his Messiah. Hence, the Isaiah passage, which urged the people to wait a little while until the Lord's wrath passed over, and the Habakkuk passage, promising that the vision would not delay, were spliced together to prove that the Lord would soon come to fulfill his "promise." The "righteous one" to whom the author referred was the reader, the Christian who had once endured a great deal of ridicule and torture but recently was tempted to give up the faith as others had done. He needed "faith" by which to "live" if he was to endure as he had in the earlier days.

39. The author confronted the reader with a choice: he could either "shrink back" and the Lord would "not take pleasure in him" or he could endure for a little while longer and obtain the promise. The expression "not take pleasure" is a "litotes" expression. It is softened to an understatement by a double negative. It means the Lord *will* pay back and judge his people (Deut 32:35, 36). It is something dreadful to fall into the hands of the living God (10:31). Therefore the author exhorted the readers to dismiss the possibility "of shrinking back for destruction," but rather to have "faith for [the] acquisition of a soul."

Summary.—This transition passage centers around three important words: (a) "endurance," (b) "shrinking back," and (c) "faith." The first two words are related to that which had been said before. The readers had been warned to hold fast unmoved (10:23) to their confession of hope (10:23) and were reminded of the trials they had endured when they first were enlightened (10:32). The third point is "faith for [the] acquisition of a soul" (10:39), which is the introductory word leading into the next chapter, lauding the faith of the great saints of the past. The author had already warned his readers of God's punishment for those who did not endure. Here he reminded them of the reward they would receive for enduring. They would gain the promise (10:36). The promise was that they would enter into his rest (4:1). This promise had never been satisfactorily fulfilled. Its full and final realization was still to come. The exodus generation did not receive it because of that generation's unbelief (3:12). The next chapter (11) was designed to show the virtues of the great saints in their great faith and endurance, because those were the most necessary qualities for the readers if they were to receive the fulfillment of the promise that God intended for his chosen people.

V. THE FAITH OF THE FATHERS (11:1–12:29)

The fathers

The meaning of faith

11 1 Now faith is [the] groundwork of things hoped for, [the] basis for testing things not seen, 2 for in this the men of old were attested. 3 By faith we consider the ages to have been put in order by [the] word of God, so that what is seen has not come into existence from things that are visible.

Pre-Abrahamic saints

4 By faith Abel offered to God a better sacrifice than Cain,
through which he was attested to be righteous, God himself witnessing to his gifts, and through it, while dying, still he speaks. 5 By
faith Enoch was changed so as not to see death, and "he was not found [dead] because God had changed him," for before the change it was attested [that he was] "pleasing to God." 6 Now,
without faith it is impossible to please him, for it is necessary for the one who approaches God to believe that he is and [that] he becomes a wage-payer to those who seek him. 7 By faith, Noah,
having been solemnly warned about the things not yet seen, since he was cautious, prepared an ark for [the] salvation of his house, through which he condemned the world, and of the righteousness according to faith, he became an heir.

The patriarchs

8 By faith Abraham, when he was called, obeyed [the command]
to go out to a place which he was about to receive for an inheritance, and "he went out," not knowing where he was going. 9 By
faith he dwelt in the land of the promise as a stranger, living in tents with Isaac and Jacob, joint heirs of the same promise, 10 for
he was expecting the city which had the foundations, whose builder and constructor was God. 11 By faith also Sarah herself received
power for [the] foundation of seed, even beyond the time of

productivity, since she considered the one who made the promise
faithful. 12 Wherefore they also came into existence from one, and
these from one [who was] dead,

> "just as the stars of heaven (in their multitude)
> and as the sand which is along the sea shore
> (which is countless)."

13 According to faith these all died, not having acquired [the fulfillment of] the promises, but they saw and greeted them from a
distance and confessed that they were "strangers and wanderers in
the land." 14 For those who say such things as these make [it]
clear that they are seeking a fatherland, 15 and if, on the one hand,
they had kept in mind that [fatherland] from which they had gone
out, they would have had opportunity all along to return, 16 but
now, on the other hand, they are reaching out for a better [father-
land], that is a heavenly [one]. Therefore God is not ashamed to
be called their God, for he has prepared for them a city.

> 17 By faith Abraham offered Isaac, being tested
> and the one who received the promises offered
> [his] only one,

18 [with reference] to whom it was said, "In Isaac shall your seed
be called," 19 considering that God is able to raise [people] from
[the] dead, from which he got him back, parabolically. 20 By faith
also concerning the things to come, Isaac blessed Jacob and Esau.
21 By faith Jacob, dying, blessed each of the sons of Joseph, and
"he worshiped at the top of his staff." 22 By faith Joseph, dying, reminded [his brothers] about the exodus of the sons of Israel and
gave orders concerning [the care to be given] his bones.

From Moses to Joshua

23 By faith Moses, after he had been born, was hidden three
months by his parents, because they saw [that] the child was attractive, and they were not afraid of the decree of the king. 24 By
faith Moses, when he had grown up, refused to [let it be said that
he was] a son of the daughter of Pharaoh, 25 choosing rather to
be badly treated with the people of God than to have transitory
enjoyment of sin, 26 since he considered the insult of the Messiah
greater wealth than the treasures of Egypt, for he was looking out
for the reward. 27 By faith he left Egypt, not having feared the
wrath of the king, for he endured as [one who] saw the invisible.
28 By faith he instituted the Passover and the pouring out of the

blood, in order that the one destroying the first-born might not
touch them. 29 By faith they went through the Red Sea as through
dry land, by which the Egyptians, when they made [the same]
attempt, were swallowed up. 30 By faith the walls of Jericho fell,
having been circled for seven days. 31 By faith Rahab the harlot did
not perish with the unfaithful ones, having received the spies in
peace.

The significance of the saints

32 Now what more shall I say? For the time will fail me to tell
about Gideon, Barak, Samson, Jephthah, David, Samuel, and the
prophets, 33 those who through faith

struggled against kingdoms,
achieved righteousness,
obtained promises,
stopped the mouths of lions,
34 extinguished power of fire,
fled [the] mouths of [the] sword,
received power from weakness,
became strong in war,
upset the military camps of foreigners.

35 Women received their dead by resurrection, but others were
beaten, not accepting the release [offered], in order that they might
obtain a better resurrection.

36 And others received [the] trial of mockings
and whips,
and still [others], of fetters and prison.
37 They were stoned, tested, sawed in two;
they died by slaughter of [the] sword,
went around in sheepskins,
in skins of goats;
they were deprived, afflicted, badly treated,
38 (of whom the world is not worthy,)
wandering in deserts, mountains, caves
and openings of the earth.

39 Now these all, attested through faith, did not acquire the
promise, 40 since God had foreseen something better concerning us,
so that without us they might not be perfected.

The cloud of witnesses and the call for endurance

Jesus the greatest leader

12 1 Therefore, we also, since we have so great a cloud of witnesses [as this] surrounding us, after we have put aside every weight,
even the sin that clings to us very readily, let us run with endurance the course that is laid out before us, 2 keeping our gaze directed to Jesus, the prime leader and perfecter of the faith, who,
instead of the joy laid out before him, having despised [the] cross
of shame, endured [it], and is seated at the right hand of the
throne of God. 3 Just consider the one who has endured so great
an opposition [as this] against himself, from the sinners, so that
you may not become exhausted, being depressed in your souls.

Necessity of discipline

4 You have not yet stood up against sin to the extent of blood,
5 and you have utterly forgotten the comfort which is offered to
you as sons:

> "My son, do not depreciate [the] discipline of the Lord,
> nor become depressed when you are corrected by him,
> 6 for whom the Lord loves, he disciplines,
> and he whips every son whom he accepts."

7 With reference to "discipline," [you must] endure; as "sons" God
deals with you; for who is [the] son whom [his] father does not
discipline? 8 But if you are without discipline (of which you have
all become sharers), then you are illegitimate children and not sons.

Comparison and challenge

9 Therefore, since we have had our fathers of the flesh [as] disci-
plinarians, and we became respectful, shall we not much more subject ourselves to the father of spirits and live? 10 For they used to
discipline us for a short time, as it seemed [wise] to them; but he
[disciplines us] insofar as it is beneficial for sharing his sanctity.
11 At the present, all discipline seems not to be joy, but pain; later,
however, it produces a peaceful fruit of righteousness for those
who have been trained through it.

12 Therefore, "set straight the collapsed hands and the paralytic
knees," 13 and "make straight tracks" for your feet, so that the lame
may not be turned off [the road] but rather be healed.

Truth and its consequences

The root of bitterness

14 Pursue peace with all, and sanctification, without which no one
will see the Lord, 15 checking carefully lest anyone fall back from
the grace of God, "lest any root of bitterness, growing up, should
cause trouble" and through this the many become defiled, 16 lest
anyone [become] a fornicator or defiled person, like Esau, who, in
exchange for a single meal "gave up his own birthright." 17 For you
[may] be sure that even afterwards, when he wanted to inherit the
blessing, he was rejected, for he did not find a place for repentance,
even though he sought it with tears.

The consuming fire

18 For you have not approached a fire that is touched and kindled,
[nor] deep darkness, gloom and tempest, 19 a reverberated sound
of a trumpet, and a voice of words, of which those who heard
pleaded [that] no word be added to them, 20 for they could not
bear that which was commanded. "Even if a beast touches the
mountain he will be stoned," 21 and so dreadful was that which appeared, Moses said, "I am afraid and trembling." 22 But you have
approached Mount Zion, even [the] city of [the] living God,
heavenly Jerusalem, myriads of angels, a national assembly, 23 a
church of first-born [people], enrolled in heaven, God [the] Judge
of all, [the] spirits of the righteous, perfected, 24 Jesus [the] mediator of a new covenant, and [the] blood of sprinkling, speaking
better than that of Abel. 25 See that you do not request [exemp-
tion from] the speaker,

for if those requesting [exemption from]
the one who warns upon earth did not escape,
how much more [shall] we [not escape] who
turn away from the one [who warns] from heaven,

26 whose voice then shook the earth, but now has promised, saying,
"Yet once [more] I will shake [not only] the earth [but also] the

heaven"? 27 Now the [expression] "yet once [more]" points to the changing of the things shaken as of things that are made, in order that the things not shaken might remain. 28 Therefore, accepting an unshakable kingdom, let us have grace through which we might worship in a way that is pleasing to God, with reverence and fear, 29 for our God is "a consuming fire."

COMMENT

THE FATHERS

The meaning of faith

11:1. The word "groundwork" (*hypostasis*) was used to describe God's "nature" (1:3) and the Christian's "faith." Accordingly, it is an integral part of the author's message and related to the rest of the document. "Groundwork" is a good description of "faith" as it appears in Hebrew concepts. The Hebrew word for faith is *'ᵉmūnāh* which suggests solidity, firmness, stability. *'mn* means "support" or "confirm." One who has faith has support; if he believes in someone or something, he has supported himself in or found support from that person or object. The word *elegchos* ("basis for testing"), however, is a Greek legal term used in debates or cross-examinations. Both terms were used here in parallel as complementary parts of the author's definition of faith.

For the author of Hebrews faith was closely related to doctrine, creed, confession, or catechism. The message of good news did not help the exodus generation because the people lacked faith (4:2). The "rest" which was denied the exodus generation was available during the author's time for those who believed (4:3). Without faith it is impossible to please God (11:6). This means that it is necessary for one who approaches God to believe that he is (11:6). Faith in God is one of the elementary doctrines of Christ (6:1). It is through faith that people become heirs of the promises (6:12), which is another way of saying they become members of the elect. One who has a true heart in fullness of faith (10:22) is ritually cleansed and prepared to enter holy precincts. He should hold fast unmoved the confession of hope (10:23), because those who are of faith do not shrink back from destruction (10:39). Those who believe are those who trust the promises of God, but they also accept the right doctrines, hold fast to the confession (4:14) and hold fast unmoved the confession of hope (10:23), because Jesus is the high priest of the confession (3:1). Those who held fast the confession of hope (10:23) were those who hoped that the promises of God would soon be fulfilled and confessed this belief, even though their fulfillment did not seem likely to most. They endured, showing forth the same zeal toward the full conviction of hope to the end (6:11). The promise and the oath (6:17) given in the Old Testament provide the believer with strong encouragement to seize the hope set before him (6:18). Only the Christian has faith; he is the one who has accepted the correct doctrines, has mastered the confession to which he holds fast. His doctrines are such that he is required to have hope that God will soon fulfill his promises. The proximity of faith to creed for the author requires the reader of chapter eleven to try to understand the shade of meaning intended for each usage. The word blends together concepts of trust, creed, confession, hope, expectation, and confidence. It is not always clear just which of these concepts is emphasized in each particular instance, but an attempt will be made to understand these in a way that is consistent with the rest of the author's message.

For the author, faith was the opposite of shrinking back into apostasy (10:39). A person who once became a Christian either held fast the confession (10:23) or became an apostate and surrendered his faith; he belonged to the faith or shrank back (10:39). "Things hoped for" and "not seen" involve the coming of the coming one (10:37) or gaining the promise (4:1; 10:36) of entering into his rest (4:1). Not only were these "hoped for," but they were anticipated soon (10:25, 37). "The groundwork," foundation, or "basis for testing" this hope is the confession to which the believers were obligated to hold fast (10:23), which is another way of saying "the groundwork of things hoped for is faith."

2. "This" in which "the men of old were attested" seems to have been some kind of confession or creed that told about them, i.e. this creed or confession. Some early texts (P^{13} 103 1908) read "in it" (*en autē*) rather than "in this" (*en tautē*), because the antecedent seemed obvious. "This" refers to "faith" (11:1), which here deals with something that holds doctrines or articles of faith which provided for the community the "groundwork" of their hope and a source which members could examine to learn about unseen things. If a person wanted to know what he should expect or for which he dared hope, he could check the confession (3:1; 4:14; 10:23) which he was obligated to hold fast (4:14; 10:23), and on the basis of this creed or faith, test the things not seen. This confession or faith (3:1; 4:14; 10:23; 11:1) contained a list of the community's orthodox doctrines and hopes, and it seems to have been closely related to, identified with, or included in the Old Testament, because "the men of old" who "were attested" "in this" were also attested in the Old Testament and in the very same order given in the list that follows, beginning with the first events in Genesis and continuing up to the conquest of Palestine by Joshua, who was a prototype for the new Joshua.

3. "The ages" were "put in order" (*katartisthai tous aiōnas*), not created, as one might expect when the report covers the creation stories in Genesis. As in 1:2, the reference is to the creation, but the author considered time to have been organized in the same act, and he was more interested in the sequence of events and God's purpose associated with the calendrical happenings than with the material nature God created (see COMMENT on 1:2). On the first day of creation God created light, which he separated from

darkness, forming day. Since a thousand years in the sight of the Lord are as one day (Ps 90:4; II Peter 3:8), and since a thousand years might be thought of as an age, one might consider that the Lord arranged the ages or the millennia the way he arranged the days of creation, so that the ages would conclude with an age of rest, just as creation ended with a day of rest. This would suit the author's eschatology. The "word of God" was the "word" spoken by God when light came into existence and was separated from darkness so that there could be temporal divisions or "ages" (Gen 1:3–5). That God was the source of "what is seen" is widely attested (Gen 1; Rom 1:20; Wis 9:1; 11:17; 13:4). It did not "come into existence" from idols, nature, or any of the "things that are visible." This is the witness of the scripture and also the confession of faith.

The contrasts between the "things not seen" and "what is seen" (11:1, 3) do not reflect a Platonic viewpoint as some have thought. Plato would not have "considered" in "faith" or "by faith," as Hebrews has done, since "considering" is the intellectual understanding of unchanging ideas, according to Plato, and "faith" is the uncritical, sensible grasp of data belonging to the physical world. Neither would Plato have thought of "what is seen" as not coming "into existence from things that are visible." For Plato, God brought order out of the then existing, chaotic, visible world, but he did not bring it forth from invisible essence.[1] The author's concern for the unseen was not primarily that which was invisible or intangible, but that which was future, that which had not yet happened (see COMMENT on 1:2). It was a concept of time rather than of substance or essence.

Summary.—The definition of faith summarized in these three verses was important to the author's doctrine, but he did not organize this definition as a separate unit. In *his* outline, the unit consisted of 11:1–7 and was thus indicated by an inclusion. From the standpoint of the exhortation in chapter ten, chapter eleven seems to be something of an intrusion, which could easily have been omitted and have the exhortation of 12:1 continue immediately after 10:39, but the author regularly related his doctrine to his homiletics, and his conclusion of chapter ten contained catchwords preparing the reader also for chapter eleven. Furthermore, chapter eleven is closely related to the introduction of the entire document, and it is consistent with the theology expressed throughout. If it was originally composed separately it has been well integrated into its present position.

Pre-Abrahamic saints

4. The scripture did not tell what was inferior about Cain's sacrifice, but, according to the LXX, Cain was told that if he did not offer sacrifices correctly (*orthōs*), he sinned (*hēmartes*) (Gen 4:7). "God looked upon" (*epeiden*) Abel and upon his gifts" (Gen 4:5), according to the account. This provided basis for the author of Hebrews to deduce that God attested him

[1] Williamson, pp. 421–22.

"to be righteous." The text told only about the sacrifice he offered, not about his righteousness, but since to offer incorrectly was sin (Gen 4:7), to offer correctly must have been considered righteousness. The author of Hebrews claimed that Abel's "sacrifice" was "better" by faith. According to the Old Testament, the question of Cain's and Abel's faith was not raised, but in the Palestinian targumim, this was important. According to Neofiti:

"*When both of them had gone out into the field* Cain answered and said to Abel: 'I understand that the world was created by mercy but not governed according to the fruits of good works and there is respect of persons in judgment. For which reason your offering was received favourably and my offering was not received favourably from me.' Abel answered and said to Cain: 'I understand that the world was created by mercy and is governed according to the fruits of good works. And as my works were better than yours my offering was received favourably.' Cain answered and said to Abel: 'There is no judgment and there is no judge and there is no other world; and there is no giving of good reward to the just nor is retribution exacted of the wicked.' Abel answered and said to Cain: 'There is a judgment and there is a judge and there is another world and there is giving of good reward to the just; and retribution is exacted of the wicked in the world to come.' Over this matter both of them were disputing *in the field, and Cain rose up against his brother Abel and slew him.*"[2]

The author of Hebrews was evidently acquainted with one of the Palestinian targumim and, on that basis, concluded that Abel's gift was "a better sacrifice" than Cain's "by faith." The faith involved was not trust but a doctrinal confession. I John concluded that Cain "was from the evil one and he slew his brother." The reason given was that "Cain's works were evil and those of his brother were good" (I John 3:12). This can be justified from the Old Testament alone. The beliefs about good works, judgment, reward, punishment, and mercy were introduced by the targumist and accepted by Hebrews. The "it" (*autēs*) through which "Abel still speaks," while dying, is not the gifts (plural), but the "faith." The report of God's judgment is still on record for those who will read Gen 4:4 and in greater detail in targum. This is the faith through which "still he speaks," and it is the faith through which he was attested "to be righteous."

5. The Hebrew text said of Enoch, "Enoch walked with God, and he was not (*'ēnennū*), because God took him" (Gen 5:24). This is a rather unclear statement: it looks as if some verb had been omitted. The LXX has either preserved that verb from a text written before the verb was lost, or it has conjectured one to make sense: ". . . and he was not *found*, because God *changed* him" (LXX Gen 5:24). Even with the LXX alterations, the question still arises: what happened to Enoch? It is uncertain. His case is somewhat like that of Melchizedek, leaving later believers plenty of room to speculate. According to some traditions, Enoch was even more righteous than Noah (Jub 10:17), so God took him from among the children of men

[2] This insight and English translation are from M. McNamara, *The New Testament and the Palestinian Targum to the Pentateuch* (Rome, 1966), p. 159.

and transferred him to the Garden of Eden in majesty and honor. There he functions as the court scribe, recording all the deeds of men to use on the day of judgment (Jub 4:23; 10:17; Enoch 15:1; II Enoch 22:12). The reason why Enoch was taken to God was his perfection (Sir 49:14; see also *Ant.* I. 85). He was changed into an example of repentance for all generations (Sir 44:16). According to Hebrews, "Enoch was changed so as not to see death," just as Elijah had been. This is a fair interpretation of the LXX, since the idiom "being found" was used as a euphemism for "being found dead" (see Epictetus iii 5–6; iv 10, 12). The basis for this statement is "by faith," which may mean that, according to the creed, confession, or religious tradition, "he was not found [dead] because God had changed him" (LXX Gen 5:24). This "change" came as a reward to Enoch, because in the LXX it says that Enoch was "pleasing to God" (Gen 5:24a) *before* it says "God changed him" (Gen 5:24b). Using a *post hoc propter hoc* (that which precedes is the *cause* of that which follows) argument, the author reasoned that Enoch was "pleasing to God" first, and the "change" came later as a reward.

6. In the author's judgment no one could please God without "faith." Therefore Enoch had faith. Since Enoch was so handsomely rewarded for pleasing God, which could not have happened without faith, it follows that "it is necessary for the one who approaches God to believe that he is." This was probably a basic doctrine of the group. The "one who approaches God" is either the worshiper approaching the altar with his sacrifice, as Cain and Abel had done, or an initiate approaching God by taking regular steps of advancement toward full membership in the sect. Since this is a very elementary doctrine, it was probably intended here to mean the initiate who would accept this in an early stage of his catechetical training or faith. The initiate must not only believe that God is, but like Abel according to the targumist, he must believe that God "becomes a wage-payer to those who seek him."

7. The Greek for "having been solemnly warned" is *chrēmatistheis* (used also in 8:5). The verb generally means "to do business with," "consult," "negotiate," "advise," or "obtain an answer." In biblical concepts it is generally used in communications from God to his people and means "to advise," or "to warn solemnly" as in Matt 2:12 and here. The word rendered "ark" is *kibōton,* "box," "chest," or "coffer." The box that contained the tablets of the covenant was such a chest. The box that Noah built, however, was some sort of wooden box that would float and hold passengers, more like a houseboat. The term "heir," here applied to Noah, was also applied to Jesus the Son, who was "heir" of all (1:2), and to the believers who would obtain the fulfillment of the promises (6:17). The heirs are those who inherit a name (1:4), salvation (1:14), the promises (6:12, 17; 11:9) or the blessing (12:17). Although not an heir of the promise, Noah was the first man recorded in scripture as righteous (Gen 7:1). The author of Hebrews interpreted this as meaning that he acted according to the solemn warning, which was the right way to act; it was according to faith.

In his characteristic fashion the author related his illustrations to his definition. Since faith is the basis for "testing things not seen" (11:1), Noah was given as an example of one who acted according to the faith regarding "the things not yet seen." He had "not yet seen" the flood that was to come, but since he had "been solemnly warned," "he was cautious." Not taking any chances, Noah believed that God rewards those who seek him (11:6), and he "prepared an ark for [the] salvation of his house." This act which provided "salvation" for his own family, however, provided no assistance for the rest of the people who belonged to "the world." Instead, it was "through" that very act that "he condemned the world" (see also John 3:17), whereas he himself "became an heir" "of the righteousness according to faith." The significance of this teaching for the Christian contemporary with the author was that the Christian, like Noah, had a basis for testing things not seen (11:1). This was the word of God, which Noah received directly and the Christian received from reading the scriptures, which is "by faith." As Noah was "solemnly warned," so the Christian who read his scripture properly was shown what the future would be and was obligated to hold fast unmoved the confession of hope (10:23). Like Noah, he was required to endure in faith when others saw no danger, but in the end the Christian would be vindicated and the apostate "condemned."

Summary.—The list of exemplary personalities which begins with Abel is similar to those recorded in IV Macc 16:20–23 and Sir 44–50. In IV Maccabees, Abraham, Isaac, Daniel the righteous (*ho dikaios*), Hananiah, Mishael, and Azariah were those who were courageous enough to face death for their faith, and the mother of seven sons encouraged them to be willing to die, as these heroic men had been, rather than transgress God's commandment. Since the story was told to encourage Jews to withstand the persecutions of the Gentiles, the list included only Israelites. Sirach began his long list with Enoch (Noah, according to the Hebrew text) and ended it with Simon, the son of Onias, the high priest shortly before the Maccabean Revolt. The author of Hebrews began earlier than the other two and continued listing names specifically until the time of Joshua, to correspond with Jesus, the new Joshua, who would usher in a new kingdom and the promised rest. Unnamed were many who suffered for their faith in Maccabean times and probably also at the time the author wrote.

These first three men constituted the testimony before the patriarchs, but they also provided the author of Hebrews an occasion to substantiate his own rigorous doctrine and ethic. The theology of Abel according to the targum was precisely that of the author. The enduring faith of Noah was exactly the ethic which the author repeatedly urged for his readers. The rewards of Enoch and of Noah were for their faith, even though some circular reasoning was required to deduce this from the Old Testament report of Enoch. The reward of Noah for his righteousness and lack of concern for the world reflects the author's sectarian attitude toward the elect and the world. He only urged the readers to stay among the elect. There is no missionary message in this document.

The author intended 11:1–7 as a unit, and he framed it as an inclusion, using the words "faith" and "things not seen" (11:1, 7) for this purpose. Some of the important words in this unit are "faith" (11:1, 3, 4, 5, 7), "witness" (11:2, 4, 5), and "God" (11:3, 4, 5, 6).

The patriarchs

8. Like Noah, Abraham was called upon to act "by faith" regarding things not seen (11:1, 7). Abraham's faith was a virtue frequently praised by later Jews and Christians (Sir 44:19–21; Wis 10:5; Rom 4; Gal 3; Acts 7:2–5; *Heres* XVIII. 90–93). "An inheritance" is a lot, fortune, or possession which may be acquired as a gift, from labor, or by plunder and conquest (see COMMENT on 1:2, 4). The place from which he left was Haran (Gen 12:4) in the northern region of the Fertile Crescent.

9. The Greek word for "dwelt" is *parǭkēsen,* "dwelt beside," as though he were not one of the nation's citizens. "The land of the promise" is the land Abraham was promised that he would receive as an inheritance, namely the Davidic kingdom, Palestine. Nowhere else in scripture is Palestine called "the land of the promise," although the land was regularly understood as the promised inheritance. According to Genesis, it was not "Isaac and Jacob" but Lot who lived (*ǭcheto*) with Abraham. The author probably did not mean literally that Abraham, Isaac, and Jacob lived together "in tents," but that they all shared the experience of living in tents as strangers "in the land." The confirmation of "Isaac and Jacob" as "joint heirs of the same promise" is reported in Gen 26:3 and 28:13.

10. "The city which had the foundations" (*tēn tous themelious echousan polin*) was probably Jerusalem. According to Ps 87:1, Zion's foundation (*yᵉsūdātō*) was in the holy mountain. The wall which Agrippa began to build around Jerusalem would have been very strong, had he been allowed to finish it. Josephus said it was constructed of stones twenty cubits long and ten broad (i.e. about thirty by fifteen feet). Recent excavations have shown that Josephus was not exaggerating.[3] When Claudius learned the dimensions of the planned wall, he made Agrippa stop the construction after he had laid only the foundation (*themelious monon balomenos*) (*Ant.* XIX. 326–27; *Wars* V. 152–55). Of course the city had other walls, but none so firm as these had been designed to be. Jews probably dreamed of completing the walls at the first opportunity. After the fall of Jerusalem in A.D. 70, an unknown seer had a vision of a constructed city that had large foundations (*fundamentis magnis*) which turned out to be Zion (IV Ezra 10:26–27, 44). Resh Lakish said that in the future the Lord would add to Jerusalem a thousand gardens, a thousand towers, a thousand palaces and

[3] About the same size as those uncovered in the Herodian wall on the south side of the temple platform. These are 10–11 meters long. See B. Mazar, "The Excavations South and West of the Temple Mount in Jerusalem—the Herodian Period," BA 33 (1970), 52–53.

mansions, and that each of these would be as big as Sepphoris in its prosperity (BB 75b). Tobit dreamed of a new Jerusalem whose gates would be built of sapphire and emerald and its walls of precious stone, its towers would be made of gold and its streets of carbuncle and stones of Ophir (Tobit 13:16–17), which is an extension of II Isaiah's vision (Isa 54:12). The New Testament seer envisioned a new Jerusalem whose walls had twelve foundations (Rev 21:14), and "the foundations of the wall of the city [were] decorated with every precious stone" (Rev 21:19). He described the city still more gloriously than Tobit had done (Rev 21:19–21). Like the temple not made with hands (see COMMENT on 9:11), "the city which had the foundations" was one "whose builder and constructor was God." "Builder and constructor" are synonyms forming a *hendiadys.* The city was also called "Mount Zion, even [the] city of [the] living God, heavenly Jerusalem" (12:22). The author of Hebrews was not the only one to attribute a divine origin to Jerusalem. Tobit (13:9) called it the "holy city," and John of Patmos dreamed of "the holy city, a new Jerusalem, coming down from heaven, from God" (Rev 21:2). The author of II Macc 3:39 said that God "whose dwelling place is heaven" was a guardian and aid of Jerusalem. Pseudo-Clement urged his readers to follow a leader that was acquainted with the road that enters the holy city (*Hom.* III.xii). Since the author of Hebrews had earlier referred to the "rest," the land of the promise, and the inheritance in association with the Davidic kingdom, and since the temple administered by the levitical priests was undoubtedly the temple at Jerusalem, "the city which had the foundations" was also probably Jerusalem, the capital city in the land of the promise (11:9). The stability of "the city which had the foundations" was set in contrast to the existence of the patriarchs in tents (11:9). Many scholars, however, spiritualize "the city which had the foundations," making the contrast, instead, between the land of Canaan and heaven. Delitzsch, however, was so much impressed by the similarity between the description given in Hebrews and other descriptions of Jerusalem that he had to admit that it was tempting to consider the city that had the foundations to be Jerusalem, but his theology required him to deny their identity.[4] More recently, Montefiore said, "They also show that *the city with foundations* cannot be Canaan, for God is no more the *maker and designer* of Canaan than of any other part of the earth, while he is in a special sense the author of the heavenly Jerusalem."[5] Since Canaan was not a city, it would seem unreasonable to claim that it was, but in Canaan was a city of Jerusalem about which the author of Hebrews was affectionately concerned and was convinced of its divine origin. Moffatt said, "Abraham had yearnings for a higher, spiritual bliss, for heaven as his true home,"[6] and Williamson said, "For the writer of Hebrews the 'city' of Abraham was clearly heaven itself."[7]

[4] Delitzsch, II, 238.
[5] Montefiore, p. 193.
[6] Moffatt, p. 170; see also Spicq, II, 348–50; Bruce, pp. 305–6; and Stuart, p. 262.
[7] Williamson, p. 491.

11. Scholars have had difficulty with the passage "Sarah . . . received power for [the] foundation of seed" because the expression "foundation of seed" (*katabolēn spermatos*) visually appears to mean the ejection of seed, which is the role of the male. Therefore, they say, this passage was once a continuation of the passage dealing with Abraham.[8] But the word "katabolēn" can mean simply "foundation," without any attempt to etymologize the idiom. The Vulgate renders this expression *in conceptionem seminis.* Although *katabolē* is not the same word for "foundation" as *themelious* used in the preceding verse, the author may have intentionally compared the two. On the one hand, there was the city which had the foundations, which was the capital of the nation; and, on the other hand, there was Isaac, the "foundation" of the chosen people, the seed of Abraham, who were destined to be heirs of the land of the promise (11:9) and the city which had the foundations (11:10). *Hēlikias* refers to the age of maturity, the prime of life. It generally distinguishes adulthood from childhood. In early years it would mark the beginning of menstruation for a woman, but it also refers to the entire period from the beginning of menstruation to the beginning of menopause, namely, the period of fertility. Since Sarah was "beyond the time of productivity," her menopause had already occurred. "The one who made the promise" in Sarah's hearing was one of the men whom Abraham had entertained as a guest (Gen 18:1–10), and Sarah certainly did not consider him "faithful," but laughed at the suggestion (Gen 18:9–15). It also is a generous interpretation of the text to assume that Sarah did all of this "by faith." The author of Hebrews probably meant that the one who made the promise to Abraham (Gen 15:5; 22:17) was "faithful," and that one was God. The author had earlier claimed that God was faithful (10:23).

12. Those who "came into existence" were the sons of Abraham who originated "from one," namely Abraham. "These are the seed (plural) of Abraham, who was called "dead," meaning sterile. The poetic couplet which included Gen 22:17 has been expanded while still preserving the poetry by adding "in their multitude" to one line and "which is countless" to the other. The author may have made these additions himself, or he may have used a couplet already formed from these stock phrases.

13. "According to faith" perhaps means according to the creed or report on which their faith was based. "These all" were Abraham, Isaac, and Jacob and possibly Abel, Enoch, and Noah. The author probably meant only the patriarchs (plus Sarah), because they were the ones involved in "the promises." They all received "the promises," but they did not acquire their fulfillment, and that is what the author had in mind. The author of Hebrews confessed that they were "strangers and wanderers . . . in the land" (*gērīm . . . wᵉtōšābīm . . . ʿal hāʾāreṣ*) even after they were established on the land (I Chron 29:15). "The promises" about which the author was interested involved entering the "rest" (4:1), being blessed, and be-

[8] For this discussion see Bruce, pp. 299–302; Michel, pp. 262–63.

coming a great and numerous people to whom others would defer (Gen 22:17–19; Josh 21:43–45; Heb 6:13–20), or receiving the "land of the promise" (11:9). These are all related to the reestablishment of the land of Palestine under the control of the chosen people, as an exalted nation. Since this never happened, even for a short time, until the reigns of David and Solomon, the author was correct in saying that "these all died, not having acquired [the fulfillment of] the promises." Moses, who was called the servant of the Lord (Deut 34:5), was not allowed to lead the children of Israel from the wilderness into the land of Canaan, but he saw the land from afar, from the top of Mount Pisgah (Deut. 34:1). The land which he saw was that which the Lord swore to give to "Abraham, to Isaac, and to Jacob" (Deut. 34:4). The first generation of Jews in Babylon was also called the Lord's servant (Isa 53:11).[9] That servant was not allowed to return to "the land of life" (i.e. Palestine), but made his grave with the wicked in Babylon (Isa 53:8–9). Like Moses, however, these Jews were allowed to see their seed (Isa 53:10) who would be allowed to return. The author of Hebrews classed the patriarchs with Moses and possibly the suffering servant, when he said they "saw and greeted" the promises "from a distance" even though the distance was temporal rather than geographical, as was true of Moses and the Isaianic servant. They lived in the very land they hoped to inherit, but only as "strangers and wanderers" in the land, not as citizens.

14–15. The author of Hebrews thought people would not call themselves such depreciative names as "strangers and wanderers" if that was their highest goal. To him it was "clear that they [were] seeking a fatherland," but they had already left one fatherland. If they were not particular, they could have returned to Haran and had a fatherland again. This "opportunity" had been open to them "all along," but these were not satisfied with Haran.

16. When they left Haran, they were "reaching out for a better [fatherland], that is a heavenly [one]." Just as the author of Hebrews was the only author in the Bible who called the land of Canaan "the land of the promise" (11:9), so he was the only one to call it a "heavenly" land (11:16), but it is clear in both instances that Palestine was the land intended. In the covenant, the Lord promised Abraham:

> "To your seed I have given this land,
> from the River of Egypt to the Great River (the
> River Euphrates)" (Gen 15:18).

The explanatory passage, "the River Euphrates," is a later gloss made by someone who thought the only great river was the Euphrates. The same glossator probably made the same identification in Josh 1:4 and Deut 1:7 as well. Initially, the author of the poetic couplet had some other river in mind that was either called great or was one he considered to be great. In all probability that river today forms the northern boundary of Lebanon

[9] CC, pp. 123–31.

and is still called "The Great River" (*Nahr el-Kebir*). All the known biblical sites listed in the northern boundaries are in the area of this river: Lebwe or Labwah Ḥamath, Riblah, Lebanon from the river, Hethlon, Zedad, and Kadesh (Josh 13:3–5; I Chron 13:5; Gen 15:18; Amos 6:18; Isa 27:2; Exod 23:31; II Kings 14:25; Ezek 6:24; Deut 11:24; I Kings 5:1; Ezek 47:15–19; Deut 1:7; Num 34:3–9; Ezek 48:1–2, 28). None of these is near the Euphrates River. The southern border was the River of Egypt (probably Wadi el-Arish or perhaps a distributary of the Nile), the Shiḥor opposite Egypt (perhaps also—Wadi el-Arish), Kadesh-barnea, the wilderness of Zin, Ḥalak, the Ascent of the Akrabbim ("Scorpions"), and the Arabah—all sites from the Mediterranean Sea toward the Dead Sea, via the wilderness south of Mount Ḥalak. Between the River of Egypt and the Great River lay the land of Canaan and the land of the Hittites, which together comprised the territory ruled by Solomon.[10] This was the land Israel was able to conquer, so it was the land she believed to be her true heritage. This was the land she was promised, so the author of Hebrews called it "the land of the promise" (11:9). Its capital city was Jerusalem, called the holy city or "city of our God" (Ps 87:2–3). It was the city which comes down from heaven, from God (Rev 21:2), or, as the author of Hebrews called it, "Zion, even [the] city of [the] living God, heavenly Jerusalem" (12:22). It was the "city" God "has prepared for them," a "city which had the foundations, whose builder and constructor was God" (11:10, 16). IV Ezra promised that the time would come when the city that was then invisible would appear, and the land which was then concealed would be seen (7:26). This implies that both Jerusalem and the promised land were hidden, perhaps in heaven, to be disclosed when they were restored to the chosen people under the establishment of conditions of glory. Along with other encomiums, the author of Hebrews called "the land of the promise" (11:9) "a heavenly [one]." This does not mean it is not on earth any more than the "sharers in [the] heavenly calling" (3:1) who had "tasted the heavenly gift" (6:4) were not those who lived on earth. Indeed, it was the very land on which the patriarchs dwelt as "strangers and wanderers" (11:13), but the expression means that it is a divine land which God himself has promised. D. N. Freedman, who has taken his cue from F. I. Andersen, further supports this interpretation with his thesis that the land of Palestine itself was called the temple of the Lord (*bēt YHWH*).[11] Delitzsch said, "It must be confessed that we nowhere read of the patriarchs, that they expressed a conscious desire for a home in heaven. The nearest approach to anything of the kind is in Jacob's vision of the angel-ladder, and his wondering exclamation (Gen 28:17) *zeh šaʿar haššamāyim* [This is the gate of heaven]; but even there no desire is expressed for an entrance into the heavenly land, but the promise renewed of future possession of earthly Canaan: 'The land whereon

[10] See further CC, pp. 91–109.

[11] Unfortunately, neither of these scholars has published his defense of this position at this time. Freedman, who received the idea from Andersen, plans to use it in his commentary on Hosea (AB, vol. 24).

thou sleepest will I give to thee.'"[12] Stuart, however, thought 11:16 so clearly denied Palestine and Jerusalem as the goal of Abraham that his comment was only, "The explanation of the writer in respect to the country which the patriarchs sought, is so plain, that nothing can add to its perspicuity."[13]

The Greek word *gē*, used in 11:13, like the Hebrew word *'āreṣ*, can mean either "earth" or "land," signifying the promised land, depending on the context. Moffatt[14] and the RSV both render *gē* "earth" in 11:13, and Michel gives it the German *Erde*.[15] Consequently Moffatt interprets 11:13–16 quite differently from the above exegesis. The patriarchs were, according to Moffatt, *"strangers and exiles upon earth."*[16] They aspired "to the better land in heaven" (11:16). Moffatt correctly observed that Jacob told Pharaoh, "The days of the years of my sojourning are a hundred and thirty years" (Gen 47:9), and that Abraham confessed to the Hittites, "I am a sojourner among you" (Gen 23:4–5). Moffatt erroneously concluded that "the words *epi tēs gēs* 'upon the earth' or 'upon the land' start the inference (vv. 14–16a) that the true home of these confessors was in heaven."[17]

Moffatt reached these conclusions by ignoring the immediate contexts of the Old Testament references he quoted, accepting "heavenly" as a place description, and overlooking the major theme of the author of Hebrews. Jacob was talking to Pharaoh about his life which had been spent traveling from place to place throughout most of the Fertile Crescent. There is no indication that he was contrasting his earthly sojourning with a heavenly habitation. Neither did Abraham consider himself to be a sojourner on earth whose home was in heaven. He was sojourning in the land of the Hittites, where he was not a citizen.

Michel identified the heavenly city with Jerusalem and related it to the Old Testament expectations of II Isaiah, Ezekiel, and Zechariah, as well as Tobit, IV Ezra, and II Baruch. He also called it the future Jerusalem of rabbinic literature. He claimed, however, that this was an apocalyptic and transcendent reality, rather than a restoration of Jerusalem to its political position in Palestine.[18] He was correct in relating all these eschatological hopes of Judaism with Hebrews, but he was mistaken in his belief that apocalyptic hopes did not anticipate the restoration of Jerusalem to a geographic position. The transcendent city in heaven was to be brought down to its former location when the nation was restored. So Jerusalem could be called a heavenly city and Canaan a heavenly land, as the author of Hebrews seems to have done.[19]

[12] Delitzsch, II, 246.
[13] Stuart, p. 265.
[14] Moffatt, p. 173.
[15] Michel, p. 257.
[16] Moffatt, p. 173.
[17] Moffatt, p. 174.
[18] Michel, pp. 261–62.
[19] CC, chs. 1–4.

The author of Hebrews had basically one hope or aspiration: receiving the promised land in its full glory and prosperity, free from foreign rule or threat from enemies. This was called inheriting or acquiring the promises (6:11, 15–17; 11:13, 33, 39) and entering into the "rest" (3:11, 18; 4:1, 3, 5, 8, 11). The promise is that which was given to Abraham that his seed should inherit the land and be blessed with power, wealth, and number (Gen 15). This is also the "rest" (4:1), and the reception of the land was called an inheritance (11:8). The "rest" which the Israelites might have had if they had not rebelled in the wilderness is the very rest still available. The good news announced to the Israelites under Moses' leadership is the same good news related to Jesus (4:1, 6). Moses and Jesus were related to the same "house"—Moses as a servant and Jesus as a Son (3:2–6). Since the term "rest" was so closely related to the acquisition of Canaan, the intended readers were expected to object that Israelites had received their promised rest when Joshua led the conquest of Canaan after forty years in the wilderness. The author of Hebrews had two answers: (a) If Joshua had really given them rest, at a later time God would not have spoken through David of another day (4:8); and (b) whoever finds rest, ceases from his labors (4:10). Since Israel had never had a continuing period of settlement free from threat or "labor," she had not received her full and final rest that had been promised. That did not mean the "rest" still expected was different from the one early Israelites expected, but only that it would at last be completely received.

This promise-rest-inheritance was inextricably tied to the land of Canaan, which is the place where the patriarchs wandered as sojourners (11:13). It was called the land of the promise (11:9) and the heavenly country (11:16), which is better than Haran. There God has prepared for them a city (11:16), which has foundations (11:10). That city was called by other authors "the holy city" (Tobit 13:9) or "the holy city, new Jerusalem, coming down from heaven, from God" (Rev 21:2).

The RSV and Moffatt in translating 11:13 "strangers and wanderers on the earth" failed to notice that this was a partial repetition of 11:9: "By faith he dwelled in the land of the promise as a stranger." Just as the earlier passage (11:9) refers to Canaan, so also the later (11:13) passage refers to Canaan. Since only context determines whether *gē* should be translated "land" or "earth," the context here clearly required 11:13 to be rendered "strangers and wanderers in the land," namely "the land of the promise" (11:9).

17–19. The Greek for "only one" is *monogenē,* which is different from LXX Gen 22:2, "beloved" (*agapēton*). The Hebrew *yāḥīd* means both "only one" and "beloved," so both are fair representations of the Hebrew, but their differences indicate that the author had access to a variant LXX text or else translated at times directly from the Hebrew, or even substituted a synonym he preferred. The Greek for "he got him back" is *komizein* and can mean either "acquire," "receive," "carry off" or "get back," "recover, "return."

The author's sensitivity for poetic expression is shown in the couplet in vs. 17. His effective use of repetition echoes 11:11–12, though with different meanings:

a. Sarah was "one [who was] dead" (12)	a. God could "raise [people] from [the] dead" (19)
b. Sarah "received power" (11)	b. "God is able" (19)
c. God made the "promise" (11)	c. Abraham "received the promises" (17)
d. Sarah "considered [*hēgēsato*] the one who made the promise faithful" (11)	d. Abraham considered (*logisamenos*) "that God is able even to raise [people] from [the] dead" (19).

Since both subdivisions deal with Isaac, and since the author consciously used similar terminology in both, perhaps the rabbinic rule, *gazara shawa*, whereby one unit is employed to clarify the other, may be applied here. In 11:19, Abraham was said to have offered Isaac because of his faith in God who was "able even to raise [people] from [the] dead," and parabolically Abraham "got him back." What is this parable? How was it intended? How did Abraham get Isaac back from the dead? This may refer to the original acquisition of Isaac from Sarah, i.e. "from one [who was] dead" (11:12). If *komizein* were intended to mean "receive," it would refer to Isaac's birth; if it meant "get back," it would mean the rescue of Isaac from sacrifice. The context suggests the latter, but the relationship between 11:11–12 and 11:17–19 indicates the former. Some rabbis said that Abraham and Isaac learned that God would raise the dead when Abraham received the command not to hurt Isaac. At that time Isaac's soul really left his body and was then restored, and he was raised from the dead to bless the Lord (PRE 31, 16b). This may be the interpretation the author intended, but it is not certain. The choice of interpretations is not clear. The rabbinic explanation makes good sense for an author who believed in the resurrection as the author of Hebrews did (6:2; 11:35), but the author's skill in literary artistry is also a strong argument to relate the parable to Isaac's birth. Without further evidence the choice is almost arbitrary. In any case, the author's understanding of the resurrection from the dead to be parabolic did not mean the real resurrection of a corpse.[20]

Whereas Paul held that Abraham was reckoned righteous because he

[20] For a convincing analysis and thesis of the importance of the binding of Isaac as a virtue for which God was expected by Jews and Christians to reward Israel in the future, see N. A. Dahl, "The Atonement—An Adequate Reward for the Akedah? (Ro 8:32)," *Neotestamentica et Semitica,* eds. E. E. Ellis and M. Wilcox (Edinburgh, 1969), pp. 15–29.

believed against all odds that Sarah would bear a son (Gal 3:6–19; Rom 4:1–25), others believed that the real basis for his justification was his willingness to offer Isaac (James 2:20–22; Sir 44:20; Wis 10:5; Aboth 5:4; IV Macc 16:18–20). The Genesis narrative began by announcing that God tested Abraham (Gen 22:1). The word used for testing (Hebrew *nsh*, Greek *peirazein*) is the same word used to describe the Israelites' rebellion in the wilderness (Exod 17:2–7; Num 14:22) and the devil's testing of Jesus (Matt 4:1). It is not surprising that the author of Hebrews admired Abraham's willingness to offer Isaac. He would have considered it enduring in faith or holding fast the confession of hope.

20–22. The author was kindly disposed toward his spiritual ancestors, so he did not tell about the way Jacob cheated Esau out of his blessing (Gen 27:1–29). When Esau asked Isaac to bless him also, Isaac could only predict the future for Esau after Jacob had already been promised the blessings intended for the first-born (Gen 27:36–40). The author rather obscured this deceptive event when he generously reported that "Isaac blessed Jacob and Esau." According to Jub 17:15, this had the approval of Abraham who did not want his posterity to follow Esau's line or to have Esau's children called by his name. In his report of Joseph, the author of Hebrews copied directly the LXX version of Gen 47:31, which does not make much sense. The LXX, working with an unpointed text, confused the words *hammiṭṭāh* (bed) with *hammaṭṭeh* (staff). Although the Greek implies that Joseph considered the staff as some object of worship and bowed himself down before it, the Hebrew simply meant that he was lying prostrate on the top of or at the head of his bed (MT Gen 47:31), a normal position for a dying man.[21] According to Jewish tradition, a miracle was performed by which Joseph's bones were recovered and taken with the children of Israel when they escaped from Egypt (Mekilta *Beshallaḥ* 1:86–98; 106–7).

Summary.—Verses 20–22 form a small subdivision, all unified by death scenes, blessings, and orders. In relationship to the whole unit, 8–22, these verses complete the topic. This unit began with the promise of "the land of the promise" (11:9) which Abraham "was about to receive" (*ēmellen lambanein*) "for an inheritance" (11:8). The topic concluded with blessings concerning "the things to come" (*mellontōn*) (11:20) which involved a reminder of "the exodus of the sons of Israel" (11:22) when they would return to take possession of the land of the promise, which they were to receive as "an inheritance" (11:8). It also prepared the readers for the topic on Moses and the exodus, which was to follow. In between these sentences that introduce and conclude the unit as well as prepare the reader for the following topic, was the history of Abraham, Isaac, and Jacob, and even Joseph in Egypt, according to the author's

[21] See also Delitzsch, II, 256. For a strong defense of the LXX translation, see Stuart, p. 269.

interpretation. This involved not only the history of the chosen people, but their relationship to the promise and the land of the promise from Abraham's promise in Haran to Joseph's providence in Egypt. These patriarchs were famous for their faith and endurance, but they did not receive the fulfillment of the promise.

From Moses to Joshua

23. The Greek for "three months" is *trimēnon* which means the same as the LXX Exod 2:2 but is different in form (LXX *mēnas treis*). This is another indication that the author of Hebrews had access to a different LXX text from any that is extant today. "The decree of the king" was that every male child born of Hebrew parents should be drowned in the Nile (Exod 1:22).

24. The expression "when he had grown up" (*megas genomenos*) literally means "having become great" and could refer to Moses' prestige and political or material greatness, but it probably only means that he had become an adult so that he could make decisions for himself. Josephus says "when he came of age" (*parelthōn eis hēlikian*) (*Ant.* II. 238). At that time he was free to choose to remain in a leading position in Egypt or he could reestablish his identity with the Israelites, who were in disfavor with Pharaoh. He chose the latter, refusing "to [let it be said that he was] a son of the daughter of Pharaoh." This must have seemed like ingratitude, sabotage, and insurrection to Pharaoh, but it seemed heroic to the Israelites.

25. The Israelites, like the author of Hebrews, probably considered having "transitory enjoyment" of a position of importance in Egypt to be "sin." Anything that helped the chosen people was considered virtue, and anything that hindered them was thought to be sin.

26. The scripture quoted in this verse is from Ps 89[88]:50–51:

"Remember, O Lord, the insult of your servants,
which I have borne in my bosom, of many nations,
which your enemies have hurled, O Lord,
with which they have mocked the retaliation of your Messiah."

The author of Hebrews took the words "the insult" from vs. 50 and the words "the Messiah" from "your Messiah" (*meššîḥékā*) in vs. 51 and put them together in such a way as to apply to the Messiah Jesus. Just as being "badly treated with the people of God" (11:25) was contrasted to having "transitory enjoyment of sin" (11:25), so "the insult of the Messiah" was contrasted to "the treasures of Egypt." Although it is unreasonable to think of Moses as anticipating the Messiah in pre-kingdom times, this did not disturb the author. Not only was he able to apply Psalms to Moses, he also assumed that Moses foresaw the Messiah Jesus and acted accordingly. Like other covenanters, he believed that all prophecy applied only to the days of the Messiah.

The chief motivation for ethical behavior for the author of Hebrews was the "reward" (see also 10:35; 11:6) involved, which was the promised rest, receiving the promises, or acquiring the inheritance. This was the reward Moses had in mind. In order to acquire possession of Canaan for the sons of Abraham, Moses was willing to leave "the treasures of Egypt," and accept instead "the insult of the Messiah."

27. The author sharpened the contrasts between the values at stake for Moses so that they appear more vivid than they were presented in the Exodus account. The author shows that Moses was not only contrasting the Egyptians with the Israelites, but Egypt with Canaan. He gave up a tangible royal post in Egypt for a potential royal post in Canaan. This involved leading an insurrectionist movement in Egypt, which was certain to arouse "the wrath of the king" and cancel any aspirations he might have had to the throne of Egypt. He left the security of Egypt for the insecurity of the exodus. He left the treasures of Egypt, its visible glory, government, power, and land, for an as yet "invisible" land, treasure, glory, government, and power. "He endured as seeing the invisible." Just as Abraham left the land of Haran for the land of the promise, so Moses left Egypt for the land of the promise. Just as Abraham wandered all of his life without receiving the inheritance, so Moses and the Israelites wandered forty years in the wilderness without receiving the promised rest. The values and emphases the author has presented regularly are given here in his typical style.

28. The Greek for "instituted" is *pepoiēken,* which means simply "made." Normally it might be rendered "observed" or "made preparations for," but the author of Hebrews understood that this was the first Passover, so it is translated "instituted." "The pouring out of the blood" (LXX Exod 12:22) refers to the activity of the Israelites in marking their houses with blood from the Passover lambs so that the one who went through Egypt "destroying the first-born" of the Egyptians would know that these homes belonged to Israelites and should be spared. This was designed as a distractive measure for the Egyptians while the Israelites escaped.

29. "The Red Sea" which the Israelites "went through" was the *yam sūph* or Sea of Reeds (Exod 15:4). That was a swampy area several miles north of the Red Sea. The LXX translators mistranslated *yam sūph* as "Red Sea," and the author of Hebrews accepted their text. The night the Israelites arrived at this Sea of Reeds, a strong east wind moved back the tide and the Israelites crossed over on foot (Exod 14:21–22) "as through dry land," meaning as if they had been walking on dry land. When the Egyptians tried to follow with their heavy chariots, they got stuck in the mud and "were swallowed up" when the tide turned (Exod 14:25–28; 15:4, 12).

Moses' acts continued as he led the Israelites in the wilderness for forty more years, but for the author of Hebrews, these years of rebellion were those that prevented the Israelites from receiving their promised rest (chs. 3–4), so they were not glamorized as examples of endurance in faith.

30. The biblical account of the fall of Jericho is so legendary that it is nearly impossible to find even a clue for trying to solve its capture (Josh 6:1–21). Archaeologists have not been able to find any trace of walls that were supposed to have fallen, and only slight evidence that the city might ever have been invaded by the Israelites in that period.[22]

31. "The unfaithful ones" include all unbelievers, non-covenanters; in this case it means the citizens of Jericho before the Israelites moved in, but the exodus generation was also "unfaithful," and Christians who became apostates would also be "unfaithful."

Many readers have wondered how a "harlot" like Rahab came to be listed among the roll call of the faithful. There are several reasons for this: (a) When she joined forces with the Israelites, she became a believer or a faithful person in the eyes of the author. (b) She had faith in the spies. Therefore she was saved from destruction by her "faith." (c) She assisted in the conquest of Canaan, led by the old Joshua. This called attention to the new Joshua, who would successfully lead the faithful into the promised rest. The importance of the entrance into Canaan and the promised rest is emphasized by the very point in time at which the author chose to conclude his specific listing of individuals. The faithful were listed from the promise given to Abraham to the entrance into Canaan when the fulfillment of that promise should have been received.

Apart from the author's judgment of Rahab was her own understanding of ethics. In the Near East then as now the responsibility of a host or a hostess to guests was extensive. Once guests are admitted, the hostess or host is responsible to protect them at the cost of his life and fortune. Lot and the Gibionite who entertained a Levite both offered their virgin daughters as ransom to protect their guests (Gen 19:8; Judg 19:22–24). Under the accepted hospitality customs, Sisera trusted even an enemy hostess enough to sleep in Jael's tent. Because Jael did not feel the same social restraints, she killed Sisera in his sleep (Judg 5:24–27).[23] Rahab was more responsible to her guests than Jael was, and therefore more ethical, from one point of view. Of course, for her to hide her guests as she did made her an accomplice in the invasion that destroyed all of her fellow citizens except her own immediate family (Josh 2:1–24; 6:22–23). Although she became a traitor to her own people, she became a believer and a trusted citizen of Israel. For this she gained favorable recognition in her own day and praise by the author of Hebrews.

Summary.—The author of Hebrews told the account of Israel's history from Egypt to the promised land by accounting for the virtues of faithful heroes who paid handsomely for their convictions. Moses gave up a position of royalty and wealth in Egypt to take a chance that he and the Israelites might receive the promised land. Similarly, Rahab gave up

[22] See K. Kenyon, *Digging up Jericho* (New York, 1957), p. 262.
[23] See further, "The Spiritual Commandment," JAAR 36 (1968), 126–27.

her loyalty to her own tradition and people so as to cast her lot with the people of God. Therefore she was classed with Abraham and Moses who did the very same thing.

Although 11:23–31 has been organized here as one unit, the author of Hebrews divided it into two. His inclusion shows 23–27 to be marked off as a separate unit. Heb 11:23 remarks that Moses' parents did not fear the decree of the king, and 11:27 reports that Moses had not feared the wrath of the king. Moses' action as seeing the invisible (11:27) refers to the parents who saw that Moses was attractive (11:23), and also refers the reader to the beginning of the chapter, to the definition of faith as the basis for testing things not seen (11:1).

The significance of the saints

32. Gideon was one of the judges who destroyed the altar of Baal and overthrew the Midianites with only three hundred men (Judg 6–7). Barak joined his troops with those of Deborah and overcame Sisera and the Philistines at Megiddo (Judg 4–5). Samson was a compulsive strong man who made many exploits against the Philistines: He burned their wheat fields (Judg 15:1–8), killed a thousand of them with the jawbone of an ass (Judg 15:9–17), and at his death pulled down the pillars of the house where there were three thousand Philistines, including leaders (Judg 16:23–31). Jephthah overpowered the threatening Ammonites and subjected the uncooperative Ephraimites (Judg 11:1–12:7). Saul was strangely omitted from the list, even though he was Israel's first king. The author may have reasoned that since the Old Testament reported that God had rejected Saul (I Sam 16:1), therefore he no longer belonged to the faithful. He was like the sinful exodus generation. After Saul and his son, Jonathan, were defeated in battle against the Philistines, David took the kingdom away from the sons of Saul and extended it to include all the territory understood to be a part of the inheritance promised to the seed of Abraham. Samuel was the last of the judges and the first of the prophets. He anointed both Saul and David as kings over Israel. Although he demonstrated some military leadership against the Philistines, he could not compete against Saul on this score (I Sam 7; *Ant.* VI. 19–44). The prophets included men like Elijah, Elisha, and Daniel, who performed some of the miraculous deeds listed in the quoted poem (33–34). The heroes were not listed in chronological order, which would be: Barak, Gideon, Jephthah, Samson, Samuel, and David.

33. Up to this point, the discussion of chapter eleven has dealt with the report of great men and women and the things they did "in faith" or "by faith" (*pistei*) (*passim*) or "according to faith" (11:7, 13), and the reading made good sense to consider faith to be "tradition," "creed," "confession," "scripture," or "God's word." Righteousness of faith was the action prompted by God's word or because of a certain confession based on the Old Testament. Here there may be a change. Instead of an

individual report for each person, there is a summary statement of their combined heroic deeds and a partial listing of the people involved. In this summary, the actions were reported "through faith" or "by faith," rather than "according to faith" (11:7, 13). In its position, this expression would be expected to mean the same as the previous terms. This is possible and would imply that these men acted as heroically as they did by means of their doctrinal profession of faith. Because of their creed they could be daring. They endured in hope. They held fast the confession. Since it is a different idiom as part of a summary, it might be the work of a different author who intended a different meaning. This possibility has some positive and negative arguments: A different author would make sense if the glossator were also the author of the basic document who used most of chapter eleven as a source. The noun "faith" occurs twenty-four times in chapter eleven, but only an additional eight times in the rest of the document. The verb "to believe" (*pisteuein*) occurs only in 4:3 and 11:6. The adjective "faithful" (*pistos*) occurs only once in chapter eleven and four times in the rest of the document. This may mean that faith was more important to the source than to the author of Hebrews who borrowed the word. It might also mean that the author of Hebrews composed all of chapter eleven and concentrated his use of the term "faith" in this chapter. In the rest of the document and most of chapter eleven, "faith" is much more closely related to creed, doctrine, or tradition than a motivating force for action. To translate "through faith" to mean something different would make it inconsistent not only with the rest of chapter eleven, but also with the rest of the document as well. These data seem to favor rendering "through faith" to mean "because of doctrinal beliefs" which include the hope that the promise made to Abraham would be fulfilled. With this interpretation all of chapter eleven makes sense and fits in well with the rest of chapters one through twelve.

Michel noted the poetic nature of 11:33–34, with three verses of three lines each.[24] He thought this passage might once have been a separate unit, dealing with victories of war.[25] Heb 11:32–33a seems like an introduction to the quoted poem, written by the author of Hebrews, giving names of some of the heroes he knew who did things listed in the poem. Those were mostly victors in battle and important leaders from the beginning of the conquest of Canaan until the establishment of the monarchy. This seemed like an unimportant period to the author, who covered it all in one verse plus a quoted poem, including the leadership of David, whom most New Testament authors considered to be the one who established the line from which the Messiah should come.

Since all six of the persons named were warriors, all would qualify as "those who through faith struggled against [*katēgōnisanto*] kingdoms." Josephus, however, used the same term as Hebrews, claiming that God

[24] Michel, p. 279.
[25] Michel, p. 280.

gave David power to save the country of the Hebrews by struggling against (*katagōnisamenǭ*) the Philistines (*Ant.* VI. 53). David would also be among those who "achieved righteousness" (*dikaiosynēn*), since there is a testimony that he administered judgment and righteousness (—justice) (*dikaiosynēn*) to all the people (II Sam 8:15). Again David is the most likely candidate for one who "obtained promises," because he was the one who extended the kingdom to its farthest limits. He was the one who achieved the situation that his son, Solomon, inherited of having "rest from all his enemies round about" (I Chron 22:9). That enabled Solomon to bless the Lord who had "given rest to his people Israel, according to all that he had said (*hosa elalēsen*) (I Kings 8:56). It was Daniel for whom "God stopped the mouths of lions" (Dan 6:22).

34. It was for Daniel's friends, Shadrach, Meshach, and Abednego, that God "extinguished power of fire" (Dan 3:19–30; see also I Macc 2:59; III Macc 6:6) so that no hair of their heads was singed. Among these victories, the author probably did not mean to list Israel's defeats when he recorded that her leaders "fled [the] mouths of [the] sword." He meant to praise them that they had successfully escaped when they were forced to flee. These events were also deliverances for which Israel should be grateful. "Mouths" probably does not refer to two-edged swords which were used against them. The plural may indicate that there were several times when Israelite heroes escaped the swords of the enemies who pursued them like a pack of wild beasts with their "mouths" open to consume them (see also Luke 21:24). This would refer to such events as David's escape from Absalom (II Sam 15:1 – 18:15), Elijah's escape from Jezebel (I Kings 19:1–18), and Elisha's escape from the Syrians (II Kings 6:11–23, 30–33). Several times Israel was delivered by a small force or overcame a stronger enemy with Israel's poorly equipped men, such as deliverance from the Egyptians at the Reed Sea (Exod 15), defeat of Sisera at Megiddo (Judg 5), Samson's slaughter of three thousand Philistines when he was blind (Judg 16:23–31), and David's slaughter of Goliath (I Sam 17:1–54). These were times when her heroes "received power from weakness." There were so many military victories when Israel "became strong in war" that the author was correct in saying the time would fail him to tell about them all (11:32).

The Greek word rendered "military camps" comes from the verb *paremballein,* "to throw alongside," "to line up in a row for battle," "to throw together in order" as a camp. The verb *eklinan* rendered "upset" means "to make bend" "to make yield or give way," "to turn back or rout." Upsetting "the military camps of foreigners" alluded to such events as Gideon's capture of the Midianite camp with three hundred men (Judg 7:15–23) or Jonathan's slaughter of the Philistine garrison with only his armor bearer (I Sam 14:6–15).

35. There were not many "women [who] received their dead by resurrection." These were contrasted to the "others" whose treatment was described. This probably refers to the resuscitation of the Zarephath

woman's son by Elijah (I Kings 17:24) and of the Shunamite's son by Elisha (II Kings 4:32–37); see also John 11:1–44; Luke 7:11–17; and Acts 9:36–43). Both children were revived only to continue living in the same conditions as before their deaths.

The Greek for "were beaten" is *etympanisthēsan,* from *tympanizō,* "to torture," derived from the verb *typtein,* "to beat," "to strike," or "to pound." A *tympanon* is a kettledrum which has a skin stretched taut for striking. Those who were tortured by some such means as this might either be beaten directly or stretched over a wheel and whirled while being afflicted with rods to break their limbs until they died. These "others" who "were beaten" were probably the mother and her seven sons who faced death by torture during the Maccabean period. Had they accepted "release" that was offered to them if they would only give up their faith, they not only would have avoided torture, but they would have received reward and position (II Macc 7). They were not raised like the sons of the Shunamite and the woman of Zarephath, but they and their mother died "in order that they might obtain a [still] better resurrection" than those sons experienced. They believed that they would be raised up to everlasting life (*aiōnion . . . zōēs*) (II Macc 7:9), which meant they would be revived to live in the land of the promise after it had been freed from Antiochus Epiphanes and the oppressive Greek rule.[26] Because the political conditions of the nation were expected to improve, this would have been "a better resurrection" than that received by the boys whom the prophets revived. Because they believed this, they willingly suffered torture and death, while they prayed that God would speedily be merciful to their nation, which meant restoring their land (II Macc 7:37). After that they would be raised again, and the mother would receive again her sons who had died (II Macc 7:11, 29). For Antiochus, of course, there would be no resurrection to life (*anastasis eis zōēn*) (II Macc 7:14). Verse 35 seems to be a summary introduction of the poem that follows (36–38), just as vs. 32 is a summary introduction to the poem in vss. 33 and 34. The word "others" of 11:35 was probably taken from the text that follows.

36. The "others" here probably included the "others" mentioned in vs. 35. The expression "received [the] trial" (*peiran elabon*) is the same idiom used in LXX Deut 28:56 to describe a woman so delicate that she would not risk (*peiran elabon*) setting her foot on the ground. These "others" were not that delicate. They did risk "mockings and whips." The way this passage incorporates the poem, the text now seems to read "others" (35) ". . . and others" (36) ". . . and still [others]" (36), as if these were all different groups of people. Originally the poem may have meant that the "others" mentioned at the beginning of vs. 36 covered all the people tortured. These were mocked and whipped, "and still" further, bound and imprisoned, but the number of kinds of torture is

[26] CC, pp. 110–49.

more than would apply to any one group. The author of the poem also seems to have been speaking of the many types of torture which different people suffered, rather than specifying the number of tortures one group suffered. In any general persecution which involved torture and death there would be some people imprisoned and others bound hand and foot so that they would be helpless. During the persecution of Antiochus, the Greeks led the women and children away captive (I Macc 1:32).

37. These faithful people who held fast the confession were "stoned," like Zechariah the son of Jehoiada, the priest who was stoned in the temple court (II Chron 24:20–21), "tested" by all sorts of tortures, like those applied to the woman and her seven sons (II Macc 7), or "sawed in two," like Isaiah during the time of Manasseh, according to tradition (Ascension of Isa 5:1–14; *Dial.* 120; Jerome *Comment on Isa 57:2*). The words "tested" (*epeirasthēsan*) and "sawed in two" (*epristhēsan*) are so similar in spelling that there are several textual variants, and some scholars have suspected that one was added by someone who placed one variant after the other in his text. Scholars who hold this view ignore the poetic features of the passage in which words and expressions are listed in groups of three, and they fail to appreciate the alliteration of the terms (see also 1:1).

Jehoiakim brought Uriah from Egypt and slew him with the sword (Jer 26:23), and Elijah complained that the people of Israel, under Jezebel's administration, had slain the Lord's prophets with the sword (I Kings 19:10). Many Jews during the Maccabean Revolt and again in the rebellions of A.D. 66–73 and A.D. 132–35 died "by slaughter of [the] sword" in battle. During the siege of Vespasian against Jotapata, Josephus reported that he (Josephus, the general in charge) sent men out for supplies past the Roman guards, crawling on all fours like animals. These had disguised themselves with sheep's fleece on their backs (*Wars* III.190–92). This may not be what the author of Hebrews or of this poem had in mind, but it was something having to do with fugitive conditions necessary because of shortage of supplies or requirements of guerilla warfare. The verbs "deprived, afflicted, badly treated" are general descriptions of conditions of hardship, such as those faced by the Jews during the Maccabean Revolt or the revolts against Rome (A.D. 66–73; 132–35). The word "badly treated" (*kakouchoumenoi*) is the same as that used to describe the conditions of the Israelites in Egypt when Moses chose to identify himself with them (*synkakoucheisthai*) (11:25).

38. Moffatt called the passage "(of whom the world is not worthy)" "a splendid aside."[27] It not only is an aside, but it is one that breaks the poetry and was probably made by the author of Hebrews rather than the author of the poem he used. The aside may have been suggested by the story of Eleazar or of the mother and her seven sons, all of whom were called worthy ("axios, axia") (6:23; 7:20). R. Eliezer ha-Kappar said Israel pos-

[27] Moffatt, p. 189.

sessed four virtues, "than which nothing in the world is more worthy" (*kl h'wlm kd'y*). Two of these were their unwillingness to change their names or their language (Mekilta *Pisḥa* 5:15–17). Temptations to make such changes would occur in times of persecution.

Those engaged in guerilla warfare in Palestine were destined to wander "in deserts, mountains [*horesin*], caves (*spēlaiois*], and openings of the earth," because that kind of terrain was available. These places were used by David and Saul (I Sam 22:1; 23:14; 24:3), the Israelites during the time of the judges (Judg 6:2), and various prophets (I Kings 18:4, 13; 19:9, 13). Isaiah warned Jews to flee to such places of refuge to escape the Lord's wrath (Isa 2:10–22). Jesus warned the inhabitants of Judea to flee to the mountains when certain conditions presented themselves (Matt 24:15–16). After Mattathias killed the Jew who offered pagan sacrifice and the Greek who encouraged it (I Macc 2:23–27), he and his sons fled to the mountains (*eis ta horē*) (I Macc 2:28), from which position they led the revolt (see also II Macc 5:27; 6:11; 10:6). Because the mountainous regions of Palestine are honeycombed with caves, guerilla warfare is easy to conduct and difficult to suppress. When Herod was first made king of the Jews, he was faced with the task of forming "a campaign against the cave dwelling brigands (*epi tous en tois spēlaiois hōrmēto lęstas*) who were infesting a wide area and inflicting on the inhabitants evils no less than those of war" (*Wars* I.304). Herod finally conquered the caves (*ta spēlaia*) by sending his soldiers in baskets hanging by ropes from the tops of the cliffs to the caves in the sides of the mountains, where they fought the guerillas in hand-to-hand combat or smoked them out with firebrands (*Wars* I.309–11). Josephus described these guerilla insurrectionists as "brigands," and used similar disparaging names, but to the author of Hebrews these were religious heroes who held fast the confession and endured in the faith.[28]

39. "The promise" they wanted to receive was that made to Abraham (Gen 15). Of the names listed, none achieved the promises which involved permanent acquisition of the land, freedom, prosperity, and "rest." The nearest approximation of "rest" came during the rules of David and Solomon. David's name was mentioned only once as a hero (11:32) along with other judges and prophets. No effort was made to show his faithfulness, possibly because of his sin or because he did not show the same qualities of trust and endurance in hope demonstrated by people like Abraham, Moses, and even Rahab. Solomon was not even mentioned, possibly for the same reason. On the other hand it would have been difficult to praise them very highly without acknowledging that they were recipients of the promise. The author picked his heroes to suit his needs and emphasized the qualities he admired. "These all" included such people as Rahab and excluded such people as Solomon and Saul.

40. Just as the mother and her seven sons died with the expectation that they might receive a better resurrection than the sons of the woman of

[28] See further "Mark 11:15–19: Brigands in the Temple," HUCA 30 (1959), 169–77.

Zarephath or the Shunamite, so the author anticipated "something better" awaiting fulfillment for the Christians of his day than any of the previous Israelites or Jews had ever known (11:35). The promise made to Abraham involved the things not seen (11:1) by men, but these were all "foreseen" by God, which he had withheld so far for two reasons: (a) the exodus generation was unfaithful, and (b) "God had foreseen something better concerning" contemporaries of the author. All of the efforts in the past on the part of the Israelites had been to acquire the promise. It had not yet happened. Without the rigorous endurance in faith of the author's generation of believers, all the earlier endurance in faith would be futile. If Christians of the author's generation became apostates and lost the promise again, all these other believers "might not be perfected" or fulfilled. The author was consistently urging that his readers endure in faith more rigorously than any of their predecessors had ever done, because the guarantees for great reward were greater, their responsibility to their heritage was greater, and their sin at failing would also be greater than the sins of any other generation of covenanters.

Summary.—Heb 11:32–40 forms a unit enclosed by the words "through faith" (11:33, 39). This seems to be a unit largely based on two poems or two verses of the same poem. These may have been taken from longer poems or ballads describing the heroism of the fathers generally, or of the Maccabean heroes particularly. There may have been the same kind of relationship between part of the poetry and the story of the mother and her sons in prose (II Macc 7) as exists between Judg 4 and 5 as prose and poetic accounts of the victory over Sisera. The author of Hebrews seems to have been responsible for the summarizing introductions in vss. 32 and 35, possibly the gloss in vs. 37, and quite certainly the concluding statements in vss. 39 and 40.

The conclusion of this unit also forms an end to the whole eulogy on the faith of the fathers, as the author has shown by his inclusions. These all who were attested through faith (11:39) are the same men of old who were attested in faith (11:1–2). The greatest of the heroes were the ones like Noah, Abraham, Moses, and Rahab who took chances on the promises of God, even though the evidence for their fulfillment did not seem strong. Not only did they accept God's word as valid, but they paid high costs of giving up status, position, and social security, to act as God had commanded. They stood in direct contrast to the exodus generation that was unfaithful, and, as a result, was denied the promise God had intended for it. The author's purpose in making this strong case was to urge his readers to imitate the faithful fathers who held fast their confession of hope against great odds rather than become apostates like the exodus generation.

The author continued his consistent style of concluding one section while, at the same time, preparing the reader for the topic that follows. His last word in chapter eleven is "perfected" (*teleiōthōsin*) to prepare the reader to look to Jesus the pioneer and perfecter (*teleiōtēn*) (12:2) of the faith.

The cloud of witnesses and the call for endurance

Jesus the greatest leader

12:1–2. The word "cloud" (*nephos*) was used metaphorically, giving expression to the immense size of the group. Herodotus (VII.109.12) also described an enemy's army as "so mighty a cloud (*nephos*) of men." No intention was implied that these heroes were in heaven like a cloud. "Witnesses" (*martyrōn*) occurs also in 10:28, and the verbal form, witnessing (*martyrein*), occurs eight times (7:8, 17; 10:15; 11:2, 4 (twice), 5, 39). It is an important term for one who urged boldness in holding fast to the confession. The expression "clings to us very readily" is *euperistaton,* the superlative degree of the passive participle of *periistēmi,* "to surround," with the prefix, *eu,* meaning "good," "well," "easily," or "readily." This which surrounded the believer very readily was an obstacle of some kind, like reeds or moss getting in a swimmer's way and impeding his progress; or cords, reeds, or some kind of binding and repressing clothing that "clings to us very readily" and hinders our progress. Since this obstacle was "sin" that should be "put aside" like a "weight," the image is not so much like clothing as something the runner or swimmer might start with unknowingly or pick up along the way, or possibly weights used in practice to build up muscle, but removed for contests.

The word "endurance" (*hypomonēs*), in nominal (10:36) as in verbal forms (10:32; 12:2, 3, 7), occurs only in exhortation sections.[29] It was never applied to any of the saints of the past. *Karterein* was used to describe Moses' enduring qualities. The author effectively repeated the word *keisthai,* "to lay," "to place," or "to lie." So "a cloud of witnesses" is "surrounding" or lying around (*perikeimenon*) us; "the course . . . is laid out before" (*prokeimenon*) us and "the joy [was] laid out before" (*prokeimenēs*) Jesus. "Keeping our gaze directed to" (*aphorōntes eis*) is literally "looking away toward" Jesus. The context in Hebrews requires a continuing force for this expression. The same is true of Philo, who used the term in relationship to Moses, to whom rulers looked as an archetype or in relationship to a pattern which a builder followed (*Op.* 18). The Jewish martyrs of Maccabean times vindicated their race, "keeping their gaze directed toward God (*eis theon aphorōntes*) and enduring until death" (IV Macc 17:10). The "looking away" of the martyrs, like the "looking away" of the early Christians, involved a continual, steady gaze. Therefore the expression was translated "keeping our gaze directed to" Jesus.

"The course" (*agōna*) "laid out before" Christians was a contest (*agōn*).[30]

[29] Bruce, p. 349, observed that *hypomonē* occurs eleven times in IV Maccabees and the verb, *hypomenein,* an additional fifteen times.

[30] For other examples of *agōn* as a religious contest in which martyrs engage, see IV Macc 11:20; 13:15; 16:16; 17:11.

Eleazar and the woman with her seven sons who faced torture and death rather than submit to Antiochus were called "athletes of the divine legislation" (IV Macc 17:16) who had been engaged in a contest (*agōn*) (IV Macc 17:11). The author encouraged his readers to participate seriously in such a contest, struggle, race, just as they had done earlier, after they had been enlightened, when they endured (*hypomeinete*) a great struggle of sufferings (*athlēsin . . . pathēmatōn*) (10:32). The picture given is of athletes running a race or fighting in an arena for their very lives, but it refers to the religious struggles of believers who must fight against the world for the faith. At times this is not just a mental, emotional, or social struggle, but involves real physical torture. In any case it required removal of sin, endurance, and direction.

"Prime leader" (*archēgon*) might also be called "initial leader," "primary leader," or "chief leader," implying either first in time or first in rank. For Christians, Jesus was given both emphases. He was earlier called the initial leader (*archēgon*) of their salvation whom God made perfect (*teleiōsai*) through sufferings (2:10). Jesus was also the perfecter of the faith (*ton tēs pisteōs . . . teleiōtēn*) in contrast to the heroes of the faith who might not be perfected (*teleiōthōsin*) (11:40). Since he learned obedience from the things he suffered (5:8), and was made perfect (*teleiōtheis*), he became a cause of eternal salvation (5:9). By the word of the oath Jesus was established as the Son made perfect (*teteleiōmenon*) for the age (7:28). Perfect, in the religious sense, meant one who had completed requirements for membership or prepared a sacrifice which completely removed all sins. It did not have the force of scientific perfection as in making a perfect circle or a perfect square. Pseudo-Clement told of a certain Maro who was perfect in all things, so Peter appointed him bishop (*Recog.* VI.xv).

Jesus' willingness to accept the "cross of shame" rather than "the joy laid out before him" fitted perfectly the author's ideal of righteousness. In this way, Abraham left Haran for the promised land where he remained a stranger; Moses left a royal position of wealth in Egypt to identify himself with the Israelites who were badly treated; and Rahab denied her countrymen to become identified with a tribe that had no country. The author implied, as did Paul in II Cor 8:9, that Jesus, like Moses and Abraham, gave up a position of wealth and prominence to accept the position of leadership that he had.[31] In his letter appealing to the Corinthians to give money, Paul told them of the sacrificial giving of the Macedonians for this project (II Cor 8:1–6) and also of "our Lord Jesus Christ, that on account of you he became poor, being a wealthy man" (II Cor 8:9). The likelihood that Jesus was originally from a wealthy family and that he gave up his wealth for the movement he led seems greater when his relationship to the wealthy tax collectors and rulers is considered. Most of his parables and teachings seem to have been directed to an upper class of people who had money to lend, give, and use for hiring servants. His willingness to surrender this for the Kingdom of God would have given

[31] See further *Novum Testamentum* 8 (1964), 195–209.

him more authority to ask others to give up all they had than he would have had if he had been reared in poverty. It would have been difficult in the Near East for a poor man to gain a hearing with the rich as Jesus evidently did. So he won Paul's admiration for his act, and Paul was able to use this as an example for the Corinthians to follow in their contributions to Jerusalem saints. The author of Hebrews, who admired Moses for his willingness to give up wealth, security, and position to be faithful to God, also admired Jesus for the same kind of willingness to give up everything he had to enable the promises of God to reach fulfillment.

Others have interpreted this differently: Westcott said, "The joy was that of the work of redemption accomplished through sacrifice."[32] If that had been the case, Jesus would not have faced an either/or situation at all. He could have "endured the cross" as "the joy laid out before him" rather than "instead of" it. Moffatt thought "the joy" involved was pre-incarnate bliss which Jesus renounced to become human.[33] This agrees with some interpretations of Philip 2:6–7, but the author of Hebrews never suggested such an idea in the rest of the document.

When Jesus "despised [the] cross of shame" he may either have sloughed it off as if it were nothing, as Michel believes,[34] or it may mean that he did not like it; he wanted to avoid it; this was anything but his choice; but nonetheless he "endured [it]," just as Moses endured the wrath of the king (11:27). The author has not given this the same theological force of the confession in Philip 2:5–11, which also deals with Christ's mission in terms of glory, debasement, and greater glory. The word "cross" occurs only here in the entire document (1:1 – 12:29), and the word "crucify" does not occur at all. This is quite different from the Pauline documents in which the meaning of the cross is a central point of faith. The author of Hebrews instead emphasized the ascension in terms of a sacrifice (4:14; 6:20; 7:26; 9:11–12, 24) and Jesus' position, seated at "the right hand of the throne of God" (1:3; 8:1; 10:12). Although the author has seemed fond of the perfect tense, this is the first time he used the perfect tense in alluding to Ps 110:1, which seems to be the basic text on which his entire message is built. "The throne of God" may have been the mercy seat on the cover of the ark or it may have been structured so that the ark was the footstool in relationship to it. Because the Lord's presence and his throne were in the holy of holies, the expression "throne of God" or just "the throne" came to be periphrastic euphemisms for God, just as was true of other expressions like "heaven" (Luke 15:21), "the place" (*māqōm*) (Gen R. 68b), and "the holy One, blessed be he," (*haqqādōš bārūk hū'*) (Gen R. 68c). People took oaths by some holy object, with the understanding that this meant God. So Jesus said, "The one who swears by heaven swears by the throne of God and the one seated upon it" (Matt 23:22). He prohibited his disciples from swearing "by heaven, because it is the

32 Westcott, pp. 395–96.
33 Moffatt, p. 197.
34 Michel, p. 294.

throne of God" (Matt 5:34). The throne in heaven was like "the throne of God" in the holy of holies. Like the one in the temple, the throne in heaven had lampstands before it (Rev 4:5) and also a gold altar (Rev 8:3). The one who sits upon this throne would dwell with his faithful martyrs (Rev 7:15), just as he dwelt with the Israelites in the wilderness, in the promised land, and in the temple (Exod 25:8; 29:42–46; Num 5:3; 35:34; I Kings 6:13; 8:12–13).

3. "Just" is the translation for *gar,* a conjunction meaning "for" or "because." Because the author used this conjunction frequently, to avoid repetition in English a free translation has been given. The Greek for "consider" is *analogizesthai,* "to count up," "reckon," or "calculate." It means to consider in the sense of "taking account of." The author seems to have made allusions in this verse to LXX Num 17:2–3, which is a report of the conclusions of Korah's rebellion. Korah and his immediate followers were swallowed when the earth opened up under them. Those followers who tried to get away were caught by a fire sent down from God to consume two hundred and fifty of them (LXX Num 16:30–35). These followers were called men who had sinned against their souls (*tōn hammartōlōn en tais psychais*). The author of Hebrews seems to have identified the "opposition" to Jesus as being a rebellion like Korah's against Moses, Aaron, and God. The sinners (*tōn hamartōlōn*) were members of the insurrectionist movement. The rest of Israel accused Moses and Aaron for their action against that group of sinners, and the Lord was prepared to destroy them all in a moment with a plague, but Moses and Aaron began at once to make atonement for them, and part of the congregation was spared (LXX Num 17:6–15). Under even more difficult conditions, Jesus also "endured so great an opposition [as this]." The author reminded his readers of this so that they might "endure" as Jesus had done. Those who might "become exhausted" (*kamēte*), "worn out from work," "weary from annoyance," "afflicted," or "distressed" were like those who supported Moses and Aaron. They were on the side of Jesus and were losing hope that their persecutions would ever be replaced by the fulfillment of the promise. They were also becoming "depressed" (*eklyomenoi*), "unstrung," "broken up," "exhausted," or "despondent," "in" their "souls" (*tais psychais*).

Summary.—Like the first three verses of chapter eleven, 12:1–3 forms an introduction to the whole chapter, but the author did not separate it as such. Instead, he formed his first unit in this chapter by an inclusion at 12:1 and 12:13. In addition to its introductory value 12:1–3 helps relate chapter twelve to chapter eleven. The "we" (12:1) is related to "us" (11:40), and the "witnesses" (12:1) refer to those who were attested through faith (11:39).

As the author regularly related his doctrine to ethics, he here gave the consequences of such a faith as that affirmed in chapter eleven. In chapter eleven, the witnessing was not done by the heroes of the faith themselves, but rather a witness was made about them in this confession (11:2) by God himself (11:4) or through the faith (11:39). Heb 12, however, speaks as though these heroes were all witnesses surrounding Christians (12:1), who themselves attested to the faith, and because they did, Christians were also obligated to prepare themselves to "run." This involved putting "aside every weight" (12:1), the way a ship is relieved of its cargo in emergencies, so that it can stay afloat or travel more rapidly (see Jonah 1). For the Christian, the weight that must be unloaded is the sin that clings very readily (12:1), weighing us down, encumbering us, impeding us, and keeping us from running with "endurance the course that is laid out before us" (12:1). The image of a believer pictured as an athlete of virtue seems to be dependent upon IV Maccabees and reflects an admiration for the Maccabean martyrs that has been evident before.

Necessity of discipline

4. In trying to prevent apostasy among his readers, the author has already told of the many faithful heroes of the past who did endure in the faith through all sorts of physical tortures to the extent of death. Jesus also endured against a great opposition from the sinners (12:3) until death. Therefore the readers should have been expected to be willing to do the same thing, but they had not been tested until "blood" in their efforts to stand "up against sin" (see IV Macc 17:10).

5. In the author's judgment, the readers had become dull of hearing (5:11); they had "utterly forgotten" their earlier instruction; they were urged to remember the earlier days after they had first been enlightened (10:32). "The comfort" they received when they were enlightened enabled them to endure many kinds of hardship, but they had forgotten all of this (10:32–35). Hardship should have given them a sense of belongingness. They should have taken "comfort" that they were being treated "as sons." They were not denied the necessary "discipline" parents provide their children. Proof for this was found in the scriptures. The word translated "discipline" (*paideias*) might also be rendered "instruction," "training," or "child development." In a context that deals with the responsibility of standing up against sin until blood, the particular type of training involved was more than quiet meditation. It involved painful drilling and discipline to prepare the readers for the life they must face. The Greek root for "become depressed" is the same as that used in vs. 3 (*eklyein*). The word "are corrected" (*elegchomenos*) means "being tested" "reproved." It is from the same root as that rendered "basis for testing" (*elegchos*) in 11:1. It is a Greek legal term sometimes used in debates and cross-examinations. Being "corrected" may mean being exposed, being shown up in public, or being criticized (see John 3:20; Eph 5:11, 13). These are all painful experiences which were considered necessary preparation for Christian living. For the meaning of "loves" see COMMENT on 6:10 and 10:24. Prov 3:11–12, quoted here, is also freely quoted in Rev 3:19 in a context

of exhortation to Christians in the face of persecution. Hebrews quoted the LXX *verbatim,* adding only the possessive adjective "my" to "son." The word translated "he whips" (*mastigoi*) renders the Hebrew *k'b,* which the MT points *k*^{e}*'āb,* "like a father," which makes good sense in the context. Pointed *kā'ēb,* this Hebrew means "he caused pain," or "he made suffer." Freedman has noticed that thus rendered the Hebrew forms a chiasm:

"For whomever the Lord loves, he chastises

and he disciplines the son he desires."

A person who disciplines the one he makes to suffer might whip him. Therefore the LXX translation is valid and has just about as strong an argument for being the intended meaning for *k'b* as the MT form.

The interpretation of hardship in terms of discipline was appreciatively offered earlier to Jews in time of trial:

"Now, I appeal to those who happen to come upon this book, not to be cast down by these misfortunes, but rather to consider that these were retributions not intended to destroy, but rather only to discipline our people. As a matter of fact, it is a mark of favor not to leave impious ones alone for any length of time, but to inflict immediate punishment on them. When it comes to other nations the Lord shows his forbearance, and delays punishing them until they have reached the fullness of their iniquity, but for us He had determined differently, in order that He may not be compelled to punish us later when our sins have reached finality" (II Macc 6:12–16, Tedesche's tr.).

It is on the basis of this kind of theology that Paul could encourage the Romans to let God vindicate them against their enemies (Rom 12:19), while they themselves heaped coals of fire upon the heads of their enemies by doing good to them (Rom 12:20). The more good they did, the more harm God would do to their enemies. Since God rewards people for suffering and punishes them for sin, Christians should be glad when they face trials (James 1:2). The experience of trials not only builds character for the Christians (James 1:3–4; I Peter 1:6–9), but it cancels their sins, since "whoever has suffered in the flesh has ceased from sin" (I Peter 4:1). Being beaten up unjustly wins God's approval (I Peter 2:19), and therefore adds merits to the treasury of merits. Although this type of theology was part of the background of the author's understanding as reflected in other parts of the document, the emphasis here was not on adding merits to the treasury, but rather the positive value to the reader himself of these sufferings. It attested his acceptance as a "son," and it corrected his faulty views, improving his character and understanding.

7. The Proverbs passage on discipline prompted the author to interpret this passage also in terms of endurance. The Greek *eis paideian* is translated with the understanding that *eis* here means "with reference to," as

would be normal in a midrashic context, commenting on one word from the text just quoted. The author's paraphrastic elaboration on the relationship of sonship to "discipline" is fair to the text he used.

8. The negative aspect, that the Proverbs passage did not mention, is that if a "son" cannot be "without discipline," then the undisciplined ones would be "illegitimate" and not true "sons." Since this is the case, the readers, all of whom "have become sharers" of discipline, should be comforted. They have not been rejected by God. This suffering is the sure sign of their sonship.

Summary.—This small unit was centered around sonship and discipline. It was framed by an inclusion, using the word "son" (12:5, 8), which also occurs within the unit (12:6,7). The next unit will elaborate on this analogy, so the word "son" in 12:8 also is a catchword introducing the next topic.

Comparison and challenge

9. This verse constitutes an *a fortiori* argument which contrasts "our fathers of the flesh" with "the father of spirits" and also becoming "trained" to being alive. To "live" religiously means more than eating, breathing, and taking up space. Only those who are under the covenant and on the promised land (the land of life) when it is free from foreign rule are really alive. Others are "dead," and those who are "alive" can let the dead bury their own dead (Matt 8:22). Christians know that they have been changed from death to life because they love their brothers (I John 3:14). The one who has the Son has life and the one who does not have the Son does not have life (I John 5:12). If any one commits a sin, not unto death (i.e. a pardonable sin), his fellow should pray and God will give him life (i.e. restore him to the community where alone life is possible) (I John 5:16).[35] Christians who subjected themselves to "the father of spirits" would become approved believers, which means they would "live." If they were subject to God, of course, they would have to accept discipline, a reasonable expectation, according to the author.

10. Still dealing in contrasts, there is a carry-over from the *a fortiori* argument in vs. 9 which is apparent in this verse. The "short time" during which the fathers of the flesh disciplined the members did not refer to individual events, but rather the whole training period from birth to adulthood, which was not very long. During this period the fathers used whatever methods of discipline "seemed [wise] to them." It was generally believed that this was to the advantage of the children, so that they might learn to behave properly. In the same way God disciplines his sons "insofar as it is beneficial," in God's judgment, to prepare them to share in "his sanctity." "Sanctity" (*hagiotētos*) usually refers to levitical purity, especially observed by the priests, so that the temple where they minister might be

[35] CC, pp. 110–49.

"clean" or ritually undefiled, and the Lord would be willing to dwell there. It also described the condition of holiness observed by soldiers in camp, because they wanted the presence of the Lord with them in battle. When the temple was no longer standing, believers tried to keep their homes as ritually clean or holy as the temple, which meant observing rules as strict as those observed by the priests. This was the priesthood of all believers. Not only priests but all true believers were supposed to be saints or holy people. This condition of holiness or "sanctity" was "life." Heb 12:10 is a partial repetition and extension of the argument of vs. 9. Those who accepted God's discipline would live. God would discipline these sons as much as was necessary to produce "sanctity" which was religious life. Those who took these holiness rules seriously were strongly motivated toward monasticism. Judging from the advice given and the demands made upon the readers, the author of Hebrews seems to have been a member of some rigorous monastic society that expected "sanctity" of its members.

11. The third contrast of this unit compared immediate results to far-reaching results. The person who learned something new was forced to practice and train endlessly until he became proficient. This was not always easy or enjoyable, but the satisfaction that came from being able to perform well was worth the practice. The implication is that those who faced social and physical torture for their faith would become "trained through it" until they accepted his sanctity and the new life associated with it. This meant producing "a peaceful fruit of righteousness." Jews and Christians were frequently faced with the need for endurance during the current evil era, but they endured in the hope that the future would hold pleasant rewards. They could hasten the time when the reward would be granted by laying up treasures in heaven (Matt 6:20). This might prompt the Lord to pardon his people and shorten the term of their "captivity" (Mark 13:20; Enoch 80:2; II Bar 20:1). Whenever this "training" period was over, and the people were all holy and perfect, then they would receive their promised reward of rest and prosperity on the land.

12–13. The author followed the LXX more or less in his quotation of two Old Testament passages (Isa 35:3; Prov 4:26). In the Proverbs passage the main variant is that the LXX *poiei* ("you [sing.] make") became *poieite* ("you [pl.] make"), a variant which the author of Hebrews may have made himself to suit his context. The same may be true of the substitution of "collapsed" (*pareimenas*) for the related LXX "slack" (*aneimenai*) in Isa 35:3. In Hebrew, the Isaiah passage formed a chiasm in a well-balanced couplet.[36]

"Strengthen the weak hands, *ḥazzeqū yādayim rapōt*

the feeble knees make strong." *ūbirkayim kōšelōt 'ammēṣū*

[36] D. N. Freedman called my attention to this.

As Freedman has suggested, the LXX text is clearly secondary in this passage. The LXX has dropped out the word "make strong" (*'ammēṣū*) when a scribe passed over it, since the next word in the text began with the same two consonants, *'aleph* and *mēm* (*'imru*) (Isa 35:4); this is a simple case of homeoarcton error. The author of Hebrews followed the LXX structure in making his first verb (*anorthōsate,* "set straight," instead of *ischysate* in the LXX) take two objects.

The author's choice of texts was excellent from several points of view. He associated "set straight" (*anorthōsate*) with "make straight" (*orthas poieite*), one dealing with bodies and the other with paths that individuals take. While urging his readers to hold fast to the confession (4:14; 10:23) and reminding them that the time of waiting was almost over (10:25), he quoted from a passage reflecting the end of the captivity in Babylon. The poet was announcing the good news that the promise was just about to be fulfilled; Jews could return and reestablish the homeland in Palestine. This encouragement applied perfectly to the author's understanding of his own time. The author of Prov 4:26, like the author of Hebrews, urged his hearers not to fall away from the faith. They must follow right paths, keep the commandments, and hold fast to the right doctrine. The lame in the Babylonian community were physically lame, but the author of Hebrews used the term metaphorically to go with the Proverbs passage. The "tracks" about which the proverbial poet wrote were religious rather than geographical paths. Therefore the "lame" who might "be turned" away from this true path would be the religiously weak. They would be the same group of people called the "little ones" (Matt 10:42; 18:6, 10, 14) who might "stumble." Believers should walk carefully themselves so as not to mislead others. Instead of being "turned off [the road]," the weak feet should "rather be healed," which meant, metaphorically, that the believers should "set straight the collapsed hands and the paralytic knees" of the religiously insecure. This was the type of healing expected just before the "captives" entered their promised "rest."

Summary.—This unit was composed of three contrasts, concluding with two quotations of scripture. The first comparison was between the human fathers and the father of spirits; the second showed the purpose of the types of discipline that were contrasted; and the third, the immediate pain involved in discipline which was compared to the lasting advantage. The passages of scripture were introduced to relate their character to the reward of the promise, which was always before the author's eyes.

These three small units: 1–3, 4–8, and 9–13 really belong together, but they are partially subdivided by subject matter and steps in argument. The first unit is introductory so far as the exhortation is concerned, but presents conclusions of action based on previous arguments and doctrine. The main thrust of the author's exhortation is an urgent appeal for endurance, which involves discipline. The second unit related discipline to the

Christian's relationship to God, and the third unit provided applications and elaborations on the discipline urged. Although the actual quotation of Prov 4:26 forced the author to use a different word for "track" (12:13) than for "course" (12:1), the imagery of a runner staying on his course and running hard to reach the right goal was maintained throughout 12:1–13, comprising one unit, set off by an inclusion.

Truth and its consequences

The root of bitterness

14. The words "peace" and "sanctification" relate this unit to the peaceful fruit (12:11) and sanctification (12:10) of the previous unit. Ps 34:14 [LXX 33:15] says, "Seek peace and pursue it." The author of Hebrews used only the second verb, "pursue" (changing it to a *present* imperative and *plural,* to fit his context). Hillel counseled his students to "be disciples of Aaron, loving peace, and pursuing peace" (Aboth 1:12).

Pursuing "peace with all" meant that the believer should see that all of his sins committed against his brothers had been forgiven, so that God could effectively forgive his sins on the Day of Atonement. The covenanter who desired forgiveness for his sins had to know that he had not sinned with any conscious intention of seeking release on the Day of Atonement. He also first had to be reconciled to his brother for his sin; he had to repent; and he had to bring his sin and guilt offerings to the temple of the Lord. Because of these terms, Christians were told, "So if you are offering your gift at the altar, and there remember that your brother has something against you, leave your gift there before the altar and go; first be reconciled to your brother, and then come and offer your gift" (Matt 5:23–24). God's forgiveness was dependent upon the believer's reconciliation to his brother. Because this was true, the one who had sinned could not be forgiven by God if his brother refused to forgive him for the sin he had committed against him. With this understanding it was necessary for members of the community to forgive one another (Matt 6:12, 14–15) even seventy-seven times (Matt 18:22; Luke 17:3–4; see also T. Gad 6:3–7). God would not redeem Israel while she was still in her sin. Therefore it was important for all members of the community to be sinless, to be reconciled to their brothers, to repent, and to offer the required gifts on the Day of Atonement, so that Israel could be forgiven and the land restored.[37] Those who pursued "peace" were those who tried to cancel the debt of sin against Israel. They were the poor in spirit, the mourners, the meek, the merciful, those who hungered and thirsted for righteousness, the pure in heart, the peacemakers, or those who were persecuted for righteousness' sake (Matt 5:3–10). "Sanctification" involved levitical purity, primarily required for priests. The author of Hebrews, however, said that all sons of God were to be disciplined until they shared "his sanctifi-

[37] CC, pp. 229–33.

cation" (12:10)." Matthew promised that the pure or clean (*katharoi*) in heart would see God (Matt 5:8), whereas the author of Hebrews said "no one" who was not sanctified, or ritually clean, would "see the Lord." Since I John 4:12, following Exod 33:20, said that no man had ever seen God, the promise that anyone would ever "see God" seems strange; but the same inconsistency occurs in the Old Testament. On the one hand no one could see the face of God and live (Exod 33:20), whereas Moses, Aaron, Nadab, Abihu, and the seventy elders of Israel "saw the God of Israel" (Exod 24:9–11); the Lord was seen "eye to eye" (Num 14:14); in the temple, Isaiah "saw the Lord" (Isa 6:1). Exod 23:17 should probably be pointed to read: "Three times a year all your males will see the face of the Lord Jehovah." The priests were required to walk blamelessly in certain ways (Ps 15:1–5); the priest who ascended the hill of the Lord was required to have clean hands and a pure heart (Ps 24:3–4).

Rabbis understood the passage "Because in a cloud I will be seen on the ark cover" (Lev 16:2) to refer to the cloud of smoke made by incense which the priest offered on the Day of Atonement when he entered the holy of holies. The incense was to be offered in such a way that the priest's vision there would always be blurred by the smoke, lest he "see God" improperly (Sifra 81b; JYoma I, V.39a–39b; see also Exod R. 34:1; RH 31a; Mekilta *Shirata* 10:24–43).[38] Matt 5:8, then, in a context of Old Testament promises that were expected to be fulfilled, evidently meant that those who had clean hearts would live to worship in the temple, where they, like Isaiah and the priests, could "see God," not in his ultimate reality, but in the way others had done who worshiped in the temple. The author of Hebrews dealt with the same promise, negatively: without sanctification "no one will see the Lord." Just as persistently as the Gospel of Matthew urged that covenanters be perfect, continually repenting and forgiving, so that the community might be without sin, the author of Hebrews encouraged his community to "pursue peace." The author of Hebrews was even more severe than Matthew. He did not allow for continual forgiveness with repentance. For the brothers there must not be *any* evil in *any* of them (3:12). *No* one could see the Lord who was not sanctified. It is difficult to conceive of any group other than a monastic brotherhood who would even attempt to maintain this severely rigid ethic.

15. The Greek for "checking carefully" is *episkopountes*, "watching over," "supervising," or "inspecting." The author's emphasis on absolute perfection is evident again in his use of "any one." No single person dare slip in any way (3:12; 12:14), lest there be *any* root of bitterness within the group.

The "root of bitterness" in Deut 29:18[17 MT and LXX] probably referred to anything that led to idolatry and apostasy. In New Testament times, however, this term came to be identified with the tree of knowledge of good and evil (Gen 2:9), and this was considered marriage. The sect

[38] CC, pp. 74–75, n. 10.

that lived according to the Gospel of the Egyptians was evidently ascetic. According to its teachings, the Savior said, "I came to destroy both the works of sexual lusts and the works of creation and destruction." A certain Salome asked how long men would continue to die. The Lord answered, "As long as women bear children." She responded, "Then I did well not to bear children." The Lord answered "Eat every plant, but do not eat the bitter plant" (*Strom.* III.ix.63.1–67.2).

Another sectarian had drunk from the water of life, given up folly, was clothed in a new garment, had his eyes enlightened, and was taken to the Lord's Paradise. He was one of the Lord's servants who turned away from the bitterness of the trees (Odes of Solomon 11:9–18). Another psalmist thanked God for not reckoning him with the sinners and asked the Lord to save him from the wicked sinful woman, not to let the beauty of a wicked woman lead him astray, and to remove him from all anger and unreasonable passion (Pss Sol 16:7–10).

In opposition to these celibate sects, Clement of Alexandria (*Strom.* III.x.73:3–4) said Moses' commandment not to touch anything unclean did not refer to those who were married, but to those nations who were still living in "fornication."

This implies that the celibate sects called the marrying Christians "fornicators." In addition to its normal use, "harlotry" was used metaphorically in Old Testament and New Testament times to refer disparagingly to social mingling. Idolatry was called "whoring after strange gods" (Deut 31:16; Assump. Mos. 5:3). When Judah made international agreements with Egypt and Assyria, Ezekiel interpreted her faithlessness to the covenant to be harlotry (Ezek 16). The Shepherd of Hermas (*Mand.* IV. i.9) said adultery referred not only to defilement of flesh but also to behavior like that of the Gentiles. In the gospels, Jesus was reportedly mingling with the "harlots" and tax collectors, the former of whom probably were not women at all, but rather Jews who mingled with Gentiles and were thereby defiled. Masculine harlots (*pornoi*) were listed together with "dogs" (*kynes*), sorcerers, murderers, idolators, and liars (Rev 22:15; see also Philip 3:2) as those not admitted to the New Jerusalem. The "dogs" probably were Gentiles who mingled with Jews, and "masculine harlots" or "fornicators" were probably Jews who mingled with Gentiles, terms used in derision by orthodox covenanters who would mingle with neither.[39]

There are some clues in Heb 1:1 – 12:29 that suggest the author of Hebrews was himself a celibate monk who addressed a group of similar celibate monks. These clues are implied in his teachings, even though he nowhere directly speaks of himself or his readers as celibates. The author referred to the readers as "brothers" (3:1, 12; 7:5; 8:11; 10:19) as was customary in monastic brotherhoods. Like communal brotherhoods, he stressed the importance of work and love for one another (6:10; 10:24). His emphasis on holiness (3:1; 9:7; 12:10, 14), discipline (12:6, 7, 10, 11),

[39] CC, pp. 184–89.

defilement (2:14; 9:13), and sin as fornication (12:16) points toward a celibate group that was required to be strongly disciplined to avoid any kind of defilement. His requirement of absolute sinlessness could hardly be taken seriously by any but a rigorous, monastic group. Not *any* member dared to commit *any* evil deed (3:12); not *any* of the group dared to fail in achieving the promises (4:1); *no* one dared backslide into disobedience (4:11); *all* must be sanctified with *no* one failing to obtain the grace of God (12:14–15); *no* one dared to shrink back (10:38–39); there could be *no* root of bitterness allowed in the group (12:15); there was *no* chance for second repentance or forgiveness (6:4–8; 12:17). The picture of Jesus as a priest without a family or posterity (7:3), who was separated from sinners, unstained, holy, and blameless (7:26), seems to fit the ideal of monasticism. Since Jesus was criticized for mingling with sinners in the gospel reports, the picture given in Hebrews seems to fit the author's ideal rather than the facts. It is not just that he called the members "brothers," or spoke of brotherly love, that suggests monasticism. Christians who married also did the same, but the extent to which he emphasized these terms that were more customarily used in monastic communities than generally, and the rigorous discipline he required, indicate a background of associations that would fit better into a monastic community than any other.

The Greek word translated "should cause trouble" is *enochlē*. P. Katz has made a good case for holding that the best reading of the LXX is *en cholē* (in anger),[40] but the author of Hebrews evidently used a text that read *enochlē*, and he preserved it with that meaning. "The many" is a technical term which means the whole congregation. Just as one rotten apple spoils the whole basketful, so one defiled person would, "cause trouble" by defiling the whole community. This meticulous care for sanctity and avoidance of defilement is the kind of legalism expected in a monastic group.

16. Verse 16 is partly repetitious and partly an elaboration of vs. 15. Thus the "root of bitterness" (12:15) is in parallel construction to "a fornicator or defiled person," which is a hendiadys composed of two synonyms. In this context, the root of bitterness is the fornicator who is also the defiled person—different names for the same offender. Esau, in New Testament times, was identified with Rome, and all sorts of sinfulness were attributed to him (see *Virt.* 208 and Jub 25:1, 8). He was considered wicked because he had no Day of Atonement to remove his defilement as Jacob did (Gen R. 65:15). The Roman state was called a pig because it posed as if it were clean when it was not, according to R. Simon. In the same context, Esau was accused of having violated many married women (Gen R. 65:1; Jub 25:1, 8). This was an insulting way of illustrating the extent of Rome's defilement from the rabbinic point of view. The author of Hebrews agreed with the rabbis in attributing

[40] P. Katz, "The Quotations from Deuteronomy in Hebrews," ZNTW 49 (1958), 213–23.

to Esau defilement which he described in terms of fornication.[41] The word translated "meal" is *brōseōs,* literally "an eating." *Brōma* is "food." Therefore he was reported to have given up "his own birthright" for a single "eating" or "meal." The author of Hebrews referred to the story of an occasion when Esau was extremely hungry, and Jacob took advantage of the situation. He bargained with him on the basis that he would give him the food he wanted at the moment in exchange for Esau's birthright. As the eldest son, Esau was entitled to a double portion of his father's inheritance (Deut 21:15–17), but Jacob bought this from him under the pressure of hunger (Gen 25:29–34).

17. Jacob also tricked Esau out of his father's blessing, to which Esau was entitled, but which he could not recover, even though "he cried out with an exceeding great and bitter cry" (Gen 27:34). An objective judge might sympathize with Esau and criticize Jacob for his malice, but the author of Hebrews was not critical of his religious ancestors. He used the example to warn his readers of the ease with which a Christian could make one mistake, which would be fatal. When Esau "wanted to inherit the blessing, he was rejected" even though this happened a long time "afterwards." The mistake made earlier had not been forgotten. There was no "place for repentance" either from God or from Isaac. Esau might be sorry for his mistake, and seek even "with tears" to make restitution or to revoke an earlier decision, but there was no possibility.

The point of this illustration was to warn the readers against making the same mistake the exodus generation or Esau had made. It was not his concern for Esau's activity but for the behavior of the readers that caused the author to warn against becoming a defiled person, a fornicator, or a root of bitterness. Esau was compared to the one who fell back from the grace of God because both would be guilty of giving up their own birthrights. Esau lost his birthright by dealing with an unscrupulous brother at a weak moment; the Christian might become weak also and break covenant, which meant he would be defiled or without sanctification. The lot of the Christian was also like that of Esau in that once his fate was sealed, he could not change it.

Summary.—The ethical demand in this unit did not differ from that offered several times in other exhortatory parts of the document. It is rigorous, unrelenting, and complete. There was no room allowed for mistakes, weakness, or oversights. Here, however, the specific terms used in defining that ethic more carefully seemed even more likely than earlier to be those appropriate to a monastic group that opposed marriage,

[41] Montefiore, p. 224, seems mistaken in his analysis: "*Pornos* is more likely to have its literal sense here of the one who is sexually immoral (cf. 13:4) rather than the metaphorical meaning of apostate." He may have been misled by assuming that 13:4 was written by the same author as 12:16.

fornication, defilement of every kind, and worked steadfastly for sanctification. This was an either/or type of segregationism characteristic of communal, celibate groups like the Essenes, the community governed by the Rule of the Community, and many early ascetic Christian monastic groups.

The consuming fire

18. The words "fire" (*pyri*), "deep darkness (*gnophǭ*), and "tempest" (*thyellę̄*) are terms used to describe Mount Horeb when the commandments were given (Deut 4:11). The word rendered "gloom" (*zophǭ*) is very similar in meaning to deep darkness (*gnophos*). In the LXX, *zophos* occurs in only a few places and only according to Symmachus' text. This may have occurred in a version of the LXX Deut 4:11 which the author used, or it may have been an elaboration by the author. Several of these terms were frequently used together in theophanies (Deut 4:11; 5:22; Exod 10:22).

19. "A reverberated sound of a trumpet" is a slight variation of a quotation from LXX Exod 19:16, describing a similar scene around Mount Sinai when the commandments were given. The author's willingness to parallel the two accounts is shown by his addition to the passage from Exod 19:16, "a voice of words," taken from Deut 4:12. This may have meant the proclamation of the ten commandments, called "the ten words" in Deut 4:13.

20. There is no report in the scriptures to the effect that the people groaned about accepting the ten words and begged that the Lord add no more "to them." They were afraid, but according to Deut 5:27, they responded: "We will perform; we will obey." The author may have had access to a tradition or targum not available today that described the people's response as he has reported it. One of the traditions related to the giving of the Torah held that the Lord first offered the Torah to all the nations of the world, but when they heard its demands, they rejected it. Finally it was offered to Israel, and the people responded, "We will perform; we will obey" (*Sēpher hā'aggādāh* 59b). Commenting on "these words" (Exod 19:7), rabbis said, "You shall not diminish; you shall not add" (Mekilta *Baḥodesh* 2:78). There are many narratives that have developed around the giving of the Torah. Different accounts tell of different responses. The scripture reports that the people, hearing, were afraid and trembled (Exod 20:18). The author of Hebrews may have accentuated the fear a bit for his own polemical purposes. The reference to the beast touching "the mountain" is a summary statement of LXX Exod 19:12–13, which says that anyone who "touches the mountain" will be put to death. He should "be stoned" with stones. This would be true whether it be man or "beast" (*ktēnos;* Hebrews has *thērion*). The author's summary reveals his *a fortiori* logic. If even a beast that touched the mountain would be stoned, how much the more would such severity apply in the case of a covenanter!

21. There is a slight play on words in the Greek between "dreadful" and "afraid." "That which appeared" was "so dreadful" (*phoberon*) that Moses said, "I am afraid" (*ekphobos*). The author had to strain his sources a bit to bring about this play. In the context on Mount Sinai the people were afraid (Exod 19:16). Still at the mountain, but after the people had made a molten image and Moses had broken the tablets that bound the people in covenant relationship with God, then Moses fasted and "was afraid" (Deut 9:19) because of the Lord's wrath.

22. At Mount Horeb, which the author of Hebrews, following a widely held tradition, identified with Mount Sinai, the Lord was called the "living God" (*theou zōntos*) (LXX Deut 5:26). The expression "living God," when used in a descriptive context, describes a wrathful, militant deity (Deut 5:26; Josh 3:10; Jer 10:10; see also Heb 3:12; 9:14; 10:31). Here the author, in contrasting Mount Sinai with Jerusalem, called Jerusalem "[the] city of [the] living God" (*theou zōntos*). As in Gal 4:24–26, Mount Zion was contrasted to Mount Sinai (Horeb), and by implication, the old covenant with the new. Although only a few words of 12:18–21 are actually identical to the ones describing the theophany in Exod 19–20 and Deut 4–5, the description was accurately paraphrased, with an additional notation from Deut 9:19. The solemnity of the occasion was marked by fear, natural sounds, fire, and darkness. It was like the holy of holies before Christ entered through the curtain. Although the holy of holies was a dreadful place where only the high priest was allowed to enter, after Christ had renewed for Christians a new and living way through the curtain, Christians were urged to draw near (10:19–22). In a similar way, knowing the fear and dread that surrounded Sinai, Christians were assured that it was not Mount Sinai or Mount Horeb, but "Mount Zion" which they had "approached." Philo called Jerusalem "The City of God" (*hē de theou polis*) (*Som.* II. 250). That was the city of David which the author of Hebrews called "[the] city of [the] living God." This was none other than the capital city of the promised land, "heavenly Jerusalem," where the Lord had chosen to dwell. Zechariah had promised that when the Lord became king, Jerusalem would remain aloft upon its site as a city without a curse (Zech 14:9–11). In Ezekiel's vision of the restored temple (40 – 48), he saw the glory of the Lord entering the temple (43:4), and Ezekiel was told that the temple would be the place of the Lord's throne where he would dwell with his people forever (43:6–7, 9). "Heavenly Jerusalem" was not used to mislead the reader into thinking Mount Zion was in heaven, although Jews and Christians believed there was a Jerusalem in heaven as well, but to affirm its divine origin, just as in 6:5 the heavenly gift was something believers on earth had tasted, meaning it was a teaching considered divine or heavenly (see COMMENT on 11:13–17).[42] "Myriads of angels" were be-

[42] Bruce, *Interpretation* 23 (1969), 11, was not justified in calling Mount Zion "spiritual" nor in presuming the unity of intention between Heb 13 and 1:1 – 12: 29. This same is true of Stuart, p. 293, who said, "The epithet *epouraniǫ* here

lieved to hover over Mount Zion (see note at the end of chapter nine), especially at every "national assembly" or feast.[43] At these gatherings the saints, believers, heirs of the promise, or "church of first-born [people]" were congregated. Those "enrolled in heaven" were Christians believed to be listed in the book of life, a membership roll of the elect which God kept and brought up to date at the beginning of each new year.[44] Also present was "God [the] Judge of all" at every gathering at Mount Zion, but particularly in his role as "Judge of all" on the Day of Atonement and New Year's Day. If the sacrifices were properly performed so that atonement really took place, on the Day of Atonement "[the] spirits of the righteous" were "perfected," meaning that all their sins were removed and they were sanctified (10:1, 10, 14, 29). The readers, who had been called "holy brothers" (3:1), were given the further honorific titles of "first-born," those "enrolled in heaven," "the righteous," "perfected" ones. Other covenanters who were similarly impressed with their status made similar affirmations: "To those whom God chose, he gave an inheritance of [the] age, and he made them heirs in the lot of the saints, and with the sons of heaven he bound their foundation for [the] council of [the] community" (1QS 11:8–9).

24. The picture of a congregation of saints gathered at Jerusalem on the Day of Atonement or New Year's Day was related to the perfection that takes place because of the atoning blood of Jesus. Jesus, the great high priest, had acted as "[the] mediator of a new covenant," bringing as a sin offering his own "blood of sprinkling." This was a better covenant than that made through the mediation of Moses at Sinai, and it was inaugurated with a better offering. This offering was compared to the gifts offered by the innocent Abel, because of which, while dying, he still spoke (11:4). The "blood of sprinkling" offered by Jesus spoke "better than that of Abel."[45] Those who had received the benefits of Christ's atonement joined the throng of those saints gathered at Mount Zion when Jesus was crucified and thereby removed the debt of sin that prevented Israel from receiving her promised "rest." Although the crucifixion is reported in the gospels to have taken place at Passover, the author of Hebrews interpreted this whole act in terms of a priestly sacrifice, similar

---

determines, of course, that a *spiritual Jerusalem*, a *heavenly city*, is meant." Also Montefiore, p. 230, said, "But God's habitat is not the earth. He lives in heaven, and so Mount Zion must be a heavenly reality. It is *the heavenly Jerusalem*." Vaughan, p. 278, however, said: "It is a mistake to treat this as a new particular, distinct from *Siōn horei*. Mount Zion and Jerusalem are not to be made two separate things (as, for instance, the one the type of the divine presence itself, and the other, that of the divine beatific manifestation)."

[43] For the relationship of *panegyris* to feasts, see Williamson, pp. 64–70.

[44] CC, pp. 120–23. See also Luke 10:20; Philip 4:3; Rev 3:5; 13:8; 17:8; 20:15; 21:27; 22:19.

[45] Montefiore, p. 233, said "Abel's blood cries for vengeance while Jesus' blood speaks for reconciliation."

to that offered on the Day of Atonement. For that reason it was necessary for Jesus to have been a priest-king, rather than a Davidic messiah.

25. The Greek translated "requesting [exemption from]" is *paraiteisthai,* which can mean, "request," "beg," or "plead for," but it can also bear a negative force, like "to beg off," "ask to be excused," or "excuse." Michel renders it "reject" (*abweisen*),[46] and RSV, "refuse." It refers to the request the people made to Moses that he not let God speak to them. They wanted to be excused or exempted from this threat (Exod 20:18–20). As elsewhere, the author of Hebrews warned his readers not to make the same mistake their fathers had made in the wilderness. Also consistently, he pressed his case with an *a fortiori* argument. "The one who warns upon earth" was Moses, who acted as the representative, mediator, or spokesman for the people of Israel (Exod 20:18–20). "The one who warns from heaven" was God who spoke with Moses from heaven (Exod 20:22).[47] The Israelites who tried to evade the demands of Moses' warnings were finally punished for their disbelief by being forced to wander the rest of their lives in the wilderness. Similar to the warnings of 2:2–4 and 6:4–6, the author held that if the Israelites who received an inferior revelation and warning "did not escape" (*exephygon;* see also 2:3), then there would be no chance at all for Christians who should "turn away" and become apostate after they had been warned "from heaven" and had received the superior revelation through Jesus. The Israelites whom Moses warned were the members of the exodus generation who failed to be admitted to their promised "rest" because they were unfaithful and turned away.

26. It was God whose "voice then shook the earth" (Judg 5:4–5; Pss 68:7–8; 114:7–8) and made the people of Israel tremble (Exod 19:16; 20:18). Just as Moses was contrasted with God, so also the voice that "shook the earth" in the past was contrasted with the promise that was effective in the author's own day. The account in the Torah applied to the Israelites and the first covenant, but the account in Haggai came later in time, and therefore could be applied to the Christians who were contemporary with the author of Hebrews. The one who once "shook the earth" promised a still more severe disruption. Haggai said he would shake the heaven, the earth, the sea, and the dry land (Hag 2:6). Since heaven and earth constitute a merism (see Ps 102:26) for the whole universe, in which sea and dry land would come under the general classification of "earth," the author of Hebrews was justified in changing a list of four items to a merism of two that have the same meaning. At Mount Sinai and Horeb there were many natural noises that involved shaking the earth. When God's voice spoke again it would "shake not only the earth but also the heaven." In Rashi's commentary on Hag 2:6,

[46] Michel, p. 321.

[47] Hanson, StEv II (1965), 402–7, by holding that the one who warns from heaven was the pre-incarnate Jesus, claimed that it was also the voice of the pre-incarnate Jesus that shook the earth (12:26–27).

he said this prophecy was fulfilled in the miracles that happened for the Hasmoneans.

27. The author seemed to use the term "once" (*hapax*), like "today" (4:7), to express something decisive. Those who had "once" been enlightened could no longer renew for repentance (6:4). Jesus appeared "once" at the end of the ages for the removal of sin through his sacrifice (9:26). The author interpreted Haggai's prophecy as a promise for the future. There would be still one more upheaval when God would upset the status quo. That would change "the things shaken." These are the ephemeral "things that are made," also called that which is seen (11:3). These all belonged to the past and the old covenant, the old law, and the old priesthood. In contrast to them are "the things not shaken" or the things not seen (11:1), which belong to the future, the new covenant, the new temple not made with hands, the perfect sacrifice, the great high priest, and other benefits associated with Jesus which "might remain." This does not mean that God is hostile to ephemeral things; it just means that they are ephemeral and designed to be changed and replaced. Indeed, the changing ages have been put in order by the word of God who created that which is seen (11:3).

28. That which is not shaken but intended to remain (4:6, 9; 12:27) is "an unshakable kingdom." This "unshakable kingdom" suggests an allusion to the "kingdom that shall not be destroyed" (Dan 7:14) which was presented to the one like a son of man by the Ancient of Days (Dan 7:13). This was understood to mean "the land of the promise" (11:9) given to the Hasmoneans by God (see note at the end of chapter two). The psalmist had the same territory in mind when he said:

"Say to the nations, 'The Lord has become King!'
for he has set straight the world (*oikoumenē*),
which will not be shaken" (Pss 96[95]:10; 93[92]:1).

In these enthronement Psalms, when a ruler was established over Israel, God set straight the "world" or administration "which will not be shaken" (Pss 96[95]:10; 93[92]:1), which was also the *oikoumenē* into which the Lord led his first-born (see COMMENT on 1:6). It would also have been at a time when the administration was changing, when the "kingdom" was being established, when the "Lord became King" (Ps 99[98]:1) that the earth would be made to shake (*saleuthētō*) (Ps 99[98]:1). That would be the time when the things shaken would be changed in order that the things not shaken might remain (12:27). The "unshakable kingdom" would be established before God's people could enjoy a sabbath rest (4:6, 9) on the land of the promise (11:9), whose capital city, Jerusalem, was the city having foundations whose builder and constructor was God (11:10).

Since Christians, "accepting an unshakable kingdom," were given another opportunity to enter into the rest (3:11), they were obliged to "have grace through which [they] might worship in a way that is pleasing to God, with reverence and fear." Having grace is the same as being thankful; therefore, Christians are urged to worship properly with thanksgiving.

Falling into the hands of the living God is dreadful (10:31). Nonetheless, Christians were urged to approach the throne of grace with boldness (4:16), approach with a true heart in fullness of faith (10:22), or "worship in a way that is pleasing to God." Moses warned the Israelites: "The Lord your God is a consuming fire, a *zealous* God" (Deut 4:24). The god who consumed the enemies of the Israelites and overpowered the Syrians for the Hasmoneans was the same zealous God who invited Jesus to sit at his right hand until God put Jesus' enemies under his feet (1:13).

29. This final unit is marked by an inclusion with the key word "fire" which appears at both the beginning and the end (12:18, 29). Its message repeats an emphasis on the contrasting conditions that the author had emphasized in different ways in his exhortations. The situations contrasted were those related to the exodus generation and those that existed for the readers. The emphasis this time was on the revelation at Mount Sinai in contrast to the one on Mount Zion, where Jesus was crucified. The crucifixion, however, was not described in terms of criminal punishment outside the city during the events related to the Passover, but in terms of a great Day of Atonement and New Year's festival when the sacrifice was offered as necessary to provide perfection and sanctification for the saints. This event was so tremendous that it shook not only the earth but also heaven. The revelation was so much greater at Mount Zion than at Mount Sinai that the believers who were contemporary with the author were under a much greater obligation to obey the commandment from heaven and not turn away into apostasy. It was only by steadfastness of faith and worship with reverence and fear that the readers could expect to receive the unshakable kingdom which was the rest promised to Abraham long ago and denied to the wilderness Israelites who stood around Mount Sinai when the first law was given. The living God who appeared at Mount Sinai was the same God who disclosed himself again when he spoke from heaven. He was a consuming fire before whom believers must stand in awe.

It was in the confidence that our God is a consuming fire (12:29) that the author concluded his book as he had begun it, calling attention to the great power of God and the glory he would give his Son, Jesus, while he suppressed his enemies. This author, who showed great skill in forming inclusions to tie his introductions and conclusions together, centered his interest in this final paragraph on the shaking that God would do and the unshakable kingdom (12:28) that would remain (12:27). The readers and the author were evidently so well versed in scripture that the author could allude to a word or passage of scripture and the readers could be expected to understand the whole context related to the reference. For example, the author may have expected the readers to relate the word "shaken" (12:27) to the *oikoumenē* which was not shaken of Ps 93[92]:1 and Ps 96[95]:10, which, in turn, would suggest the *oikoumenē* mentioned at the beginning of the document into which the Lord led his first-born (1:6). Also the church of the first-born (12:23) might have referred the reader to the initial reference to Jesus as the first-born. This may be attributing to the author more subtlety, and to the readers more perspicuity, than was intended or understood, but the author was an excellent student of scripture and he wrote as if his readers should be able to understand what he wrote. He was an artist in style, employing inclusions throughout the document to indicate his literary units. It would not have been out of character for him to write the document in such a way that there was a subtle, if not obvious, inclusion tying the end of the document to the beginning.

Heb 1:1 – 12:29 is a unified homily centered around the one text of Ps 110, which the author quoted from time to time. He never quoted the whole Psalm, but, by alluding to one verse, he presumed that the reader understood the rest of the Psalm. He also frequently drew doctrine from other Old Testament passages, preferring Psalms and prophets to the Torah. He sometimes even used the Psalms and prophets to refute or override the Torah. He regularly interpreted the passages he quoted according to their context, sometimes with meanings that would have surprised the original author and readers of the Old Testament. On the basis of his doctrine, he exhorted his readers to be faithful and warned them of the adverse consequences that would come upon them if they were not. He also assured them of the rewards promised to those who did not give up hope but were steadfast to the end. This was artfully done in a homily whose divisions were marked by inclusions which were tied together with transition sentences that contained catchwords belonging to the adjoining paragraphs.

Heb 12:29 seems to be the conclusion of the whole document, and it has no transition sentence that leads neatly to chapter thirteen. Heb 13:1 begins abruptly with an exhortation that is not directly related to chapter twelve and is not based on Ps 110. Chapter thirteen seems to be a collection of material which an editor has put together. It includes a confession of faith, some doctrinal narrative, a benediction, and some personal greetings, with some of the editor's exhortations interspersed. Some of the views of chapter thirteen contradict those of 1:1 – 12:29. Therefore, it seems not to have been a part of the original composition and should be examined separately.[48]

[48] So also Spicq, II, 414–15. Westcott, p. 429, said the thirteenth chapter "is a kind of appendix to the Epistle." Bruce, p. 386, and Vanhoye, p. 210, however, claimed that it belonged to the entire document.

VI. GENERAL EXHORTATION
(13:1–25)

Christian attitudes

13 [1] Let brotherly love continue;
[2] do not forget love for strangers
(for through this, some, when they entertained angels, were not
aware [of it]).
[3] Remember the prisoners as partners in bonds,
those badly treated, as yourselves in [the] body.
[4] [Let] marriage be honored in every [respect],
and [let] the marriage bed be undefiled
(for God will judge fornicators and adulterers).
[5] [Let] unconcern for money be the fashion,
being satisfied with the present conditions,
for he himself said,
"I will not forsake you,
and I will not abandon you";
[6] so that we may have courage to say,
"The Lord is my helper, I shall not be afraid.
What can a man do to me?"

Doctrine and ethics

[7] Remember your leaders who spoke to you the word of God; by
observing carefully the outcome of their behavior, imitate their
faith. [8] Jesus Christ, yesterday and today the same—and for the
ages. [9] Do not be carried away by means of various and strange
teachings, for it is good [that] the heart be strengthened by grace,
not by foods, in which those who walk have not benefited.

[10] We have an altar, from which those who minister in the tent
do not have authority to eat, [11] for the beasts "whose blood is
brought into the temple for sin" by the high priest, the bodies of
these "are burned outside the camp." [12] Therefore Jesus also suffered outside the gate so that he might sanctify the people through

his own blood. 13 Therefore let us go out to him "outside the
camp," bearing his insult, 14 for we do not have here a continuing
city, but we are looking for the [city] which is to come. 15 Through
him, then, let us bear a sacrifice of praise to God through everything, that is [the] fruit of lips which confess his name, 16 and do
not forget the good works and common [fellowship], for God is
pleased with such sacrifices [as these].

17 Comply with your leaders and be subject [to them], for they
are vigilant in behalf of your souls as [those who must] give an account. [Submit] so that they may do this with joy and not groan,
for this [groaning] is damaging to you.

18 Pray for us, for we are convinced that we have a good conscience, desiring to behave properly in everything. 19 I strongly
urge you to do this, so that I may be restored to you quickly.

Benediction

20 May the God of peace, "who led up" from [the] dead ones
the great "shepherd of the sheep," through "the blood of the eternal covenant," our Lord Jesus, 21 make you fit in every good thing
to do his will, doing in your midst that which is well-pleasing before him, through Jesus Christ, to whom be glory for the ages of
the ages. Amen.

Parting postscript

22 Now I exhort you, brothers, accept the word of exhortation
[given above], for I have sent [it] to you by a few [words of my
own]. 23 Be informed that our brother Timothy has been released,
with whom, if he comes quickly, I shall see you. 24 Greet all your
leaders and all the saints. Those from Italy greet you. 25 Grace be
with you all!

Comment

Christian attitudes

13:1–2. "Brotherly love" (*philadelphia*) is the concern that fellow sectarians have for one another's welfare. Especially in celibate brotherhoods where members did not have children to care for them in their illness or old age, it was necessary for brothers of the religious family to assume responsibilities ordinarily provided by families. This is not limited to personal feelings but also involves care for physical and material needs. In these communities where alone "life" was believed to be possible, those who joined the group passed from death to life when they took on responsibilities of love for one another (I John 3:14). Any member who had material possessions and saw his brother in need and did nothing about it could not claim to have God's love in him (I John 3:17).

"Love for strangers" (*philoxenias*) was a type of brotherly love. "Brotherly love" could be shown to immediate community members by personally providing needs as they were required. For the saints who lived in Jerusalem and depended on others for subsidy, gifts for the poor were sent as expressions of "brotherly love." Because some groups of orthodox Jews, like the Essenes, refused to eat with anyone whose carefulness in dietary, tithing, and purity rules was not proved by being a member of his own sect, hospitality was very important. Those who traveled from place to place had to find other members of their sect who would provide them food, clean clothing, and lodging. When "strangers" came who were of the same faith, Christians and Jews were expected to entertain them. If they did not observe the same rules, however, they were not to be admitted into the homes of the faithful, lest they defile the premises. Some were warned against even greeting them, lest they become defiled (II John 10–11; 1QS 5:16–17; 7:25; 8:23–24; 9:8–9). Leaders sometimes scolded others who neglected "strangers" (*xenous*). When they were not given hospitality, they were made to suffer because they did not dare eat food provided by Gentiles (III John 5–8).[1] Because some "strangers" took advantage of the hospitality they were guaranteed by their membership, some Christians were warned to consider any stranger who stayed more than two days to be a false prophet (*Didachē* 11). Those who generally practiced "brotherly love" rather well in their own communities might be a little selfish about "showing love for strangers"; therefore Christians were frequently admonished against neglect in this area (Rom 12:10–13; I Thess 4:1–12; I Peter 1:22–23; II Peter 1:5–7).

The couplet was evidently a poetic exhortation on love. The editor of chapter thirteen added to this his own explanatory elaboration. Not only were Christians fulfilling their religious responsiblity by showing hospitality to strangers, but some, like Abraham and Sarah (Gen 18) and Lot (Gen 19), in this way "entertained angels" without realizing it at first. The honor that comes to a Near Easterner who entertains important guests might be missed if the Christian who thought he was only refusing hospitality to a Christian from another location was really rejecting an angel in disguise.

3. Because early Christianity and Judaism were both understood as subversive movements within the Roman Empire, faithful Jews and Christians were frequently thrown into prison for their positions and activities. When some people were suffering and dying for their faith, there was a strong tendency to deny association with them (Matt 26:69–75), and in this way to avoid similar fates. The word rendered "partners in bonds" is *syndedemenoi*, "bound together with," which involves a very close identity with the "pris-

[1] See further COMMENT on 6:9 and CC, pp. 238–81, 290–305.

oners." Those who called on them, brought them food and other necessities, admitted to all that they were in sympathy with the "prisoners" and shared their political and religious views. This kind of identity was very important for the survival of the movement, and it also was considered an expression of brotherly love.

Verse 3 is a couplet, line 2 being synonymous with line 1. Therefore "those badly treated" were either "the prisoners" or those like them who were made to suffer for their religious beliefs and practices. Being "in the body" may mean that the readers should so identify themselves with those "badly treated" that they could share vicariously the pain involved. It might also refer to the church as the body of Christ, in which all members suffer if one is pained (I Cor 12:12–27; II Cor 5:6; Rom 12:4–5). This seems the more likely interpretation, giving more force to the parallelism of the verse. Being "in the body" has much the same meaning as being "partners in bonds."

4. This couplet deals with faithfulness in marriage. Letting "marriage be honored in every [respect]" probably meant the same as letting "the marriage bed be undefiled." From the point of view of levitical purity, the "undefiled" marriage bed would be one in which "those who have wives live as though they did not" (I Cor 7:29), since every act of sexual intercourse is defiling (Lev 15:16–18). This kind of temporary ethics might be expected of holy war soldiers during time of war, but when the war was over, they would be expected to return to their wives without any sense of guilt. There were followers of Jesus who had left their families to be with Jesus (Matt 19:27–30), but later, when the kingdom had not come as soon as expected, they returned and lived with their wives (I Cor 9:3–6). If the "marriage bed" were kept permanently "undefiled," the Christians practicing that ethic would be celibate. The editor who interpreted this couplet, at least, did not understand it that way. He took this to mean a prohibition against "fornicators" who were promiscuous in their sexual activity and "adulterers" who were unfaithful in marriage. Adultery was considered more sinful than fornication and was punishable by death (Lev 20:10–21; Exod 20:14; Deut 5:18).

In the main section of the document (1:1 – 12:29) there was no mention made of marriage. In fact, the references to sanctification, holiness, brotherhood, the root of bitterness, discipline, and avoidance of any kind of defilement suggest that the author and readers were celibate monks. That is not the case of chapter thirteen, which seems to have been composed by a different author or editor for a wider reading public.

5. The couplet urging "unconcern for money" is similar to other Christian admonitions and attitudes. This attitude was usually associated with a communal economy in which the individuals were dependent upon the administration of others for their provision, although it was also encouraged by early Jewish and Christian concern for widows, orphans, and others who were in need of social welfare which the community provided. Those who in the Sermon on the Mount were counseled against being anxious for

food, drink, or clothing (Matt 6:25), who were told not to lay up treasures on earth (Matt 6:19–21), and who were sent out on missions with no gold, silver, or copper in their belts, no bag for the journey, no staff, and no change of clothes (Matt 10:9–12), were traveling missionaries for whom the church had prepared hospitality stations where they could receive food, clothing, and other needs. Because the administration had laid up treasures on earth for them, the missionaries did not have to be anxious for the next day (Matt 6:34). Since this administration did not function perfectly, and because there were men like Diotrephes, who turned away missionaries (III John 5–10), not all dependent Christians found it "the fashion" to have a complete "unconcern for money." It was easier for a celibate like Paul to be content in whatever state he found himself (Philip 4:11–12) than for others who had families for whom to provide. Because not all early Christians were "satisfied with the present conditions," they had to be admonished from time to time.

In addition to the couplet urging Christians to be unconcerned about money, the author further pressed the point by quoting two passages of scripture on God's providence. Just before his death, Moses urged the Israelites to continue in their mission to capture the land. They should not be afraid of any enemies who stood in their way, because the Lord their God would go before them; he would not "abandon" them nor "forsake" them (Deut 31:6). The importance of God's presence in that case was his power in war. He was expected to overthrow Israel's enemies, and they should count on it. Here the text was used to assure Christians of God's general providence, which made concern for money unnecessary.

6. The second quotation came from Ps 118:6, and the editor admitted that it took "courage" to give up concern for money. Like Deut 31:6, the Psalm reminded Israel of the Lord's faithfulness in overthrowing Israel's enemies in war, but the editor used it to urge trust in God's financial and material providence. Like the lilies of the fields and the birds of the air (Matt 6:28–30), Christians should give up their anxiety for money and material things and instead trust "the Lord" who is their "helper." Because this was so they did not have to be anxious about what a "man" could "do" to them. The church continued to maintain a doctrine of voluntary poverty, but it has always required much pressure to convince Christians to be confident of God's care so long as the men of the church were in charge of the welfare program. The editor of chapter thirteen was one of those who added his arguments to the Christians' reading material in support of general financial sharing and lack of concern for one's own material needs.

Summary.—The editor of chapter thirteen put together in these verses four couplets and two Old Testament quotations, interspersed with his own elaborations, introductions, or connecting sentences. These dealt with brotherly love as expressed in concern and care for strangers who needed hospitality, and prisoners who needed visitation and material provisions. Contrary to the monastic ideal of the main document, one of these couplets which the editor interpreted provided counsel for married people, urging faithfulness. The note that received the most attention was against overconcern for money and material needs. There were evidently many people during the editor's time who had had second thoughts about giving all that they had to the Christian movement. Therefore the editor supported his couplet with two passages of scripture, which he interpreted to mean that Christians should trust God for their material needs and be willing to share their goods. These couplets may once have been part of one poem on Christian ethics from which the editor chose the verses that appealed to him and that served his immediate needs. If this was not the case, then the editor collected them from different sources and put them together. It is unlikely that he composed them himself, as the connecting sentences show.

Doctrine and ethics

7. The expression "outcome of their behavior" renders the Greek *hon . . . tēn ekbasin tēs anastrophēs,* literally, "the way out of their turning around." Idiomatically this can refer to their departure from life. They were evidently faithful to the end (see II Tim 4:6–8). The readers were encouraged to "imitate their faith." Although the pastoral epistles and the letters of Paul gave frequent admonitions to leaders for proper dealing with their parishioners, and Paul boldly urged Christians to "imitate" him (II Thess 3:7, 9; I Cor 4:16; 11:1), there is very little general counsel in the New Testament to the people concerning the way they should treat their leaders. There is no specification of a distinct office which these leaders filled, such as bishops or deacons. It evidently referred to all leaders who "spoke . . . the word of God."

8. This is an early Christian confession of faith. "The ages" are the ages to come. This is just a poetic way of saying that "Jesus Christ" is always "the same."

9. "Various and strange teachings" refer to some teachings that differed from those accepted by the author. They were "strange," meaning strange or foreign to the creed considered orthodox. Like the "myths and endless genealogies which promote speculations rather than divine training" (I Tim 1:4), these seem to have been teachings of the Judaizers, who, like the author of 1:1 – 12:29, were interested in keeping the law to the letter on matters of purity and foods. It was a non-Judaizer, like Paul, who emphasized salvation by faith rather than law, who minimized the importance of foods, circumcision, and Jewish birth, who would encourage the churches to "be strengthened by grace, not by foods."

To use "walk" for religious observance is customary in Jewish terminology. The way in which a person should "walk" is the rule by which he conducts his life. In this imagery, Christianity was early referred to as "the way," meaning the true way in which to "walk." Jewish legal teachings are called *halakoth*, "walkings." According to the author, the Judaizers who walked in ways that were "strange" to him did not benefit from their strict observance of food laws. This is in direct disagreement with the author of 1:1 – 12:29. It is possible that this comment was written after the fall of Jerusalem, after the religious and military efforts of the Jews had failed, because the author seemed to have some basis for holding that the Jewish way of walking had not been successful and therefore should not be practiced. He did not even have to mention his basis, because his audience would have understood the allusion. At a distance of many centuries, however, scholars can only speculate.

10. "Those who minister in the tent" are the priests who have the exclusive right to eat from certain offerings that are brought to the altar (Lev 7:6; Num 18:9–10) in the temple at Jerusalem, but the Christians to whom this writing applied "have an altar" which excludes those who worship at Jerusalem.[2] Exclusive hospitality was common among Christian and Jewish sects. Outsiders were excluded from eating with members, to prevent members from becoming defiled. There were also groups, like the Essenes, who considered the temple at Jerusalem to be corrupt and, for that reason, performed their own sacrifices (*thusias*), apparently at their own altars away from Jerusalem (*Ant.* VIII.19). The altar used by the Essenes obviously would not be permitted for use by the priests at Jerusalem, nor would these non-Essenes be permitted to eat from the guilt and sin offerings made at the Essene altar. Similarly, the group to whom this message applied had an exclusive "altar" which did not admit the Jerusalem priests to function, nor did it allow them "to eat" from its sacrifices.

11. Lev 16:27–28 describes the way the sin offerings must be treated. The "blood" was to be sprinkled on the altar for atonement, but the carcass had to be taken "outside the camp" and "burned." The person who handled the carcass became defiled by this action and was required to bathe to be cleansed before he could again enter the city.

12. The author who interpreted this Old Testament passage compared the sacrifice of Jesus to that of animals, noting some important differences. The sacrifice of animals took place inside the camp and the carcasses were carried out, whereas Jesus' body and blood were both kept outside the camp, since "Jesus . . . suffered outside the gate." This is one of the few allusions to the historical Jesus, either in chapter thirteen or the major part of the document (see also 5:7 and 7:14). As with the references in 1:1 – 12:29, the reference to Jesus was made only as a basis for formulating doctrine.[3] The blood of animals atoned for those inside the camp, whereas Jesus "suffered outside the gate so that he might sanctify the people" outside the camp through his own blood. Dead bodies defile; sacrificial blood atones. For this reason the Pentateuchal rules had the carcass taken out so

[2] So also H. Koester, "'Outside the Camp' Hebrews 13:9–14," HTR 55 (1962), 313.

[3] See further Grässer, pp. 82–91.

as to remove all defilement from the "camp," which in New Testament times meant Jerusalem. In the case of Jesus, the blood was shed outside the city and never brought in. Therefore it would not cleanse the people inside the city, but it would "sanctify the people" who were outside the city. Koester missed the point slightly when he contrasted the defilement of the area outside the camp with the sanctifying of Jesus' sacrifice.[4] The point of the difference was the location of the atoning blood (Lev 16:27).

13. Since the blood of Jesus was poured on an altar "outside the camp" to sanctify the people outside the camp, Christians were admonished to "go out to him outside the camp, bearing his insult." The insult or disgrace involved came from association with one who had claimed to be the great king, but who was instead crucified as an insurrectionist. To most this seemed like a failure; to Christians who interpreted his death in terms of an atoning sacrifice, this meant victory, so they were willing to bear "the insult." Bruce also missed the point slightly when he said people were to leave the city in search of a city which had foundations (11:10).[5] The author of chapter eleven thought Jerusalem was the city having the foundations. The annotator who wrote chapter thirteen, or at least the author of this part of chapter thirteen, felt differently about Jerusalem. He thought Christians should leave that city. This presumes that there was a city to leave. After A.D. 70 there probably continued to be a few people in Jerusalem,[6] but not nearly so many as before the destruction, and there is no record of Christians in Jerusalem after that time. This seems to be a pre-A.D. 70 appeal, urging Christians to leave the wicked city as other covenanters had done who moved to such other religious centers as Qumran and Pella. If this is not the case, then this passage was written as if there were still a Jerusalem and still Christians there—a possibility even after A.D. 70, but not a great one.

14. The main thrust of vss. 10–16 is anti-Jerusalem. In the judgment of this author, in opposition to the author of 1:1 – 12:29, Jerusalem was *not* the city having the foundations, whose builder and constructor was God (11:10). Since Jesus suffered outside the gate, "here [at Jerusalem]" we do not have "a continuing city, but we are looking for the [city] which is to come." The location of that city was not given. The author told Christians to leave the city that was not a "continuing city." That was Jerusalem as it existed during the time of this writing. The city that was "to come" may have been the new Jerusalem, "the holy city . . . coming down out of heaven from God" (Rev 21:10). There was a strong belief among Jews and Christians of New Testament times that the temple and the city that then existed would have to be destroyed, or at least cleansed, before true worship could take place there. Pious covenanters objected to the lineage of the high priests, the purity practices, the calendars observed, or the affiliation of the priests with Rome. Some of these people conducted their own

[4] Koester, HTR 55 (1962), 300.
[5] Bruce, p. 404.
[6] See K. W. Clark, "Worship in the Jerusalem Temple after A.D. 70," NTS 6 (1969–70), 269–80.

religious services in exile, according to rules they accepted. One of these groups met somewhere in Judah (1QpHab), possibly at Qumran, under the leadership of its own priestly teacher of righteousness; another was organized by the high priest Onias in Heliopolis, Egypt.[7] Some Jews prayed daily that God would root out foreign worship from the land and bring holy worship in its place.[8] These people thought of the temple on Mount Zion as the temple made with hands (Acts 7:47–48). They refused to worship there under those conditions, just as the Jews refused to worship there after Antiochus Epiphanes had defiled it. As soon as Judas drove out the Greeks, however, and the temple had been properly cleansed, Jews rejoiced at the opportunity to renew sacrifices. Similarly, Jews and Christians, who had left Jerusalem and worshiped in exile, would have been glad to return to the same temple in the same city under conditions they believed to be proper. The temple that was defiled was considered idolatrous, but the same temple could have been cleansed and considered a temple "not made with hands." A complete change in administration would change the whole character of the temple and the city. The Jerusalem which was to come down from heaven, "the city which [was] to come," was the cleansed city, the holy city, Zion city of our God. That was to be the "continuing city." The city that then existed, however, had no future in their judgment. It should not be supported or encouraged in any way to continue. Christians who were there should leave. Some thought the conditions were so bad and so deeply ingrained that the new temple and the new Jerusalem could not come unless the old temple was completely destroyed (Matt 24:1–3; Mark 13:1–2, 24–27; Luke 21:5–6, 25–28; John 2:19). Whatever the variation in details of the changes required for the new Jerusalem "to come," there is no necessity in understanding it to be a city to which Christians would "go" when they reached heaven, as Michel and others hold.[9]

15. The two Old Testament passages quoted here both use the imagery of sacrifice to speak of praise and confession. The psalmist insisted that God was not hungry and did not need the sacrifice of goats and bulls (Ps 50:12–13). Therefore, the believer should offer to God "a sacrifice of praise" (Ps 50:14). Hosea urged Israelites to confess their sins while they rendered the "fruit of lips" (Hosea 14:2), as Heb 13:15 repeated.

Whenever the temple was burned, defiled, or doctrinally rejected as a place where sacrifices might be offered effectively, covenanters could substitute only "a sacrifice of praise to God . . . , that is [the] fruit of lips which confess his name." They could pray, read scripture, sing Psalms, and do good works. The unknown author of 1QS 9:4–5 said, "an offering of lips [*trwmt sptym*] [is considered] as a reckoning like a fragrant offering of righteousness." The wise man was to bless the Lord with an offering of lips

[7] See further "The Priestly Teacher of Righteousness," RQum 6 (1969), 556–58.

[8] CC, pp. 63–65, 76–80.

[9] Michel, p. 349.

(1QS 9:26).[10] When R. Yoḥanan ben Zakkai and R. Joshua left Jerusalem after the temple had burned, R. Joshua said, "Woe for us, because the place which atones for the iniquities of Israel has been destroyed!" R. Yoḥanan comforted him: "We have one atonement that is like it, deeds of loving kindness, as it is said, 'For I desired loving kindness and not sacrifice'" (Hosea 6:6; ARN 7:30–34, 11a). In a conjectured conversation between the Lord and Abraham concerning the way Israel could have her sins removed so as not to be like the generation of the flood or that of the division of tongues, Abraham responded, "Master of the age, this is all right at a time when the temple is standing, [but] what will happen to them when the temple is not standing?" The Lord replied, "I have already prepared for them a list of sacrificial [duties]. Whenever they read them, I will credit them as if they were offering sacrifices to me, and I will forgive all their iniquities" (Meg. 31b). Rabbis held that God said to Israel, "Be strict [in your observance] in prayer, for there is no measure more acceptable than it; it is greater than all sacrifices" (Tanḥuma *Wayera* §1, 24b). The author of Heb 13:10–16 had an ancient tradition of the type of worship that was acceptable when there was no temple. This probably went back to the Babylonian captivity when Jews had to adjust to life without the temple. Since the author rejected the Jerusalem that then existed as a continuing city (13:14), Christians were left with the substitute means of pleasing God.

D. N. Freedman has called attention to a background for this concept of divine judgment in Old Testament theology and in Canaanite mythology. In a setting where the chief god ruled in a court, part of his function was to judge men. Cases came up annually, and at death a final disposition was made. The traditions concerning the New Year and the Day of Atonement revolve around this understanding. At the turn of the year a preliminary verdict was given, and then after or on the Day of Atonement it was made final. In the period in between, men could pray, repent, and request intercession from the angel who served that function. There were two main officers of the court, the prosecuting attorney or Satan and the defense attorney, who pleaded the case for men. The author of Hebrews urged Christians to behave as if the judgment had been made and they were still given the chance to offer "praise to God" and make confession in his name, hoping to have some influence on the final decision at a time when their consciences required them to leave the city of Jerusalem and find temporary exile elsewhere until the new Jerusalem should come and remain. Other covenanters also related confession to praise:

"For who is strong, O God, if he does not confess you in truth?
and what man is able [to do anything] if he does not make confession in your name?
[Sing] a new psalm with an ode with a joyful heart,
a fruit of lips with [the] harmonious organ of [the] tongue,
a first fruit of lips from a pious and just heart" (Pss Sol 15:3–5).

[10] The Old Testament bases for rejecting blood sacrifice are reported in Amos 5:21 ff.; Hosea 6:6; Micah 6:6–8; Isa 1:11 ff.; Jer 7:21–22; Pss 50:7 ff.; 51:16–17.

16. It was "such sacrifices [as these]" which "pleased" God: praise, confession, "good works," "common [fellowship]" or community worship, and reading the scripture. When it was not possible to sacrifice at Mount Zion, God would still accept these as if they were offerings made in the temple.

Verses 10–16 seem to comprise a separate unit of literature which the editor of chapter thirteen collected together with other materials to compose this chapter. It includes many terms employed by the author of 1:1 – 12:29, such as "minister" (13:10), "tent" (13:10), "blood" (13:11), "temple" (13:11), "sin" (13:11), "high priest" (13:11), "insult" (13:13), "city" (13:14), "sacrifice" (13:15), and "confess" (13:15). The methods of exegesis in both sections are similar, but the point of view is somewhat different. The Jerusalem which the author of 1:1 – 12:29 considered the city which had the foundations, Mount Zion, and the city of God was considered by the author of this section to be so defiled that Christians must leave in search of a continuing city. Until that city should come they must live in exile, observing the religious duties that were possible without a temple.

17. The admonition in behalf of leaders is one leaders had to make frequently. The case made here was that the responsibility of the leaders was great. They were responsible for watching over the "souls" of all those under their supervision. They had to "give an account" to God and to their superior officers concerning the spiritual and, in the case of communal communities, material and physical welfare of the people under their jurisdiction. Since the leaders were responsible for the outcome, it seemed reasonable to allow them to be the ones who decided how things would be done. In so doing, however, they were obliged to enforce discipline and call attention to members' faults so that they might correct them and maintain perfection in the community (Matt 18:15–17). Some members may not have liked this fault-finding and may not have been willing to "comply with" their "leaders and be subject" at every point. This kind of insubordinate behavior made the leaders "groan" while carrying out their necessary obligations. This irritation not only prevented the leaders from enjoying their work, but it was also "damaging" to the rest of the group.

18–19. The author of these notes urged the readers to "pray for us," probably meaning that they should pray for the leaders mentioned above of whom he was one. He further assured them of the sincerity and intended good character of the leaders.

Summary.—The words "behavior" (*anastrophēs*) and "leaders" at the beginning of this unit (13:7) and "leaders" (13:17) and "behave" (*anastrephesthai*) (13:18) at the conclusion form an inclusion typical also of the author of 1:1 – 12:29. In between is a doctrinal discussion about the sacrifice of Jesus and contemporary worship and witness (13:10–16), a small confession (13:8), practical advice about behavior in relationship to leaders (13:7, 17–19), and warnings against heretics (13:9). This is a scissors-and-paste composition of collected bits of literature, that changed from first person pronouns to second person pronouns. Admonitions from 7–9 are directed in the second person plural: "remember your leaders" (7); "do not be carried away by means of various and strange teachings" (9). Then the shift is made to first person plural: "we have an altar" (10); "let us go out to him" (13); "we do not have here a continuing city, but we are looking" (14); "let us bear a sacrifice of praise to God" (15). With vs. 16, however, the subject returns to the second person plural: "do not forget," and vs. 19 is in first person singular. This suggests the work of an editor who used sources. Important for use in dating is the doctrinal statement of 10–16. This seems to have been written before the destruction of Jerusalem. The question is, "Did the editor use it because it was a condition still true in his time?" If we knew the answer to that question it would be easier to conjecture the dates for the composition of the whole document, "To the Hebrews."

Benediction

20. "Peace" is related to being "paid up" in Hebrew. In a treasury-of-merits system, the person who had atoned for all his sins had paid for all his iniquities. His books balanced, so he had peace with God. His debts of sin had been paid in full. "The God of peace" (also Rom 15:33) was the one who made peace by forgiving or canceling sins so that there was no barrier of sin between himself and his people. II Maccabees paraphrased the benediction in Num 6:24–26 thus: "And make peace—may he pay attention to your supplications and become reconciled to you and not give you up in an evil time" (II Macc 1:4–5).[11] The ascription to the deity includes some scriptural passages put together in such a way as to express the liturgist's desires.

Some words came from Isa 63:11, referring to God who led the Israelites from Egypt through the Reed Sea. According to the MT: "where is he who brought up from the [Reed] Sea the shepherds of his flock?" The LXX has: ". . . who brought up (*anabibasas*) from the land [of Egypt] the shepherd of the sheep." Heb 13:20 has for "who led up," *ho anagagōn* rather than *ho anabibasas* as the LXX has, but its author agreed with the LXX in making "shepherd" singular. The next two ascriptions related Jesus to the deliverance from Babylon: "And you in [the] blood of [the] covenant have sent out your captives from a pit, not having water" (Zech 9:11). From another passage of redemption, the liturgist took the term "eternal" (Ezek 37:26) to modify the covenant mentioned in Zech 9:11.

The covenanter who composed this benediction did not use Old Testament phrases "quite apart from their original setting" as Moffatt says.[12] He intentionally alluded to passages referring to God's deliverances of Israel and ascribed them to the deity to whom he made his request. To be sure, he

[11] CC, pp. 237–40.
[12] Moffatt, p. 242.

understood "the great shepherd" to be Jesus rather than Moses, because he had a later redemption in mind. He also considered "the eternal covenant" to be the covenant of "our Lord Jesus." The editor who added this benediction to the discussion on leaders may have intended to relate the leaders with whom the readers were expected to comply (13:17) to Jesus, "the great shepherd."

21. The editor may also have wished to remind the readers that the leaders were vigilant in behalf of the covenanters' souls by offering a prayer that the covenanters be made "fit in every good thing to do his will, doing in your midst that which is well-pleasing before him." The benediction was concluded according to the counsel given earlier, with lips which confess his name (13:15), that is "through Jesus Christ, to whom be glory for the ages of the ages. Amen." This conclusion is similar to other New Testament ascriptions: "To the one who loves us and released us from our sins through his blood, and made us a kingdom, priests to God and his Father, to him be glory and power for the ages of the ages. Amen." (Rev 1:6). "Grace to you and peace from God our Father and [the] Lord Jesus Christ, who gave himself for our sins, so that he might deliver us from the present evil age, according to the will of our God and Father, to whom be glory for the ages of the ages. Amen" (Gal 1:3–5). ". . . in order that God might be glorified in everything, through Jesus Christ, to whom is glory and power for the ages of the ages. Amen" (I Peter 4:11). ". . . and increase in grace and knowledge of our Lord and Savior Jesus Christ. To him be glory both now and to [the] the day of [the] age. Amen" (II Peter 3:18).

The word "glory" (Greek *doxa*—Hebrew *kābōd*) primarily means "weight" in Hebrew. Since a man of substance and wealth would have the external appearance of a man weighted down with wealth, his wealth demanded respect and honor from his contemporaries, and this position of respect was called glory. "Glory," then, included the meanings of weight, substance, wealth, power, splendor, dignity and good reputation, such attributes as would be given a king or a messiah. This glory was to be his "for the ages of the ages," usually rendered "forever and ever." An age was a period of time, temporally; it usually meant a generation or a jubilee —about fifty years—but ages changed whenever administrations or fortunes changed, so they were not all the same length. A standard greeting for kings in antiquity was "O King, live for ages" (Dan 2:4; 3:9; 5:10; 6:6–21), wishing that the king would live more than the expected time of one generation.[13] This was the same kind of hyperbolic prayer which prayed that Jesus, as the established king, be given "glory" that would continue one generation after the other, or "for the ages of the ages."

"Amen" was a term used in taking oaths to affirm that the conditions were accepted or the things said were true (Num 5:16–22). When a leader of the congregation offered a prayer to which members agreed, they responded with, "Amen!" Rabbis said when the leader was an Israelite (i.e., a Jew), the congregation should say "Amen" after each benediction, but if he was

[13] CC, pp. 15–18.

a Samaritan, they must wait until the whole benediction was completed to be sure he did not add something that would be contrary to the faith of Jews (Ber. 8:8). Paul criticized those who prayed in the Spirit (i.e., in "tongues"), because those who were not able to understand the speech would not know when to say the "Amen" for the prayer (I Cor 14:16). The prayer might be one that was a standard part of the liturgy; the "Amen" was the worshipers' personal approval of the request.

Summary.—The benediction included in these verses was probably a standard liturgical expression. It was well formulated, ascribing to God attributes from the Old Testament that were related to his deliverance of Israel from Egypt and Babylon. To these acts of deliverance was added the deliverance brought about through the blood of Jesus who instituted the new covenant. The prayer was that this God who had delivered Israel in the past would now enable the readers to do his will.

Parting postscript

22. "The word of exhortation" (*tēs parakleseōs*) which the final editor employed to "exhort" (*parakalō*) his "brothers" was probably the main document (1:1 – 12:29), to which he added "a few [words]" (*dia bracheōn*) of his own. These included such poetic exhortations as 13:1, 3, 4a and 5a, a confession of faith (13:8), an anti-Jerusalem midrash (13:10–16), and a benediction (13:20–21). To these items he added his own exhortations, interpretations, expansions, and connecting sentences to complete chapter thirteen. Heb 13:22 seems to be a statement recommending Heb 1:1 – 12:29 plus the items collected in chapter thirteen to the readers. It is much like the recommendation given in Rev 22:6–7, urging the readers to consider seriously the document included in Rev 4:1 – 22:5: "These words are faithful and true. . . . Blessed is he who keeps the words of the prophecy of this book." It is not likely that the same author who had earlier said his message on one point alone was "extensive" (5:11) should later refer to the entire document as brief. The items added in chapter thirteen are "few" as the author says, and it seems reasonable to believe that it was to these that his reference was made. Stuart asked many years ago, "But how . . . could Paul say this, when this epistle is longer than any one of his, that to the Romans, and the first to the Corinthians, excepted?"[14] Even if Paul is not considered the author, it does not seem reasonable for any one author to write of the whole message "To the Hebrews" as if it were only something briefly said. Westcott excused the reference by saying, ". . . that is, relatively to the vastness of the subject," but even that is not valid, because the author covered the material very thoroughly, frequently repeating for effectiveness.[15] Moffatt said the author was probably referring to his brief words rather apologetically, realizing

[14] Stuart, pp. 309–10.
[15] Westcott, p. 451.

that they were really quite extensive and might have aroused some resentment because of the length of the message. Then, justifying the author from the opposite direction, Moffatt said, "*Pros Hebraious* may be read aloud easily in one hour."[16] Both of these arguments assumed that the comment was made by the author himself, even though Moffatt had earlier said the main document ended with 12:29![17] Bruce followed Moffatt basically, also reversing the implications of the data that puzzled Stuart, saying that the document was not so long as Romans or I Corinthians, and concluded, "There is no need to suppose that the 'word of exhortation' might be confined to the concluding admonitions of Ch. 13:1–19; they are so brief that no writer would think it necessary to ask his readers to bear with them."[18] Michel believed the statement was made as an indication that the author had actually and deliberately limited himself, even though the document was long.[19] In dealing with indefinite matters such as these, complete agreement is seldom reached, but the simplest and most obvious interpretation is to assume that chapter thirteen was written by a different author from the first twelve chapters and that the final author's reference to brevity was accurately made to describe his own additions.

23–24. The personal reference to Timothy and the author's proposed visit and greeting were added to give this the appearance of a Pauline letter, even though the theology and style of Heb 1:1 – 12:29 are certainly not Pauline. The "leaders and all the saints" of the community may or may not have been the same people. The "leaders" were among the ones with whom the readers were exhorted to comply (13:7, 17). "The saints" originally referred to the holy ones who were separated from defiled people, according to levitical purity rules to maintain levitical cleanliness. These were the soldiers, separated from women and children while at war to keep the camp holy, or the priests, who kept themselves free from defilement to minister at the tent of meeting or the temple. After the temple was destroyed, and there was no longer a specific place that was kept holy for the Lord to dwell, the hearth was substituted for the altar, and the believers were substituted for the priests. The priesthood of all believers took place when laymen undertook the responsibility of keeping themselves as levitically pure as priests and their homes as free from defilement as the temple. These believers, then, were also "saints." By New Testament times, this term evidently was extended in meaning in some circles to include all believers, even if they did not keep all the levitical rules (Rom 1:7; I Cor 1:2). It is not clear in 13:24 what limitations were required in the editor's definition.

"Italy" may have been the residence of the final editor as well as that of the committee that compiled the canon, but it says nothing about the place

[16] Moffatt, p. 244.

[17] Moffatt, pp. 224, 244–45, was inconsistent. He also held (pp. xxvii–xxx) that the whole document was written by one author.

[18] Bruce, p. 413

[19] Michel, p. 366.

of origin of 1:1 – 12:29. The location may have been fabricated to give the letter the appearance of originality.

25. The prayer for "grace" was frequently used in complimentary closes and is a prayer needed by all authors, editors, and readers. Amen.

Summary.—John Knox has made an impressive case for believing that Marcion's canon was the first New Testament canon and that it forced other Christians to establish a canon that was not Marcion's and to begin to establish an orthodoxy among all the various Christian beliefs held up to that time.[20] Marcion was such a strong Christian leader in the second century that he could not be ignored. Anti-Marcionites had two alternatives if they were unwilling to accept Marcion's canon: (a) They could have declared his works heretical and opposed their use in churches. This would not have been very successful, and it would have opposed teachings preserved in Paul's ten letters and the Gospel according to Luke that most Christians treasured. (b) The second alternative seems to have been the one employed: they followed Marcion's canon as a basis, but neutralized it by extending it in size.

Marcion's canon contained the writings of the apostle Paul, which were all letters, and the Gospel of Luke. This set a strange pattern of literary forms to follow, but the later church seems to have followed it. It added to the Gospel of Luke three other gospels, and to the epistles of the apostle Paul other epistles of other apostles, with the Acts of the Apostles as a unifying factor. In this way the committee on canon could present a more balanced representation of Christian views and literature, but it is not likely that all of the best literature had been composed in gospel and epistle form. Therefore, the committee had to adapt otherwise useful and acceptable writings to the required literary form. Since the church lacked unity, there may have been more than one committee on canon. It is certain that some books, like Hebrews, were late in being admitted by some churches. Knox believes that Luke was expanded from Marcion's document to include some pro-Jewish material Marcion would have opposed. The Fourth Gospel probably originated as a historical prophecy that pictured John the Baptist and Jesus as the new Elijah and Elisha, but was edited so as to abbreviate the document and add an introduction and conclusion to make it appear to be the same kind of document as the Synoptic Gospels.[21] Some documents which were needed to represent various branches of Christianity may have been composed in the form of letters at the time the canon was being decided. Other important literature, like confessions of faith and brief catechisms, may have been added to some portions of letters that had been composed previously. Other more extensive documents that were complete units and too large to be included

[20] J. Knox, *Marcion and the New Testament,* Chicago, 1942.

[21] "The Samaritan Origin of the Gospel of John," in *Religions in Antiquity,* pp. 149–75.

as only a part of another document were given introductions and conclusions to make them have the forms of letters. "To the Hebrews" and the Epistle of James originally seem to have been examples of a type of Christian wisdom literature and were used as such by Clement of Alexandria and Irenaeus. To James was added an introduction (James 1:1), and to Hebrews was added this conclusion, to make both documents appear to be letters and thus qualify for the canon. The introduction to Hebrews was so integral to the entire message (1:1 – 12:29) that it would have been impossible to replace it with an epistolary salutation or to have a separate salutation prefixed to the present introduction without seeming very awkward and artificial. Therefore the best alternative was to add a complimentary closing and let the introduction stand.

The homily section of Hebrews 1 – 12 was used at the end of the first century by Clement of Rome, but not included in the Muratorian list at the end of the second century. The church at Rome did not accept it as Pauline as late as the fourth century. Either chapter thirteen was added very late as the necessary requirement for inclusion in the canon, or the person who added it to the homily with the "Pauline" conclusion did not at first succeed in convincing all of the churches of its genuineness. Because the author was not an eye witness of Jesus (2:3) the document could not have been accepted as apostolic from any apostle other than Paul.

All attempts to reconstruct the literary forms of New Testament documents before the formation of the canon are necessarily conjectural. The evidence is not sufficient to know precisely what the sources were or how they were changed to fit the canon. Scholars have recognized for many years, however, that the epistolary character of some New Testament documents, like Hebrews, was artificial and forced. The literary forms now in the New Testament canon seem to be a strange basis for a religious literary canon. Religious literature coming from a Jewish sect might be expected to consist of psalms, laws, history, wisdom literature and prophecy. The fact that the canon that was accepted was quite different from normal expectations requires some explanation, such as the Marcion movement which Knox has proposed.

Marcion had evidently been a strong Pauline Christian leader for many years before the Bar Cochba Revolt of A.D. 132–35. It was probably the bloody militarism of that revolt that aroused Marcion's anti-Jewish convictions. He held that the Christian God was a God of love and not a God of war, as the Jewish God was. All Jewish literature, including the Old Testament, should be dismissed as Jewish and a new canon established for Christians that had none of that Jewish militarism. Although Marcion gathered a strong following, he did not represent all Christendom at that time. The pro-Jewish forces in Christianity were strong enough in Rome, at least, to force his excommunication in A.D. 144, but the very forces that excommunicated Marcion were obligated to displace his canon or assimilate it into a larger canon that included such Jewish documents as Matthew, James, and Hebrews, as well as such military, holy-war prophecies as the Book of Revelation. Sometime in the process of forming that canon, a member of the committee may either have added only this Pauline postscript to Hebrews or have created the entire thirteenth chapter, using some undatable poetry and confessions of faith that had already been composed as well as some pre-A.D. 70 doctrinal material (10–16) and exhortations, to which he added a few comments of his own plus an epistolary conclusion.

This conjectural reconstruction of chapter thirteen's formation may not be accurate, but it is not possible to deal in certainties with literary problems such as these. If this was not done by an unknown committee member, it was done by some other churchman who wanted the document included in the canon.

CONCLUSIONS

Kind of document

The first twelve chapters of Hebrews constitute a complete homiletical midrash, similar to those in Pesikta de Rav Kahana. It seems originally to have been independent of chapter 13, which will be considered separately. This unit begins and ends like a sermon rather than a letter and will be considered as a homily here rather than a letter.

Basic message

"How to acquire the fulfillment of the promise God made with Abraham" is the topic which held the interest of the author of the first twelve chapters of Hebrews. God promised Abraham the land of Palestine, although he did not intend for Abraham to receive it during his own lifetime. It was intended for Abraham's posterity. Consequently the patriarchs all dwelt in the land of the promise as strangers. God intended to fulfill his promise to the generation of Moses in Egypt, and he announced to those Hebrews the good news that their captivity was over. They could at that time leave Egypt under the leadership of Moses and take possession of the land of Canaan. Thus motivated, the exodus generation left Egypt and reached the border of the land. Instead of entering the land, the leaders sent spies to see what probabilities there were for success in their venture. All of the spies except Caleb and Joshua reported that it would be impossible for the Hebrews to take the land, so that generation disobeyed God and refused to enter. This disobedience was the way they tested God. God, in turn, withheld the promise. Under oath, he swore that all of the adult males except Joshua and Caleb would die in the wilderness and never see the good land the Lord had promised to give them.

Later Joshua led the Israelites into Canaan, but the author did not consider that to be a fulfillment of the promise, because God spoke through David in Ps 95 as if the "rest" had not been received. David wished that people in his day might receive it. If the promise were received it could never be taken away. (Gen R. 65:23; Exod R. 15:21,

31; 50:5; Rashi and Eben Ezra on Dan 7:11–18; Yalqut Shimoni Dan 7–8, 513c–d). Since Israel had never had secure and lasting possession of the land, it was clear that the promise of God was still pending.

The good news that had been given to Israel through Moses had again been renewed through Jesus, who, through his sacrificial offering of himself, prepared a new way whereby the new Israel could be recipients of a new covenant and the fulfillment of the old promise that had never been achieved. Like Moses before him, Jesus had done all that was necessary to make the fulfillment of the promises available. The Christians who were contemporary with the author were obligated to learn an important lesson from history: The exodus generation had been disobedient. Therefore the author urgently exhorted his recipients to be faithful so that the precious reward might not be missed again.

The author outlined his message in a well-structured manner, dealing first with one topic and then the next, as is evident from the general outline. Within this outline he transposed a series of types and antitypes, and, in a typically midrashic manner, he effectively repeated themes that were especially important to him. Some examples of these are as follows:

1. The Origin of the Ages

a) "In the last of these days he has spoken to us through a Son, . . . through whom he also made the ages" (1:2).

b) "By faith we consider the ages to have been put in order by [the] word of God" (11:3).

2. Exaltation

a) "When he had made a purification for [his] sins, sat down at the right hand of the Majesty in exaltation" (1:3).

b) "Since, then, we have a great high priest [who] has gone through the heavens, Jesus the Son of God, let us hold fast the confession" (4:14).

c) "For such a one also became high priest for us,
holy, guileless, undefiled,
separated from sinners,
and become higher than the heavens" (7:26).

d) "Most important of the things said [is that] we have such a high priest [as this] who sat down at the right hand of the throne of Majesty in the heavens" (8:1).

3. High Priest

a) ". . . so that he might become a merciful and faithful high priest [regarding] divine services" (2:17).
b) "Direct [your] attention to Jesus, the apostle and high priest of our confession, [who] was faithful to the one who made him" (3:1–2).
c) "Since, then, we have a great high priest [who] has gone through the heavens, Jesus the Son of God, let us hold fast the confession. For we do not have a high priest [who is] unable to sympathize with our weaknesses" (4:14–15).
d) ". . . where Jesus entered [as] a forerunner in our behalf, since he is a high priest for the age according to the order of Melchizedek" (6:20).
e) "For such a one also became high priest for us,
holy, guileless, undefiled,
separated from sinners,
and become higher than the heavens" (7:26).
f) "We have such a high priest [as this] who sat down at the right hand of the throne of Majesty in the heavens" (8:1).
g) "But Christ, having become a high priest of the good things that have happened, . . ." (9:11).

4. Holding Fast

a) ". . . if we hold fast the confidence and boasting of hope" (3:6).
b) ". . . if indeed we hold fast the initial doctrine until the end" (3:14).
c) "Let us hold fast unmoved the confession of hope" (10:23).

5. The Promises

a) "The promise of entering into his rest is left [unfulfilled]" (4:1).
b) ". . . so that you may not become dull, but [rather] imitators of those who inherit the promises through faith and long suffering" (6:12).
c) "And thus, after he had suffered patiently, [Abraham] received the promise" (6:15).
d) "So when God wanted very much to show the heirs of the promise the unchangeableness of his will, he imposed an oath [on himself]" (6:17).
e) ". . . as he is also a mediator of a better covenant, which has been made into law on the basis of better promises" (8:6).
f) "And, because of this, he is [the] mediator of a new covenant,

so that, . . . those who are called might receive the promise of the eternal inheritance" (9:15).

g) "For you must have endurance so that, after you have done the will of God, you may obtain the promise" (10:36).

h) "By faith, he dwelt in the land of the promise as a stranger, living in tents with Isaac and Jacob, joint heirs of the same promise" (11:9).

i) "According to faith these all died, not having acquired the promises" (11:13).

j) "By faith Abraham offered Isaac, being tested,
and the one who received the promises offered [his] only one" (11:17).

k) "Now these all, attested through faith, did not acquire the promise, since God had foreseen something better concerning us, so that without us, they might not be perfected" (11:39–40).

It is evident from the above quotations that the author has woven and interwoven his major emphases so that they cannot be completely separated from one another. The same is true of the types and antitypes.

Typologies

Revelation. The author began his homily by setting forth the various ways God had spoken to the fathers as a type for which his revelation through the Son was an antitype. When God spoke to Noah (11:7), Abraham (11:8–19), Moses (11:23–29), and Rahab (11:31), he asked them to act in ways that seemed unreasonable. Nonetheless, when they obeyed at great personal cost, their faith was rewarded. In the same way, Jesus, the Son, had been asked to offer himself as an atonement to enable the seed of Abraham to receive the necessary salvation. Like the faithful fathers, Jesus obeyed. This type of perfect, unquestioning obedience at any cost was the model that Christians of the author's day were expected to imitate.

The Gospel. The exodus opportunity for the Hebrews in Egypt was a type for which that available to the recipients of the document called "To the Hebrews" was the antitype. Both received the good news that the promise given to Abraham could be fulfilled for them. Both were placed in situations where the achievement seemed incredible. In both cases, success depended upon the faith of the covenanters and their ability to hold fast to their confession and never give up hope that God would fulfill his promises and give the children of Abraham the land promised to Abraham. Both were tempted to doubt God's ability to fulfill his promises. Of the exodus generation, only Caleb and Joshua were confident and refused to give up hope. The rest of the Hebrews perished in the wilderness. The author urged his readers to learn from the exodus generation so that they might be different from it in the ways necessary for success.

The high priesthood. The levitical priesthood was a type for which Melchizedek, and consequently Jesus who belonged to his order, was the antitype.[1] The levitical high priest was sympathetic (5:2), appointed by law (5:1; 7:28) to offer gifts and sacrifices on earth (8:3) of bulls and goats (9:12, 19–22) and to sprinkle blood from them every year (9:25–26) or every day (10:11–12). The priest offered a gift to cleanse his own sin (5:3; 7:27), but he was unable to cleanse the conscience, remove sins, or perfect anything (9:7, 25; 10:1–4). The Levites received tithes (7:5) and the people were governed by the Levites (7:11). The high priest entered the holy of holies (9:7). Jesus, the antitype, was an apostle and high priest who could be sympathetic because he had been tempted, but since he had been cleansed (1:3), he was without sin (4:14–15). He was appointed by God (7:28), ministered in a greater and more perfect tent not made with hands, in the heavens (9:11). He entered the holy of holies as a forerunner (6:19–20). Melchizedek received tithes (7:5–10) even from the Levites by extension. Jesus offered himself as the perfect sacrifice once, pouring out his own blood to cleanse, sanctify, and perfect himself and the people (7:26–27; 9:14, 23, 26; 10:14). He cleansed not only earthly, but even heavenly, things (9:23) since he had gone through the heavens (4:14). As the perfect priest, he was holy, undefiled, separated from sinners (7:26). His purpose was the same as that of the levitical priesthood. He belonged to the same type, but he succeeded where they had failed. Therefore he was a superior antitype for their inferior type.

The covenant. The first covenant was renewed in the wilderness with the sprinkling of the blood of bulls and goats, whose deaths made the covenant valid (9:16–22). Christ was the mediator for the new covenant (9:15). The new covenant was confirmed by the blood of Christ, whose death made the covenant valid and whose blood redeems transgressions against the old covenant (9:15). Because of the covenant that Jesus made and his death that made it valid, those who are called may receive the inheritance (9:15). The antitype is superior to the type.

The tent. The earthly antitype tent was at Jerusalem. It was made with hands. There goats and bulls were offered and ashes of the red

[1] Williamson, p. 532, correctly says Melchizedek was a type of Christ for the author. See also p. 534.

heifer were sprinkled (9:13). The high priest entered this tent once a year with the blood of another (9:25), but this tent was only a model of the heavenly tent which was its true archetype, not made with hands (9:11). Christ entered this true tent where heavenly things were cleansed by better sacrifices (9:22–24). Christ appeared at the end of the age to cleanse sins with his own blood which was offered as a blameless sacrifice (9:14, 26).

There are more types and antitypes than these in the homily, because there is an overtone of comparison that implies both a typology and an *a fortiori* relationship between the things related to the old covenant and the new. The comparison of the Hebrews in the wilderness with the Hebrews to whom his homily was addressed was so central to the message that the author of this document may have originally given the sermon that title. Its title may have been "The Hebrews" before this homily was associated with a collection of letters, but that is only an imaginative suggestion.

Christian ethics

The kind of Christian behavior approved by the author is made evident both from the positive and the negative examples he gave and from the exhortations he supplied. The negative examples include such foolish people as Esau who lightly gave up his inheritance and later suffered the unalterable consequences (12:16–17) and the disobedient exodus generation that received the good news, had the opportunity to receive the promised rest, could have been the recipients of the inheritance promised to Abraham, but doubted God's ability and willingness (3:16–19; 4:6). They did not hold fast to their confession. They gave up their confidence in hope.

Examples of those who were approved were people of the opposite attributes. They took advantage of the first opportunity given them to obey God's command. They never wavered but did exactly as God ordered, without losing hope. Noah built an ark to save his family, when there was no sign of rain in sight (11:7); Abraham left his native land without knowing where he was going; he trusted God that he would become the father of a numerous posterity when he and Sarah were too old to have children; he was prepared to offer Isaac as a sacrifice at the commandment of God (11:8–19). At God's direction, Moses left a position of comfort, wealth, prestige, and power to lead the Israelites out of Egypt toward the promised land (11:23–29). At her first chance, Rahab betrayed her countrymen to destruction to become identified with the recipients of the promise. Like these faithful ones was also Jesus, who gave up the joy that was his to endure the cross necessary for the salvation of the covenanters (12:2). The emphasis on Jesus, God's Son, as an offering may have been intended to relate God's offering of his Son to Abraham's willingness to offer his son Isaac.

The author was not interested in providing salvation for others. He thought Rahab (and probably Jacob) was to be admired for her skill in becoming an heiress when she did not deserve the inheritance from the standpoint of birth. The author admired Noah for saving his own family. He had no sympathy for the misfortunes of those destroyed by the flood, for Esau's misfortune, for the Egyptians killed at the Reed Sea, or for the citizens of Jericho who were destroyed by the invading Israelites. His ethics were limited to his concern for the sons of Abraham and the behavior required for them to achieve the promises given to Abraham.

The ethics required were strict obedience, unwavering faith, and consistent hope. Like the heroes of Old Testament times were the martyrs who resisted Antiochus Epiphanes, endured all kinds of torture and death, but refused to give up their faith, religious practices, or hope in a resurrection on the promised land (11:32–39).

Since the author believed these were the ethics God required, he urged the readers to be very careful lest they fall into any kind of sin, give up love, or forsake the faith. They must not be indolent or careless. The group could tolerate no unbelief (3:12), "hardening" (3:13), falling behind (4:1), dullness (4:11; 6:12), deliberate sin (10:26), or avoidance of God's command (12:25).[2] Every single member of the group was required to be rigidly disciplined to avoid any misdemeanor. Positively, they were also urged to hold fast to their confession or doctrine to the end (3:14; 10:23), approach the throne of grace with boldness (4:16), press on to maturity in faith (6:1), show forth love, minister to the saints (6:9–12), encourage one another and maintain regular attendance in community gatherings (10:24–25), be willing to face insult, sacrifice, and suffering for the faith (10:32–36), and accept discipline gladly (12:5–11). They were obliged to strive for ritual purity for the whole community and maintain peace with all (12:14–15).

The goal of all Christian ethics, according to the author of Hebrews, was to please God so that he would bless the sons of Abraham with the fulfillment of his promise to grant them rest on the promised land. The faithful heroes of the past had acted in the way that would bring

[2] The author's list of prohibitions deals with more than just apostasy, as Williamson, pp. 250–51, 261, and others say.

about that event while the unfaithful were negligent of their opportunities and responsibilities in relationship to the covenant.

The significance of Jesus

Jesus was important to the author of Hebrews, not primarily for the things he said and did during his lifetime, but for the offering he made which renewed the possibility of receiving the promise. It was Jesus who first announced salvation (2:3). Jesus, according to the author, arose from Judah, but the author may not have received that information from local tradition about the historical Jesus at all. Since Jesus was accepted as the Messiah, and the prophecy stated that from Judah would come the Messiah (Gen 49:9–10; see also the targumim), this information may have come from his use of scripture. Since Jesus was identified with Melchizedek, whose residence was in Jerusalem according to Jewish tradition, the author may also have deduced Jesus' Judaic origin from that tradition (7:14). The apparent report of Jesus' agony in the Garden of Gethsemane could be the result of the exegesis of LXX Ps 114 without any knowledge of the prayer in Gethsemane as recorded in the gospels (5:7–10). The author mentioned only once the cross which Jesus accepted instead of the joy that could have been his (12:2). Hebrews is different from the letters of Paul in that the cross itself had little theological significance, and no mention was made of the resurrection. It was only when Jesus' death was reinterpreted in terms of an atonement offering that it captured the attention of the author of Hebrews. The one mention of the cross was given only as an example similar to that of Moses, who was reported to have accepted disgrace instead of the position of wealth available to him (11:24–25).

For the author's doctrine, it was important that Jesus be understood as a high priest so that his sacrifice could be understood as an atonement offering. Since Jesus was not from the priestly line of Aaron, the author attributed the office of high priest to him on the basis of Ps 110 (5:10). As a priest of the confession (3:1) he became forerunner and pioneer (2:10; 6:19–20), having gone through the veil as the high priest did when he entered the holy of holies. As a priest he offered blood, but not that of bulls and goats. He offered his own blood in the greater and more perfect tent (9:11–12). This offering was made only once, but as a once-for-all sacrifice it successfully cleansed the consciences of the believers (9:14) who thereby became sanctified and perfected (10:10–14). Jesus was a sympathetic high priest who was tempted and learned obedience through the things he suffered. It was in this way that he was perfected and made sinless, since his offering was the perfect gift to atone for sins (4:15; 5:8–9). Like other offerings that went up to God in the heavens, Jesus, the perfect sacrifice, also went through the heavens to God (4:14), and by his ascension was seated on the right hand of God as the Son of God (1:3, 13; 4:14; 5:8; 8:1; 10:12; 12:2). His self-offering not only opened the heavens to him, but it also provided a cleansing for his sins so that he could be sinless (1:3; 4:15), holy, undefiled, and separated from sinners (7:26–27). Although he claimed the sons of Abraham as his brothers (2:10–18), he was without any family lineage or dynastic succession (7:3). He was the ideal monk who had denied his family to join a brotherhood. Since he was celibate, he would have no family to succeed him. That meant to the author that he himself remained forever (7:3), never to be replaced by other mortals the way levitical priests were (7:8).

As a high priest, Jesus successfully atoned for his own sins and those of the people. His self-offering caused his ascension to the right hand of God where he was installed as Son. As Son he received all the attributes of an ideal king of Israel. He was to rule over all his enemies, who would become as a footstool for his feet (1:13; 2:7–9). His willingness to give up his life for his religion made him a martyr, like one of the faithful who resisted the Greeks in the Maccabean Revolt. Like the Hasmoneans, he filled the role both of high priest and of royal leader for his people. The author reached these conclusions by his clever use of scripture. Although other tradition classifies Jesus as a son of David who had been teamed with John the Baptist, a son of Aaron, in accordance with the two-messiah expectation (Luke 1:5–13, 26–33) the author of Hebrews made no mention of Jesus as a son of David.[3] Messiahship based on the son of David would rule out the possibility of Jesus as a high priest as well as a king. Although the gospels relate Jesus' death with his crucifixion near the Passover feast, the author of Hebrews interpreted his death in terms of an offering given by himself as the apostle and high priest of our confession on the Day of Atonement. It was the death of Jesus that was important to the author. Interpreted as an atonement offering, his death could justify the claim that he was a true martyr, whose sins had been cleansed, leaving him sinless, holy, undefiled, perfect, and sanctified. Since his ascension was interpreted as an atonement offering going up to heaven to God, the author reasoned that he was seated at the right hand of God and should be called God's Son on the basis of Ps 110. This is ingenious exegesis in accordance with acceptable rab-

[3] W. R. Farmer, "John the Baptist," IDB, II, 959–62.

binic use of scripture, but the entire picture provides only slight information, indirectly deduced, about the life, activity, and teaching of the historical Jesus.

The original readers

The original hearers or readers of this homily were not among those who had seen and heard Jesus themselves, but the salvation which Jesus announced had been confirmed to them by those who had actually heard his voice (2:3). Although this may mean that the original hearers had written down that which they had heard so that it was confirmed for all generations, it seems more likely to mean that the readers were close enough in time and space to have heard the testimony of the original eye and ear witnesses of Jesus and his message. This homily was prepared for certain sons of Abraham (2:11, 16) who had begun training in the Christian faith. They were neither Samaritans nor Sadducees, because they accepted the Psalms and prophetic books as inspired scripture. They had already been enlightened (6:4), which means they had received the training necessary for baptism. They had tasted the heavenly gift (6:4), which might mean they had been admitted to the common meal. They had become sharers of the Holy Spirit, suggesting that they participated in the ceremony whereby others laid their hands upon them (6:5); and they had tasted the good word of God and the miracles of the coming age (6:5), assuring them that the promises were about to be fulfilled. They had apparently expected the promises to have been completely fulfilled before this document was written, because some were leaving the faith and needed the strong warning of the author to enable them to hold fast to the confession to the end (3:12; 4:1, 11, 14; 6:6–8, 11; 10:23, 35–36; 12:1, 3). In the early days of their faith, they had been courageous, suffering physical torture and disgrace from outsiders. They may have also had their goods confiscated by outsiders. They boldly called on prisoners, sharing with them their embarrassment and probably their provisions (10:32–34), but they had not yet resisted to the blood, perhaps meaning that no one of them had received the death penalty for his faith (12:4). They had been in training long enough to have been teachers, but the author chided them because they seemed to have lost interest and had not moved ahead as rapidly as they should have (5:11–14). Some of them were neglecting attendance at congregational gatherings (10:25). Their earlier training involved doctrines familiar to Judaism: repentance, faith in God, teachings about ablutions, laying on of hands, resurrection of the dead, and the judgment at the end of the age (6:1–2).

There are some indications that the original readers belonged to a very strict, communal, monastic sect. They were called "brothers" and "beloved," terms not restricted to brotherhoods, but regularly used by them (6:10, 19). They had shown their brotherly love by ministering to the saints, as was customary among brotherhoods. The joy they experienced when their goods were confiscated suggests that they may have been confiscated with their own approval by the communal order, rather than by outsiders. The custom of forfeiting all possessions by initiates when they were fully admitted to the sect was usual among groups like the Essenes whose goods were shared communally (10:34). Recipients of Hebrews were urged to strive for sanctification, to go on to perfection (6:1; 12:14). This communal sharing was not usually called "confiscating" (*harpagēn*) (Heb 10:34), but there were negative feelings about it. Some resisted it and falsified the extent of their possessions (1QS 6:24–25; Acts 5:1–11). They were under strict legal discipline, like that of monastic brotherhoods. Not one of the members dared to fall behind in the disciplines necessary to receive the grace of God; absolutely no ritual defilement was allowed (12:15). It is true that terms like "perfection," "brothers," "beloved," and "sanctification" were also used by less rigorous Christian groups with less strict meanings than were applied by monastic groups, but the fact that all of these were used together with admonitions about brotherly love, and since approval was given for the joy that came when goods were confiscated —all fit together with the strict discipline demanded of this group that would be expected of a monastic order.

The recipients had been reminded that they had come to Zion (*proselēlythate Siōn*), the city of the living God, heavenly Jerusalem (12:22). Unless this be understood in some metaphorical sense, as has been frequently done, it would be normal to presume that the readers were still in Jerusalem when they had access to this document. They had arrived at Jerusalem too late to have heard Jesus personally, but in Jerusalem they and the author could receive the message of salvation secondhand from those who heard it from Jesus himself (2:3). Like Abraham of old, these faithful Zionists had left their homeland to come to the promised land. They had expected the promise made to Abraham to be fulfilled in their day. This raises the question, "When did these migrants come to Jerusalem?"

Date and place of origin

In response to the oath that God took prohibiting the Israelites from entering into the Lord's rest (Ps 95:11), rabbis said they would not enter that particular rest but that they would enter another rest, meaning the promised land, at a different time under different conditions. R. Levi, in the name of the Bar Qappara (third century A.D.), compared the situation to a king who, in his anger, said his son could never enter his palace with him. After his anger subsided, the king tore down the palace, rebuilt it, and then brought his son into it with him. In this way he kept his oath and still allowed his son to enter into the palace. In the same way, rabbis believed God would rebuild Israel and readmit the sons of Abraham in the messianic age (Lev R. 32:2). The nature of the analogy reflects a composition after the destruction of Jerusalem in A.D. 70. The rabbis expected the land to be restored and "rest" to be allowed, but the destruction had already taken place and the analogy necessarily reflected it. The author of Hebrews also expected God's people to enter into the rest, in spite of the oath in Ps 95:11, but he had no need to consider a destruction of the temple, city, or land to prevent this oath from admitting the promise of Abraham to be fulfilled. In fact there is nothing at all in the homily "To the Hebrews" (chs. 1–12) to require a post-A.D. 70 composition. The author's reference to the sacrifices that the priests were then making presumes the existence and function of the priests in the temple (9:6–9; 10:1–2).[4] To presume that the author wrote after A.D. 70 to meet the needs of Christians without a temple *as if* he had written before the fall seems unjustified. There is a long history of apocalyptic literature composed pseudonymously *as if* it had been written many years earlier, but the homily "To the Hebrews" is neither pseudonymous nor apocalyptic, nor are there any mistakes in the document that betray any intention of giving the impression that the document had been written earlier than it really had. Since this is the case, it is fair to accept as much of the message as possible on the basis that the author meant what he said. This allows the following information to be considered: (1) The author referred to the death of Jesus which occurred during the reign of Pontius Pilate (A.D. 26–36). The sermon could not have been written before then. (2) The priests were still functioning in the temple. That would be true only until the destruction of the temple in A.D. 70, so the homily must have been written before then. (3) The readers themselves were in Jerusalem, the city of the living God.

For hundreds of years Jerusalem has been a place where pilgrims and migrants have gathered, particularly at times when they expected the Messiah to appear and restore the kingdom to Israel (see Pss

[4] Scholars who have spiritualized many parts of Hebrews have held that the tents referred to in Hebrews had nothing to do with the temple in Jerusalem. A comparison of Hebrews with Philo and Josephus, however, shows that there were two tents that were considered separate, connected parts of the temple in Jerusalem (see COMMENT at the end of ch. 9).

42:4; 68:35; 84:1–7; 122:1–7).[5] Whenever Jews believed that the signs of the times were just right for God to gather the Jews from the Diaspora and return them to the homeland, some of the most pious and sincere were willing to give up their positions, sell their land, and move to Jerusalem. In order to stimulate these movements rabbis said those who died outside of Palestine would not live again (Keth. 111a, b) or would experience a twofold death (Gen R. 96:5), whereas the dead of the land of Israel would be the first to rise in the days of the Messiah (Gen R. 96:5; Exod R. 32:2). The concern the author of Hebrews had shown for the promised land and the heavenly city would have been attractive to such Jewish idealists. The merit which the author placed on Abraham's willingness to leave his homeland in search of a city that had foundations would have been shared by migrant sons of Abraham who had done the same. If they had been attracted by the Christian message to believe that Jesus provided the merits needed for salvation and moved to Jerusalem, they might afterwards have become discouraged by the delay and begun to wonder if their hopes had been mistaken.

"But you have approached [*proselēlythate*] Mount Zion," the author said to these migrants, "[the] city of [the] living God, heavenly Jerusalem, . . . a national assembly, a church of first-born [people]" (12:22–23). Since Israel was called the first-born, and Paul observed that the gospel came to the Jew first and also to the Greek (Rom 1:16), the "church of first-born [people]" was probably the name given to the Jewish Christian church at Jerusalem. Zion was the capital city of the promised land. It was the city which had the foundations. It was the heavenly city in the heavenly fatherland which was the goal of Abraham's migration. In the author's judgment, it was the ultimate goal of all sons of Abraham.

The author not only related the migration of the readers to the migration of Abraham, but also their opportunity to that of the exodus generation which wandered forty years after its arrival at the border of the promised land. Had as many as forty years elapsed since the sacrifice of Jesus, he might have been expected to mention that fact and interpret his analogies accordingly. The length of time that had elapsed since Jesus' death is not given in any specific way. The readers had been enlightened, which meant they had undergone a short period of training

[5] Just before going to press, R. Jewett's "Pilgrimage in the Bible: From Ur to the City Which is to Come," in the *1971 Ministers' Seminar, Morningside College*, pp. 96–116, was brought to my attention. Jewett traced the wanderings of the Hebrews, beginning with Abraham, and, interestingly, concluding with the homily "To the Hebrews." He thought of Heb 12 in terms of a pilgrimage like those taken to Jerusalem, although he thought of this as an existential Christian pilgrimage rather than a real migration to Zion.

before baptism. With the Essenes this period lasted one year. Some of the group were losing faith and needed the author to assure them that the end was very near (10:25), but he did not have to justify the delay in terms of thousands of years as II Peter (3:8–9) did. The extremely strict behavior expected of the readers seems like a possible "interim ethic" that had not yet made modifications to deal with normal living.

Without insisting on the historicity of the description of the Pentecost experience in Acts, it is reasonable to presume that it was written with the intention of being accepted as true. The gathering of Jews at Jerusalem from many parts of diaspora was customary during times of religious festivals. The necessity of establishing an emergency group economy to meet the material needs of pilgrims also made sense to those acquainted with pilgrimages and messianic beliefs (Acts 4:32; 6:7). During the first century messianic expectations were high, and many Jews were prepared to put their faith into action. Messianic pretenders had no difficulty luring Jews to the wilderness, promising that there God would show them signs of deliverance. One Egyptian Jew led thirty thousand followers through the wilderness on the way to the Mount of Olives (*Wars* II. 258–63; *Ant.* XX. 168–72). Christians were warned against such enticements (Matt 24:25), but they were probably as credulous as other Jews of that time and place. Later Christians, who believed the advent of Christ was imminent, broke family ties, dissolved marriages, and observed severe rules of asceticism. In the days of Hippolytus (third century A.D.), there was a bishop of Pontus, Asia Minor, who indicated a particular year when the end would come. His people believed him so implicitly that they sold their cattle and left their fields uncultivated to prepare for that great day. In the third century a prophetess in Cappadocia started a large group of pilgrims on the way to Jerusalem (Hippolytus *In Daniel* 4:18; Cyprian, *Epistle* lxxv 10). At periods when their calculations seemed right for the Messiah to come, later rabbis advised Jews not to buy a field in Palestine worth a thousand dinars for even one dinar, because during that very year the Messiah would redistribute the property (AZ 9b).[6] The immediate followers of Jesus had left families, houses, and fields to follow Jesus (Matt 19:27–29). This kind of wholehearted commitment was characteristic of those who held messianic beliefs. There were many who left everything they had to come to Zion, the city of the living God, heavenly Jerusalem (12:22).

The author depreciated the effectiveness of the levitical priests who

[6] See further, L. Duchesne, *Early History of the Christian Church,* I (London, 1957), I, 196–200; A. H. Silver, *A History of Messianic Speculation in Israel;* (Boston, 1959), pp. 3–35.

he claimed were beset with weakness (5:2–3), were unable to attain perfection (7:11), perfect the conscience (9:9), or cleanse from sin (10:1–4, 11). This was not a unique opinion in the first century. There were other covenanters who had severe criticism for the Jerusalem priesthood. Members of one group apparently gathered in Judah under the leadership of its own priest, whom they called "the teacher of righteousness." They called the Jerusalem high priest "the wicked priest" and refused to observe the rules directed under his leadership (1QpHab 11–12).[7] One of the prayers offered at that time was that God's kingdom would reign, his salvation spring forth, his Messiah draw near, and that God would complete the temple, root out foreign worship from the land, bring holy worship in its place, and that the Holy One, blessed be He, would rule his kingdom.[8] The atmosphere and attitudes prevalent in Palestine prior to the fall of Jerusalem closely resemble those of the sermon "To the Hebrews."

These data support Flusser's opinion that the author of Hebrews was indebted to pre-Pauline concepts for his theology.[9] Flusser found some of these theological views in the Dead Sea scrolls. The similarity between the teachings of Hebrews and those of some of the Dead Sea scrolls has led Kosmala to conclude that the recipients of Hebrews were Jews like the Essenes who had been attracted to Christianity and had even begun training but had not fully accepted the Christian faith.[10] Yadin held that they were former Essenes who had become converts to Christianity.[11]

It is natural for scholars who have worked in the Dead Sea scrolls to notice the close resemblances between the rigorous "orthodox" theology of the Rule of the Community (1QS) and that of this homily "To the Hebrews," but the groups represented by these two documents were not the only sects of Jews and Christians who expected the fulfillment of God's promise to Abraham, believed ascetic discipline was necessary to do God's will, and thought that the temple in Jerusalem was defiled. These were the normal conclusions reached by serious Jews who studied the Old Testament carefully and tried to follow the Pentateuchal rules. Faithful Jews could be found in the diaspora just as readily as in Palestine. In fact, those who left important positions in the diaspora to migrate to Palestine would have testified by the

[7] RQum 6 (1969), 555–56.

[8] *The Traditional Prayer Book for Sabbath Festivals*, ed. D. de Sola Pool (New York, 1960), p. xii.

[9] D. Flusser, "The Dead Sea Sect and Pre-Pauline Christianity," *Scripta Hierosolymitana* 4 (1958), 236–42, 265–66.

[10] H. Kosmala, *Hebräer-Essener-Christen* (Leiden, 1959), pp. 1–43.

[11] Y. Yadin, "The Dead Sea Scrolls and the Epistle to the Hebrews," *Scripta Hierosolymitana* 4 (1958), 38.

price they paid to the seriousness with which they accepted their faith. It may have been in praise of the Jews who migrated to Palestine that Jesus said, "Many will come from east and west and sit at table with Abraham, Isaac, and Jacob in the kingdom of heaven" (Matt 8:11). The document that praised Abraham for migrating to Israel to receive the promise for his posterity may have been delivered to later Christian migrants to the promised land who also came because they believed it was God's will that they be there to receive the fulfillment of God's promise to Abraham.

A Palestinian origin before A.D. 70 for this homily has the support of the early church. Eusebius said Hebrews could not have been composed late because Clement of Rome utilized it for the composition of his first epistle to the Corinthians (near the end of the first century, *HE* III.xxxviii.1). These parallels all belong to chapters one to twelve of Hebrews.[12] Clement evidently used this sermon in Hebrews in the same way he used the Old Testament, as if he accepted its authority. Stuart listed in adjoining columns both the parallels between Clement and Hebrews and also the parallels between Hebrews and the Epistle of Barnabas, the Shepherd of Hermas, and the works of Polycarp and Ignatius. Some parallels are more striking than others, but in general Stuart has demonstrated that the homily in Hebrews gained a wide reading public at an early date.[13] This was not true of chapter thirteen. In the fourth century. Eusebius said he recognized the fourteen letters of Paul, including Hebrews, but that Hebrews was rejected by the church of Rome, because it was not Pauline (*HE* III.iii. 4–5). There were church officials who said Paul initially wrote Hebrews in Hebrew and that it was translanted into Greek either by Luke or by Clement of Rome, since many had noted the similarity between Hebrews and Clement's epistle (*HE* III.xxxviii.1–3). According to Eusebius, Clement of Alexandria thought Hebrews was originally written in Hebrew by Paul and translated into Greek by Luke (*HE* VI.xiv.1–2). Some heretic named Proclus did not consider Hebrews to be Pauline (*HE* VI.xx.3). Origen said Hebrews was so well written that everyone accepted it as Pauline, although it lacked the apostle's rude speech, as anyone who could discern differences of style could easily recognize (*HE* VI.xxv.11–12). Clement of Alexandria used such sources as the Wisdom of Solomon, Sirach, Barnabas, Clement of Rome, and Jude, together with Hebrews, for the composition of his *Stromateis* (*HE* VI. xiii.6–7). Irenaeus used Hebrews together with the Wisdom of Solomon for one of his works (*HE* V.xxvi.1). Hebrews seems early to have been

[12] Stuart, pp. 63–78; see also Moffatt, pp. xiii–xiv.
[13] Stuart, loc. cit.

recognized as some kind of wisdom literature and used as a valid authority.

The homily "To the Hebrews" seems to have been accepted as an important document without anyone knowing its author or place of origin. The reasons for losing the identity of an author in antiquity are legion. If the homily had been first composed before the war of A.D. 66–73 in Jerusalem, for instance, it is a miracle that it survived at all, since the community from which it would have originated was probably destroyed in the war. The existence of a copy outside of Jerusalem would allow for its continuation, but the community would no longer have been available to identify its author. It may have circulated with no information about it except that it was a surviving document from the Hebrew community at Jerusalem or that it bore the title "The Hebrews." The fact that it was classed among Pauline writings may mean that it did not come from any of the apostolic communities in Palestine, such as the church headed by James, Peter, or John. Since the author had never heard or seen Jesus personally (2:3), the only *apostolic* author to whom the homily could have been attributed was Paul. The author may have been originally from the diaspora and have ministered to a small monastic group of migrants at Jerusalem, so his name and status would not have been well known.

Stuart has argued strongly for a Palestinian origin of Hebrews (Caesarea), noting that the title indicates that it was identified at an early date with Palestinians who were called "Hebrews" (Acts 6:1; 21:40; 22:2; John 5:2; 19:13, 17).[14] He argued further that the persecutions in Hebrews (10:32–34) might have taken place outside of Palestine, but inside Palestine there were certainly early persecutions of Christians (Acts 9:2; 18:12–17).[15] This criterion is not sound enough to be useful. Our knowledge of the number and extent of Christian and Jewish punishments in New Testament times is very limited. By whom were the Christians mentioned in Hebrews punished? By Jews for deviation from accepted beliefs, or by Romans for political offenses similar to those committed by other Jews? Many peripheral events like these were never reported by the major historians, so the answer is unknown. Josephus did not even mention the entire Christian movement. How much less would he have reported such small details as these! There were undoubtedly many conflicts between Jews and Christians and between both groups and the Romans in many parts of the Roman Empire. Therefore events as small as these might be attributed to any locality which was concluded for other reasons to be the location for the original readers. The account of persecutions alone is no clue to the

[14] Stuart, p. 37. [15] Stuart, p. 47.

origin of the homily. Even if it were possible to know all the occasions for Jewish and Christian imprisonments, once the possibility is entertained that a group of migrants was the original body of hearers or readers, it is still unknown whether these events took place in Palestine after their migration or in the migrants' lands before coming to Jerusalem. Stuart's choice of Palestine as a location is meritorious, but not for the reasons he has given.

From internal evidence, the most likely place of composition and delivery of this homily "To the Hebrews" is Jerusalem, sometime after the death of Jesus (A.D. 26–36) and before the destruction of the temple (A.D. 70). External evidence supports this conclusion.

THE AUTHOR

Judging from the advice he gave to the original hearers or readers of this document, the author held some position of respected authority. He was a very sincere, pious, rigorously disciplined Jewish Christian. He was not a Sadducee or a Samaritan, because he considered the Psalms at least as valid as the Pentateuch for holy scripture. He trusted the validity of God's promise to Abraham and believed also that Jesus' sacrificial death provided the necessary merits to cancel all the sins that had been held against Israel. He was convinced that it was only a matter of a short time until God's promise would be fulfilled (10:36–37). He interpreted scripture on the basis that it was the only source for religious knowledge; that which was not in the scripture was not in the world. He was acquainted with I, II, III, and IV Maccabees and considered the unyielding faith of the Maccabean martyrs to be an ideal for Christian behavior. To some degree the Hasmonean priests and rulers formed a type for which the author's interpretation of Jesus was the antitype. His description of Jesus was more carefully based on scriptural interpretations than on historical fact.

Judging from his literary style, the author of Hebrews was an excellent scholar, well-versed in Jewish customs, midrashic exegesis, rabbinic logic, and Greek. His vocabulary includes 151 *hapax legomena* not found anywhere else in the New Testament.[16] Not only is his homily well organized into major units and minor subdivisions which have well-structured connective sentences that relate one to the other, but major themes are effectively repeated and clarified throughout the document. Leading sentences are so well written that the important words are alliterative to aid in memory. Spicq has correctly suggested that the author must have been a professor of biblical studies.[17]

Since chapters 1 – 12 give no indication of being an epistle, there is

[16] See Williamson, p. 11, for the list. [17] Spicq, I, 25.

no need to conjecture that the author had a different location from that of the readers or original hearers. The author may have prepared the homily for discouraged migrants who had come to Zion in the last days, fully prepared to observe every jot and tittle of the law for the few days remaining until the kingdom should come. Since the author seems to have held some position of respected religious authority, he may have been one of the leaders of a Christian monastery in Jerusalem to which these migrants had come. Those who had been enlightened and were later relaxing in their religious studies were given a lecture or an assignment to consider before giving up hope and returning to their former homes or participating in the Day of Atonement services.

Some objections to the conjecture are as follows: (1) Why would anyone in Jerusalem, writing to others in Jerusalem, write in Greek? and (2) If the author had been close to the historical surroundings of Jesus, why is there not more evidence of the historical Jesus in the document? Some considerations are as follows:

1) Ever since the Babylonian captivity, Jerusalem has been occupied by Jews from many places in the diaspora, if it was occupied by Jews at all. It has also been a city where many languages were spoken. Among the Murabba'at letters of Bar Kochba were those written to two different persons in three different languages: Hebrew, Aramaic, and Greek. The scribes who wrote the letters assumed the readers could understand all three. The geographical location of Palestine on a land bridge between great nations has made Jerusalem a commercial city where languages of great nations were spoken in order to negotiate business. The centrality of Jerusalem in Jewish traditions has encouraged Jews and Christians to migrate to that city whenever it was possible to do so. Consequently this has traditionally made Jerusalem a city whose inhabitants were cosmopolitan. Some of them had been born and trained in other lands and languages before moving to Jerusalem. Because of this constant migration it has been possible for people to move there and settle among others of the same language and continue to speak in their native tongues. The scholar who wrote the homily "To the Hebrews" may have spoken more than one language well, or he may have been born, trained, and have lived many years of his professional life somewhere else in the Roman Empire before he, like his readers, migrated to Jerusalem so as to be there when the kingdom came and the promises of Abraham were fulfilled. In either case, he would have been able to write in the language of the new migrants. Normally it requires a few years for adults to learn the language of a new country. The community of pilgrims at Pentecost did

not expect to be able to understand one another in Jerusalem when they first arrived (Acts 2:3–12).

2) The author's interest, rather than his familiarity with the historical facts of Jesus' life, dictated the content of this homily. If the original readers or hearers were in Jerusalem and had heard about Jesus directly from those who knew Jesus personally, they did not need another lecture on that subject. The author's message was theologically-ethically oriented. The author was primarily interested in the fulfillment of the promises made to Abraham. It was Jesus' death that was important to the author's theology and the current needs of the recipients, not his life and teachings. The author found adequate biblical bases for his interpretation of the death of Jesus as an atonement offering.

Lenski's objection that "it is impossible that any Christian in Palestine should think of going back to these Jews . . . and to a Judaism in such a state" reflects a tendentious Christian viewpoint.[18] That which seems impossible to Lenski in twentieth-century U.S.A. may not have seemed impossible to first-century Christians in Jerusalem. Ignatius warned Christians who were in communication with Jews, "But if anyone interpret Judaism to you, do not listen to him; for it is better to hear Christianity from the circumcised than Judaism from the uncircumcised. But both of them, unless they speak of Jesus Christ, are to me tombstones and sepulchers of the dead, on whom only the names of men are written" (*To the Philadelphians* 6). If there had been no danger, there would have been no need to issue such a warning. There is little reason to think that Judaism in Jerusalem would have been less attractive than anywhere else in the Roman Empire. It is not clear, however, that the author was primarily interested in keeping Christians from reverting to Judaism, as Lenski presumed. The author seemed more emphatic in warning the readers against giving up their messianic zeal and discipline than in returning to Judaism. The consequences of their relaxation may have been to have them return home rather than to stay at Jerusalem until the promise was fulfilled.

This conjecture, of course, is only one of many that could be imagined to account for its anonymity. It will be necessary for scholars to continue to deduce the authorship from the contents of the document and to accept the wisdom of Origen's observation: "But who was the author of the epistle? Truly God only knows" (*HE* VI.xxv.13). From the internal evidence there is a good deal to be learned about the author—his ability, tendencies, points of view, basic beliefs, and national allegiance, but any attempt to identify this anonymous person with some of the few known Christian leaders of that time, like Paul,

[18] Lenski, p. 13.

Barnabas, Silas, Philip, or Apollos is, according to Moffatt, "in the main due to an irrepressible desire to construct New Testament romances."[19] Such attempts also presume that there were no important Christian leaders in the early church whose names are not recorded in the New Testament. It is quite likely that there were many significant leaders whose names will never be known. On the other hand, sources are not so limited that it is necessary to follow Williamson's agnosticism and concede that the author might even have been a woman. The odds that a learned monk who would have been able to compose a document such as this homily in the first century might have been a woman are very low, as even Williamson would probably allow.[20]

Purpose

The author wanted to persuade the original hearers or readers to hold fast to their faith and not give up hope that Jesus' self-sacrifice was the perfect gift needed to motivate God to fulfill for them the promise he had made to Abraham. To achieve this purpose, he warned, threatened, pleaded, encouraged, and interpreted scripture doctrinally to convince them to hold fast. He wanted them to realize that they were, at that very time, standing in the same position where the Israelites stood when they reached the border of the promised land. If they would just hold on a little longer, they would succeed where the exodus generation had failed. This much is apparent regardless of the time and place conjectured for the composition.

The centrality of Jesus' sacrifice as an atonement offering, if first read or written for a group of migrants in Jerusalem, may have been made to prevent these formerly Jewish migrants from observing the Day of Atonement with other Jews in Jerusalem. They may have been asking whether Jesus' sacrifice had really been effective. Since the kingdom had not yet come, perhaps they should repent again and offer still more sacrifices to add to the treasury of merits. Even Paul reasoned that his own sufferings were added to the afflictions of Christ to fill up what was lacking for redemption (Col 1:24–25). The author's response was that Jesus' sacrifice was once-for-all. It did not need to be repeated and it could not. To make such an attempt would be an insult to Christ and be unpardonable. The original readers probably had not planned to give up Christianity by participating in these Jewish customs any more than the Galatian Christians had when they became circumcised after they had received the gospel (Gal 3:1–5:21).

[19] Moffatt, p. xx.
[20] Williamson, p. 579.

Another danger the author may have wanted to prevent was that the migrants who were becoming discouraged may have considered going back to the place from which they had come. Perhaps their hope was mistaken, and they were simply wasting time in Jerusalem. The author's counsel was that they should be studying harder, making greater advances in the faith so that they would have less time to wonder and doubt. They had come to the promised land as Abraham had. If they did not lose faith they would certainly receive the promised reward.

Chapter Thirteen

The nature and message

Chapter thirteen is an addition prepared for a different group from that for which the homily in the first twelve chapters was written. It includes a collection of various literary compositions (13:1–19), a benediction (13:20–21), and a "Pauline" postscript (13:22–25). Verses 1–19 seem once to have been structured as a unit enclosed by an inclusion. Within these verses is a doctrinal discussion about the sacrifice of Jesus and contemporary worship and witness (13:10–16), a small confession (13:8), practical advice about behavior in relationship to leaders (13:7, 17–19), and warnings against heretics (13:9). This is a scissors-and-paste composition of collected bits of literature that changed pronouns more than once. The benediction and "Pauline" postscript may have been added to the first twelve chapters at the same time 13:1–19 was, or they may have been added later.

Readers

The homily made no mention of marriage. In fact, references to sanctification, holiness, brotherhood, root of bitterness, discipline, and the avoidance of any kind of defilement point to a monastic community. Chapter thirteen, however, addressed a different, wider, and more general reading public, composed of married people (13:4) who had ongoing concerns for practical matters like money (13:5–6) and administrative problems (13:7, 17–19). The readers were not leaders themselves.

The author

The author seems to have been a church leader in some capacity of responsibility to the readers. He was not a monk; he was opposed to Jerusalem as it then was administered; he was opposed to the dietary practices of the Jews.

Time and place of origin

Verses 10–16 were evidently composed while the temple was still standing, and other sources used to compile 13:11–19 may have even been pre-Christian, but its editor wrote after the initial expectation of the parousia had cooled and the church faced ongoing problems of finance, continuing morality, and relationship of leaders to other members of the group. Any attempt to say how much later this was composed than the first twelve chapters would be a guess. No quotation from chapter thirteen occurs in the writings of the early fathers. It may have been composed as early as before A.D. 70 or as late as the second or early third century. It was included in P^{46}, a third-century text, so it was certainly written before then. Verses 10–16 seem to have a non-Jerusalem, Palestinean setting, but the final edition of 13:1–19, 20–21, and 22–25 may have been composed anywhere in the Roman Empire. The greetings from Italy may have been a fictitious addition intended only to give Hebrews the appearance of a letter. Even if they were genuine, this would provide no indication that the author or readers were from Italy, but that the author was in contact with some unknown people whose home was in Italy. Any attempt to be more specific about the time and place of chapter thirteen's composition would be guesswork.

Purpose

Chapter thirteen may have been composed partially to give a homily the appearance of a letter to allow its admission into the canon. Other purposes may have been to encourage financial support for the church, moral support for the leaders, and good moral conduct among Christians.

KEY TO THE TEXT

Chapter	*Verses*	§
1	1–4	I
1	5–14	II
2	1–18	II
3	1–19	III
4	1–16	III
5	1–14	IV
6	1–20	IV
7	1–28	IV
8	1–13	IV
9	1–28	IV
10	1–39	IV
11	1–40	V
12	1–29	V
13	1–25	VI

INDEX OF AUTHORS